ENGLISH RENAISSANCE TRAGEDY

By the same author

SHAKESPEARE AND DECORUM

ENGLISH RENAISSANCE TRAGEDY

T. McAlindon

MALCOLM. Now we'll together; and the chance of goodness
   Be like our warranted quarrel! Why are you silent?
MACDUFF. Such welcome and unwelcome things at once
   'Tis hard to reconcile.

(*Macbeth,* IV.iii.136–9)

THE UNIVERSITY OF BRITISH COLUMBIA PRESS
VANCOUVER   1986

First published 1986

Printed in Hong Kong

Canadian Cataloguing in Publication Data
McAlindon, T. (Thomas)
English Renaissance tragedy
Includes index.
ISBN 0-7748-0253-7
1. English drama (Tragedy) – History and criticism.
2. English drama – Early modern and Elizabethan,
1500–1600 – History and criticism.   3. English
drama – 17th century – History and criticism.
I. Title.
PR658.T7M2   1986   822'.3'09   C85-091630-5

ISBN 0-7748-0253-7

To M. A. McA

*'What I have done is yours,
what I have to doe is yours.'*

Contents

Preface

This study of English Renaissance tragedy differs from others of its kind in the degree of attention given to the seminal achievements of Kyd and Marlowe. Although I have not included a chapter on Shakespeare (it is difficult to see how justice could be done to him in a work of this scope), I do believe none the less that his tragedies and those of his contemporaries are mutually illuminating. I have tried to establish this point in my long opening chapter (Part I), an account of recurrent elements in Renaissance tragic tradition which draws on both Shakespearean and non-Shakespearean texts.

T. McA.

Acknowledgements

For patient reading and helpful criticism I am indebted to three friends: Peter McClure, Robin Headlam Wells, and (especially) Rowland Wymer. My principal debt, of course, is to the many editors, scholars, and critics who have been in this field before me. The limits of space and the imperfections of memory mean that the extent of my dependence on their work is indicated in the endnotes less fully than true justice would require.

List of Editions Used

Francis Beaumont and John Fletcher, *The Maid's Tragedy,* ed. Howard B. Norland, Regents Renaissance Drama Series (London: Arnold, 1968).

George Chapman, *Bussy D'Ambois,* ed. Nicholas Brooke, The Revels Plays (London: Methuen, 1964).

——, *The Plays and Poems,* vol. I: *The Tragedies,* ed. Thomas Marc Parrott (London, Routledge, 1910).

John Ford, *The Broken Heart,* ed. Donald K. Anderson, Regents Renaissance Drama Series (London: Arnold, 1968).

——, *The Chronicle History of Perkin Warbeck,* ed. Peter Ure, The Revels Plays (London: Methuen, 1968).

——, *'Tis Pity She's a Whore,* ed. N. W. Bawcutt, Regents Renaissance Drama Series (London: Arnold, 1966).

Ben Jonson, *The Works,* ed. C. H. Herford and P. and E. Simpson (Oxford: Clarendon Press, 1925–52).

Thomas Kyd, *The Spanish Tragedy,* ed. Philip Edwards, The Revels Plays (London: Methuen, 1959).

Christopher Marlowe, *The Plays,* ed. Roma Gill (London: Oxford University Press, 1971).

John Marston, *Antonio and Mellida,* ed. G. K. Hunter, Regents Renaissance Drama Series (London: Arnold, 1965).

——, *Antonio's Revenge,* ed. G. K. Hunter, Regents Renaissance Drama Series (London: Arnold, 1966).

——, *The Malcontent,* ed. Martin L. Wine, Regents Renaissance Drama Series (London: Arnold 1965).

Thomas Middleton, *Women Beware Women,* ed. J. R. Mulryne, The Revels Plays (Manchester: Manchester University Press, 1975).

——, and William Rowley, *The Changeling,* ed. N. W. Bawcutt, The Revels Plays (London: Methuen, 1961).

William Shakespeare, *Complete Works,* ed. Peter Alexander (London and Glasgow: Collins, 1951).

Cyril Tourneur, *The Atheist's Tragedy,* ed. Irving Ribner, The Revels Plays (London: Methuen, 1964).

——(?), *The Revenger's Tragedy,* ed. R. A. Foakes, The Revels Plays (London: Methuen, 1966).

John Webster, *The Duchess of Malfi,* ed. John Russell Brown, The Revels Plays, 2nd edn (London: Methuen, 1964).

——, *The White Devil,* ed. John Russell Brown, The Revels Plays (London: Methuen, 1964).

List of Abbreviations

CQ	*Critical Quarterly*
EIC	*Essays in Criticism*
E&S	*Essays and Studies*
ELH	*English Literary History*
ELN	*English Language Notes*
ESC	*English Studies in Canada*
ETh	*Elizabethan Theatre*
ILR	*Iowa Law Review*
JEGP	*Journal of English and Germanic Philology*
JWCI	*Journal of the Warburg and Courtauld Institutes*
MLQ	*Modern Language Quarterly*
MLR	*Modern Language Review*
MP	*Modern Philology*
N&Q	*Notes and Queries*
OED	*Oxford English Dictionary*
PBA	*Proceedings of the British Academy*
PLL	*Papers on Language and Literature*
PMLA	*Publications of the Modern Language Association of America*
PQ	*Philological Quarterly*
REL	*Review of English Literature*
RenD	*Renaissance Drama*
RES	*Review of English Studies*
s.d.	Stage direction
SEL	*Studies in English Literature*
Shaks	*Shakespeare Studies*
ShS	*Shakespeare Survey*
SP	*Studies in Philology*
SUAS	Stratford-upon-Avon Studies
TDR	*Tulane Drama Review*
TLS	*Times Literary Supplement*
TSL	*Tennessee Studies in Literature*
TSLL	*Texas Studies in Language and Literature*
YR	*Yale Review*

Part I

1 Common Elements

In the period beginning with Kyd's *The Spanish Tragedy* (c. 1585–90) and Marlowe's *Tamburlaine the Great* (1587–8), and ending with Ford's *The Broken Heart* and *'Tis Pity She's a Whore* (c. 1626–33), English tragedy is remarkable for its variety of form and outlook. Yet it is clear that Renaissance tragedians found a major stimulus to creative endeavour in each other's work and were quick to borrow and adapt what they saw there. Indeed, so numerous are the connections – conceptual, thematic, and formal – between their work that it is very difficult to make a classification of different types of tragedy in the period without ignoring some fundamental and illuminating analogy between major plays assigned to separate groups. This is not to deny that the various categorical divisions – into revenge tragedy, villain tragedy, domestic tragedy, love tragedy, and so on – have provided us with useful analytical tools. It is to suggest rather that something might now be gained from approaching the diverse but interdependent tragedies of the Renaissance in the light of a broad referential framework drawn from their shared ideas, preoccupations, and methods, and clarified where necessary by appeal to their cultural context.

I propose to deal here with these common elements under the following headings: (I) Violent Change; (II) The Noble Death; (III) The Violation of Justice and Love – (i) Justice and Law, (ii) Love and Marriage; (IV) Treacherous Entertainment: The Symbolism of Rite and Play; (V) Treacherous Words: The Language of Tragic Reality. This arrangement reflects a certain logical order and unity of perspective. In no sense, however, have I attempted to provide a fully coherent schema of Renaissance tragedy; and I am well aware that the material could have been otherwise divided and presented with substantial differences of emphasis as well as interpretation.

I VIOLENT CHANGE

An outstanding feature of Renaissance tragedy is its preoccupation with violence. This can be ascribed in part to the influence of Senecan tragedy.[1]

3

Seneca's sombre, oratorical studies of inordinate passion and unnatural crime so impressed the Elizabethans that they seem to have felt from the outset that violence is tragedy's defining attribute. Writing before the advent of Kyd and Marlowe, the fastidious Sir Philip Sidney himself located the chief attraction of the form in its 'sweet violence'.[2] But the violence of the popular stage at this time was due also to the needs of the audience. Nurtured on a steady diet of bear-baitings, public executions, and readings in Foxe's martyrology (a book whose text and vivid woodcuts attuned it to such scenes as the blinding of Gloucester), this was an audience with a pronounced taste for ritual horror.[3] In fact violence is presented in Renaissance tragedy with a directness which openly affronts the neo-classical doctrine, upheld by Sidney and his likes, that all such action should take place off stage and be communicated to the audience by means of narration and monologue (in the Senecan manner). Even for us the best tragedies of the period sail perilously close at times to gratuitous and melodramatic sensationalism.

The reasons why they can usually be absolved from this charge are simple but worth rehearsing. In the first place, their bloody and unnatural deeds are so firmly grounded in an imaginative exploration of the destructive potencies of passion and will that they tend to assume a symbolic or quasi-symbolic status (often emphasised by a stylised mode of presentation). As a rule, too, violence is meaningfully juxtaposed – or meaningfully confused – with everything antithetical to it: with eloquence, gracious manners, friendly entertainment, ritual, and all the panoply of the law. Explicitly or implicitly, too, it is made indigenous to its context by means of a world view in which strife and amity are held to be the governing forces of nature. Finally, the complex meanings assigned to the word 'violence' by the dramatists could be said to endow the phenomenon itself, as we understand it, with a special inevitability. For 'violence' signifies not only vehemence and the destructive or unlawful use of force, but also rashness in the sense of untimeliness. Of this type of violence there is an abundance in the tragedies, and the constant suggestion is that it can resolve with treacherous ease into the kind which brutally transforms the whole complexion of life.[4] To conflate the choric wisdom of Friar Lawrence and Iago, violent (i.e. hasty, untimely) commencements are likely to have very violent (i.e. bloody) endings.[5]

The violence of Renaissance tragedy may be taken as symptomatic of the dramatists' belief that the essential tragic phenomenon in life is change. Not graduated change, of course, but change which is sudden, deeply painful, and calculated to undermine all faith in the essential justice and benevolence of mankind and of whatever powers rule the world. In keeping with a tradition inherited by Christian culture from the Greeks, the tragedians tend to see evil and suffering in terms of change, and all change as degenerative.[6] As they present it, the tragic experience is one in which the suffering protagonist seems thrust for the first time into the horrors of the Iron Age or the Fallen World, his agony sharpened by consciousness of a lost state of perfection.

What I should like to emphasise is that tragic change is commonly defined in terms of a clash and confusion of contraries, the ideal or pre-tragic state being understood as a stable bond of opposites. Behind this twin idea, forming a kind of imaginative and philosophical matrix, lies the anthropomorphic conception of nature as a system of interacting, interdependent opposites – the four qualities, elements, and humours. According to the old cosmology, the inherent antagonism of the opposites (nature as egoism and strife) is kept in check and assimilated to a process of 'concordant discord' which is at once love and justice (nature as partnership and law). The balance, harmony, or 'well-tempered' mixing of the opposites is the condition of full and enduring life, their unchecked strife the source of all decay and death in nature. The former ensures that change will be regulated and timely; the latter is productive of change which is both sudden and extreme, with one opposite eclipsing the next in a condition comparable to primal Chaos.[7]

In historically oriented studies of Renaissance drama, it has been customary to assume that the essential feature of pre-modern cosmology as understood by the Elizabethans was the principle of hierarchical correspondence (or analogy). Viewed in the light of this principle, however, the universe presents itself to the imagination as a straightforward model of order and stability, inducing a mood of philosophic confidence and optimism in any consideration of the human condition. There has, therefore, been a strong reaction against those critics who have assumed that the so-called 'Elizabethan world picture' exercised a substantial influence on the tragic dramatists' delineation of man, society, and universe; it is commonly held now that the tragedians' vision of a terrifyingly unstable world where good and evil and right and wrong are confusingly entwined could only have evolved in spite of or in reaction to the conditioning effects of traditional cosmology. I would suggest, however, that the full implications of pre-modern cosmology were never taken into account in the interpretation of Renaissance tragedy (and tragical history) in the first place. For in the 'theoria of the world' – to borrow Marlowe's phrase – which the Elizabethans inherited from the Middle Ages and the Greeks, polarity was a principle of at least equal importance with that of hierarchy (analogy, correspondence, degree). To put the matter in elemental terms, the disposition of earth, water, air, and fire in a stratified order throughout the universe does not alter the fact that they are opposites whose nature always inclines them to strife and mutual domination. Without the strife of the elements there would, in fact, be no accounting for change and death; moreover, given their instinct for strife, there can be no knowing what convulsions lie ahead in the order of nature. At the end of the sixteenth and the beginning of the seventeenth century, the pessimistically inclined, looking at the evidence of contemporary history (Christianity at war with itself) and of scientific discovery (changes in the changeless heavens of 'the fixed stars'), decided that man's moral character, human institutions, and external nature were all in a state of incipient disintegration, that the promised end was at hand. Automatically, they explained this cosmic disaster in terms of an uncontrolled acceleration in the strife of the contraries. The explanation suggests that, while their cosmology conditioned them to admire and cherish harmonious stability, it also conditioned them to dread and expect violent change, 'Chaos come again'.[8]

The effects which the cosmological principles of analogy and contrariety had on Renaissance drama are incalculable. Of the two, however, the principle of contrariety etched itself more deeply on the art of the tragedian, and for reasons which are not hard to perceive. The idea of the universe as a dynamic system of opposites speaks to the imagination not only of order but also of the fragile and impermanent nature of life's harmonious patterns. And, since subject and object are held to be duplex and always liable to change, it speaks too of a radical uncertainty in every attempt to interpret and evaluate man's nature and experience. Viewed in the light of this cosmic model, unity – and all that it entails in terms of order and intelligibility – may seem no more than the effect of a truce in a war that can have no end. It was perhaps inevitable, therefore, that Renaissance tragedians should exploit the contrarious model of man and universe. Beginning as they did with the medieval tragic idea of man as the victim of an inherently treacherous world (the world of Fortune),[9] and adjusting it to their own conviction that he is betrayed also by the conditions of his nature, they created a complex and comprehensive view of the tragic to which the notion of universal contrariety contributed both as stimulus and validation.

The Renaissance inclination to interpret and shape tragic experience in the light of universal contrariety does not become gradually apparent. Rather, it leaps to attention at the outset in *The Spanish Tragedy* and *Tamburlaine the Great*. The principle of polarity dominates the vision of man and his world presented by each of these two plays and is unfolded in boldly formalised designs which no Elizabethan could have failed to perceive and appreciate. Among subsequent dramatists, perhaps only the Elizabethan Shakespeare (in *Romeo and Juliet, Richard II*, and *Julius Caesar*) relates the extremes, oppositions, and confusions of the tragic world to the model of the contrarious universe with an emphasis and clarity approaching that of Kyd and Marlowe. However, the lack of overt emphasis on the model in the later drama is of no significance, since the danger for the seventeenth-century tragedian in this matter lay in labouring the obvious rather than in excessive reticence. Adequate reminders of the relevant frame of reference could easily be supplied through elemental imagery, humoral detail, or implicit allusion to the ancient tradition of marriage and dance as symbols of cosmic unity-in-contrariety. In tragedies with a martial hero, the Mars-Venus myth, conventionally interpreted as an allegory of nature's concordant discord, provided a singularly appropriate means for tactfully invoking the universal dialectic of Strife and Love: it is used to this end in *Othello* and *Antony and Cleopatra* – as it had been, however, in *Tamburlaine* and *The Spanish Tragedy*.[10]

Given the wealth of scholarly investigation into the development of medieval and sixteenth-century drama in the last few decades, one is necessarily hesitant about locating the origin of anything in either of these two plays. In particular, it has to be acknowledged here that a tendency to play with opposites in the spirit of intellectual inquiry is noticeable in comedy and tragedy alike before Marlowe and Kyd.[11] This dialectical propensity, however, has its roots in the techniques of rhetorical disputation and not in a metaphysical and scientific doctrine which postulates that nature itself is a system of opposites. Thus it is impossible to find in the extant plays which antedate *Tamburlaine* and *The Spanish Tragedy* any attempt to identify the tragic process with the terrible potentialities of life in a contrarious universe. One might have expected to encounter just such an attempt in the learned *Gorboduc* (1561), where tragic violence and change are identified with the undoing of unity; but no trace of it can be seen there. Indeed, to discover anything in imaginative literature comparable to the grand contrarious vision of Kyd and Marlowe, one has to go out of the drama altogether and back as far as the first of the Canterbury Tales. Chaucer's tragi-comical romance is founded on an elaborate dialectic of love and hate, war and peace, male and female, Mars and Venus, 'ernest' and 'pleye', violence and law, irregularity and ritual, funeral and marriage, chance and fate. Because of this dialectical complexity it has been confidently interpreted not only as an affirmation of Boethian providentialism but also as an absurdist vision of a world in which men are the deluded instruments of powers who care little for them.[12] It is probable that Kyd and Marlowe, like the author of *A Midsummer Night's Dream*, were deeply impressed by the superbly contrarious art of *The Knight's Tale*.[13] But to them alone must go all the credit for showing how the metaphysics of polarity could nourish tragic drama. Basically, what they discovered was this: that the concept of *discordia concors*, and the whole habit of thought which goes with it, allows the tragic dramatist to move to and fro across a spectrum between essential optimism, implying the inevitability of reintegration and the growth of unity out of strife, and an essential pessimism, implying the inevitability of violer ~e and the utter fragility of those bonds which exclude confusion from the objective and subjective worlds.

The notion of reality as a process of interacting opposites has proved to be one of the most fruitful in the whole history of ideas (its dissemination in modern times by way of Hegelian and Nietzschean influence needs no emphasis). Its chief virtue, perhaps, lies in its efficacy as an instrument for counteracting rigid orthodoxies, undermining monocular vision, and encouraging the acceptance of contradiction and uncertainty. It is not surprising, therefore, that some of the more adventurous and heterodox thinkers of the Renaissance – among them Paracelsus, Bruno, and Montaigne – were greatly attracted by it, and knowledgeable too about its origins and variations in Pythagoras, Heraclitus, and Empedocles. To suggest, however, that the contrarious aspect of Renaissance tragedy was due mainly to the influence of such thinkers would be mistaken. Moreover, it would have the effect of underestimating the high degree of intellectual rapport which must have existed between the dramatists and their audience – even those of their audience who might not accept their more disturbing conclusions. The contrarious view of nature, after all, was inherent in accepted teachings on the microcosm and the macrocosm, and its liberating potential had been fully perceived and richly communicated in the Middle Ages by the Father of English Poesie.[14]

Moreover, although it could be used to support un-Christian sentiments, it had long been officially accommodated to Christian doctrine. In the Creation, it was explained, God had imposed perfect harmony on the warring elements. This concord was permanently impaired – though not wholly undone – by the curse on nature which followed original sin, the damage being most apparent in the sublunary world and above all in man himself.[15] Thus uncontrolled contrariety, and so changefulness and confusion, are essential characteristics of life in the fallen state. The devout Christian, however, could find comfort in contemplating the changeless order of the celestial world and in particular of Heaven itself, even though that ideal order heightened his gloomy consciousness of this world's discordant and unstable conditions.

A particularly instructive example of this type of devout Christian is Sir Thomas Browne, a younger contemporary of Webster and Middleton, and a great admirer, it would seem, of Shakespeare.[16] His most famous work, *Religio Medici* (written c. 1635) is both a testament of religious faith and a sensitive mind's response to the profound effect of the Reformation on the whole climate of contemporary life. Browne declares that his faith rests on the Bible, or written word of God, on the providential ordering of historical events (which merely seem to be governed by chance or Fortune), and on the wonderful order of nature – the 'setled and constant course' ordained by the divine wisdom for all created things. He perceives 'in this Universe a Staire, or manifest Scale of creatures, rising not disorderly, or in confusion, but with a comely method and proportion', stretching up from the mineral, vegetable, and animal worlds through the human to the angelic and the divine (p.101). But the universal model which dominates his imagination throughout is not the vertical model of hierarchy but the primarily horizontal one of interacting opposites. The world 'is raised upon a masse of Antipathies'; yet its 'divided Antipathies and contrary faces doe yet carry a charitable regard unto the whole by their particular discords, preserving the common harmony, and keeping in fetters those powers, whose rebellions once Masters, might be the ruin of all' (pp.144, 146). Man himself is 'another world of contrarieties'. As well as 'publike and . . . hostile adversaries without', he has to contend with 'private and domestic enemies within'. Indeed, within the compass of himself Browne finds another 'battell of Lepanto, passion against reason, reason against faith, faith against the Devill, and my conscience against all' (p.145). But he has also found that unity and peace within are possible: by the exercise of 'a moderate and peaceful discretion', the rival claims of the opposing forces can be so stated and ordered 'that they may bee all Kings, and yet but one monarchy, every one exercising his Soveraignty and Prerogative in a due time and place, according to the restraint and limit of circumstance' (p.85). Having pacified 'the unruly regiment within', Browne has no trouble with adversaries without. Being blessed with an equable temperament inherited from his parents, he naturally 'affect[s] all harmony': his disposition 'consorts, and sympathizeth with all things', he has no 'antipathy' or 'repugnances' to any nation or clime, he dislikes quarrelsome disputation and 'cannot conceive why a difference in opinion should divide an affection' (pp.133, 138).

But Browne perceives all too well that the peace and harmony he enjoys with himself and the rest of the world are exceptional. Mankind is split into four religions – Christianity, Judaism, Mohammedanism, and heathenism – which mutual hatred, persecution, and war have driven progressively further apart: 'It is the promise of Christ to make us all one flock: but how and when this union shall be, is as obscure to me as the last day' (p.93). Christianity itself is similarly afflicted. Having been 'decaied, impaired, and fallen from its native beauty', it required 'the carefull and charitable hand of these times to restore it to its primitive integrity'. But the careful and charitable hand did not prevail, and the effect of the Reformation seems to be that the original integrity or wholeness of the Church is further away than ever: the two parties spend their time 'violently defending' their own positions and 'with ardour and contention' attacking their opposite. The hope of moderate souls that by 'dividing the community' in gentle fashion, rather than by 'rending' it apart, there would remain 'an honest possibility of reconciliation', has turned to hopelessness: 'that judgement that shall consider the present antipathies between the two extreames, their contrarieties in condition, affection, and opinion, may with the same hopes expect an union in the poles of Heaven' (p.61–4). In the spheres of morality and philosophical knowledge, as in theology, the history of mankind tells the same story. Men 'naturally know what is good, but naturally pursue what is evill' (p.129). All the great philosophers have disagreed on fundamentals, and the wisest of them 'prove at last, almost all Scepticks, and stand like Janus [the two-faced god] in the field of knowledge' (p.148). Given his longing for unity, harmony and stability, Browne's melancholy conclusion is not surprising: 'there is no happiness under . . . the Sunne' (p. 160). What sustains him is his faith in an afterlife where all doubts and discords will be resolved, and where he will be united with God, who is Unity itself.

There is very little comfort of this kind in Renaissance tragedy. The dramatists often adumbrate the presence of a stable pattern behind the violent and confused course of things, but their imaginative emphasis on the convulsions which it encompasses is such as to render it of secondary importance. On the whole, too, they are conspicuous for their refusal to suggest that eternity will compensate for the agonies of time; indeed, they are likely to invoke the afterlife only as a horrifying extension of existential loss and misery. Nevertheless, these dramatists do present the tragic environment in a manner which the convinced Christian would have found consistent with his image of the fallen world. God's curse on nature would have been heard in Timon's curse on Athens: 'Decline to your confounding contraries / And let confusion live' (*Timon of Athens*, IV.i.19–20).

Confusing and treacherous change being the chief source of suffering and evil in the tragedies, constancy features as a moral and psychological quality of supreme significance: to a large extent, the wickedness of the villain and the greatness as well as the fallibility of the hero or heroine are defined in terms of it. Constancy is not a quality which admits of easy definition, for it can be involved in every virtue. But its etymological meaning – 'standing together' – provides the clue to its essential significance in the drama and in Renaissance thought generally: it is constancy in human behaviour which makes for unity and integrity. Constancy, therefore, implies fidelity to self and to others, psychic and interpersonal harmony; and, since fidelity may entail strength of mind and purpose, it also implies fortitude. Being a binding force, however, it is closely associated with justice, amity, and moderation (finding a mean between opposites or extremes). Its full range of meaning is concisely indicated in that speech of Hamlet's where the faithful Horatio is fervently praised as a 'just . . . man' in whom passion and reason are so well mixed that Fortune cannot alter him (*Hamlet,* III.ii.52–71).

The true villain is the personification of inconstancy and therefore of duality and division. Usually he compounds his own viciousness by presenting himself as an apostle of unity and concord – loyal, truthful, kindly.[17] Moreover, he seeks to universalise inconstancy by entangling the noble in the dualities of their own nature and of the world at large. Behind him stands the figure of Satan, the archetypal traitor and seducer whom the Fathers of the Church, turning Plato's attack on rhetoric and drama to theological account, had made into something of a glib-tongued orator.[18] Like Milton, the tragedians developed this aspect of the archetypal villain to the full, adjusting it to the humanist doctrine that the tongue is the greatest instrument for evil as well as for good known to man.[19] Since 'change' and 'motion' were synonymous philosophical terms, and since rhetoric was by definition 'the art of moving', they found it singularly apt that the most terrible changes in the individual and society should be ascribed to Satanic masters of persuasion. Shakespeare has a brilliant sequence of characters who fall into this category – Richard III, Cassius and Antony, Claudius, Iago, and Lady Macbeth. To name them in conjunction with Heywood's Wendoll, Jonson's Sejanus, Chapman's La Fin, Tourneur's(?) Vindice, and Middleton's Livia is undoubtedly to underline Shakespeare's transcendence in dramatising the power of language. Yet all these characters belong to the one family and can profitably be looked at in conjunction. In the characterisation of Vindice and Livia, for example, there is as clear an emphasis on the connection between inconstancy, degenerative change, and the art of moving as there is in that of Iago.

Evil persuasion, especially of the kind which encourages some fundamental betrayal, is a natural attribute of the Machiavel. And the Machiavel is Satan in modern (i.e. Renaissance) dress precisely because in the eighteenth chapter of *The Prince* the author avers that keeping faith is a noble ideal which has no place in the real world of politics. Fidelity would be worthwhile if others could be relied on to practise it; since they cannot, the ruler who would combat change and build his state on stable foundations (all Machiavelli's advice has this end in view: he too sees change as the great enemy) should not hesitate to break faith when expediency requires. However, since fidelity commands public respect, the ruler should conceal his treacheries and cultivate a reputation for this virtue.

It is perhaps too easy to dismiss the popular horror with which these recommendations were greeted in England as a simplistic reaction based on complete ignorance of Machiavelli's motives and of the grim socio-political context which shaped his disillusioned empiricism. For not only did Machiavelli rip out the cornerstone of Christian–humanist teaching on political morality; he became in effect the official propagandist for practices which were threatening to undo the English state – its civil and religious institutions, its law, its unity. The papal bulls releasing Englishmen from their oath of fealty to the monarch, and the deliberate use of equivocation in the courts by Catholics accused of treason, seemed proof – in a context of plots and rumours of plots to assassinate Elizabeth – that the Machiavellian doctrine of the unbinding oath had to be taken very seriously.[20] The dramatists undoubtedly concurred with Machiavelli's view that the ruler who can be relied on to keep his word is a rarity, and that in the world of politics generally the way things are and the way things ought or seem to be 'divides more wider than the sky and earth'. But the Italian's prescription for a stable and enduring rule must have seemed to them a desperate paradox, and on the evidence of their plays it emerges as a sure recipe for convulsive change. 'Nothing violent . . . can be permanent',[21] remarks Marlowe's Machiavel sagely; but he neglects to add what his own history shows all too clearly: that nothing breeds violence like treachery.

Since Machiavelli endorsed the necessity for absolute power, Machiavellianism on the stage is given its classic embodiment in the figure of the tyrant, usually a usurping one. And, since Machiavellianism came to be seen as the doctrine of violent change, the tyrant is a ruler who makes and unmakes laws at will ('I seal, I cancel, I do what I will') and impersonates Fortune even while purporting to be her master ('I'd make you what you would be', 'Rise but in this and thou shalt never fall').[22] It is true that Machiavellian 'policy' and duplicity are practised by a variety of evil characters who have no political ambitions of their own. Usually, however, such characters operate under the tutelage of a tyrant: with upright subjects to dispose of, and insatiable lusts to gratify, the tyrant creates a greasy élite of spies, panders, and hit-men to whom cynical and scheming treachery is a way of life.

It is a simple rule that the more noble the tragic character who falls, the more degenerate the society or the more cunning the mover he has to stand firm against. Like Caesar and Othello, however, virtually every tragic character has 'the falling sickness', and his tragedy is due to some extent to his own capacity for degenerative change. Thus, although the greatest cries of anguish and rage in Renaissance drama are cries against treachery, the tragic sufferer usually makes the same discovery as Shakespeare's Richard II: 'I find myself a traitor with the rest' (*Richard II*, IV.i.248). Self-forgetting and self-loss are key motifs in this tragic tradition.[23]

In the depiction of character degeneration, as in that of outward fortunes, an antithetical principle often obtains;[24] from Kyd's judge-turned-assassin the dramatists learned just now theatrically impressive and poignantly ironic the transformation of the protagonist into his own opposite might be.[25] The broad pattern of complete change can, however, be complicated or even replaced by one of continuous oscillation between opposite emotional and behavioural extremes, a method which emphasises from the start the uncertain coexistence of contrary attributes and tendencies in the protagonist: the prototypal character here is Tamburlaine, a furious conqueror susceptible to the gentle claims of love and friendship.[26] In non-Shakespearean tragedy, the change from one extreme to the other can be so ungraduated as to appear – especially from a purely naturalistic point of view – implausible or even downright grotesque. On the whole, however, it is rendered acceptable by symbolic elements in the dramatic style (such as disguise or costume change) and above all by the underlying assumption that man's nature is constituted of opposites each of which forever threatens to eclipse the other.[27]

The kinds of transformation can be very varied. Common to most of them, however, is change caused by a conflict in which reason is overcome or perverted by passion: the mythographer who identified Proteus, god of change, with the passions, would have found his interpretation vividly endorsed by English tragedians.[28] As has already been remarked, the major part played by passion in the downfall of the tragic character owes much to the example of Seneca. More specifically, the dramatists seem to have been affected in their treatment of extreme passion by the Senecan attitude of mingled horror and fascination, as well as by a radical contradiction in the significance which Seneca attaches to it. This contradiction stems from the nature of Stoicism itself. As a good Stoic, Seneca insists (especially in his choruses) on the need for rational control of the passions in accordance with the law of nature. But, being a Stoic, Seneca is also a fatalist; and nothing shows his fatalism more clearly than does his representation of passion as a dark and irresistibly destructive force, a curse from the gods. Perhaps the contradiction does not run so deep in Renaissance tragedy, but one does not have to look far for signs of a double attitude. In plays such as *Othello* and *'Tis Pity She's a Whore*, we see clearly enough that the loss of judgement and understanding marks the beginning of the end; but we see too that the pales and forts of reason provide poor protection against the full onslaught of the passions.

What the dramatists acquired from Seneca, however, was modified in the light of ideas about passion disseminated in the Renaissance by the flourishing science of ethical psychology and by Christian teachings on the effects of the Fall on man's nature. In their elaboration of traditional microcosmology, the ethical psychologists adhere to the fundamental Galenic (and ultimately Empedoclean) principle that health of mind and body depends on a proper balance of the four humours and qualities. They hold above all that right action requires a harmonious relationship between the higher faculties of the soul and the lower: between reason and will on the one hand, and 'appetite' (the passions, 'affections', or 'motions'), imagination, and memory on the other – but especially between reason and passion. However, the ethical psychologists give the impression that few men ever achieve this harmony. They postulate a never-ending conflict between reason and passion, and between the passions themselves; and they describe in great detail the ways in which disordered passion ('perturbation') can 'alter and change the whole estate of man . . . transform and disfigure him'.[29] Thoroughly indicative of this bias in their thinking is their special interest in the related conditions of wrath (by definition a temporary form of madness, liable to become permanent), melancholy (close to madness, and of all humours 'fullest of variety of passion',[30]) and madness itself (total unreason). In general, the ethical psychologists see man as a creature of passion, and for that reason they see him also as a creature of change – contrarious, variable, and recalcitrant to the stable laws of nature and God:[31] it is not surprising that their favourite term for passion is 'motion'. One might reasonably conclude that, although they give formal allegiance to medieval, *a priori* assumptions concerning the naturalness of rational conduct and the unnaturalness of inordinate passion, their Renaissance empiricism gets the better of them when they look closely at their subject.[32] But the inference can be only partially correct, for the notion of unity in contrariety and contrariety in unity on which their micro- and macrocosmology is based made it easy for the observer of nature to move between rationalist and empirical positions without risking the charge of philosophic inconsistency. He could stress pattern or process, permanence or change, rational order or passionate unruliness just as the circumstances or his purpose required.

The ethical psychologists' vision of passionate, contrarious man was sustained by, and in turn sustained, the theologians' account of the Fall. The principal effect of original sin on man's nature was that his reason and will were weakened and his passions became rebellious. Thus a harmonious relationship between the higher and lower faculties was transformed into one of almost permanent strife, which in turn became the chief source of human misery and imperfection.[33] In one theological tradition, echoed by Milton, the contribution of passion to the whole process of degenerative change is emphasised to the extent that it is made a cause of original sin: thus in *Paradise Lost* the eating of the apple is presented as a voraciously passionate act (IX.780–94, 990–1033), a 'Thystean banquet' (X.688) ending in an orgy of lust.

The extent to which these two related currents of thought fed into the drama was substantial. It shows in the dramatists' image of tragic man as a volatile creature whose integrity is rapidly undone by passion, imagination, and blind will; in their predisposition to interpret character (like history) in the light of a 'devolutionary' or deviationist principle; in their constant endeavour to show the transformational power of passion and to delineate precisely the physiological as well as the psychological changes it effects (the way voice, bodily movement, and countenance reflect the turmoil in the soul); and in their natural gravitation towards characters afflicted by melancholy, madness, and the extremes of wrath or grief. This is not to imply that the characters of Renaissance tragedy are fully explicable in terms of the psychological theories of the time; these plays contain psychological insights which have not been conceptually defined until recently. The fact remains, however, that the basic conceptions and categories of traditional psychology or 'microcosmology' did have a strong, general effect on the dramatists and are of use to the modern interpreter.[34] Some knowledge of them, for example, might have prevented E. E. Stoll from arguing that steep, tragic contrast in characters such as Othello and Macbeth, whose actions contradict their essential nature, is basically implausible, could never have been determined by psychological considerations, and was dictated mainly by the desire to create a powerful emotional effect. And it would have obviated the necessity for apealing to modern, depth psychology in the attempt to refute Stoll's argument.[35] 'We know what we are, but we know not what we may be', remarks the mad

Ophelia; and in Renaissance psychology what we may be–when reason and will succumb to the intensities of emotion and imagination–is our own antithesis.

Of course the attitude of the Renaissance tragedian towards inordinate passion, unlike that of the ethical psychologist and the theologian, is not one of simple disapproval.[36] The tragedians offer an abundance of choric and, more important, of dramatically ironic commentary on the sheer folly of headlong passion, and are unflinching in their depiction of the self-loss and cruel injustices it occasions. Yet they are acutely conscious that the greatness of men and women is tied up with their capacity to feel greatly and can present the passionate excess of their tragic figures as awe-inspiring if not in some sense blameless. Often, indeed, their plays adumbrate deep sympathy for the view that passion ('blood') and change rather than reason and permanence are the marks of what is most valuable in character and experience:

> The blood turns in my veins; I stand on change,
> And shall dissolve in changing; 'tis so full
> Of pleasure not to be contain'd in flesh:
> To fear a violent good, abuseth goodness,
> 'Tis immortality to die aspiring,
> As if a man were taken quick to heaven;
> What will not hold perfection, let it burst;
> What force hath any cannon, not being charg'd,
> Or being discharg'd?[37]

I do not think, however, that any play ever finally endorses this view: certainly not the one just quoted, and not even *Antony and Cleopatra*. And it appears to me that attempts to interpret Renaissance tragedy in the light of Nietzsche's theory of passion and reason as opposed but equally valid moralities are ultimately misleading.[38] For the dramatists, it would seem, remain convinced that human greatness resides in a harmony or partnership of psychic opposites, and that the force which destroys the noble self is unbound passion (or impassioned reason and will). And they seem similarly convinced that redemption entails the recovery of rational understanding and control.

Of all the passions which motivate the characters of Renaissance tragedy, ambition is perhaps the most illuminating. That it should have been considered a passion at all must be ascribed to the fact that passion itself was conceived as a 'rebellious' force always pressing for change. Its prominence in the tragedies recalls a feature of the Fall of Princes literature, but points even more to the dangerous actualities of life in the competitive, fast-changing society of Tudor and Stuart England. Any one of the passions which impel men and women to seek what is beyond them is likely in the tragedies to take on the complexion of worldly ambition and be so named: the word is used so loosely that it becomes a blanket term for 'the huge army of the world's desires'. In the tragedies of Marston, Chapman, Tourneur, and Webster, this universalising of ambition stems from the conception of the court as a sinister place where everyone who enters must of necessity climb on to a restless wheel which will hurl him down as surely as it will take him up: the incarnation of endless promise and duplicity, the corrupt court is the last palace of Lady Fortune. However, since the court is an image of the world at large, the meaning of ambition in Webster is essentially the same as it was in Shakespeare and Marlowe. Bosola, 'fed worse than hoping Tantalus', Macbeth 'drunk' with the 'hope' of a gilded future, and Barabas awaiting the return of his rich ship *Speranza*, alike suggest that men are all too easily seduced by hopes that in the nature of things can only beget despair.[39] Their hopes may be doomed because the history of human endeavour is ultimately the story of 'virtue in labour with eternal chaos / Press'd to a living death'.[40] More likely it is because all hopes erected in a corrupt society, or in defiance of some fundamental bond, are built on quicksand.

II THE NOBLE DEATH

Yet fall and despair seldom determine the final imaginative impression: even the gloomiest of Jacobean tragedies intimates that there is some sense in which loss converts to its opposite – defeat becomes victory, death renewal, fall transcendence. The reasons for this alteration of perspective are partly aesthetic (the artist's desire for balance and harmony) and partly emotional (his need to assuage the lacerated feelings of the audience). But they are partly metaphysical as well. As can be seen in two early tragedies which deeply affected the conception of tragic death in the tradition as a whole, *Tamburlaine the Great* and *Romeo and Juliet*, the possibility of change for the worse resolving into change for the better (hope creating from its own wreck the thing it contemplates) is inherent in a tragic structure which associates calamity with the universal dialectic of amity and strife.

It is appropriate to recall here that in the infancy of Greek cosmology Heraclitus claimed that the stability of the universe is founded not on a harmonious mean between the opposites, as the Pythagoreans taught, but on their strife: 'War is the father of all.' Although it is common to see in this disagreement two mutually exclusive world views, it should really be taken as early evidence of the elastic nature of a cosmology in which it is possible to emphasise either concord or discord. Heraclitus is not the total iconoclast he is often made out to be, for he explained that universal strife is a process of *measured* change between the elements of fire and water, and so characterised it both as harmony ('a hidden attunement') and as justice.[41] In consequence, the most ardent exponents of universal concord in the Renaissance – the Neo-Platonists – never felt embarrassed by his teaching and would even cite him as an authority. Although they held that unchecked strife is the source of all evil, they would also acknowledge that strife is necessary to the scheme of things and can be productive of good (in the sense that poisons can be used as cures).[42] That there is 'some soul of goodness in things evil, / Would men observingly distil it out' (*Henry V, IV.i.4–5*) was, in fact, a commonplace idea; but it was known to be grounded in natural science and metaphysics. Thus the terms in which the compensatory, regenerative motif is expressed at the end of *Timon of Athens* (when confounding contrariety has done its worst) must be related to the intellectual conventions of an age which – with the help of Empedoclean and Platonic teaching – had fully assimilated the contrary insights of Pythagoras and Heraclitus: 'Make war breed peace, make peace stint war, make / Each prescribe to other as each other's leech' (V.iv.83–4).

Although by no means peculiar to it, a regenerative or redemptive note is of singular importance in Renaissance tragic tradition. A measure of its importance can be found in the manifestly conscious efforts of several dramatists to ensure that it does not dilute tragic effect (e.g. Shakespeare in *King Lear*, Chapman in *Bussy D'Ambois*), and in the inability of some others to avoid being led by it into the sentimental harmonies of religious and secular romance (e.g. Heywood in *A Woman Killed with Kindness*, Ford in *The Broken Heart*). Indicative too of its powerful appeal to the age is the astonishing last act of *Antony and Cleopatra*, where tragedy is all but subsumed in cosmic comedy.

The characteristics of the tragic experience being strife, inconstancy, and confusion, the chief signs of regeneration are concord, constancy, and clarification. And they are found mainly in the noble manner with which the protagonists confront death.[43] For some of them death is a happening which makes a nonsense of all they have done. But for the majority it is a happening which one must strive heroically to shape and control so far as is possible. They turn it from a meaningless or unchosen event into a significant, chosen action, a deed which enshrines a clear image of their true selves and by means of which they distil something of permanence from change itself. Thus the protagonist dies at one with Fate, with others (or another), and above all with himself: as the phrase goes (and even Milton relies on its ritual resonance in *Samson Agonistes*), he dies 'like himself'. This does not mean dying in a recognisably individual manner, but 'like a man'; and like a man as distinct from a beast, with rational fortitude rather than passionate defiance or any kind of rage against the dying of the light.

The ritual of the Noble Death in Renaissance tragedy drew on a rich complex of cultural ideals and experiences and seems to have exercised a correspondingly potent hold on the imagination of contemporary audiences. Behind it lie centuries of iconographic, hagiographic, and dramatic tradition in which the death of Christ and the martyrs is made to yield a vivid contrast between the bestial frenzy and frustrated cunning of the tormentor and the complete serenity of his victim. This tradition was kept vigorously alive in the sixteenth century by the sectarian persecutions of the time and by the immensely popular *Acts and Monuments* (1563) of John Foxe. Foxe's pages abound in heroic images that are likely to strike the student of Renaissance tragedy with a curious sense of *déjà vu*:

> And when the woode was kindled, and the fire began to burne neere him, stretching out hys arme, he put hys right hand into the flame: which he held so stedfast and immoueable . . . that all men might see hys hande burned before his body was touched. His body did so abide the burning of the flame with such constancy and stedfastness, that standing alwayes in one place without moouing his body, he seemed to mooue no more than the stake to which hee was bound.[44]

These images of perfect constancy, however, may have contributed less to the conventions of Renaissance tragedy than did the pervasive implication of martyrological literature that violent death is the one test of heroic authenticity, the event which above all others can give meaning and value to life.

Yet the archetype of the Noble Death which most directly influenced the dramatists was that of the demi-god Hercules as interpreted by Seneca – in the light of Stoic tradition – in his *Hercules Furens*. (Given the fact that there had been from the beginning a strong admixture of Stoic constancy in the Christian ideal of patience, this influence was an eminently natural process.[45]) Some salient features of the Senecan treatment of Hercules's end were to become standard elements in the Noble Death of Renaissance tragedy: the great change of mood which overtakes him as the end approaches, his sense of decorum or of what befits his manhood and reputation, his upright stance, and the use of music metaphor (denoting the resolution of a great conflict).[46]

The first of these made a particularly deep impression on the imagination of the Renaissance dramatist. Hercules's initial response to the poisonous death which has been treacherously prepared for him is one of raging, boastful, and incredulous resistance; but this gives way to a mood of calm acceptance. The change springs from his realisation that although his body must perish his greatness will survive; and it culminates in his active participation in the process of his own destruction. During the Renaissance, the Herculean pattern of passionate resistance and rational acceptance is noticeable – as one might expect – in the deaths of martial heroes and men of action such as Marlowe's Tamburlaine, Shakespeare's Othello and Antony, and Chapman's Bussy D'Ambois and Pompey. But its influence is at work in the deaths of other tragic characters who do not fall into this category at all. It is wonderfully expanded in Hamlet's progress from the furious bravado of the graveyard scene ('Let Hercules himself do what he may') to the resigned yet active co-operation with divine providence evident in his response to the challenge of the duel ('The readiness is all'). It even affects the characterisation of the great heroines. Some of them seek desperately to escape the inevitable; all rise in the end above the fickleness and frailty for which the daughters of Eve are excoriated in seventeenth-century tragic satire, assuming a 'marble constant' and 'masculine virtue' which gives a special lustre to the paradox of the transcendent fall.[47]

There is something unmistakably suicidal in the final attitude of Seneca's Hercules to his own death (as there is in Hamlet's). This reflects the Stoic presumption that no real difference can be made between the uncomplaining acceptance of the worst that Fortune can offer and the ending of one's own life where survival would mean tolerating injustice and unreason – each postulates the constancy of purpose entailed by respect for universal law. The motives for suicide in Renaissance tragedy are not always of the purely Stoical kind, but Stoicism certainly determines the general colouring of the more memorable acts of self-slaughter: they are presented in a noble light as supreme gestures of constancy at a time of change; as assertions of justice or defiances of injustice. In view of Christianity's unqualified condemnation of suicide, this laudatory attitude might well seem baffling. Theodore Spencer's explanation was that the dramatists tacitly accepted two strict conditions for the favourable presentation of suicide: it had to take place in ancient Rome or to be committed under the stress of violent emotion.[48] There are, however, some striking exceptions to this rule: not only Chapman's *The Revenge of Bussy*

D'Ambois (acknowledged as an exception by Spencer) but also *Romeo and Juliet* and *Othello*. In both Shakespearean tragedies the emotional state of the hero as he prepares to kill himself is not violent at all; it is one of marmoreal calm, an achievement in manly self-control which the structural pattern invites us to contrast with the unseemly passion of his symbolic and literal fall near the centre of the action.[49]

A more workable explanation might be that the dramatists' interest in suicide does not operate on a literal level of meaning at all: that the calm suicide is essentially a grandiose symbol dictated by the fervency of their desire to show that great men and women, when put to the test, are capable of throwing away the dearest thing they own as if it were a careless trifle. The theme of the Noble Death generated a rhetoric rich in hyperbole and paradox and in a logical sense suicide is its culminating point of development. After the spectacle of death accepted with perfect equanimity comes that of death embraced eagerly. Assassin and executioner are then greeted as courteous friends: violated welcome (the guest or host at the Treacherous Entertainment) becomes welcomed violence, bloodshed becomes bloodletting and healing, disturbance rest, dying coition, funeral marriage. The baroque extremes to which this rhetoric can go in the presentation of deaths which are not suicidal at all can be seen in such plays as Heywood's *A Woman Killed with Kindness*, Beaumont and Fletcher's *The Maid's Tragedy* and Ford's *The Broken Heart*. In these plays we are invited to extend all our admiration and pity to characters (mostly women) who conspire to bring about, and joyously participate in, the 'pastime . . . majestical' of their own untimely ends.[50] To say that suicide is the next logical step in depicting the Noble Death is not, however, to postulate a simple process of chronological development. It is to point to the prevalence of stage conventions whose effect is to remove from suicide its everyday significance as the ultimate expression of despair and misery and to turn it into a figure of perfect constancy. Given the force and acceptability of such conventions, it seems unlikely that the dramatists would have felt the need for rules which would have squared the presentation of self-slaughter with Christian doctrine.

The equivalence of Aristotle's 'recognition' – a 'change from ignorance to knowledge' – is an obvious component of the Noble Death. Like Middleton, most of the dramatists believe that 'man's understanding / Is riper at his fall than all his life-time';[51] they see him rising above calamity not simply by accepting it with total constancy but by perceiving the extent to which he himself has worked it or by recognising the operation of a universal law from which no one is exempt. This stress on 'acquist of knowledge' is not Aristotelian in origin; nor is it primarily Christian. It was probably inspired by Seneca's interpretation of Hercules's death and by the related Stoic doctrine of 'right reason'. As the greatest of Renaissance Neo-Stoics explained, 'right reason' is the 'verie roote where uppon is setled the high and mightie bodie of that fair oake CONSTANCIE'. Its complete opposite is 'opinion', by which it is continually being obscured. This is 'naught else but a vaine image and shadow of reason'; and unlike 'right reason' it does not signify strength of mind but rather 'a certaine hardnesse of a stubborne mind proceeding from pride or vaine glorie'.[52] It is from something very like obstinate opinion that many of the confused protagonists of Renaissance tragedy escape in their constant and clear-seeing acceptance of the inevitable.

The process of recognition is frequently modified, however, by the Christian assumption that repentance and forgiveness are prerequisites for spiritual renewal: 'Penitence . . . throws men down, only to raise them up.'[53] Yet the implications of the idea are more this-worldly than other-worldly. Those who in dying freely acknowledge the wrongs they have done to others, and are eager to exchange forgiveness, are both 'Christian and noble', but the stress is on their nobility.[54] The qualities they display are the essentially secular virtues of candour and magnanimity; the effect of such virtues is to resolve earthbound conflicts and to redeem the dying in the eyes of their fellow men, even when they seem damned from a religious standpoint.

So important is the motif of forgiveness that it often extends beyond the death of the protagonist to form the basis of social reintegration or – a key word and stage image – 'joining'. Thus the dying hero actively seeks to ensure that the reconciliation he has achieved is extended to all who survive him.[55] The living spontaneously pledge themselves to renewal in a ritual where the sufferings of the dead are felt as a kind of sacrificial incense:

> Let us make noble use
> Of this great ruin; and join all our force
> To establish this young, hopeful gentleman
> In's mother's right.
>   (*Duchess of Malfi*, V.v.110–13[56])

Or, where the protagonist dies unreconciled, appalled survivors draw together to advocate a 'change . . . from an ignorant wrath / To knowing friendship' and to commit themselves anew to the bonds of social unity.[57] But the more severe tragic vision strains against such conclusions and we may be given cause to remember the false hopes and 'politic' reconciliations which have gone before. The endings of *Hamlet* and *King Lear* are notable in this respect; so too is the conclusion of *Bussy D'Ambois*, with the difference that Chapman spells out with emblematic emphasis what is implicit in Shakespeare. The dying Bussy succeeds in effecting a 'Christian reconcilement' in the marriage he has helped to undo, to the extent that Tamyra asks and Montsurry grants forgiveness. But when Bussy dies Montsurry refuses to 'conjoin in one' with his wife, and the pair *'Exeunt severally'*: we are to understand that the only enduring and indisputably authentic reconciliations are those which belong to the dying and the dead.

The model of the Noble Death, or any of its principal features, may be used implicitly and negatively in order to emphasise the fact that a character dies unredeemed or incompletely redeemed. Failure to respond to this strategy is not uncommon and its effect is to diminish appreciation or understanding of the crucial last scenes of a tragedy. If, for example, we observe that in his last hours Faustus oscillates between cowardice and bravado, that his penultimate wish is to be 'chang'd / Unto some brutish beast', and that he is dragged off stage screaming, yet do not perceive in these details a fiercely ironic glance at the manly, constant, upright death of the true hero, then some of the astounding force and spiritual significance of that tragic finale will be lost on us.[58] Unfamiliarity with the relevant heroic pattern is more likely to contribute to straightforward misinterpretation of the conclusion of such plays as *Macbeth* and Chapman's *Byron's Tragedy*. Macbeth's dying ferocity and contemptuous refusal to 'play the Roman fool' have often been taken as reassertions of his essential, soldierly self.[59] Such an interpretation, however, ignores several important points. Macbeth has been full of change almost to the last moment; his final stand is not manly but 'bear-like' (*Macbeth*, V.vii.2); and if he had committed suicide (in the Othello manner) it would probably have been taken by Shakespeare's audience as a redeeming resurgence of that respect for limit and justice which once made him pre-eminent among soldiers. Byron's dying rage is even more impressive than Macbeth's, but it too is a flawed greatness. Like Macbeth's, it is inhuman – the fury of 'a savage boar' – and part of a pattern of emotional extremes and instability ('He alters every minute'); and it is tinged with bravado (*Byron's Tragedy*, V.iii.187, 229). One is more likely to misinterpret Byron's death than Macbeth's, for, whereas Chapman's allusion to the heroic model is entirely implicit, Shakespeare's, like Marlowe's in *Doctor Faustus*, is not. In dying, Young Siward is to Macbeth what the Old Man is to Faustus: not (as has been claimed) his mirror image, but rather his spiritual antithesis ('like a man he died' – *Macbeth*, V.viii.43). Moreover, just what 'manly fortitude' (*Faustus*, I.iii.85) consists of is a crucial issue on which Macbeth, like Faustus, has been deeply confused from the start.

Like constancy and manliness, recognition can be conspicuously absent or imperfect just when it is most expected. The Stoic hero of *Julius Caesar* is said to die 'like Brutus, like himself' (v.iv.25), yet his boast that he found no man but was true to him is sadly delusive (v.v.35); more than that, it is proof that he has failed to appreciate the significance of what 'Caesar's angel' did to Caesar and that he is still possessed of a subtly false notion of constancy: the phrase 'like Brutus' is deeply ambiguous, implying as it does that the noble Roman who commits suicide at Philippi is the same confused man who killed his friend because of the crimes he might commit and out of love for his fellow Romans. In plays with a Christian setting, such failures are usually failures to admit guilt and ask pardon from those wronged. Again, *Macbeth* and *Byron's Tragedy* are illuminating. Although Macbeth never deludes himself about his guilt, and cryptically acknowledges some of it to Macduff, his bitterness and despair are such that a redeeming candour is beyond him: in a play packed with retrospective contrasts, 'the deep damnation of his taking off' (*Macbeth*, I.vii.20) has to be measured against the death of the first Thane of Cawdor, whose 'deep repentance' and imploring the King's pardon won him an undying epitaph: 'Nothing in his life / Became him like the leaving it' (I.iv.7–8). Much more emphasis is placed on Byron's failure to confess. His is a deliberate refusal reinforced with angry and specious denials of treachery, and it prevents him from getting the royal pardon he so confidently expects. Indeed it is mainly what keeps him a figure of 'impossible mixtures' and 'contraries' to the end (*Byron's Tragedy*, v.iii.180), the microcosmic reflection of a

> Wretched world
> Consisting most of parts that fly each other,
> A firmness breeding all inconstancy,
> A bond of all disjunction.
>   (V.iv.62–5)

Byron dies unreconciled to his fate, to himself, and to the good king he betrayed.

It is doubtful, however, whether the failure of the protagonist to achieve constancy, self-knowledge, or reconciliation necessarily means that he or the play is not tragic in the full sense. Such failures stir us deeply with the spectacle of total self-loss or alienation. They usually pertain, moreover, to heroes of a special type, that of the 'fallen angel', and so are imaginatively appropriate; for the death of such a hero should leave us with a final impression of greatness and imperfection hopelessly confused. Furthermore, the hero's failure to achieve self-knowledge is usually calculated to enhance *our* understanding of what has happened; and the knowledge that matters in tragedy is surely that which is acquired by the audience.[60]

Just how much tragic potential there is in the death of a hero who fails to achieve self-knowledge and full reconciliation is best seen perhaps in a play which the author himself did not venture to call a tragedy – Ford's *The Chronicle History of Perkin Warbeck*. Nowhere does the hero of this play approach more nearly the stature of the great heroes of Renaissance tragedy than in the sublime impenitence of his 'taking off'. If Warbeck repents and renounces his counterfeit self, a royal pardon awaits him. But he will not; and his refusal is neither furious nor despairing but calmly confident, proceeding as it does from absolute faith in his claim to royalty. Moreover, Warbeck acts out this faith with quite compelling decorum: even when the ignominious rope is placed on his neck, he is utterly dignified and quietly eloquent. So, although we are given good reason to see the former boatman as a creature deluded to the depths of his soul, we cannot but accord him unqualified admiration and compassion. In what is perhaps the most amazing metamorphosis effected by the Noble Death on the Renaissance Stage, a specious claim to royalty is here changed into a genuine one. We find justice in Warbeck's opinion that 'illustrious mention / Shall blaze our names, and style us Kings o'er death' (V.iii.206–7); and we may suspect that the final truth of what men are is enveloped in mystery.

III THE VIOLATION OF JUSTICE AND LOVE

(i) *Justice and Law*

The tragic protagonists' response to the forces which threaten their identity and their view of the way things are is played out in a context of problematic relationships. Whether openly or secretly, and whether because of the protagonist's actions or not, society itself is convulsed with violent change. Although the play may end on a note which reaffirms the idea of enduring and fruitful human relationships, this, like the Noble Death, is essentially consolatory. The vision of human life presented here is a grim spectacle of broken bonds; in the thematic terms most characteristic of this drama, what we have been witness to is the violation of justice and love, law and marriage.

Justice and law are, of course, a perennial tragic theme. Most tragic writers dwell on the sufferings of those who defy accepted rule; they ask whether the harsh reversals of life conform to any reasonable pattern, and they gravitate naturally towards such concepts as lot, necessity, and fate (which are legal in essence). For a number of historical reasons, however, Renaissance tragedy is preoccupied with this theme to an extent that is exceptional. During the sixteenth and seventeenth centuries, the heady new doctrines of individualist self-assertion were countered on every side by an almost obsessive concern with the nature and the necessity of law. In religion the predestinarianism of Luther and Calvin drastically reduced the measure of spiritual freedom conceded to man in the Catholic dispensation and presented him with an inexorable divine judge whose perfect justice is so inaccessible to human reason that he can consign to eternal damnation souls created with no choice but to break the law. In moral and political philosophy, the socio-political turmoils incident to the Reformation occasioned an urgent quest for the substratum of unchanging law below all the variable rules of human societies, and so to a revitalising of Stoic and Scholastic doctrines of natural law. The new scepticism, however, like the ancient scepticism from which it drew much of its inspiration, insisted on the purely conventional and arbitrary nature of man's laws and ridiculed the notion of a common law rooted in the nature of things and available to reasonable men everywhere. Yet the most influential spokesmen of this attitude were more convinced than anyone else that man must be 'bridled and fettered' by laws of whatever kind if he is to be saved from the urge towards 'volubility and dissolution' that forever rages within him.[61]

All this belongs to the social and intellectual history of Western Europe and was not peculiar to England alone. But the sixteenth–seventeenth century period was also the most vigorous and momentous in the whole history of English law.[62] The great struggle between the claims of the Royal Prerogative and the Common Law (and their respective courts and conceptions of law), the struggle which culminated in the Civil War and regicide, had begun. At the same time the law courts and the legal profession expanded and flourished as never before. For ambitious young men with few ready-made social advantages, the law thus became the main road to affluence and political success.[63] And, in a way which harmonised nicely with the forensic colouring of the rhetorical treatises on which contemporary education depended so heavily, a spell at the Inns of Court came to be regarded as a prerequisite for the complete man. Predictably, the new secular intelligentsia was dominated by lawyers.[64]

Developments such as these would have indirectly affected any drama sensitive to its own environment; but the connection between the law and the drama was intimate and direct as well. On the negative side, the popular dramatists were keenly aware of the brutal severity with which the law might descend on anyone who penned speeches held to be seditious or irreligious: Kyd's subjection to the horrors of *peine forte et dure* was exemplary. On the positive side, several of the popular dramatists were themselves former students of the law, and some even conducted their own legal cases. Most of them, too, were probably on friendly terms with the Inns of Court men, for these were among the liveliest patrons of the new drama and had fostered its development from the start. The development of native tragedy in particular owed much to them. *The Mirror for Magistrates* (1559) and *Gorboduc* (1566; acted 1561), those twin landmarks in the history of sixteenth-century tragedy before Marlowe and Kyd, were composed by lawyers and given a legal orientation which directly or indirectly affected everything written thereafter in the genre. Thus, when Kyd devised his own immensely influential fable about a great lawyer demented by injustice to the point where his violence leaves two kingdoms without an heir-apparent, he was certainly not belittling the legal profession or the law. He was pointing to the need for just and effective law ('Where words prevail not, violence prevails' – *Spanish Tragedy*, II.i.108) and remembering both the succession theme in *Gorboduc* and the subject of the *Mirror's* first tragedy – 'The fall of Robert Tresilian chiefe Iustice of Englande . . . for misconstruynge the lawes, and expounding them to serve the Prince's affections.' He may also have been remembering the *Mirror's* warning that 'For lack of Iustice kyngdomes are transmuted.'[65]

Retribution is by far the most conspicuous manifestation of the justice theme in the tragedies.[66] Being almost always violent and secret – a sudden reversal of the victim's fortunes rather than a formal procedure – it contradicts the very nature of law; but it is justice of a kind, none the less, and may be seen as the effect of a universal or divine law which works in spite of and also through the violence of men and the accidents of chance. The overriding interest in retribution points to the combined influence of Seneca and the Fall of Princes tradition, but the idea of an alliance between retribution and mischance (Fortune) is very much an inheritance from the latter. In Lydgate's *The Fall of Princes* (c. 1431-9) and in *The Mirror for Magistrates*, the treacheries of Fortune in a world made mutable by Adam's infringement of divine law are afflictions which every man is liable to, irrespective of his moral condition. The main concern of the *Mirror* authors, however, is to show that Fortune reserves her most shattering blows for tyrannical rulers and ambitious or rebellious subjects whose crimes provoke the divine wrath; they see Fortune as the instrument of divine justice operating with considerable precision in the theatre of history.

This comforting doctrine bears very little resemblance to the austere account of the relationship between historical happenings and divine providence offered by such authorities as Boethius, Thomas Aquinas, or Richard Hooker: properly interpreted, the Christian doctrine of divine providence offers no guarantee of poetic justice in this life either for the virtuous or the wicked. But the notion of Fortune as the retributive agent of the Almighty was a handy instrument for writers intent on influencing political behaviour (as were Lydgate and the *Mirror* authors); and plenty of support for it could be found in the Old Testament. Moreover, it was given new life in the sixteenth century – and so passed into the drama – by virtue of its relevance to one of the most pressing moral questions in the political consciousness of the time: whether it is right to overthrow a lawful but wicked ruler. The answer given to this question by Protestant theologians (most notably Calvin) in the so-called doctrine of non-resistance reflects the age's desperate desire for stability and correspondingly desperate respect for law. Under no circumstances was forcible resistance to be offered to a lawfully constituted ruler or 'magistrate', however vicious his conduct might be: the correction of such men was to be left to God who, as his treatment of biblical tyrants had shown, would probably act against them in his own good time through the torments of conscience, the agency of evil men, or one of his own servants specially called and commissioned for the purpose.[67] It was a doctrine by no means free from ambiguity: how does the tyrannicide know whether he is prompted to revenge by Heaven or by Hell? But it suited the needs of the time, and it was treated with considerable respect by the dramatists.

Indeed, the dramatists' devotion to the poetry of justice as it affects the vicious is even more pronounced than that of the narrative tragedians: every common villain as well as every tyrant and rebel gets his deserts. Nevertheless, even the most superficial examination of the way in which retribution functions in the plays cannot but serve to emphasise how much the old theme has been changed by its context. Just as the mutabilities of Fortune are assimilated to the process of universal contrariety, so retribution becomes part of a comprehensive view of justice and injustice in relation to the dynamics of human nature and social interaction as well as the design of man's life in time. Didacticism has largely vanished and moral disapproval of those who ruthlessly impose their will on the world is largely taken for granted: the response called for is one of mingled awe and dread at the passion or will which drives such men and at the energy and cunning which brings them success. Moreover, in plays which depict the fall of a tyrant or arch-villain the wonderful efficacy of divine law is of far less account than is the total inadequacy of human law. Correspondingly, there is a large extension of interest from the wickedness of great men who ignore or abuse law to the sufferings and moral dilemmas of their victims, especially those who are driven to carve out justice for themselves: the great problem of 'resistance' is brought into the open. In this way, the tyrant and the noble revenger emerge as complementary types and interacting extremes – law without justice and justice without law – through which the dramatists can explore the major evils that threaten man-in-society.

Of the two types, the revenger has by far the more dramatic potential. He is gripped by emotions which are singularly intense and transforming and can provoke in us a conflict between sympathy and moral presupposition that ensures imaginative involvement with his predicament at the deepest level. Indeed, the dramatists are often so successful in securing our imaginative identification with the revenger's viewpoint that many critics have argued that the dramatists and their audience – unlike the law, the Church, and all thoughtful moralists of the day – considered revenge-killing not only morally acceptable but even, in certain circumstances, a sacred duty. Other critics have found this quite implausible; and, although careful scholarship has investigated every allusion to revenge inside and outside the drama in order to resolve the problem, we are still left with intelligent critics holding diametrically opposed views on the matter.[68]

Whatever position one adopts, it may be useful to keep clearly in mind that most revenge heroes are pitted against tyrants or other 'great men' who use rank to frustrate justice, and that in consequence the revenge theme was very much a means by which the dramatists tied the melodrama of popular tragedy to the great contemporary problem of forcible resistance to unjust authority as well as to the perennial problem of the relationship between justice and law. This said, however, I would wish to express agreement with the view that the great majority of spectators and playwrights did accept orthodox teaching on revenge and tyrannicide, holding it better to endure injustice under the law than to risk the miscarriages of justice, and the moral and social disintegration, which are likely to occur when legal restraints and procedures are thrown aside. This much seems evident from such plays as *The Spanish Tragedy, Julius Caesar, Othello,* and *The Revenger's Tragedy*, where the hero's absolute conviction of the rectitude of his extra-legal justice is symptomatic of a profound intellectual and moral confusion induced by emotional distress (or humoral disorder). Admittedly, however, there is enough evidence in the plays to suggest that allegiance to the orthodox teaching on revenge and tyrannicide could not have been unqualified and that those who did accept it were willing to regard it as inapplicable in exceptional circumstances. In *Tamburlaine the Great*, for example, the hero is frequently accused of being a murderous usurper, yet he sees himself as a fully justified, divinely

ordained destroyer of tyranny and corruption. Marlowe leaves us to judge
him for ourselves, but gives him (at the least) a very good case. In *Antonio's
Revenge* – by John Marston 'of the Middle Temple', be it noted – the two
viewpoints are not artistically controlled in this way but emerge instead as
an awkward though revealing inconsistency. Marston begins by approving
Stoic endurance in a reign of tyranny, then seems to decide that this is a
preposterous ideal in the real world, and concludes by presenting a
revenger who emulates the archetypal barbarities of Atreus and Medea as a
glorious champion of civil and religious order – a Herculean Protestant in
Augean Italy. One might wish to dismiss the evidence of this play on the
ground that it is some kind of literary joke.[69] But then there is Chapman,
who changes his position from one play to another. In *Bussy D'Ambois* he
presumably endorses the King's trenchant refutation of the argument that
honourable men have the right to 'imp out' the law when it fails to do them
justice:

> This would make every man that thinks him wrong'd
> Or is offended, or in wrong or right,
> Lay on this violence, and all vaunt themselves
> Law-menders and suppliers though mere butchers;
> Should this fact [i.e. crime] (though of justice) be forgiven?
> (II.i.160–4)

Yet in *The Revenge of Bussy D'Ambois* Chapman ingeniously provides
moral justification for a Stoic hero who avenges the murder of his brother,
the justification being that he kills his enemy with the passionless
detachment of a judge-*cum*-executioner, turning violence into law itself.

It would be wrong, then, to assume that commitment to the orthodox
view of revenge was absolute and unwavering; but the notion that the
revenge hero is presented as a man who in the circumstances has no real
alternative to revenge hardly seems tenable either. It is valid only in the
sense that revenge has become an apparently irresistible emotional
imperative. The alternative to revenge is what the spokesmen of the
orthodox ethic habitually recommend to those who chafe under gross
injustice: the Christian virtue of patience. In the tragedies – with the
possible exception of Heywood's *A Woman Killed with Kindness* – this
virtue does not savour of milk-and-water piety, for it merges into the Stoic
virtue of constancy. It is a positive virtue which implies a disciplined refusal
to act until such time as action is compatible with one's moral values; and it
may also imply faith in the ultimate justice of the universe. Those who
practise patience in the face of injustice are often accused by other

characters of despair and timidity, but the accusation is not endorsed by the dramatist. Jonson, for example, connects 'the plaine and passiue fortitude, / To suffer and be silent' with the Herculean 'stand upright', and implicitly contrasts it with the sound and fury of an ostentatious valour which only makes a bad situation worse.[70]

Patient constancy, however, is an inherently undramatic attribute, as the heroes of Tourneur's *The Atheist's Tragedy* and Chapman's *Chabot* clearly demonstrate. It is dramatically acceptable as a dominant quality only when assigned to characters of a second order of importance: men who represent the virtues of a better age, such as 'time honour'd' Gaunt in *Richard II* and Lepidus in *Sejanus*; or who undertake the burden of rule when the violent hero is dead, as does Edgar in *King Lear* or Antonio in *The Revenger's Tragedy*. Such characters make splendid dramatic foils to the heroic men of action, and their personalities tend in consequence towards a colourless sobriety; but this should not obscure the fact that they provide an ethical perspective on violence which has to be taken seriously.

That many tragic heroes and heroines move beyond violent passions to become monuments of patience is one obvious indication of the high place which that virtue holds in the dramatists' scale of values.[71] That it is indistinguishable in practice from respect for time – 'seasonableness', 'ripeness', 'readiness', 'opportunity' – is another. It would be difficult to exaggerate the extent to which this concept contributed to the whole Renaissance sense of right conduct and fruitful procedures: its importance seems to have been confirmed from whatever standpoint human behaviour was studied. In the doctrine of decorum so much emphasis is placed on the need for adjustment to the circumstance of time that propriety in behaviour becomes almost synonymous with a discriminating sense of the fitting moment.[72] Elsewhere, timeliness is noticeably associated with justice and law. In didactic applications of the providential theory of history it is underwritten by the much-used formula that 'God is the patient avenger of all unrighteousness' who 'will in his due time' act against the unjust, carefully choosing 'his fittest time to revenge'.[73] A closely related theme in moral philosophy – one which goes back to the Stoics – makes timeliness a cardinal virtue of the truly just man: those with responsibility for punishing crime are exhorted to avoid 'all beastly violence; and hastiness . . . taking to counsell Time, which seldom or never is accompanied with repentance'.[74] For reasons peculiar to the native legal system, this notion became a refrain in English law courts; thus it was set down as a major principle of jurisprudence by Francis Bacon, who claimed that 'untimely and hastie passing of sentence' was first among the four main causes of 'instability of judgements' in law.[75] All three traditions associating time with justice converge in a proverbial motif widely disseminated during the Renaissance in the iconographic forms of moral allegory – 'Time is the author both of truth and right'.[76]

Respect for time is no ordinary moral or pragmatic rule in Renaissance thought. It has metaphysical implications and predicates a capacity to cope with or transcend the moment by intuiting its place in the unfolding drama of existence. In the great variety of cosmographical writings produced by the Renaissance, there is general agreement that the essential purpose of all study of the universe is an understanding of time, that being the chief means outside of revealed religion for an understanding of man's relationship with nature and the Creator.[77] The cosmographers endow Time with a two-fold character which is everywhere reflected in Renaissance literature. As the measurement of cosmic motion it is identified with destructive mutability. But as a cyclical process of balanced opposites (day and night, summer and winter, spring and autumn), identical in design to the pattern of the four elements and humours, it is seen as the cosmic law of regulated change. The heavenly bodies, the linking factor in this spatio-temporal order, have the same double character. As the universal clocks and calendars, they are the agents of mutability and decay. But being steadfast in their motions they are timeless too – images of eternal constancy which might inspire bewildered mortals when it seems that the world has returned to its 'First chaos'. 'Look you, the stars shine still' (*Duchess of Malfi*, IV.i.99).[78]

In the tragedies, time is sometimes perceived as a controlling force intermediary between divine providence and man. But in keeping with the secular outlook of the drama it seems to stand more and more on its own for whatever suggestions of an enduring order the tragedians can detect behind the convulsions of tragic experience.[79] Almost by definition tragic action is untimely in itself and the result of actions which are also untimely. Untimely action may be dilatory or rash, but rashness – or 'violence' – is what prevails. Being a distillation of the compulsive element in the passions, it has the effect of making tragic characters seem the victims of their own nature and so of neutralising criticism of their actions without making ethical concepts irrelevant to an understanding of their fall.

The encompassing rhythm of time, and the divergence of tragic action from it, are signalled in a variety of ways. (1) Warnings, predictions, and omens draw out the rash nature of a crucial choice or deed; when placed near the beginning of the play, they have the effect of turning the two hours' traffic of the stage into a period fixed for time to bring in its revenges. The same effect is obtained in more intense form when the action is placed from the outset within a specific time limit which the hero ignores or is unconscious of, his rashness having given way to the hope that time will stand still.[80] (2) Nature imagery, music imagery, music, astrological reference, casual questions as to the time of day or night, and the ringing of bells and striking of clocks all work as reminders of a law from which the tardy and the rash cannot escape.[81] (3) Transfer of the action to the hours of darkness is a favourite device for indicating departure from time's law.[82] Those who confuse temporal opposites by becoming creatures of the night seem death-marked or sinister or both. (In *Hamlet* this kind of confusion is indigenous to a realm where action is so frenzied that the funeral meats furnish the wedding-table and it is scarcely possible to 'divide the Sunday from the week' – I.i.76.) (4) But the most popular method of relating tragic action to the norm of timeliness is the conspicuously ironic one of endowing the agents of violence with a self-approving and even fastidious care for 'opportunity' and 'occasion'. This is an outstanding peculiarity of vigilant revengers and cunning Machiavels – 'Catch Occasion by the front for she is bald behind' is their favourite motto;[83] but it can be found in any character blind to the true nature or likely consequences of his impulsively chosen course of action.[84] That rash and violent action should be conceived as patient and timely is, of course, a notable sign of the confusion which characterises the tragic world.

The dramatists' sense of time as an inescapable frame of order has much to do with the brilliant and often pitiless irony which informs the process of retribution. For irony is an awareness of the unexpected changes that lie in wait for us, and is nourished by anticipation of time future ('Aye, think so still, till experience change thy mind'), and by remembrance of time past ('I wasted time, and now doth time waste me'). The irony of retribution colours the whole psychology of the revenger: his imagination feeds on the memory of past misdeeds and on the expectation of a moment when punishment will be delivered in a manner ingeniously fitted to the crime that was. But it is remarkable how often and how cruelly past errors and faults are echoed when no conventional revenger is present, and at moments of supreme agony in the lives of those who at that moment merit nothing but compassion. Such ironies seem to occur spontaneously, as if part of the scheme of things; and they evoke the presence of a punitive spirit as cruelly mocking and endowed with as long a memory as any crazed revenger. But there is a difference of effect. Whereas at the fall of villains retrospective irony intensifies the impression of poetic justice, at the fall of noble characters it throws a sharp light on man's blindness and on the terrible disporportion between his errors and frailties and the price he may have to pay for them. Always, however, the ironic echo points to a process of cause and effect in human affairs and to the remorseless operation of a law which demands limit and restraint even where obedience to that demand seems humanly impossible – when perhaps the time itself is out of joint.[85]

We have now considered two aspects of a development in which the traditional theme of retribution becomes part of a much more comprehensive and dramatically oriented response to the problem of justice and law in the tragic world: first, the extension of interest from the inevitable downfall of the great law-breakers to the sufferings and dilemmas of those whose wrongs the law will not redress; and, second, an emphasis – arising out of the antithesis between reason and passion, patience and revenge (rebellion) – on time (natural law, the historical process) as a source of ironic Nemesis and a corrective order. A third aspect of this development is the dramatists' recognition that justice is twofold, being distributive as well as corrective. Their ideal society (seldom glimpsed) is governed by a legitimate ruler who not only punishes all crime impartially within the form of law but also seeks to ensure that 'just guerdon may befall desert' in the distribution of honours and benefits.[86] Tragic society is defined accordingly: dominated by the classic types of injustice (tyrant, usurper, Machiavel), it shows innocence persecuted and crime unpunished while at the same time the unworthy are rewarded and patient merit is spurned. There are clear signs of this comprehensive grasp of the nature of justice in Kyd and Marlowe, but it is in the Jacobean period, when the economic ills of the nation are echoed from the stage, that it really commands attention. Here the neglect of true worth combines with the legality of crime to produce the outraged man of violence. The combination produces also a general mood of melancholic introspection and satiric bitterness which leads in turn to a disillusioned world-weariness undermining all optimistic assumptions concerning the nature of man and the universe. There seems to be no justice anywhere, of any kind.

The problem of justice in its distributive aspect is associated above all with the figure of the malcontent, the stage version of a psycho-social type frequently identified in late-Elizabethan and Jacobean times with a dangerous yearning for change of any kind.[87] There are relatively few pure or even nearly pure examples of the malcontent in the tragedies, but there is a strong smack of him in a variety of heroes and villains, and consideration of the composite model is undoubtedly useful for analytical purposes. He may be seen initially as a diminished version of another tragic type, the ambitious overreacher. In fact both types are present in Chapman's Bussy and Byron, Chapman being the first dramatist to perceive the tragic possibilities of the malcontent and the theme of distributive justice. Like the overreacher, the malcontent is dissatisfied with the way things are because he is obsessed with the disparity between his natural endowments and his place in the world; and like the overreacher he is turned by this obsession into a lawless resolute. But the malcontent is no imaginative Titan who will challenge kingdoms or 'the universal body of the law'. What he wants is a lucrative place at court, and his offences are the consequence of his inability to find employment with great men other than as pander to their vices and executant of their vendettas. A cynical mercenary rather than an impassioned leader in the rebellion against the bonds of moral order, the malcontent is at once spectator and actor, moralist and villain; he thus brings into sharp focus the nature of evil as understood by the dramatist. As voyeuristic procurer he becomes the ironical anthologist of seductive promises and broken vows. As hired revenger and assassin he exemplifies the utterly perverted nature of 'courtly reward and punishment'. As the chronically unpaid servant of great lords who forfeits his freedom and self-respect, he makes the old discovery that some bonds are mere bondage. Misanthropist and misogynist, he is the spiritual bastard of a self-seeking society in which no attempt is made to confine will to law or to 'let distribution undo excess'. When he turns against his patrons to become the instrument of their downfall he is very much the sins of the past come home to roost: 'The dark and vicious place where thee he got / Cost him his eyes' (*King Lear*, v.iii.172–3).

At the end of every Renaissance tragedy the rule of just law is formally reasserted, with due punishment and often due reward being meted out to those who survive. What has been seen, however, allows little hope that lawful authority will espouse justice or control the violence in man's nature for long. Life at its best seems to be a delicate state of balance in which the opposites of law and violence are liable to fall at any moment into explosive confusion: law then becomes violent, violent will becomes law, and only through more violence is just law made possible again.

Since the processes and the representatives of human law inspire so little respect, one might be tempted to conclude that law itself is a concept of secondary importance which never escapes from the sceptical periphery of the dramatists' minds. One might also contend that the real purpose of the legal element in the tragedies can be inferred from the dramatists' shrewd awareness that the theatrical impact of violent change – their main concern – is keenest when set in an elaborately civilised context of rules, prohibitions, customs, and institutions. Both positions would be mistaken. The dramatists are fully conscious of the fact that violence is meaningless except in relation to the idea of law. And, however alert they are to the violence latent in every civilised individual – to man's innate recalcitrance to law – they seem unreservedly convinced that man is a creature of law or he is nothing, one who finds his personal identity and his happiness in the bonds which tie him to others and others to him. Despite their ruthless analysis of the workings of law in society, law itself is a supreme value with the dramatists; ultimately it comprehends or merges into all the values by which they identify tragic evil: unity and concord, justice, constancy, and regulated change. Ben Jonson stands apart from all his great contemporaries in his refusal to put violence on the tragic stage, but is fundamentally at one with them in this dual perspective on law. He shows with grim clarity how the law can be turned into 'a meere ingine / to take ... life by a pretext of iustice' ('fraud ... worse then violence'), yet defines his ideal man as one who 'do's nothing but by law'.[88] Law might be confused with everything it is naturally opposed to, but that is a measure of the extent to which the tyrannies of will and passion can pervert man's noblest ideals and achievements.

The only law which proves reasonably dependable in the play-world of the tragedies is the law that evil rebounds upon the doer; there is an even-handed justice which works independently of lawfully constituted authority, making the torments of conscience and the passions and errors of desperate men its only instruments. In some tragedies this retributive process is ascribed to divine providence and taken as proof that there is a superior 'Star Chamber' above where every crime is properly dealt with either in time or eternity.[89] Whether such religious allusions are part of the play's total attitude, or simply expressions proper to the character who makes them, may be open to dispute; however, the important point is that the dramatists consistently endeavour to make the retributive process fully intelligible in terms of natural cause and effect. Moreover, there are only a few plays (one thinks of *Tamburlaine, Faustus, A Woman Killed with Kindness, Hamlet*, and *Macbeth*) where it might be said that the retributive process is related to a religious view of the universe consistently and in depth. It is largely through the conception of time as an immanent yet transcendent moral law that the pattern of justice acquires the metaphysical resonance proper to tragedy. Although his own tragedies are something of an exception in this regard, Chapman's *sententia* is strikingly applicable to Renaissance tragedy as a whole: *'the use of time is Fate.'*[90]

The dramatists' faith in the operation of a retributive process is by no means such as to eliminate a sense of the power and the mystery of evil, or of life's ineradicable injustices. When they look closely at those who wilfully violate the most fudamental spiritual and moral laws – at characters such as Faustus, Macbeth, or Beatrice-Joanna – they find desires so overmastering as to suggest a blind compulsion to evil; their handling of such characters leaves the observer free to speculate on the possibility (familiar enough to those who lived in the shadow of Luther and Calvin) that the ultimate law of the universe wills some to do what it commands all not to do. Above all, there is no attempt to show that the fall of those who are persecuted and driven to desperate deeds conforms to any human conception of justice. Such characters contribute something to their own destruction – and that something may be of the utmost interest to the dramatist; but they are essentially victims of an enveloping evil caught up in a retributive action which that evil engenders.

(ii) *Love and Marriage*

It should be inferred from what has been said here on the theme of justice and law that the concept of 'the revenge play' is a very restrictive one. To analyse even the most famous examples of the type in terms of their commitment to the revenge theme is usually to simplify their thematic design and to conclude that they suffer from structural imbalance.[91] Yet to devote all one's attention to the larger theme of justice in such plays may also entail a regrettable narrowing of focus, for one of the most remarkable features of thematic patterning in Renaissance tragedy is the intimate relationship which is regularly established between justice and love, law and marriage. What the Renaissance tragedian is characteristically concerned with is a process in which violence is done to these twin manifestations of the principle of harmonious coherence.

Tragic action, in other words, is synonymous with the violation of bonds. The bond signifies love and friendship on the one hand, obligation and limit on the other. In the ideal or pre-tragic phase of experience these two dimensions of meaning are coextensive: the ties of natural affection on which society is founded are spontaneously confirmed by mutual assurance, and the duties which such assurances prescribe are performed as a labour of love (see *Macbeth*, I.iv.14–27). But in the tragic phase, where polarity and conflict prevail, self-love and true love alike rebel against external constraints, while lawful authority itself tramples on natural rights and affections. The divisive factor is wilful passion or passionate will, the impulse to reject all bonds or to turn the bonds of others into mere bondage.

Two paradigms of ordered and disordered relationships, one natural and the other supernatural, regularly serve to extend the imaginative significance of the bond motif. There is, of course, the idea of nature as a system of warring opposites held together in the bonds of unity by means of a sympathetic or harmonising force. And there is the religious conception of a man's relationship with God as both a legal covenant and a marriage, with its corollary notion of sin as a form of bondage to, or adultery with, the spirit of evil. This conception of ordered and disordered spiritual relationships originates in the Old Testament, where the Babylonian captivity of the chosen people is ascribed to their 'adulterous' lapse into polytheism and their concomitant breaking of the covenant. It was scarcely less familiar to audiences in the sixteenth and seventeenth centuries than the idea of nature as a system of bound opposites in which strife and confusion are always imminent. Pauline theology had made it an integral part of Christian teaching on sin and redemption. Following Luther's *De captivitate Babylonica ecclesiae praeludium,* it was regularly used by reforming preachers and theologians to characterise the degeneracy of Roman Catholicism. Moreover, it had enjoyed widespread popular expression for centuries in the multiform legend to which Doctor Faustus of Wittenberg has given his name.

In *Doctor Faustus,* Marlowe shows all the sensitivity to the theological and symbolic implications of this legend that one would expect from a former student of divinity. Having denied God's love and grace, Faustus becomes enchanted with stellar gods and mythological fables and commits himself to a demon whose name, Lucifer, is that of a Babylonian tyrant in 'Jerome's Bible' (Isa.14:12; *Doctor Faustus,* I.i.38); he is easily persuaded that 'Marriage is but a ceremonial toy' (II.i.147), and finally seals his damnation by embracing the succubine Helen. But Marlowe's great achievement was to have seized on the legend's core of universal truth and tragic irony. What his play communicates with terrible force is that there can be no such thing as autonomy of action in the real world: every act either confirms an existing bond or creates a new one; it has binding consequences and is a deed in two senses of the word. Thus the tragic design of *Doctor Faustus* turns on the appalling peripeteia whereby the rejection of a bond whose grant of limited freedom (the freedom of the sons of God) has begun to seem intolerably constricting and servile leads not to liberty and power but to a condition of claustrophobic and degrading servitude: the hero becomes the deed's creature, a prisoner of what he himself has willed.

This tragic law is operative in plays as diverse as *Macbeth, Othello, The White Devil,* and *The Changeling,* its presence signalled by the symbolism of the demonic pact or marriage, or by the Marlovian pun on 'deed' and 'will'. Even in the pagan context of *King Lear* its presence is keenly felt at the outset. The 'hideous rashness' (I.i.150) which thrusts Lear into 'the tyrannous night' (III.iv.147) involves a ritual abjuring of love, grace, and benison (I.i.265), a brutal attempt to prevent a marriage of true minds, and an act of fatal submission to the will of two women who seem to fetch their nature from 'the mysteries of Hecat and the night' (l.109).

Nevertheless the paradigm of ordered and disordered relationships that deeply affects Renaissance tragedy as a whole is the cosmological and not the theological one. The bonds undone in *Lear* are not – or not primarily – those between men and gods. As in *The Spanish Tragedy*, they are familial, matrimonial, and national bonds, as well as bonds of service and hospitality; and, as in Kyd's play, their universal model is the union of contrary elements in a just and fruitful relationship where individuality and mutuality are simultaneously acknowledged. Here the sign of catastrophe is the sudden eruption of a fiery, primordial hatred which would consume its opposite or consign it to the void: 'No contraries hold more antipathy / Than I and such a knave'; 'as a stranger to my heart and me / Hold thee from this for ever' (II.ii.82–3; I.i.114–15). Here too the experience of Hell is the discovery that a human bond of incomparable value has been violently and irrevocably broken: 'Thou'lt come no more, / Never, never, never, never, never' (V.iii.306–7).

Although marriage and family are of obvious importance in both *Lear* and *Macbeth*, these plays – unlike *Hamlet* and *Othello* – are untypical of the tradition in that their treatment of the bond theme does not give central attention to the sexual and matrimonial relationship. When Kyd tied love and justice, marriage and law, into a firm thematic knot, and linked them to the universal principle of harmonious contrariety, he showed his contemporaries and successors how to combine in a richly significant pattern the elements of romance and intrigue attractive to a popular audience with those matters of state traditionally thought proper to tragedy. As a result of his design, the interaction of socio-political and sexual disorder is a constant feature of Renaissance tragedy. What happens in courtship and marriage is reflected in or directly affects what happens in the state. Thus the changing configurations of sexual intrigue echo the great world's uncertainty as to who's in and who's out in the palaces of favour and fortune. The parent or guardian who enforces or prohibits a marriage is a domestic tyrant; sometimes too he is a political tyrant whose scorn for Hymen's laws is indicative of his contempt for law in general.[92] The stock figures of the melancholy bride and the melancholy, dispossessed lover parallel the gloomy malcontent.[93] The villain who seizes another's throne may usurp – or seek to usurp – his bed as well.[94]

Remorseless lust too is a conventional attribute of the tyrant; in the kingdom of ungoverned will, the idea of rape is always present, if only metaphorically. The dramatists are in touch here with an ancient but still vital popular symbolism which goes back through the *acta* of the virgin martyrs to the myths of archetypal tyrants such as Tereus and Lycaon. Shakespeare's Lavinia is the first of many heroines whose suffering evokes memories of Philomela and Astraea and re-enacts in one way or another the wanton violation of human dignity and basic human rights by brute power and authority.[95] Even the unscrupulous heroine of *The White Devil* can be placed in this category, for she is to some extent a victim of male will and an unjust society, and is tried for adultery by a court as corrupt as herself. There is truth as well as hypocrisy in her indignant protest: 'A rape, a rape! . . . you have ravished justice, / Forc'd her to do your pleasure' (III.ii.273–5).

In the seventeenth century, there is a marked shift of emphasis from the political to the sexual and marital side of the thematic pattern created by Kyd. This development reflects a more naturalistic interest in character and relationships and a breaking-down of the barriers between tragedy and comedy.[96] But it reflects, too, an almost Calvinistic obsession with the anarchic power of sexual appetite – a belief that all passions are included in lust and that Paradise itself was lost by man's inability to control 'the flesh'. Sexual desire becomes a dark tyrant under whose spell the past is forgotten, promises crumble, people abandon their accustomed roles, and the whole scenario of human relations is rapidly transformed. The logical *terminus quo* of this line of imaginative inquiry is incest. Subtly handled by Shakespeare, by Webster (perhaps), and more boldly by Middleton, it is given a stark centrality in Ford's *'Tis Pity She's a Whore*. Ford's handling of the incest theme in *'Tis Pity* puts a definitive touch to the close of a tradition in which tragic experience is closely identified with the idea of confusion: for incest is 'confusion' – Ford's key word in this play – where the natural order of society was thought to begin.

This subordination of the political to the sexual and marital in the later seventeenth century undoubtedly entails a shrinking of the tragic vision. But that shrinking is not so substantial as it might have been in a different tradition. For the symbolic status of marriage – 'that first good deed began i' the world / After man's creation' (*Duchess of Malfi*, I.i.385–6) – as a microcosm of society and a reflection of cosmic unity-in-contrariety was such that the shadow of sexual tragedy could be thrown as far back as the Fall and reflected on a screen as wide as the universe:

> My wife! my wife! what wife? I have no wife.
> O insupportable! O heavy hour!
> Methinks it should be now a huge eclipse
> Of sun and moon, and that th'affrighted globe
> Did yawn at alteration.
> (*Othello*,V.ii.100–4)

That Providence that has made ev'ry poison
Good for some use, and sets four warring elements
At peace in man, can make a harmony
In things that are most strange to human reason.
O but this marriage!
(*Women Beware Women*, I.ii.179–83)

IV   THE TREACHEROUS ENTERTAINMENT: THE SYMBOLISM OF RITE AND PLAY

Any account of the core elements of Renaissance tragedy must necessarily inquire into the function and significance of its most characteristic and conventionalised scene, the Treacherous Entertainment (as I have called it). This scene may coincide with the major point of change near the centre of the action, but as a rule it forms the catastrophe. It may consist simply of a banquet or a game; more often it is a play or masque performed in conjunction with a marriage. But, whatever its position or form, it is always a ritual affirmation of love and union which turns out to be a monstrous negation of everything it affirms.

Fashioned by Thomas Kyd with great originality out of elements drawn from Seneca's *Thyestes* and *Medea*, the Treacherous Entertainment is a dramatic device whose popularity must be ascribed to its symbolic function as well as to its great theatrical potential. Every dramatist who uses it seeks to give it some original twist, but all follow Kyd in shaping it as an elaborate model of the play-world to which it belongs. Thus, however much it may differ in detail from play to play, its guiding principle is always a lightning confusion of opposites which summarises the essential nature of life in its tragic perspective. Hospitality and violence, love and hatred, marriage and mourning, play and earnest, and comedy and tragedy are all likely to be involved here in a sudden and 'huge eclipse'.

Although by far the most important, the Treacherous Entertainment is seldom if ever the only action of its kind in a tragedy. Usually there are two or three well-distributed ritual scenes, standing out clearly from the rest of the action and related to each other by analogy and contrast and sometimes cause and effect: indeed, it is difficult not to see in this pattern a basic constructional formula on which the dramatists are heavily dependent. Some ritual scenes exhibit an achieved order; but they are the exception rather than the rule, and even they are darkened by external threats or flawed by some subtle internal discord. The general impression given by ritual scenes, an impression which transfers to the tragedies built round them, is an impression of rite gone wrong: the pun, facilitated by interchangeable spelling in the seventeenth century, is ubiquitous.

It has been argued with great persuasiveness that in the symbolic strategies of Renaissance drama, ritual and play serve to express two quite different conceptions of life. Whereas rite, ceremony, and pageant, it is said, stand for the traditional view of the world as a stable and immutable order, play signifies the new and disturbing notion of life – embraced in their different ways by Promethean heroes and Machiavellian politicians – as a historical process in which nothing is stable and the individual is free to assume ever-new identities.[97] I would suggest, however, that the operative distinction is not between rite and play (drama) but between the proper and the improper use of each. The Treacherous Entertainment in its most typical form exemplifies this point. Ritual and play are both presented in it as accepted signs and instruments of harmonious order, and both are either violently truncated or wilfully perverted for destructive ends. As in Renaissance tragedy generally, they function in this scene as symbolic partners.

Nevertheless, ritual and play do have obviously distinct implications which have to be taken into account. To begin with ritual, clear indications of Renaissance thinking on its purpose and value can be found in Chapman's characterisation of Ceremony in his continuation of *Hero and Leander*, the poetic narrative of tragic love begun by his friend Marlowe. According to Chapman, Ceremony is an 'all-states-ordering' goddess whose alliance with 'all the bench of Deities' (i.e. the divine lawgivers), and in particular with natural order as time, makes her the guardian of 'all the sweetes of our societie'. Without her co-operation, no bond of union can prove either fruitful or enduring; and, since she stands above all else for openness and timeliness in human transactions, bonds which are established in secret and with 'violence' (i.e. haste) are doomed.[98] This explication of Ceremony might well stand as a commentary on the fatal conflicts between the individual and socio-cosmic order in the tragedies. There, outright villains exhibit the depth of their wickedness by deliberate abuse and misuse of secular and religious rites. Moreover, passionate lovers and revengers whose nobility is not in question alike make secret vows which take them outside the ritual order of justice and love down labyrinthine paths spelling error and death.

Yet, as an elucidation of what ritual meant to the dramatists and their audience, Chapman's allegorical portrait of Ceremony is incomplete. Despite the very high value placed on rites and ceremonies in this period, there was at the same time a historically exceptional – perhaps unique – consciousness of the fact that they are instruments of social control and can, in consequence, become little more than a tool for legitimising and sustaining corrupt power. Here, of course, we are speaking of the Reformation rather than the Renaissance: of the Protestant conception of Roman Catholicism as a universal tyranny which kept all men in bondage by means of a vast system of largely ostentatious rites and ceremonies. With the help of biblical typology and polemical simplification, this interpretation of history acquired the status of a myth. The popes were Babylonian tyrants and usurpers, Catholic ritual was Babylonian (Babel-like) pride, and the Reformers were spiritual heroes who rebelled against monstrous power and sham to restore freedom to the sons of God and efficacy to the rites of Christendom.[99]

The effects on the tragic drama of this reading of conflict and change in Christian Europe were substantial. It helped to ensure that consummate evil would take the form of usurped and tyrannous authority, would be identified more and more with Catholicism and Italy, and would habitually clothe itself in 'popish tricks and ceremonies' on the supposition that 'fair accomplishments make foul deeds gracious'.[100] A corollary effect was that the tragic hero often has in him a smack of the Reformer. The model of the age's spiritual hero can be traced, for example (though the example may astonish), in Marlowe's Tamburlaine the Great, a historically predestined figure who exposes hollow claims to supreme authority, frees Christians from bondage to idolaters, and crowns his career with the sack of Babylon. The influence of the model is more easily discerned in moralising avengers and malcontents who are deeply at odds with the ethos of a corrupt court (sometimes characterised as 'Babylon').[101] Whatever their excesses and delusions, these men usually seek to assert truth and justice against lies and tyranny, and even to 'root out sin'.[102] Often they are the mouthpieces of a bitter Calvinistic sense of man's essential depravity and of the fantastic tricks he plays in order to conceal it:[103] their view of the degenerate and gaudy world is summed up in Hamlet's fervent exclamation, 'O, reform it altogether', and in his wish ('most retrograde' to the desires of a sanctimonious usurper) to return to *Wittenberg*.

A more general effect of Reformation attitudes is that the anti-ceremonial behaviour of tragic characters is often presented in a sympathetic light: it may be seen as the inescapable consequence of attempts at legitimate self-expression in a world where ritual order has become identified with tyrannic sham, or as the symptom of an extreme passion for authenticity and justice. Yet the dramatists do not reject ritual as such. They maintain at least an implicit distinction between true and false ritual and show clearly enough that to reject it (however heroically) can be as disastrous for the individual and society as is its systematic manipulation in the interests of despotism. Their attitude is broadly comparable to the mean position advocated by the new English church and state as they tried to steer their way between the oppressive ritualism and legalism identified with Rome and the fierce hostility to almost all ritual and legal procedures shown by overzealous Protestants who clamoured for 'reformation without tarrying'.[104] But, however we define the dramatists' attitude to ritual (and it admits of many shifts of emphasis along a scale between wholehearted approbation and tacit, qualified acceptance), we must conclude that ritual action and reaction dominate their plays partly because they were a potent means of relating perennial tragic questions concerning the individual and society to the doubts, conflicts, and hard-fought convictions of contemporary experience. Is plain-speaking Cordelia right to undo her father's childishly tyrannous ritual of dower-giving? Should the Duchess of Malfi remarry, not only against the wishes of her tyrant brothers, but also in secret and in defiance of what she calls 'all vain ceremony'? In asking these questions we must no doubt recall that anti-ritualism is a primary expression of social dissent in every age,[105] and that protesting nonconformity is a predictable feature of all tragic heroes and heroines. Nevertheless, it is certain that such questions as these registered with special sharpness on audiences in a nation which felt menaced within and without by forces identifiable in terms of their perverted or mistaken attitudes towards 'rites and ceremonies'.

The broad distinction in the tragedians' theatrical symbolism and metaphor between the proper and the improper use of play is more closely linked with the parallel distinction in ritual than I have so far indicated. The closeness of the connection can be made clear if we speak in terms of the dramatists' manipulation of two traditional attitudes towards play, the Christian–humanist and the puritan (using that word in its general as well as its particular sense). In the first tradition, play and pageant constitute an art of social harmony; they are rituals of celebration and hospitality which flourish naturally at court and at royal progresses, in the banquet halls of the nobility and the inn yards of the people. Drama in this tradition is seen as an art of controlled change and co-operative endeavour. On the platform, men create new worlds and assume new identities, but their freedom to do so is subject to a variety of restrictions, including the time limit, the nature of available resources, the fitness of the entertainment to the audience, of actor to role, and style to subject. As Shakespeare graciously acknowledges in the epilogue of *The Tempest*, to be on stage is to be in 'bands', to accept a covenant. It is to perceive a fundamental affinity between art and life and to sympathise with the Stoic idea of the world as a stage where every man must accept his allotted part and play it to the best of his ability.[106] Lastly, in this tradition drama is an art of feigning and changing whose effect is to reveal and affirm unchanging truths and values.[107]

The puritan attitude to play begins with Plato's condemnation of rhetoric and drama (already referred to in part) and has been present at all times in the more severe forms of Christian thought and sentiment. The Fathers of the Church regarded plays and spectacles as – quite literally – the art of the devil; closely associated with the feasts and fables of the old gods, they were seen as snares which could lure the faithful back into idolatry.[108] Using Plato's arguments against drama and rhetoric for their own purposes, the Fathers engaged in a bitter attack on all forms of the dramatic that was to have one very important effect on the evolution of Christian myth, specifically the myth of the devil. Very quickly, the archetypal figure of evil – on whom all really vicious characters in Christian legend and literature were to be modelled – acquired a unique persona which was to stay with him for over fifteen hundred years: that of a theatrical and oratorical artist who ensnares his victims by means of beguiling shows, cunning impersonations, and persuasive speech. This model of demonic evil is commonplace in the ascetical writings, hagiology, and folklore of the Middle Ages.[109] It lies behind the sportive, smooth-talking Vice of the English moralities, and through him influenced the later drama. However, since traditional demonology was still very much alive in the sixteenth and seventeenth centuries (as the witchcraft mania testifies), the idea of evil as sportive and histrionic would probably have affected the tragedians' image of villainy anyhow.[110] Moreover, it was given a startling new lease of life – such indeed that it eventually closed the theatres – as a result of the Puritan diatribes against the stage. In these writings and sermons, all the old arguments which the Fathers had mobilised against the diabolical art were relentlessly reproduced.[111] Of course, the hostility of the Puritans to the stage was of a piece with their attitude to ritual (Calvin had dismissed 'the unmeaning ceremonies' of Rome as 'theatrical display', 'a mask of useless splendour'.)[112] But we need not think of this twin hostility as exclusive to a small religious minority, for in this as in many other matters the line between Anglicanism and Puritanism could be very thin. The twin hostility stands for something deep-rooted in Protestant culture: a suspiciousness of show as such and a tendency to detect in it the taint of pretence and degeneracy.

In the tragedies, the theological identification of play with treacherous change and mere evil is regularly endorsed. But the playfulness of the demonic villain is also 'placed' or interpreted in the light of the humanist idea of play. Overtly or by implication, a distinction is made between play which works in the service of truth and harmony, and play which deludes in order to divide and destroy: the entertainments presented by Hieronimo in Acts I and IV of *The Spanish Tragedy* vividly embody this distinction; so too do the contrasted disguisings and plottings of Edgar and Edmund in *King Lear*. To perceive the distinction is to recognise that the villain or villain–hero of the tragedies is not quite the actor–dramatist of genius he is often said to be, but rather an undisciplined artist who perverts great natural talent and violates the elementary principles of dramatic art. Thus Shakespeare's intending usurper Richard of Gloucester (taking his cue in this from Kyd's Lorenzo) jocularly decides to 'entertain these fair well-spoken days' with 'tragic violence' just when war has ended and the King has called for 'stately triumphs, mirthful comic shows, / Such as befits the pleasure of the court'. This determination involves him in appropriating noble and pious roles for which, as the embodiment of physical and spiritual deformity, he is manifestly unsuited ('Thou [art] unfit for any place but Hell').[113] And, although his comical tragedy is accepted by the frightened and the gullible, its strained incongruities of style are fully perceptible to judicious, off-stage spectators. In *The Revenger's Tragedy* the pejorative implications of the theatrical metaphor are elicited by means of other basic rhetorical concepts as well as style – invention, ordering, and memory: because his plots are uncontrolled and extemporal, Vindice forgets where he is going and finally gets lost in his own inventions.[114] It is clearly implied by both plays that the theatrical–rhetorical art of the villain–hero stands for qualities of mind which are directed towards chaos. This is an art which asks from us an educated, double response, one in which our delight at its non-stop plotting is balanced by an awareness that all its charm as art depends on the art of the larger play which confines it to a coherent and meaningful form.

The radical discrepancy between self and role (or style) which the villain cheerfully ignores becomes a source of painful self-consciousness, of division within and alienation without, in characters of tragic stature; and we may include in this category introspective 'tool villains' such as Webster's Bosola, specifically described as 'a good actor . . . playing a villain's part'.[115] Such characters come to adopt roles at variance with their true or better selves not knowingly and eagerly, like the villain, but blindly and in response to powerful compulsions. These compulsions may be objectified in the figure of the tyrant or usurper, who characteristically redistributes roles at will, or the Machiavellian tempter, who would make a change of role seem no change at all.

Because conceptions of the self and its relation to society have changed enormously since the seventeenth century, and are much more variable today than they were then, the significance of role as a metaphor in the characterisation of the Renaissance tragic hero and heroine seems bound to give rise to doubtful interpretations and critical dispute. I would draw attention here to two critical tendencies which, although obviously distinguishable, share the common assumption that the hero is presented as unable in the nature of things to find his personal identity in any one socially defined role. One of these approaches stems from romantic and existentialist positions suggesting that the individual life in a developed community is necessarily inauthentic, and that social alienation is a prerequisite for self-realisation; it encourages us to see the hero of Renaissance tragedy advancing towards self-discovery as a result of his refusal to play out a given role. The other approach stems from socio-anthropological perceptions concerning the plasticity of human nature; it suggests that the hero discovers or uncovers the truth about his self – that it is multiple rather than single, artificial rather than innate – in the very process of acting out many roles.[116]

There is much in the texts to justify these critical perspectives. Moreover, they have the great virtue of highlighting the dramatists' often profound sense of the elusive complexity of the individual personality, as well as their recognition of the multiple forces which continually threaten the integrity of the individual. But it may be that they help to conceal at least as much as they reveal. In the first place, it is surely incorrect to speak of the protagonist as moving out of role into character (or vice versa), since the dramatists and their contemporaries took it as axiomatic that character without role, like thought without language, is in practical terms non-existent. It is true that role-playing usually begins to catch attention when it is clear that the hero and his world are out of joint. But that is not because playing a part is in itself considered to be unnatural; it is because a part well played is felt to be a harmony of nature and art and so does not call attention to itself. We begin to reflect on the problems of 'acting' when characters have disqualified themselves from playing the part which is properly theirs (Richard II arbitrating in a dispute where he himself is the chief culprit, Beatrice-Joanna rebuking the insolence of a servant whom she has hired to commit murder); or when they assume an alien role in order to reassert themselves (Lear kneeling in mock petition to Goneril, the usurped Duke Altofronto disguised as a railing malcontent); or when their self-regard is ominously tainted with self-ignorance or pride (Othello affirming that Cupid's toys will not interfere with his martial duties, Bussy D'Ambois indulging in 'bravery'); or when self-will and desperation have compelled them along the path of deceit (Juliet playing the obedient daughter to Capulet, the Duchess of Malfi going through the charade of dismissing Antonio as a dishonest servant). Thus, instead of moving from role to character (or character to role), the tragic protagonist is more likely to be seen as exchanging or having to exchange a role which harmonises with the conditions of his nature for another or others which do not: so that in losing his original role he loses himself.

Moreover, rather than uncovering a suppressed identity, or creating a new one, the tragic character more probably acquires a new understanding of his lost self and of those elements in his own and other men's nature which separated him from it. This understanding is often embodied in what is arguably the only perfect piece of theatre and ritual in the Renaissance tragic world – the Noble Death, in which the protagonist is sublimely constant and true to himself. Despite the splendour of this final 'act', the new understanding which gives it moral substance embraces a recognition that the individual is bound and limited, not only self-made but shaped and held in being by a context of relationships – interpersonal, social, and cosmic. Thus the famous words uttered by Webster's heroine at death, 'I am Duchess of Malfi still', are not simply the triumphant assertion of an indestructible personal identity. They are also a reminder from the dramatist that, despite her marriage to her steward, this great lady will always find her identity in the name and duchy of her dead husband. And they are but a prelude to the complete revelation, which comes when the Duchess accepts – on bended knees – Bosola's suggestion that aristocratic pride debars her from self-knowledge and lasting glory. She dies 'like' the Duchess of Malfi indeed, but in a manner which shows what that means in terms of nobility, frailty, and dependence.

One cannot, however, ascribe to the dramatists of this period any firm belief that the individual will be true to himself, or maintain a sense of his own identity, for very long. Because the self is an unstable synthesis of opposites, 'None can be always one'.[117] The psychic life seems here to be a kind of continuing Fall: a banishment from the person one would and should be, and in some sense was; a restless search for self-realisation in roles which too often have the effect of making one feel 'cabin'd, cribb'd, confin'd, bound in / To saucy doubts and fears' (*Macbeth*, III.iv.24–5). But however subtle and unremitting their sense of the strange mutations in man's character, the tragedians stop short of abandoning the notion of psychic continuity and making metamorphosis a positive. Like Montaigne, who explores with such acuteness the mercuriality of the self, they '*Esteeme it a great matter, to play but one man*'.[118] In the closely related spheres of psychology and ethics, constancy – which presupposes unity and harmony – remains their primary value.[119]

V   TREACHEROUS WORDS:
THE LANGUAGE OF TRAGIC REALITY

Apart from the ubiquitous play metaphor, there are many aspects of imagery and diction which bear the imprint of shared ideas on the tragic. There is, for example, the device of flooding the dialogue with antithetical terms whose literal, metaphorical, or etymological meaning introduces ideas of the high and the low (*Edward II, Romeo and Juliet*), or the gentle and the savage (*The Spanish Tragedy*), or resolution and dissolution (*Doctor Faustus*), or peace and strife (*Women Beware Women*): despite its concentration, figurative diction of this kind does not call attention to itself, but works at a semi-conscious level to ensure our responsiveness to the play's vision of confounding opposites and sudden change. Literal and figurative allusions to sealing and tying, wax and knots, are commonplace but almost always effective. The imaginative value of these mundane images lies in the ease with which they can be made to evoke (the one metonymically, the other metaphorically) the bonds of justice and love, and to suggest how quickly all such bonds can dissolve, slip apart, or become as a noose around the neck. And there are favourite puns too. The words 'fast' (secure), 'speed' (success), 'quick' (alive, pregnant), and 'violent' (hasty, vehement) are all used contiguously and punningly by Shakespeare, Webster, Middleton, and Ford as ironic omens to the effect that bonds entered impulsively are doomed to a violent end. In the seventeenth century, too, virtually every tragedian exploits a particular pun which conjoins ideas of bewilderment, horror, secrecy, confusion, and loss, and points in the direction of a myth that boldly acknowledges the terrible duality of human nature and the labyrinthine complexities of life. The tragic experience, for these dramatists, is to find oneself in a spiritual wilderness without path or friendly clue to be one's guide, to be entangled in 'deeds to make heaven weep, all earth amaz'd', to be 'amaz'd to death'.[120]

But wordplay in general is a major instrument in establishing the nature of tragic reality. Although a great deal of punning in the plays is a form of rhetorical skill which serves to confirm the wisdom or wit of the speaker, much of it is a function of deception and self-deception and has the reverse effect. Like the symbolism of treacherous play (with which it regularly combines), it is indicative of the unseen menace in a contrarious, insidiously changing world. Particularly in Kyd and Shakespeare, this strategy is reinforced by implicit appeal to classical and humanist doctrines which make clear speech the index of sound judgement, and a stable vocabulary the life-blood of a wholesome society.

In so far as it involves particular words (rather than style in general), the disease of semantic uncertainty and confusion takes roughly three forms, not all of the punning kind. There is the antonymic nominalism associated with the topsy-turvy world of tyrants and usurpers who redistribute titles and names at will. In their reign, words such as 'grace', 'gentle', 'noble', 'honour', 'true' and 'traitor' are habitually assigned where 'antiquity and custom' – 'the ratifiers and props of every word' – would require their opposites.[121] There is the equivocation of the Machiavellian who loves to 'moralize two meanings in one word' (*Richard III*, III.i.83): such as it is, his word is his bond and his morality. And lastly there is the unconscious equivocation of tragic characters who use words with sinister, 'other' meanings which become available to their understanding only when they are confronted with the 'amazing' consequences of their rash vow or 'deed'. Such equivocation is, of course, a form of dramatic or Sophoclean irony; but it is much more than that.

Like the writings of Montaigne and Giordano Bruno, Renaissance tragedy is haunted by the spirit of the pre-Socratic philosopher who said that the way up is the way down and that we cannot enter the same river twice. But, if we consider the superb play on the words 'move' and 'motion' in *Othello*, or the sudden splintering of Beatrice-Joanna's name with her father's recognition that he has two daughters, not one ('An host of enemies enter'd my citadel / Could not amaze like this: Joanna! Beatrice! Joanna!' – *The Changeling*, V.iii.147–8), then we might add that it is haunted also by the spirit of Cratylus, Heraclitus's disciple. For Cratylus (reports Plato) maintained that the most important names and words were all devised by the original lawgiver in accordance with his belief that everything is motion, everything changes. Such a belief, Socrates told Cratylus, might be correct and probably was not; but to accept it as correct, he added, would be to deny the permanent nature of goodness, beauty, and the like, and to be drawn into a whirlpool.[122] Not least by the semantic flux which so enriches the language of their plays, Renaissance tragedians bring us very close to the metaphysical and moral whirlpool that was Plato's nightmare.

VI SUMMARY

To summarise, then, I have suggested that a useful way into the thinking of many Renaissance tragedians is through that part of their cosmological inheritance which represents the world as a dialectical structure of strife and amity, discord and concord. The order of life rests on a system of concordant discord wherein strife is limited and change gradual or timely; for these dramatists, tragedy is a form which isolates the moment when that system suddenly shows signs of collapse, with violence, confusion, and wildfire change becoming the dominant facts of experience. Although one could not claim that any one of the playwrights, let alone many, had a carefully formulated set of guiding ideas, it is worth pointing out that the root concept of universal contrariety meshes easily with other ideas which are of obvious importance in the plays. Fortune or chance is the element of treacherous uncertainty which characterises life in a contrarious world. Time is not just change or flux but a patterned process of contrarious unity (day and night, spring and fall, summer and winter), identical in structure to the spatial cosmos of the four elements; more, it is the law of graduated change and of movement within defined limits which reacts retributively against violent and overreaching acts. Providence is the mysterious system of divine government which accommodates the opposites of freedom and necessity and operates through the medium of time to draw justice out of violence and concord out of discord.

The stark contrarieties of tragic life are imprinted in the characterisation of villain and hero alike. Not only is the villain the opposite of what he seems: he is often a professed advocate of unity who is dedicated in reality to the creation of discord within and between others. Tragic characters become their own anithesis, or oscillate between opposite extremes of feeling and conduct, or both. They are thrown into a state of intellectual and moral confusion verging on madness, find it impossible to distinguish between right and wrong, friend and foe; they feel betrayed, but betray themselves. Responsive to Nietzschean tragic insights, we may be inclined to locate the positive aspect of these plays in the energy and courage with which the protagonists defy the constrictions placed upon them by the world they inhabit. On balance, however, the positive element will be found mainly in the regenerative movement adumbrated at the end of many tragedies. The most striking manifestation of this movement is the Noble Death, in which the protagonists strive heroically to come to terms with what they are, what they have done, what has happened to them. Here opposites are joined and violence gives birth to a moment of peace and concord: the protagonists die at one with themselves, with others (or another), with Fate (the gods, Providence). The Noble Death implies that tragedy can become a quest for knowledge culminating in a perfect gesture of self-expression, an image of constancy. But not all tragic characters recover from the experience of chaos (to borrow Eric Bentley's definition of tragedy);[123] in their case the model of the Noble Death may be used negatively or ambiguously.

The 'sweet violence' of Renaissance tragedy finds its most obvious expression in the theme of revenge. But this theme is best understood as part of a comprehensive interest in the nature of justice and law. Thus the noble revenger and the cruel tyrant may be taken as complementary types and interacting extremes through whom the dramatists explore the effects on the individual and society of justice without law and law without justice. The malcontent reflects their awareness that the indifference of the great to distributive justice can be no less productive of violence than can the problems associated with justice of the retributive kind. But perhaps the most important aspect of thematic continuity in the period is the way in which love and justice, marriage and law are treated as twin dimensions of the principle of harmonious coherence and linked together in one thematic knot. The isolation and disintegration of the protagonist is part of a general shattering of bonds which, through the symbolism of marriage, may be linked suggestively with the bonds of contrarious unity that divide Cosmos from Chaos.

The violation of rite and play is fundamental to the symbolism of the tragedies. In scenes of this kind, anarchic will and passion attack or masquerade under the customary forms of justice and love. The general use of play metaphor enforces the status of such scenes as microcosmic images of the given imaginative world. It is a world populated for the most part by people in borrowed robes. By choice or compulsion, they are divided from the role which puts them at one with others in a meaningful, joyous, solemn enterprise. The very words they use reflect and contribute to this loss of stability and certainty.

Thus, while something is to be gained by abstracting and correlating those ideas which suggest a coherent frame of reference in the dialogue between the dramatists and their audience, it is of the utmost importance to emphasise that the central experience in most of the tragedies – and also the primary effect sought by the tragedians – is antithetical to the very idea of coherence. 'Amazement' is the key pun and symbol: it connotes wonder, confusion, loss, and a face-to-face experience of life's most monstrous possibilities.

Part II

2 Thomas Kyd: *The Spanish Tragedy*

I

So little indebted to all that precedes it in the tragic medium, and so profoundly influential in relation to what follows, Kyd's *The Spanish Tragedy* (c. 1585–90) is quite the most important single play in the history of English drama. We must, of course, acknowledge its obvious flaws and distinguish between historical importance and intrinsic worth. But the impression must not be given that this is an inchoate and uncertain pioneer work, a mine of useful ideas which only others will make proper use of. It is a startling achievement in its own right, being notable for the invention and the decisiveness with which it articulates a complex tragic vision.

As Kyd indicates in his first sentence,

> When this eternal substance of my soul
> Did live imprison'd in my wanton flesh,
> Each in their function serving other's need ...

the key to its meaning and form lies in the idea of opposites and their interrelationship.[1] Kyd sees tragic action as the working-out of an inexorable chain of events in which men seem the puppets of a predetermined fate; yet much of the poignance of his tragic vision lies in its suggestion that men are the authors as well as the actors of their tragic destiny. He conjoins necessity and volition, chance and choice; and reminds us continually of the Spanish comedy that might have been.

His imaginative definition of tragic reality derives from his conception of that alternative mode. It is the sudden re-eruption of the forces of strife, hatred, and violence precisely when least expected, and their triumph over the forces of concord, love, and peace. Bonds are mocked and shattered, unity, partnership, and continuity denied. A golden, middle way is lost, 'everything [is] in extremity', total transformation becomes the norm.[2] Central to the play's many dualisms is one implicit in the opening antithesis of soul and body: that of reason and passion. Much of the play's power as drama, and no doubt the principal reason for its Renaissance popularity, stems from its recognition of the volcanic forces that slumber lightly in the souls of civilised men and beneath the elegant structures and procedures of an advanced society. Nothing, therefore, could seem easier than to analyse it in terms of the Apollonian and the Dionysiac (Kyd even uses Apollo's son as paradigm for the hero's pre-tragic self). The Nietzschean categories, however, would be misleading, for the Dionysiac here carries no suggestion of insight and wisdom; its unleashing signals bewilderment in the mind as well as chaos in the objective world. Conversely, however, Kyd gives due emphasis (in the first of the stage's great Machiavels) to the evils of reason without feeling; and he acknowledges too that much of what passes for reason in the civilised world is a deceptive, and often self-deceptive, form of driving will and desire. Thus his contrarious view of reality, and his preoccupation with the ease with which opposites can become confused, enable him to present man's nature, his world, and his tragic misfortunes in a manner which is remarkable for its blend of comprehensiveness and subtlety.

II

The sonorous expository speeches which get the play off to such a slow start suggest that Kyd's initial endeavour was to impress the audience with his classical credentials. Yet Andrea's account of his life, death, and reception in the Underworld, and the Spanish general's description of the battle in which Andrea was killed, repay careful attention, for they provide a complete introduction to the conceptual and symbolic bases of the play. The battle was fought, we are told, 'where Spain and Portugal do jointly knit / Their frontiers, leaning on each other's bound'. From ordnance and musket came liquid fire resembling 'ocean's rage' when it 'gapes to swallow neighbour-bounding lands', so that a grassy field was soon turned to a purple plain where the limbs, heads and trunks of men 'lie mingled with weapons and unbowell'd steeds'. Partly because Horatio proved at a crucial moment to be the exemplar of 'Friendship and hardy valour, join'd in one', the Spaniards emerged victorious from this hellish chaos. But they did not pursue their success to the extent of swallowing up the opposition; rather, they made a 'peace conditional' promising to stay the 'fury' of their forces so long as Portugal (whose 'breach of faith' began the conflict – I.iii.34) kept its solemn vow to resume payment of the neglected tribute (I.ii.21–94).

All this echoes, by analogy and contrast, Andrea's experiences in the Underworld. Having crossed the Acheron, he becomes the subject of a dispute as to whether he should be placed among lovers or martialists. The dispute is temporarily resolved when Minos, the mildest of the three judges, proposes as a 'device to end the difference' between the other two that he should be sent to the King and Queen of the Underworld for appropriate classification. In his journey to the Elysian green where Pluto and Proserpine reside, he has to follow a middle path among three, having on his left one which leads down to deepest Hell, where sinners are overwhelmed by bloody Furies, and on his right another, which leads to 'fields where lovers live, and bloody martialists, / But either sort contain'd within his bounds'. His reward for following this Elysian path is a judgement 'seal'd with a kiss' between the royal pair (I.i.15–80).

By his symbolic shaping of character, action and setting here, Kyd prepares the imagination for its journey into a contrarious universe. He intimates that the bond of opposites is the only alternative to furious strife, utter confusion, and final loss, and at the same time shows what the bond signifies in practice. We are to understand that it is synonymous with moderation (mediating between extremes) and with fidelity; that it requires ending one kind of difference but respecting another, and so entails justice in the full sense; and finally that in its highest form it is a union of justice and love.

This, however, is to speak of contrarious unity with a kind of confidence which the dialectical subtlety of the exposition (and the play as a whole) precludes. The point for emphasis is that every such union is a 'peace conditional' whose limits and distinctions are not always understood, and are easily overstepped or ignored, by blind and impulsive mortals. This seems to be implied by the intriguing parallel between the union of Pluto and Proserpine alluded to at the end of Andrea's speech and the twin union of body and soul, and of lover and beloved, mentioned at the beginning. Like most parallels in the play, this one functions contrariously as well as analogously.

The union of Pluto and Proserpine, it will be remembered, constitutes one of the most famous agreements in classical mythology, being a legal settlement effected by Jove between Pluto and Ceres concerning their conflicting claims to the custody of Proserpine. It is also a union of opposites (life and death, summer and winter) which symbolises the ordered process of timely change enacted in what Ovid, in his account of the myth, calls 'the circling year' (*Metamorphoses*, V.565).[3] We have been prepared to respond to the implications of this myth by Andrea's opening suggestion of an ideal relationship between his body and soul and himself and his mistress. In these relationships, the inferiority of one member was rendered unimportant, and a gracious, equitable balance obtained, by virtue of mutual need, diligent service, and acknowledged merit ('Each in their function serving other's need', 'By duteous service and deserving love'). On the other hand, there are flaws in both relationships which are imaginatively, though not literally, connected with their violent and untimely termination ('in the harvest of my summer joys / Death's winter nipp'd the blossoms of my bliss, / Forcing divorce betwixt my love and me' – *Spanish Tragedy*, I.i.11–13). For, despite their mutual service, soul felt 'imprison'd' in the relationship and 'flesh' was 'wanton'. And it seems too as if courtship became a state of bondage against which the lovers rebelled, for, having won his lady's favour, Andrea 'possess'd' her 'In secret' (l. 10). Given the idea of a balanced and delicate mutuality, the word 'possess'd' is unsettling; but the real danger signal lies in the word 'secret'. Just as there is no way to Elysium for those whose funeral rites have not been performed (ll. 20–6), so there is no hope of happiness in any union of the sexes which has not been endorsed by society in the rites of marriage. Where the principle of life itself is acknowledged mutuality, secrecy is anti-life and secret possession is no possession at all. One has the impression, therefore, that Andrea does not understand fully the implications of what he has said, and this impression is supported by the fact that impatient and angry incomprehension is a feature of his response to the earthly drama which he has come to witness. However, his supernatural companion, Revenge, seems to think that poor understanding of tragic events is a universal human characteristic, for he introduces the drama to Andrea (and us) as a 'mystery' (l. 90). At this point we might conjecture that the paradox of contrarious unity is where the mystery begins.

III

The ideas implanted in the imagination by these neo-classical orations are expressed at every level of form in the rest of the play: they shape action, structure, characterisation, and style. The action proper begins with the Spanish King's judicial 'device' to end 'difference' and 'strife' between Horatio and Lorenzo concerning the capture of Balthazar, and to do it in such a way as to promote 'love' between the disputants and between them and the captive prince (I.ii.167–94).[4] This device is at once model and starting-point for the King's plan to knit the two countries together in 'a sure, inexplicable band' (III.xii.46) – the paradoxical pun is beautifully apt – by means of friendship and marriage as well as treaty. The plan of the moderate conqueror, however, is paralleled almost from the start by a secret counter-movement characterised by extremes of love and hate.[5] The origins of this counter-movement are complex. It stems from Bel-imperia's resistance to familial control of her love life; from Balthazar's killing of Andrea, her former lover, on the field of battle in a manner reminiscent of Ajax and his Myrmidons (see I.i.48–9; iv.24; III.xiii.71) and suggestive of 'a breach to common law of arms' (I.iii.47); and more immediately from the competition between Balthazar and Horatio for the favour of Bel-imperia. The combined effect of the two movements is to turn a festive court into a battlefield where differences are multiplied and confounded.

The constructional methods used by Kyd in the unfolding of this action are noticeably designed to draw attention to confounding contrariety and the imminence of sudden, unforeseen change. Starkly ironic contrast is a conspicuous feature in the sequencing of scenes.[6] In I.ii and iii, for example, the action moves from the court of Spain, with its happy and triumphant yet just king, to a Portuguese court ruled by a viceroy who is the very 'image of melancholy' (I.iii.12) and injustice. This contrast is perhaps too reminiscent of the Wheel-of-Fortune philosophy, reminding us as it does that one man's fall is the next man's ascent, and that no one must count himself secure. More typical of the play are those juxtapositions which show two groups of characters pursuing their own ends and moving in partial or total blindness towards final collision. Thus II.i ends with Lorenzo assuring Balthazar that Horatio will have to be 'removed' if Bel-imperia's favour is to be won, and II.ii begins with Bel-imperia and the favoured Horatio planning to consummate their love. More impressive perhaps (for here neither group has any idea of what the other is doing) is the juxtaposition of II.iii and iv, where the final decision of the King and his brother to marry Bel-imperia to the Portuguese prince is followed by her ecstatic union with Horatio. But there is ironic juxtaposition in the structure of the individual scene as well as in the scene sequence. The use of stage spectators (both theatrical and eavesdropping) serves to split virtually every scene into poles of attitude, understanding, and intention. The most palpable form of this technique is the constant presence on stage of the ghostly audience of two.

IV

Although the characters of the play are excellently differentiated, radical contradiction is something they all have in common. The nature of this dualism is reflected in a proliferation of certain cognate antithetical terms which never occur in conjunction but lead a deceptively separate existence: 'gentle' and 'wild', 'ruthful' and 'ruthless', 'patience' and 'fury'. Its most sinister manifestation occurs in the character of Lorenzo, the man of very gentle birth whose smooth courtliness and jovial affability obscure the fact that he can be compared to a 'savage monster, not of human kind' (II.v.19). Although untroubled by any inner conflict between the contrary tendencies in his nature (his reason and will are wholly at the service of his desires), he can be acted as a credible and well-rounded character. Aristocratic pride is what unkennels his barbarity. Resentful in the first place at his displacement in the roll of military honour by a mere gentleman such as Horatio, he is quietly outraged by the discovery that this same upstart ('What, Don Horatio, our Knight Marshal's son?' – II.i.79) is secretly undoing a prospective marriage between his sister and the Portuguese heir-apparent.[7]

Lorenzo's abrupt shifts of style from the ornate and the oblique to the plain and the blunt, manifesting a sudden impatience with the 'gentle' manner he is obliged to practise and go along with, contribute much to his credibility and liveliness as a stage character. But his impatience also relates him to an antithesis fundamental to the play's conceptual pattern: that which poises impulsive private action against respect for time, custom, and law. The antithesis is superbly dramatised in II.i, a scene which Lorenzo controls from start to finish and which, in its structure, rhythm, and sense, mirrors the larger tragedy. It opens with Lorenzo talking in his most languid and courtly style, urging his love-lorn friend to listen to reason and accept that 'in time' (the phrase is given fivefold iteration) the lady will relent and 'rue the sufferance of your friendly pain' (ll. 1–8). The scene reaches its climax with Lorenzo's successful attempt, partly brutal ('What, villain, ifs and ands?' – l. 77) and partly suave, to extract from Pedringano the name of his sister's secret lover. And it ends with his business-like injunction to the verbose and plaintive Balthazar, 'Let's go my lord, your staying stays revenge' (l. 133). Lorenzo's relationship here with the manifestly impatient Balthazar ('For love resisted grows impatient' – l. 117) is identical to that between Revenge and Andrea, shown in the preceding choric scene: 'Be still, Andrea, ere we go from hence, I'll turn their . . . joys to pain, their bliss to misery' (I.v.5–9). Like Revenge's, Lorenzo's air of quiet patience is that of a man who always has his hand on the detonator that will remove all obstacles from his path. He is fundamentally opposed to time and ripeness. This is finely suggested by the circumstances of Horatio's murder, hanged from a tree in his father's arbour and finished off in a stabbing orgy that mocks coition: 'Ay, thus and thus, these are the fruits of love' (II.iv.55).

Although it makes him an embryonic Iago (and Balthazar another

Roderigo), Lorenzo's demonic parody of patience or 'stillness' is a less important element in his characterisation than are his perverted gestures to the qualities proper to the just lord and master.[8] In his first dealings with Pedringano, he asks for fearless telling of the truth in response to 'just demand', threatens punishment if the servant is 'perjur'd and unjust' in his replies, and promises liberal reward, social advancement, and friendship to boot if he meets with 'duteous service' (II.i.43–103): the foolish Pedringano might almost confuse him with his uncle the King, whose conduct has shown strict fidelity to the principles specified in this behavioural outline. However, the service required from Pedringano entails betraying the trust of Bel-imperia and then acting as spy against her; it is secured by a combination of blackmail, bribery, and murderous threats; and it is underwritten with an oath of secrecy to which the servant is forced to subscribe. Although he has no present political role, the prospective heir to the Spanish throne is a prototypal Jacobean tyrant in every respect: that is, he violently undoes the bonds of friendship and true love, turns service into a condition of bondage, generates in society a netherworld of dark secrets, and – as we shall presently observe – either frustrates the due process of legal justice or uses it to dispose of unwanted servants. His relationship with his sister, with the socially inferior but intrinsically nobler Horatio, and with the corrupted servant Pedringano anticipates the more fully developed relationship between Ferdinand, the Duchess, Antonio, and Bosola in *The Duchess of Malfi*.

It is one of the more satisfying ironies of the play that Lorenzo, who thinks he knows everyone's 'mind' and 'humour' (III.iii.76; iv.57), is finally undone because he seriously misreads his own sister. The doubleness of Bel-imperia's name is no accident. She is beautiful and intelligent, but she is also endowed with an imperious will and with passions she is not in the habit of restraining for long. Modern attitudes to sexual morality should not blind us to the fact that her introduction to us as 'a worthy dame' possessed 'in secret' is a laconic paradox (I.i.10). Those closest to her are almost comically unaware of her unofficial self, complacently ascribing to her only those attributes conventionally associated with feminine beauty. According to brother, father, and uncle, she is 'gentle' and 'will stoop . . . In time' (III.x.12; II.i.4–5); not 'froward' but 'coy . . . as becomes her kind' (II.iii.3–5); one of the 'young virgins' (l. 43). There are layers of dramatic irony in her reassuring words to Horatio concerning her servant Pedringano: 'he is as trusty as my second self' (II.iv.9).

Not that inconstancy in love can be ascribed to her. She does indeed seem to transfer her affections from the dead Andrea to Horatio with remarkable speed; but this is because Kyd manages the development in an awkwardly condensed manner, and not because it is meant to appear unworthy. And Kyd does enough to suggest that it is perfectly credible. It seems natural that a woman grieving for the death of a lover, and alienated from her family because of their hostility to him when alive, should be strongly attracted to the sensitive hero who shares her love for the dead man. But the situation is more complex than that. For Kyd, the really important psychological fact about Bel-imperia's relationship with Horatio, and about her subsequent behaviour, is that both are propelled by a churning tide of contrary emotions. Loving grief converts to fury and hatred, these quicken new love, and new love sustains old hatred: 'Yes, second love shall further my revenge. / I'll love Horatio, my Andrea's friend, / The more to spite the prince that wrought his end' (I.iv.66–8).[9] To express the matter in humoral and elemental terms (as does Kyd: see III.x.68–75), melancholy can flow to choler, the tears of pity and love can become the fires of rage and destruction. This psychological syndrome affects Hieronimo, Isabella, and Balthazar, and so is central to the play (it is prominent in many later tragedies).[10] It means, of course, that the impulse to revenge is conceived as a dire confusion of emotional and moral opposites.

Bel-imperia's outraged love gives her a key role in the unfolding tragedy. Indeed, it makes her very like a euhemerized version of one of those classical, female divinities who habitually whip men out of their restrained and pacifist ways down the paths of violence and madness, a 'wrathful Nemesis' (I.iv.16) or 'madding Fury' (III.x.33).[11] Although Horatio was 'incens'd with just remorse' at the treacherous killing of his friend, his reaction was not extreme: he 'set forth against the prince. / And brought him prisoner from his halberdiers' (I.iv.28–9). But for Bel-imperia this subordination of personal feeling to a chivalrous ethic is the one blot on Horatio's heroic record: like Lady Macbeth, she would have her man do more than becomes a man – 'Would thou hadst slain him that so slew my love' (l. 30). It is she too who takes the initiative in the love affair; and, although this is dictated by his social inferiority, it is also indicative of her masterful nature and her intent to commit him to a course where passionate love and passionate hate are one. Thus, when he is killed as a result of his entanglement with her, his father becomes the object of those fiery persuasions he himself was due to receive:

> Is this the love thou bear'st Horatio?
> Is this the kindness that thou counterfeits?
> Are these the fruits of thine incessant tears?
> Hieronimo, are these thy passions,

Thy protestations and thy deep laments,
That thou wert wont to weary men withal?
O unkind father, O deceitful world!

(IV.i.1–8)

I am not suggesting, however, that Horatio and Hieronimo are essentially victims of this passionate young woman. Hieronimo is delighted here to discover that she is so thoroughly commited to revenge: 'Why then, I see that heaven applies our drift, / And all the saints do sit soliciting' (ll. 32–3). Since Hieronimo used to think it was the 'ugly fiends' of Hell would 'solicit' him to take revenge (III.ii.15–16), it follows that his confusion of mind and heart is just as severe as hers. As for Horatio, once he has been given the come-hither by Bel-imperia, he needs no further encouragement: it is he who lightly remarks that looks and words are very pleasant 'where more cannot be had' (II.ii.4), thus initiating the erotic dialogue which leds directly to his death in the garden. Moreover, there are suggestions that in neglecting Balthazar and pursuing Bel-imperia he is betraying the trust of the King and Castile (see I.ii.98–100; iv.55–7, 174 s.d.). At any rate, a courtier in his position would know that having an affair with the Infanta is courting disaster for oneself and one's family: Lorenzo's bitter remarks about his ambition would not have sounded wholly inept to an Elizabethan audience. It is apparent that in this tragedy, as in *The White Devil*, everyone is in some degree his own and the next person's provocative demon.[12]

Because of the baseness of both her brother and her royal suitor, Bel-imperia never forfeits our sympathy and admiration. The attitude, too, of her father and the King towards her love life contributes substantially to these positive feelings. It has to be emphasised that in virtually every respect these two brothers are models of justice and kindly concern: each seeks at crucial moments to resolve differences, make enemies friends, and acknowledge true merit. Their one fault lies in their unthinking assumption that Bel-imperia has no rights whatever in the choice or rejection of a suitor. Any opposition to their will in this matter threatens to crack the mould of their patient urbanity and humane justice. The King believes that young ladies 'must be rul'd by their friends' in matrimonial matters and urges Castile to 'win fair Bel-imperia from her will' (II.iii.42–3). He does not advise his brother how this should be done, but we can guess at Castile's preferred method. It would be a combination of emotional blackmail ('love him or forgo my love' – l. 8) and blind fury (that 'old wrath' which blighted the Andrea affair – III.x.70, 72) – like father, like daughter. In the playlet used by Hieronimo and herself to wreak vengeance on Balthazar and Lorenzo, Bel-imperia plays a 'fair Christian nymph' (IV.iv.16), and in a sense 'miss'd her part in this' (l. 140). But, given the way in which male authority disposes of Bel-imperia's natural rights as a woman, it is very apt that the Christian nymph should be driven to violence by a ruler whose name is that of a legendary, barbarous tyrant, Soliman (Suleiman) the Turk.[13] Like *Othello*, *The Spanish Tragedy* presents a contrarious world where Christian gentlemen can quickly 'turn Turk' (*Othello*, II.iii.162) in their dealings with the women they love (as with each other).

Of course, it is only in the character of Hieronimo that sudden and extreme change is exposed as a tragic fact, both pitiable and terrible. Hieronimo does not become a prominent figure until the end of Act II and so cannot be deemed a tragic protagonist in the conventional sense. Rather he is the most important individual in a tragedy which focuses on the way in which the failings of many characters interact to produce collective disaster, and where society is as much the victim of the individual as the individual is of society: a tragic model of which much will be made in the seventeenth century.[14] Nevertheless, the tragic intensity of *The Spanish Tragedy* derives almost entirely from Hieronimo's agonised responses to the horrors of a violently changing world –

> O world, no world, but mass of public wrongs,
> Confus'd and fill'd with murder and misdeeds
>
> (III.ii.3–4)

– and from his consequent protest and disintegration.

Before he is transformed by his son's murder, Hieronimo is the embodiment of all that is best in his own society. He is a father and husband of loving heart, a man of law noted for his energetic yet 'gentle' pursuit of equity (III.xiii.51–4, 93–4), and a courtly poet and entertainer who uses his art for socially binding purposes. Because of his obvious 'deserts', he has won not only royal favour but also 'the common love / And kindness' of the court and the people (III.xiv.61–2). He is thus a figure of unity in whom the twin themes of love and justice converge: very aptly, Kyd associates him with Orpheus.

Indeed, so thoroughly is the Orpheus analogy inwoven in the imaginative design of the play that it seems necessary to recall in brief the main outlines of the myth as well as the more important meanings attached to it in classical and Renaissance tradition. It was undoubtedly Ovid's version of the myth that the Elizabethans knew best: Orpheus gets more attention than any other mythological character in the *Metamorphoses*, their favourite classical poem. Ovid gracefully records the power of Orpheus's words and music to pacify the beasts and move even the trees to attend to him. He is far more studious, however, in delineating the effect which the Thracian poet had on the inhabitants of the Underworld when he went there to plead for the return of his wife, stolen from him in death on their wedding-day (or shortly after). While Orpheus sang his lament before Pluto and Proserpine, 'the bloodless ghosts were in tears . . . Ixion's wheel stood still in wonder, the vulture ceased to gnaw Tityus' liver', Sisyphus 'sat idle on his rock', and for the first time 'the cheeks of the Furies were wet with tears'.[15] Ovid thus used the myth as a tribute not only to love but also to his art and its power to civilise as well as delight the hearer; and he gives strength to this conception by effecting an implicit parallel (X.145–7) between the Orphic blend of words and music and the *discordia concors* which metamorphoses Chaos into Cosmos (on which he discoursed at the beginning of the poem). But Orpheus's loss of his wife for a second time signifies, for Ovid, the ultimate futility of mortal resistance to what is decreed by fate, or simply the necessary triumph of change and death. Moreover, the manner in which Orpheus himself dies stands, it would seem, for the inevitable triumph of the forces of envy and strife, for he is torn to pieces by an implacable mob of frenzied Maenads or Bacchic women whose clamorous howling and shrill flutes drown the harmonies of his voice and lyre (XI.1–43). Ovid does not hint at any significance in the backward glance which undid Orpheus's triumph over change and death. But Kyd and his educated contemporaries would all have remembered its interpretation by Boethius as an indication of the way in which grief can undermine one's faith in the ultimate goodness and justice of the world order, and with disastrous consequences.[16]

Pointed repeatedly by means of appropriate imagery and allusion, the broad analogy between Hieronimo and Orpheus stands out clearly in Kyd's play and greatly expands the imaginative effect of its themes. Hieronimo too is grief-stricken by the loss of a loved one snatched from him in a most untimely death. He journeys repeatedly in his imagination to the Underworld, finds that the harmonious arts are of no avail, despairs of divine justice and benevolence, and finally is destroyed in a holocaust of violence to which he has been urged by a woman as deaf to Orphic harmonies as any Maenad ('Relentless are mine ears to thy laments' – IV.iv.60). On the other hand, Orpheus dies in a vain attempt to overcome discord with concord; unlike Hieronimo, he is true to himself to the end. In fact Kyd uses the myth ironically and contrariously as well as analogically and panegyrically. Hieronimo is an Orpheus who falls: the spirit of strife invades his soul, and he even perverts the Orphic ideal, confusing discord with harmony. This conception of his tragedy (and it is the tragedy of the society which he

represents) is richly complicated by means of the Renaissance idea of
Orpheus as the father of eloquence and so of civilisation itself. Orpheus,
son of Apollo, was held to be the first orator. He was the type of those who
once used their persuasive powers to induce men to abandon their 'wyld,
stowre, hard' ways in the wilderness and to live together 'in good order . . .
Like neybours in a common weale by iustyce vnder law', and who function
at all times, by virtue of their 'honest eloquence', as 'props to uphold a
state, and the onely keyes to bring in tune a discordant Commonwealth'.[17]
Thus in the Renaissance not only poet and musician, but also lawyer,
politician and courtier – self-conscious masters in the arts of language and
'civil conversation' – would all look to Orpheus as their patron and
model.[18]

Kyd's appeal to the Orphic paradigm in its full significance is
unmistakable. Hieronimo's first two speeches mark him out with almost
programmatic emphasis as a man of loving heart who pleads effectively for
justice by skilfully controlling and expressing his feelings (I.ii.116–20,
166–72). His last sentence and his last actions in the play define, in organic
and sensationally emblematic terms, the self-destruction of an Orphic
hero: 'First take my tongue', he exclaims to his bewildered audience, 'and
afterwards my heart' (IV.iv.191); and he then bites out his tongue and
plunges a knife in his breast. His tragedy is that of a man whose heart is
poisoned by an event whose full horror he finds unendurable and
inexpressible; the discovery of his son's bloody corpse hanging from a tree
in the family arbour undoes the unity of his being and results in a
malfunctioning and perversion of his noblest gifts.[19] Kyd's concentration
on this process of degenerative change is so thorough that it is difficult to
see how he could have wished us to endorse Hieronimo's revenge, since it is
precisely the pursuit of a secret and violent form of retribution that
constitutes the loss of Hieronimo's Orphic self. This is not to say that we
are expected to sit in judgement on Hieronimo, or even that Kyd is
interested in the moral problem of private revenge. His primary concern (in
relation to this character) is to convince us of the terrible fact that the
'heart' of a loving, rational man can become 'envenom'd with such extreme
hate' (III.i.15–16) that he will revel in violence. Kyd's imaginative energies
are devoted not to the exploration of a moral problem but to a psychic
upheaval in which the protagonist oscillates between the poles of his being
until his darkest instincts take complete control, silencing his noble self or
using it as their instrument. That some audiences and readers will always
suppose we are to approve of what Hieronimo does in his distress is a
measure of Kyd's success in communicating the intensity of his hero's
sufferings and, in particular, the condition of psychic – i.e. emotional,

intellectual, and moral – confusion which makes him think his actions right and 'fit'.[20]

From the moment he discovers his son's corpse in II.iv until the end of the third act, when he has become calmly and totally committed to revenge, Hieronimo is an image of contrariety, uncertainty, and confusion. The fourth and last act is splendidly theatrical and richly symbolical, but the essence of the tragic drama lies in the tense psychomachia of the third act, where the characteristic qualities and values of Orphic man are assailed by their opposites and either overcome or seduced. Reason, communication, patience, hope, and respect for time give way to fury, silence, secrecy, dissembling, despair, and a wild desire to accelerate the moment of justice and death.

The conflict is not logically progressive; rather, it is a pattern which repeats itself over and over with mounting intensity until madness – or a kind of mad rationality – prevails. The essential features of the pattern are evident in Hieronimo's behaviour after the discovery of the body. It is Isabella and not he who says,

> The heavens are just, murder cannot be hid,
> Time is the author both of truth and right,
> And time will bring this treachery to light.
>
> (II.v.57–9)

Such thoughts have been banished from his consciousness for the time being. He thinks not of impersonal justice but of an act of retaliation which would bring 'relief' and 'joy' to his 'throbbing heart' (ll. 2, 40–1, 51–5). His advice is that they should cease or at least dissemble their grieving, and accordingly he determines that the body will not be buried until he has fulfilled his vow of revenge. Our commitment to Hieronimo as a serious and convincing dramatic character is severely strained here; but the flawed relationship between action and character does at least show Kyd's concentration on theme. We are to reflect at this point on the damage that will inevitably be done to the bereaved heart by the renunciation of communal mourning; on the function of funeral as the primary token of love and respect for the dead (see I.i.20–6; iv.34–41); and on the significance of ceremony as the antithesis of secrecy and a prerequisite for the well-being of individual and community. Hieronimo's refusal to bury his son fits oddly with his claim that the heavens will be shown unjust if the murder 'Shall unreveal'd and unreveng'd pass' (III.ii.9). In fact it is a major reason for the King's failure to listen to him when he eventually decides to get justice within the law – the King does not even know that Horatio is dead.

Far from helping him, Hieronimo's rejection of ritual and espousal of secrecy plays into the hands of Lorenzo, who has no doubts that secrecy is his best friend.

Hieronimo's sombre, Latin dirge does, however, bring the scene to a ceremonial conclusion. But it recalls the black incantations of witchcraft and confirms the ominous character of his reactions so far. For the first of many times, Hieronimo glances in two directions: towards (in Edwards's translation) 'the fair realms of light' where the sun-bred herbs provide medicine for pain, and towards the dark realm where sorceresses contrive poison and weave their spells by 'secret power' (II.v.67–73). Instinctively but solemnly he commits himself to the dark world and its heartless extremes: 'All things I shall attempt, even death, until all feeling is extinct in my dead heart' (ll. 74–5). This clearly anticipates the end of the tragedy, but so too does his belief that the solitary, unsung ritual is appropriate ('singing fits not this case'): it is his profoundly confused sense of what is fitting ('Why then I'll fit you' – IV.i.70) that accounts for his execution of the death sentence at the height of a marriage celebration.

In his next appearance, Hieronimo speaks the long, two-part soliloquy beginning 'O eyes, no eyes, but fountains fraught with tears' (III.ii.1) and broken with the discovery of Bel-imperia's letter. The elaborately patterned style of the first half indicates a reassertion of his Orphic self; it reflects a controlled endeavour to express great anguish and a corresponding effort to establish the possibility of true justice in a world that seems 'confus'd and fill'd with murder and misdeeds'. The plain, deliberative style of the second part is appropriate, too, for here Hieronimo is considering the possibility that the letter (naming the murderers) might be a trap, and reasoning towards the conclusion that it must be confirmed by circumstantial evidence before acted upon. But there are signs too that the controlled, judicious self is on the wane and that Hieronimo – to take up the metaphoric cue given in the first line – is a man whose vision of reality is being impaired by grief. The unmasking and punishment of Viluppo in the previous scene, and the King's unhesitant efforts to do justice to his soldiers and two of their quarrelling leaders, do not support his despairing conviction that the world is a chaos of 'public wrongs'. There is question-begging too in the argument that the letter must be authenticated before it is acted upon; it is, after all, a 'bloody writ' (l. 26) from an incarnate Fury, saying nothing about justice and law and calling only for revenge. Moreover the grieving part of the soliloquy culminates in a prayer for supernatural aid which makes no distinction between 'heavens, hell, night, and day' (l. 22). Hieronimo is ready for help from any quarter when it arrives – 'What means this unexpected miracle?' (l. 32) – from Bel-imperia.

One thinks of Hamlet goading himself to action with the thought that he has been 'prompted to... revenge by heaven and hell' (II.ii.580).

We find Hieronimo in his next appearance correcting public wrongs in an exemplary fashion: rebuking his prisoner for contempt of court, discharging the law 'for satisfaction of the world', and despatching the accused to execution because 'the fault's approv'd and confess'd, / And by our law he is condemn'd to die' (*Spanish Tragedy*, III.iv.25, 34–41). Simultaneously, however, he is consumed with impatience for redress of his own secret grievance and with the belief that 'neither gods nor men' are just to him (l. 10). His horror at the misplaced jocularity of the condemned Pedringano provokes some reflections which seem doubly apt. Precisely when it should be 'shrin'd in heaven', Pedringano's soul (remarks Hieronimo) is 'still wand'ring in the thorny passages / That intercepts itself of happiness' (ll. 91–4). Pedringano, it should be recalled, 'went the wrong way' (III.vii.22) in the end because he was obedient to Lorenzo's injunction to 'be merry still, but secret' (III.iv.64). Judge and criminal are less distinct here than would at first appear; and, as we shall see, time will blur the distinction a little more.

Hieronimo's next appearance suggests a considerable lapse of time in which 'restless passions' (III.vii.11) have accomplished much. At any rate, we have the clearest indication so far of a disfigured Orpheus. Hieronimo imagines that his plaintive words 'have mov'd the leaveless trees', but also that they have transformed the order of nature into a temporal and spatial chaos: 'Disrob'd the meadows of their flower'd green, / Made mountains marsh with spring-tides of my tears' (ll. 6–8). The discovery of Pedringano's letter incriminating Lorenzo and Balthazar – and rendering Bel-imperia's unnecessary – prompts him at first to acknowledge that 'they did what heaven unpunished would not leave' (l. 56). But then the mere thought of the two murderers leads immediately to a bitter curse on the day when Horatio pitied Balthazar, and so to the declaration that 'unfruitful words' must be abandoned when 'naught but blood will satisfy my woes' (ll. 65–8). The 'either... Or' decision which brings the scene to an end ('justice by entreats' or 'revenging threats') seems, therefore, an unreal commitment to alternatives. Hieronimo no longer wants or believes in Orphic justice and is heading for 'unfrequented paths' (III.ii.17). Lorenzo will find it all too easy to frustrate his half-hearted and inopportune efforts to get the King's ear.

The first onset of his madness coincides with a literal use of the symbolism of uncertain travel and contrary directions: the action emblematises his whirling confusion of mind. Asked by the Portuguese, 'which is the next way to my lord the duke's?', Hieronimo answers ambiguously. But when mention is made of Lorenzo, *'He goeth in at one*

door and comes out at another' (s.d.), purporting now to 'resolve' the
travellers' 'doubt' by directing them to 'the path upon your left-hand side'
that leads 'Unto a forest of distrust and fear', and ultimately to 'despair and
death' (III.xi.1–19). In Balthazar's phrase, he is guiding them by 'sorrow's
map' (III.x.91).

This leads naturally to the next scene, where the problem of direction is
once more Hieronimo's: 'This way, or that way? (III.xii.16): violence or
law? His attempt to follow the right path and get the King's ear (as he
passes in state with the Portuguese ambassador) is abandoned as abruptly
as it is decided upon. Suddenly, Hieronimo gives way to an outburst of
passionate frustration in which he publicly renounces his Orphic self:[21]

> Stand from about me!
> I'll make a pickaxe of my poniard
> And here surrender up my marshalship:
> For I'll go marshal up the fiends in hell
> To be avenged on you all for this.
>
> (ll. 74–8)

Here is no poet with enchanting song, no orator with civil and persuasive
words: Hieronimo is devil-driving and devil-driven, unintelligible to the
King to whom he pleads for justice: 'What means this outrage? / Will none
of you restrain his fury' (ll. 79–80).

But the climax of Hieronimo's 'incertain . . . pilgrimage' (III.x.109) takes
place in the following scene, with its 'Vindicta mihi' soliloquy and its
monologues prompted by the petitioners (who ask him to plead their cases
with the King). Like III.xii, it begins with a quiet, deliberative speech, a kind
of fragile rationality, and then moves into speech and gestures that enact a
total metamorphosis of Orphic man. In the soliloquy, Hieronimo
confronts for the first time the ethical implications of revenge, but passes
immediately through absolute confusion of mind in the direction of the
left-hand path. Citing in stark juxtaposition the Christian teaching on
revenge ('Heaven will be reveng'd of every ill . . . attend their will') and the
morality of a Senecan villainess ('Strike, and strike home, where wrong is
offer'd thee'), he proceeds by a sad parody of rational argument to choose
the latter: 'and to conclude, I will revenge his death' (III.xiii.1–20).[22] His
confusion in the soliloquy as a whole is evinced mainly by his reflections
on time and patience. 'Mortal men may not appoint their time' (l. 4), yet
'wise men will take their opportunity, / Closely and safely fitting things to
time' (ll. 25–6). He will 'enjoin' his 'heart to patience', but only in order that
he may the better exact 'revenge' (ll. 42, 44).[23]

Hieronimo's confusion is externalised in the appropriate form of mistaken identity when the petitioners arrive. He takes the Old Man with the piteous eyes to be his son: 'Sweet boy, how art thou chang'd in death's black shade! . . . Ah ruthless fate, that favour thus transforms! (III.xiii.146, 151). But he sees in him too 'the lively portrait of my dying self' (l. 85), and so construes him as an inverted Orpheus, an agent of bestial and demonic fury committed to destroy the bonds of law:

> I'll down to hell, and in this passion
> Knock at the dismal gates of Pluto's court,
> Getting by force, as once Alcides did,
> A troop of Furies and tormenting hags
> To torture Don Lorenzo and the rest . . .
> The Thracian poet thou shalt counterfeit:
> Come on, old father, be my Orpheus,
> And if thou canst no notes upon the harp,
> Then sound the burden of thy sore heart's grief,
> Till we do gain that Proserpine may grant
> Revenge on them that murdered my son:
> Then will I rent and tear them thus and thus,
> Shivering their limbs in pieces with my teeth.
> (*Tear the papers.*)
>
>   (ll. 109–23)

Hieronimo's imaginary plot to make Orpheus an instrument of revenge anticipates the use to which he will put 'fruitless poetry' (IV.i.72) (cf. 'my unfruitful words') in the final scene. But it relates also to his decision in the present scene to apply his 'tongue to / Milder speeches' than his spirit affords (III.xiii.40–1). From now on he will show himself an expert in the use of verbal art for the purposes of misleading and concealing. His elaborate reconciliation with Lorenzo – 'honey'd speech' to appease Cerberus (l. 114; I.i.30) – deludes not only Castile and his son but even Belimperia, Isabella, and the Ghost. But Hieronimo's dedication to false words results naturally and disastrously in his failure to recognise true ones: Castile's kindly sentences are taken by him as sure indications of intended treachery. Thus 'misconstered' (III.xiv.92) by the secretive judge, the innocent Duke will die with his guilty son.

Like Titus Andronicus, Brutus, and Othello, Hieronimo follows a dark path which entails a violation of all that is best in him. Like them, too, he is pitiably and terribly confused. And, although his noble image is not clearly restored at the end, we are kept conscious of it throughout. The 'monstrous resolution' (IV.iv.193) with which he carries through his plan for revenge and suicide is a pathological distortion of that constancy which he always showed in the pursuit of equity (III.xiii.53–4). Above all, his venomous hatred for Lorenzo and Balthazar, and consequent devotion to 'sweet revenge' (l. 107; IV.v.29), are inseparable from his undying devotion to 'Horatio, my sweet boy' (II.v.33): 'The cause was love, whence grew this mortal hate' (IV.iv.98).[24] Even in his moment of triumphant butchery, he is a haunting image of blasted love: 'He shrieks, I heard, and yet methinks I hear, / His dismal outcry in the air' (ll. 108–109).

V

It has been often and justly said that Kyd is a much better dramatist than poet: his imagery is unoriginal, his phrasing undistinguished, his rhythms without subtlety. He was, nevertheless, a great experimenter in adapting the strategies of language and style to the needs of the drama. Of particular interest here is his use of pun, paradox, oxymoron, and stychomythia. These serve his special purposes particularly well because they are, of course, figures of duality and contradiction. His characteristic figure perhaps, and certainly the one towards which his tragedy of confounding contrariety most naturally aspires, is the paradoxical or oxymoronic pun. We have already encountered the 'sure, inexplicable knot', which hints that in a mutable, contrarious world men often understand least what they feel most sure of.

In their phrasing and general presentation, very many of Kyd's figures evoke the style of contemporary love poetry and euphistic love prose. They help therefore to define and distinguish the characters of courtly young men such as Horatio (the eloquent and sincere lover), Lorenzo (the cool mimic of all styles), and Balthazar (the affected and self-indulgent lover). But these amatory figures all function ironically and have a special relevance to theme. Their dramatic context is always such that they acquire a literal significance, or an unintended aptness, or a stunning ineptness that instantly exposes the speaker's failure to comprehend the nature of reality: specifically, his failure to see that love and the promise of life is now strife, hate, and an assurance of death. In the bower scene of II.iv, for example, Horatio's use of the coition–death metaphor ('O stay a while and I will die with thee' – l. 48) omens the imminent transformation of sexual climax into death by hanging. Lorenzo's witty appeal to Bel-imperia on behalf of his languishing friend hits unwittingly on the true feelings of Balthazar's coy mistress: 'in whose melancholy thou mayst see / Thy hate, his love; thy flight, his following thee' (III.x.81–2). Lastly, Balthazar's rhapsody on Bel-imperia's tresses ('Ariadne's twines'), and his description of himself as a pilgrim led o'er the mountain by the lodestar of her 'heavenly looks' (III.x.89, 106–9), speak to the audience of labyrinthine loss, demonic enticement, and imminent 'downfall to the deepest hell' (I.i.64).

From *Doctor Faustus* to *'Tis Pity She's a Whore*, the language of amorous ecstasy and praise, ironically asserting the metamorphosis of Heaven into Hell and of love into strife, hate, and death, will provide the tragic stage with some of its most poignant moments. More important, however, in relation to both his own play and to subsequent practice is Kyd's combined use of stage symbols and associated image patterns. There are two dominant image clusters in *The Spanish Tragedy*, one based on the idea of natural growth, the other on play and entertainment; their corresponding stage symbols are found in the bower or garden scenes (II.ii, iv; IV.ii) and in the various scenes of dramatic performance.[25] These two symbolic sets add up to an imaginative epitome of Kyd's tragic meanings, betokening a communal catastrophe in which fruitfulness, orderly succession, and natural celebration are undone: the garden is sterile ('unfruitful'), play is joyless and corrupt.[26] There is a logical as well as an imaginative connection between the two symbolic patterns which Kyd pinpoints in his inspired pun on 'plot' (IV.ii.11–12; iv.104): what happens in *Soliman and Perseda* follows from what was done in the garden. The pun also indicates the greater importance of the play symbolism in Kyd's total design. If the paradoxical pun is Kyd's characteristic figure, its perfected form is one in which play and violence are conjoined. Just such a figure catches our attention at the beginning when the Spanish general, in his notably 'cheerful' account of that fierce battle, reports that the two armies confronted each other 'with daring shows' while 'ordnance play'd on either side' (I.ii.4, 26–7, 38).

The semantic effects of Kyd's theatrical symbolism are very complex. It contributes to the sense of tragic fatality by hinting that the characters are simply actors in a pre-scripted plot and not, as they imagine, the authors of their own actions. It points also to a continuous confusion of appearance and reality, a failure to interpret correctly what is seen and heard: most of the characters are bent on deceiving others; all are in some degree deceived. The deceptive appearance, however, is primarily that of play, signifying (like the rituals of marriage and banquet with which it is associated) a joyous desire to foster human relations; while the reality belied is a grimly earnest desire to divide and destroy. Thus it would seem that the major function of the play symbolism is to figure a root confusion of good and evil conceived in terms of love and hate or concord and strife.

This symbolism is evident at the level of diction in continuous playing on words which invoke the ancient comparison between life and the stage – 'perform', 'act', 'author', 'tragedy', 'play', 'plot', 'jest' (entertainment/merriment), 'spectacle', 'show', and (above all) 'device'. Its most striking feature, however, is its bold and original incorporation within the action itself. Most obviously, there is the continuous use of two choric, stage spectators, one of whom is at odds with the other in interpreting what he sees and hears as a comedy ('Nothing but league, and love, and banqueting!' – I.v.4). Then there are the devices placed at or near the end of each of the four acts: Hieronimo's dumb show at the banquet for the Portuguese ambassador, the love duet in the bower, Revenge's dumb show for Andrea, and the playlet at the end. Although only two of these devices are necessary to the plot, all four are connected by means of analogy and antithesis (the second and last by a cause-and-effect relationship as well); in addition, they are vehicles for the play's most important meanings.

The first two devices exhibit and celebrate the concord of opposites. Hieronimo's dumb show is designed by him to offer discreet advice to victor and vanquished on the conduct appropriate to each in the search for unity. Thus it is in perfect harmony with the spirit of the feast ('Spain is Portugal, / And Portugal is Spain, we both are friends' – I.iv.132–3) and is greeted with equal enthusiasm by the King and the ambassador when its 'mystery' (l. 139) is explained to them. The second device is not a dramatic performance in the strict sense. It is, however, an exceptionally stylised scene (or rather pair of scenes) in which the lovers playfully adopt mythological roles and are watched intently by mortal as well as immortal spectators.

As I have remarked in Chapter 1, Kyd (like Marlowe in *Tamburlaine the Great*) implicates in his tragedy the well-known interpretation of the union of Mars and Venus, and the birth therefrom of the goddess Harmonia, as an allegory of nature's fruitful and concordant discord. It is in this scene that the extreme relevance of the myth to the action as a whole is brought into sharp focus; in fact the lovers' rendezvous is turned into a duet of Mars and Venus and made the imaginative centre of the play as well as the basis for its major peripeteia. Perfectly placed towards the end of Act II (in a four-act play), it has been well prepared for and is handled in a manner designed to maximise its effectiveness as a symbol of unity (albeit a unity flawed from within as well as threatened from without). The lovers meet here to consummate a 'vow'd ... mutual amity' (II.ii.43) whose true beginning is on the battlefield, where Horatio was 'Friendship and hardy valour, join'd in one'. They have chosen time and place to fit their conception of the encounter as a moment of rare harmony, meeting in the bower when Venus begins to rise (II.ii.45) and the nightingale to 'frame sweet music' (II.iv.28–33). Casting themselves as Mars and Venus, they act out, in their formal conjunction of hands, feet, arms, and lips, and in their playful conceits, a lingering metamorphosis of martial confrontation into the kind of amorous strife that 'breaks no bond of peace' – 'a warring peace or peaceful war' (II.ii.33, 38). For the climax of this manifest dramatisation of *discordia concors*, Kyd finds a singularly appropriate verbal medium, and proceeds to use the climax as the springboard for a reversal which is devastatingly effective both as symbol and as theatre. Twenty-four lines of dialogue combining stychomythia (contrariety) and rhyme (concord), and culminating in 'O stay a while and I will die with thee, / So shalt thou yield and yet have conquer'd me', come to an abrupt end with the intervention of the murderers and the curt injunction of Lorenzo: 'My lord, away with her, take her aside' (II.iv.24–51).

The next device is the dumb show in which the Hymeneal torches are suddenly drenched with blood. An obvious prefigurement of the final device, it is symbolic not only of violent contrariety but also of incomprehension and non-communication. The show has been presented by Revenge in order to clarify the significance of the developing acting for the baffled Andrea; but Andrea understands the explanatory dumb show no better than he has understood the spoken show, and not until Revenge awakes to 'reveal this mystery' does he rest contented – 'Sufficeth me, thy meaning's understood' (III.xv.29, 36). This echoes the moment when Hieronimo revealed the mystery of his show to the King. And it echoes too the way in which Lorenzo terminated the duet of Mars and Venus. Having silenced one of the eloquent lovers forever, he exits with the command, 'Come stop her mouth, away with her' (II.iv.63); so that, when Hieronimo enters the garden, what he finds is a 'murd'rous spectacle' or dumb show with no eloquent 'author' (II.v.9, 39) to respond to his frantic questions and his even more frantic adjuration, 'Speak, here I am . . . O, speak' (ll. , 17). The dumbness of the two formal shows, therefore, is part of Kyd's complex symbolic design. It helps to express his idea that the abuse, obstruction, and final abandonment of speech, and a corresponding loss of meaning and communication, are major symptoms of tragic disintegration.

Despite the flaws which mar the conclusion (some so crude they can only be put down to textual corruption), the last device stands out as a symbolic device of remarkable inclusiveness, the complete and culminant expression of the given tragic world. Its symbolic function as an image of violent confusion – murderous entertainment, funeral marriage, act of 'mortal hate' caused by love (IV.iv.98) – is perfectly clear. But it is visually reinforced by the fact that it is a marriage play performed by *four* 'friends' whose interaction mirrors the war of the elements. Its symbolic significance, too, is ingeniously elaborated by means of the play–life analogy. Kyd follows the logic of this analogy as far as it will go, devising for Hieronimo a dramatic entertainment that comes as near to complete confusion as the intelligibility of his own play will allow. Conceiving of his revenge as the destruction of Babylon, Hieronimo is conscious of the fact that 'Babylon' ('Babel') means 'confusion' (IV.i.195–6).[27] He is conscious too that the fall of proud Babylon brought with it the curse of tongues: his treacherous play is written in four languages, one for each actor. And, although in the printed version of *The Spanish Tragedy* the playlet was '*set down in English . . . for the easier understanding*' of '*the public reader*' (IV.iv.10f. s.d.), it must surely have been acted in its polyglot form. When Balthazar protests that the performance 'will be a mere confusion, / And hardly shall we all be understood', Hieronimo promises that he will 'make the matter known' in 'an oration, / And with a strange and wondrous show besides'; at this point Lorenzo advises Balthazar to humour the old man, so the matter is dropped (IV.i.180–93). We must presume that Hieronimo has his way.

That the proud bond-breakers should both die in Babylonical confusion, with one of them playing the part of a lover pleading 'vain suits' to the 'Relentless . . . ears' of a mistress who kills him in earnest, is poetic justice indeed (IV.iv.59–60). But once more it seems that Hieronimo has become identifiable with what he opposes. Despite his 'oration' to the bewildered and horrified audience, and his wondrous strange show (Horatio's corpse), he fails to 'make the matter known' fully. Having revealed that Lorenzo and Balthazar were killed in earnest in the play for their murder of Horatio, he contemptuously denies that he was mad and then bites out his tongue, leaving the King with no explanation as to why he, of all people, should have sought justice in so barbarous a fashion. Thus the King's 'Speak . . . speak . . . I will make thee speak. . . . Why speak'st thou not' echo his own desperate appeals in the silent garden-plot for an explanation of mystery (ll. 163–4, 179, 104). Orpheus has helped to reduce life almost to the condition of an inexplicable dumb show.

The symbolic complexity of the final device is greatly enhanced by its association with decorum, the doctrine which demanded harmonious relationships and respect for differences in both life and literature (dramatic and non-dramatic). References to decorum (grace, fitness, pleasingness) occur throughout the play with almost ritual regularity, their combined effect being to strengthen the play–life analogy. However, the most overt and extended reference to propriety occurs in Hieronimo's discussion with his fellow actors of the forthcoming wedding-play. Balthazar remarks that a comedy would be more appropriate to the occasion than a tragedy, but Hieronimo appeals beyond the circumstance of time to that of persons to justify the fitness of his choice (comedy for common wits, tragedy for royalty). His argument is secretly ironic (these people will get just what suits them), but it is also openly bantering; and the banter is typical of the jesting enthusiasm with which he conducts his tragic plot and handles his intended victims. This jesting spirit is yet another symptom of Hieronimo's self-loss. We are to remember the courtier whose 'pompous jest' (i.e. 'stately show') (I.iv.137) was perfectly attuned to persons and time, and above all the grave judge who was horrified by the way in which Pedringano, gulled by Lorenzo's 'quaint device' and 'jest' (IV.v.5; III.v.13–17), clowned his way into the hangman's noose: 'I have not seen a wretch so impudent! / O monstrous times, where murder's set so light' (III.vi.89–90). Whereas in his perverted sense of fitness Hieronimo is akin to Seneca's Atreus (a revenger obsessed with the decorum of his barbarous ritual),[28] in his lethal jocularity he becomes almost indistinguishable from Lorenzo, the hated enemy who played at murder and murdered play.

Yet the final perspective on the Knight Marshal's device would seem to be affirmative; for it is the perspective of Andrea and Revenge, now alone together on stage in a spirit of complete unanimity. No longer in any doubt that he was taken to see a tragedy, Andrea expresses satisfaction for the first time with what he has been shown: 'Ay, these were spectacles to please my soul' (IV.v.12). He prepares, moreover, to lead Hieronimo to a world where friends and foes are clearly distinguished and appropriately rewarded, and to place him 'where Orpheus plays, / Adding sweet pleasure to eternal days' (ll. 23–4). It looks indeed as if Kyd has decided, for whatever reason, to put the seal of approval on the wedding-play.

But this is a tragedy which invites us to think carefully before answering the question, 'How like you this device?'[29] With a scene of great tension ended, and the stage cleared of all the actors in Spain's tragedy, the inclination to identify with the viewpoint of the two stage spectators is undoubtedly very strong. It has to be remembered, however, that the attitude of a late-Elizabethan audience to Andrea would always have been at best ambivalent and cautious: he is, after all, a nobleman who raged at the prospect of peace and happiness returning to his own war-troubled nation, and who now rejoices in effect at the almost total destruction of its royal line. And in fact, if we attend with reasonable care to what he says at the end, we must see that his sentiments – and the complaisance of Revenge – are presented ironically. The first thing to be noted is the long opening sentence in which he lists in random sequence the spectacles which pleased his soul: these include not only the deaths of Prince Balthazar, 'wicked Lorenzo', 'vild Serberine', and 'false Pedringano', but also 'Horatio murder'd in his father's bower', 'Fair Isabella by herself undone', 'good Hieronimo slain by himself', 'my Bel-imperia' slain similarly, and her father 'done to death'. This strange lack of discrimination introduces a comic note to his plan for the eternal happiness of his friends: Bel-imperia, the lady 'possess'd' in secret, is to be rewarded with all 'those joys / That vestal virgins . . . possess' (IV.v.22). But it is Andrea's planned allocation of misery to his former enemies that necessarily distances us from his ethico-aesthetic attitudes. Completely forgetting that the Underworld has its hierarchy of divinities who will carefully decide these things for themselves, Andrea asks Revenge, 'Let me be judge' (l. 30), and proceeds to sketch a scenario of torment which has nothing to do with a concern for justice but is simply an expression of undying hatred: 'how shall my hate be shown?' (l. 26). This pageant of hatred, it will be observed, looks like a copy but is in fact an inversion of the Orphic achievement: the 'sweet pleasure' felt 'where Orpheus plays' (ll. 23–4) gives way in Andrea's mind, as it did in Hieronimo's, to that of 'sweet Revenge' (l. 29; cf. III.xiii.107). For Andrea wants the vulture to cease gnawing the entrails of 'poor Tityus', and 'old wrath' to be forgotten at Ixion's wheel and Sisyphus's stone:[30] but only in order that Lorenzo, Balthazar, Pedringano, Serberine, and poor Castile can suffer the more in their 'endless tragedy' (II.v.31–48). How like we this device? To answer with Andrea, I suggest, is to rest in confusion.

Finally, then, as initially, the supernatural framework sends us back to the mundane world for an understanding of the problems which the action raises. Revenge may allude with an air of omniscience to 'What 'tis to be subject to destiny' (III.xv.28), and he undoubtedly has the last word (on the stage). But he is, after all, no more than a personification of the impulses which drove Bel-imperia, Lorenzo, Balthazar, and Hieronimo to compose the Spanish tragedy, and which now make Andrea eager for an endless one. If Revenge were asked at the end to explain the whys and the wherefores of the action, he would probably have no more to tell us than the departing Iago: 'What you know, you know.'

VI

Despite its overemphasis and its frequent clumsiness, Kyd's art is distinguished by a subtle, sophisticated self-consciousness. This stems in part from his Renaissance interest in the psycho-social significance of language, and from his related belief that tragic disaster will necessarily be accompanied by some radical failure in the symbolic systems which enable man to confront the threat of chaos and meaninglessness and so become fully human. But it may have arisen initially from his desire to defend himself against the prevailing critical view – a view endorsed by playwrights such as Jonson, Chapman, and even Webster – that tragedy must exclude comic and 'low' elements.[31] His defence lies in the implicit argument that in a play which identifies the tragic with violent contrariety the inclusion of such elements need not necessarily infringe the principle of aesthetic harmony, coherence, or fitness (i.e. decorum): they can become significant parts of an artistic *discordia concors*. Beyond this, however, Kyd seems to suggest that a play which faithfully mirrors the conditions of life in a world of confounding contrariety, and is acted before a mixed audience (and all audiences are mixed), will almost certainly provoke divided, confused, and erroneous responses – and will fulfil its task the better if it alerts its audience to this probability. His characters are involved in a search for meaning and habitually 'misconster' each other's words and acts;[32] they are witnesses to a drama which they need interpreted and even categorised. Given the restlessly ironic cast of Kyd's mind, it would be naïve to suppose that the off-stage audience is excluded from these problems.

Among his contemporaries and successors, only Shakespeare was capable of developing Kyd's metalinguistic and metadramatic treatment of tragic error and confusion (although there are some signs of it in Marlowe, Marston, and Webster).[33] This is not the place to consider that development in any depth, but a brief sketch should help both to confirm the foregoing interpretation of *The Spanish Tragedy* and to indicate just how substantial was the achievement of Thomas Kyd.

Shakespeare's first tragedy, *Titus Andronicus*, is a thorough-going exploration of Lorenzo's maxim, 'Where words prevail not, violence prevails' (II.i.108). The barbarising of Rome and Romans (including the hero) is a process in which pleadings for justice and mercy fall on deaf ears, and where the only speech to prove effective is that which serves the destructive instinct – 'stabbing' and 'siren' words. The nature of Rome's degeneracy is sensationally symbolised – we are reminded here of Hieronimo as well as Philomela – in the fate of the violated heroine, rendered tongueless and handless by her ravishers, an image of 'speechless' complaint, 'dumb action', incommunicable horror (III.ii.39–40). The Kydian pun in her last utterance (a curse and an incomplete sentence) identifies tragic disintegration with meaninglessness: 'Confusion fall –' (II.iii.184).[34]

Although Lavinia becomes for a while the object of a distracted attempt to 'interpret . . . martyr'd signs' (III.ii.36), Shakespeare's obsessive concern with the violation of humanity-as-language makes the problem of interpretation itself a secondary one; and there is no effort to vex the audience with hermeneutic problems. It is in *Julius Caesar* and *Hamlet* that the elusiveness of meaning becomes a major issue. Almost everything in these plays acquires the status of a sign, and almost every scene provokes conscious inquiry into meaning both as significance and as intention.[35] Was the increasingly feeble manner in which Caesar put by the proffered crown due to a reluctance to refuse it or to the oncoming of an epileptic seizure (or fainting-fit induced by the nauseous mob)? What interpretative comments did Cicero make in Greek, and what could be inferred from the laughter of those who (unlike the reporter) understood him? Does the ghost refuse to communicate with Horatio because he charges it to do so in the name of Heaven or because it is justly offended by his sceptical attitude to its assumption of the 'fair *and* warlike form' of the buried king (I.i.46–9; emphasis added)? When Hamlet misconstrues Claudius's show of prayerful contrition, does he postpone killing him because his nature recoils from cold-blooded murder or because he really wishes to damn his enemy's soul (something which would be utterly unworthy of him)? These are tantalising questions to which the dramatist gives no answer; instead, he involves us in a painful quest for meaning which reminds us that the *dramatis personae* are not alone in their proneness to 'construe things after their fashion, / Clean from the purpose of the things themselves' (*Julius Caesar*, I.iii.34–5). We are left with the questions of Ophelia ringing ironically in our ears: 'What means this, my lord? . . . Belike this show imports the argument of the play . . . Will a' tell us what this show meant?' (*Hamlet*, III.ii.133–9). As I have remarked elsewhere,[36] *Hamlet* itself is the sum total of all the imperfect signs, shows, rites, and plays which it contains and has been made to share in their indirect and reluctant surrender of meaning; partly in consequence, it catches the mysteriousness of tragic life in a way that no other play does. Like *Julius Caesar*, but much more so, it displays a kind of semiotic and hermeneutic self-consciousness that, in its refinement and subtlety, leaves *The Spanish Tragedy* far behind. But it must be recorded that the brilliant imaginative idea which accounts for the fascination of *Hamlet*'s self-reflexive art originates (over a decade earlier) in *The Spanish Tragedy*: not in the form of a vague or fumbled design, but firmly realised, a challenge which only the greatest dramatic genius of the age could take up. So much else in Kyd's achievement was to be assimilated, directly or indirectly, by his successors; this was for Shakespeare alone.

VII

The Spanish Tragedy then, as Shakespeare perceived, is all of a piece, but complex and richly suggestive. In construction, characterisation, symbolism and style, it figures what happens to a peninsula (a binary geo-political unit), to a nation, and to a noble individual when the untrustworthy 'second self' breaks free from the bond that controls 'difference'. One kind of difference (conflict) multiplies and prevails, the other (distinction, identity) is obliterated. A society publicly committed to love, peace, and celebration is secretly at war with itself, racked with private griefs and hatreds. Civility and cruelty, justice and barbarism, patience and revenge, reason and madness, ripeness and sterility, play and deadly earnest all become indistinguishable. Orphic man inflames the Furies and demons, domesticates Babel, and finally destroys language altogether. The dramatic poet who is the tragic hero's *alter ego* recognised that a play which adequately represents this process must risk being 'hardly understood' by some and deemed 'a mere confusion' by others. Audaciously, he took the risk, leaving it to the judicious to ask, like Theseus confronted with the artisans' comical tragedy, and no doubt like the first courtly audience of *A Midsummer Night's Dream*, 'How shall we find the concord of this discord?' Neither in prologue nor in epilogue, however, does he help us to find what we are looking for; all his clues – 'Ariadne's twines' – are in the artefact itself.

3 Christopher Marlowe

The tragedies which Marlowe wrote for the public stage were composed within a period of about six years and reflect a strongly individual artistic personality. In consequence they have tempted many a critic to present them as a more-or-less homogeneous group, with each play interpreted from the standpoint of a common theme, outlook, or character type. Yet the differences between these plays are substantial and in some cases extreme. We do well to remember F. P. Wilson's insistence that Marlowe had the true dramatist's capacity to sink himself in his material and to adapt his method and style to the nature of his chosen subject.[1]

Taken as a whole, however, Marlowe's plays do have identifiable peculiarities. They are, it is generally observed, the work of an extremist imagination. Marlowe commutes between the poles of aspiration and disillusion, hope and despair, power and impotence, audacity and timidity. His plots may demand attention to the median range of human emotions and attributes, but his treatment of these is apt to be perfunctory and conventional. He is at his best in the antithetical modes of exaggeration and deflation, hyperbole and irony.[2]

Most fundamental disagreements on the nature of Marlowe's tragic vision, and even on the interpretation of particular plays, could probably be resolved without too much simplification into disagreements as to which of these two modes predominates. The problem can be acute, since the ironist in Marlowe is liable to beckon us just when the hyperbolist is filling the imagination with dreams of magnificence and delight. We may resolve the problem by invoking the concept of ambivalence and arguing for the balanced coexistence in the text of contrary but equally valid attitudes. This, however, may be to assume that the sole function of irony is to serve as a kind of counterpoint and to ignore the fact that its modest proposals are regularly aimed at the wholesale invalidation of assumptions which are strongly held and immodestly voiced. My own view is that the rapid maturing of Marlowe's powers as a dramatist is intimately bound up with his increasingly refined and extensive use of irony, and that after

Tamburlaine the Great (1587–8) the ironist in him does indeed become predominant. Irony, however, is not central to *Tamburlaine* (Part I or II); the commonly held view that this play is an essentially sardonic and disapproving portrait of heroic conquest is no less mistaken, I believe, than the older idea that Marlowe identifies with the superhuman dreams and endeavours of his heroes. This is not to say that Marlowe suddenly becomes an ironist after *Tamburlaine*, for there is an abundance of irony in this two-part play. However, it is irony of a simple kind and its primary function is to confirm the greatness of the hero by undercutting the claims and pretences of his opponents. In fact *Tamburlaine the Great* is more heroic than tragic, while *The Jew of Malta* (1589–90), *Edward II* (1591–2) and *Doctor Faustus* (?1592–3), are tragedies with a strongly anti-heroic bias. Indeed, in some respects the protagonists of these three plays resemble Tamburlaine's opponents more nearly than they do Tamburlaine himself: their actions do not measure up to their boasts and their lofty self-conceptions, and their end is ignominious defeat. Marlowe's ironic impulse, however, is not confined to undercutting man's pretensions to heroic status; it is reflected also in a general propensity for satire and black comedy. Its strength is such that *The Jew of Malta, Edward II*, and even *Doctor Faustus* must be classed as tragedies in which the affirmative element is slight.

What we know of Marlowe's life and violent death would encourage us to give some credence to Kyd's assertion that he was 'cruel and intemperate of heart'. So too would the plays, for apart from the great closing scenes of *Doctor Faustus* they are short on genuine compassion and evince an unhealthy interest in the infliction of pain.[3] Paradoxically, however, no other tragedies of the period contain so many explicit references to pity: they abound in appeals for mercy and in fervent accusations of hard-heartedness and cruelty. Possibly Marlowe was conscious of the defect in sensibility to which Kyd drew attention (he may well have heard about it from Kyd himself) and sought to avoid the kind of imbalance it would necessarily create in his tragedies. But his attention to pity proceeds also from his preoccupation with opposites and extremes; if he was predisposed to write about the remorselessness of great men and of life itself, his intellectual habits demanded that the complaint of pity should regularly be heard. It is noticeable, however, that his incursions into this area of emotional experience often result in a feeling of artifice or sentimentality. Moreover, we are frequently left with the impression that those who cry for pity are simply demonstrating their own weakness or their failure to grasp the significance of what they have done. In fact Marlowe's imagination is stirred far less by the problem of unmerited and excessive suffering than it is by the idea of an inexorable law which operates with awesome inevitability against those who infringe its requirements. No doubt this is an aspect of his fascination with power. Just as he admires men of inflexible determination, and looks with mingled pity and contempt on the weak and the failed, so too he believes instinctively in the wrath of God rather than in his mercy and grace. It is pertinent that the heroes of his first two plays, Aeneas and Tamburlaine, are men with a divine mission which sanctions and even glorifies what in ordinary men would be deemed heartless inhumanity. Although he sometimes overcomes it triumphantly, Marlowe's deepest instinct is to justify cruelty. It is an instinct which necessarily restricts his achievement as a tragedian.

After *Tamburlaine*, and perhaps under the influence of Kyd, Marlowe structures his plays so that scene sequence emphasises a process of continuous and often extreme change in the emotional condition and the allegiances as well as the external fortunes of his principal characters. But he imposes his own stamp on the changefulness of the tragic world and its inhabitants. For him the true heroic quality is resolution. This is sometimes synonymous in his plays with constancy, but on the whole it is a less comprehensive ethical ideal. Resolution predicates clarity of purpose and strength of will, the ability to keep one's word and follow a chosen path; it suggests fidelity to self rather than to others, action rather than endurance. Marlowe measures all mankind against this ideal and finds very few who are not grossly wanting: in time of stress, the vast majority prove unstable, confused, and weak, incapable of sustaining their noble or defiant intentions. But most men are inconstant in the sense of treacherous too: the spirit of Machiavelli is omnipresent. Marlowe's mutable tragic world is thus a place of broken promises as well as of unfulfilled promise. Infidelity and disillusion prevail.

And, because it is so changeful, it is also, like Kyd's and Shakespeare's, a place of intellectual and moral chaos. Marlowe's sceptical outlook and love of shock tactics make confusion a special feature of his plays. Again and again he involves us in an attempt to disentangle contraries so as to describe qualities, actions, and men correctly. Is pitiless resolution base or noble? Are Christians blessed and Jews accursed? Are riches a sign of wealth or of poverty? Is pleasure for its own sake sweet or bitter? Is repentance to be equated with irresolution or with resolution? At the end of the play we have a good understanding of what is involved in these and other such questions, and may even feel able to answer them; but for the most part they are questions which ensnare the *dramatis personae*. The fate of Abigail in *The Jew of Malta* is exemplary: thinking that bitter experience has taught her to 'see the difference of things', she walks further than ever into 'The fatal labyrinth of misbelief' (III.iii.60–4).

II

An outstanding exception to this common fate is Tamburlaine the Great. Tamburlaine has a very clear conception of himself and of what he must do, and is able to translate these conceptions into action with stunning exactness. Never once does he waver in the belief that everything he does is morally justified. And, when he dies as undefeated conqueror and monarch of the East, he is sustained by the love of grieving sons and followers and by the conviction that Jove will reward him with an eternal throne.

Much of the play's fascination, however, lies in our uncertainty as to whether Tamburlaine's flattering self-conception is valid. Marlowe himself has induced this uncertainty with the most obvious deliberation. Throughout both parts of the play Tamburlaine acts in a manner which brings upon his indifferent head a steady stream of denunciation and curse. His enemies term him base, slavish, vile, barbarous, ruthless; a thief, a usurper, a monster, a devil. And they regularly call upon Mohammed and the gods to consign him quickly to the Hell-fire for which, they believe, he is destined. To complicate matters for the audience, Tamburlaine's detractors are not always fixed in their opinions: they can be so bewildered by his conduct as to profess themselves unable to decide 'of what mould or mettle he be made', whether he be 'god, or fiend, or spirit of the earth, / Or monster turned to manly shape' (Pt I, II.vi.9–17). Indeed, sworn enemies can become admiring friends.

These positive, negative, and ambivalent attitudes to Tamburlaine are all reflected in critical accounts of the play. Some critics hold that Marlowe wishes us to conclude that Tamburlaine's enemies are quite wrong and argue that the whole imaginative thrust of the play is to make us accept Tamburlaine on his own terms. Others insist that Marlowe presents Tamburlaine as a conqueror whose career of ruthless self-aggrandisement is essentially evil although superficially attractive: they even describe him as mad, Satanic, and marked out for damnation. Still others maintain that Marlowe does not take sides in the debate he initiates, or that his attitude is mixed, or even that it alters in Part II from approval to disapproval. As I have already indicated, my own response is of the first kind. Marlowe's attitude to Tamburlaine, I believe, is both consistent and panegyric: he means what he says when he calls him 'the Great'. As I hope to show, the two-part play is an audacious and successful attempt to justify wholly unorthodox conduct in the light of orthodox ideas on the nature of nature and the providential ordering of the historical process. It is true that Part II, written after the success of Part I, is designed to turn the whole heroic saga into a tragedy. But it is tragic only in the sense that the earthly stage is utterly impoverished by Tamburlaine's untimely death.

The argument that Marlowe's view of the Scythian conqueror is essentially panegyric finds considerable support in the fact that Marlowe's audience was predisposed to accept just such a view. In the popular accounts of Tamburlaine's life given to the Elizabethan public by Sir John Fortescue and George Whetstone, three main points are made. First, Tamburlaine was a military hero of whom the modern world can be justly proud: he deserves to be ranked with 'the most famous and worthie captaines' of all time, and was in no way inferior even to Alexander the Great. Second, although he was utterly ruthless with those who opposed his triumphal progress, and although his ruthlessness might seem to cancel out his 'many rare virtues', this was nevertheless justifiable, for 'it is to be supposed that god stirred him uppe [to be] an instrument to chastice these princes, these proud and wicked nations'. Third, Tamburlaine's astonishing achievement in rising from shepherd to king of kings is explicable mainly in terms of unity and harmony. He was able to seize power in the first place because there prevailed at that time 'a certaine discorde, or breache of amitie betwixt the king of Persia and his brother'. He himself consolidated and extended his rule because he demanded and received the utmost loyalty from his followers and was a faultlessly just and even generous and affectionate leader. After his death, too, his empire fell apart because mutual envy and dissension left his two sons vulnerable to the attack of his old enemies.[4]

Although Fortescue and Whetstone (and their continental sources) regarded Tamburlaine as a unique historical phenomenon, they obviously sought to explain his greatness and justify their admiration in terms of traditional ideas. If Tamburlaine had risen to power in Western Europe he would have had to be condemned as the embodiment of rebellion and anarchy. But when comfortably distanced behind the Iron Curtain of Islam he could be regarded as yet another instance to prove a point which was regularly made for admonitory purposes in Christian treatises on the art of princely rule: namely, that the noble titles which men inherit were originally won by noble deeds, and that if they are lost it is because of a failure to bear this in mind. The biblical notion of the Scourge of God – the pagan conqueror whose ambitions were used by God to curb and punish evil tyrants – was an established element in the providential theory of history and fitted in well with Tamburlaine's defeat of the Turk, the arch-enemy of Christendom. Lastly, the idea that the strength and durability of a regime is essentially a matter of internal harmony was a commonplace with Renaissance historians who contemplated the rise and fall of dynasties and sought to abstract from the past political lessons for the present.

It was, then, on the groundwork of this overall interpretation of Tamburlaine that Marlowe built his exuberant dramatic portrait of the conqueror. What attracted him to the story was the idea of a man whose life spanned the extremes of shepherd and king of kings. But he was attracted too by the cruelty, and far from softening this he made it a major and ever more conspicuous feature of Tamburlaine's character. However, since he employed and expanded a justifying framework known and acceptable to his contemporaries, he was able to do this without seriously threatening his panegyric perspective.

The two terms habitually used in the play to characterise Tamburlaine's greatness are 'majesty' and 'resolution'. Marlowe's understanding of majesty is similar to that of Sir Thomas Elyot, who gave two chapters to the subject in his *The Book of the Governor* (1531), the Tudor Englishman's bible on the qualities necessary to rule. Majesty is a combination of charismatic physical presence and great eloquence, and its effect is to daunt and delight, to inspire both fear and love. Whether in the awed descriptions of observers such as Menaphon, or in the suicidal despair which his angry look induces in an enemy such as Agydas, the majesty of Tamburlaine's physical appearance is always registered as a potent dramatic fact. But it is majesty of speech which makes him outstanding, and it was this which thrilled Elizabethan audiences hungry for golden words and 'high astounding terms'. Elyot insisted, too, that 'the speech of majesty' should not be all in one key but should be flexibly adjusted to persons and time in accordance with the principle of decorum.[5] Looking at Marlowe's play from the vantage point of, say, *Othello*, we might well judge that Tamburlaine fails to meet this requirement. But we must make allowances for the necessarily limited stylistic range of pioneer work and note that Marlowe would have us accept that Tamburlaine triumphantly fulfils Elyot's requirement. It is significant that two of his earliest and most important conquests, both effected by his majesty ('Won with thy words and conquer'd with thy looks' – Pt I, I.ii.228), are over an enemy general who becomes a trusted follower, and a captive princess who becomes his queen. The issue of rhetorical decorum is in fact made explicit: Agydas sneers that Tamburlaine would converse with ladies in the rattling bombast of a martial man, but Zenocrate is able to declare that his 'amorous discourse' is 'much sweeter than the Muses' song' (III.ii.40–50).

Tamburlaine's majesty, however, is inseparable from his resolution, the ability to match words and signs with appropriate deeds. Without resolution, majesty would be mere sound and show (as Shakespeare indicates in *Richard II*). Hardly less impressive, therefore, than Tamburlaine's sonorous verse paragraphs are those terse sentences into which he compresses his boundless will and his rock-like sense of his own identity:

> That which mine honour swears shall be perform'd . . . .
>
> I speak it, and my words are oracles . . . .
>
> Not for the world Zenocrate, if I have sworn . . . .
>
> This is my mind and I will have it so . . . .
>
> For *will* and *shall* best fitteth Tamburlaine . . . .

From the beginning, Tamburlaine is sharply contrasted with each of his challengers, and the essence of the contrast lies not so much in his eloquence as in his 'kingly resolution' (Pt I, I.i.55). Whereas the vows and boasts of his enemies, pitched to the height of bombast, come to nothing, his are turned into deeds with an ease and fullness that suggests historical inevitability: 'His resolution far exceedeth all' (IV.i.48). It is noteworthy that the first king he disposes of is an irresolute who relies entirely on the will of a favourite counsellor named Meander. Tamburlaine, we soon discover, never 'take[s] Meander's course' (II.v.27). Like the sun in its path, he follows the trajectory of his predestined greatness without hesitation or hindrance.

Tamburlaine's conscious preoccupation with the relationship between words and deeds is an expression of his sense of balance and justice. It is also a sign of his radical sense of fitness or decorum. A concept of considerable importance in the play, decorum appears to be essentially a question of maintaining a just relationship between sign systems and reality. Men and women must be accorded the titles, names, epithets, and similes they deserve; they must also act, speak, and present themselves in a manner which conforms to their role and name. Tamburlaine himself is never more conscious of the demands of a true and just decorum than when he is reacting to the charge of unwarranted cruelty – a charge which usually brings with it a litany of debasing names and epithets. Time and again, even to Zenocrate (who is certainly disposed to 'speak of Tamburlaine as he deserves' – Pt I, III.ii.36), he has to protest that the horrific speeches, actions, and spectacles which emblazon his path are all justified by their essential fitness to his appointed role and title. On such occasions, it is not the proud title of 'arch-monarch of the world' he appeals to. It is one which spells terror for the corrupt, the wicked, and the foolish:

> Villains, these terrors and these tyrannies
> (If tyrannies war's justice ye repute)
> I execute, enjoin'd me from above,
> To scourge the pride of such as Heaven abhors;
> Nor am I made arch-monarch of the world,
> Crown'd and invested by the hand of Jove,
> For deeds of bounty and nobility;
> But, since I exercise a greater name,
> The scourge of God and terror of the world,
> I must apply myself to fit those terms,
> In war, in blood, in death, in cruelty,
> And plague such peasants as resist in me
> The power of heaven's eternal majesty.
>
> (Pt II, IV.i.144–56)

On virtually every occasion he appears in the play, Tamburlaine reminds the world that what he does is preordained and that in consequence he cannot be defeated in battle. At first his references are mainly to the stars, the fates, the oracles of Heaven. But by the middle of Part I he is describing himself as the Scourge of God and invoking the orthodox idea that the operations of the stars, fortune, and fate are all included in the instrumentality of divine providence. So Irving Ribner's much-favoured argument that this play embodies a non-providential theory of history – history is made 'by fortune and the human strength of will which can control it' – seems a curious one.[6] There are only two ways in which it can be sustained: either by ignoring all the references in the play to providential control (as Ribner does), or by assuming (as others have done) that Tamburlaine is the victim of a gigantic and continuous self-deception. But this assumption will not stand up to textual scrutiny. From the start of his career to the end, there are a long succession of individuals who proclaim that Tamburlaine is 'misled by dreaming prophecies' (Pt I, I.i.41), that 'The gods . . . will never prosper your intended drifts' (I.ii.68–9), and that Heaven will pour down its vengeance on him in a crushing military defeat. In every case, experience changes their mind: his prophecies are fulfilled, his intents prosper, no one defeats him. The effect of this ironic strategy is to neutralise all objections to his claim that he is invincible because he is the agent of divine power.

It is often said that Marlowe would have expected his audience to disapprove of Tamburlaine's career if only because the Scourge of God type was traditionally held to be an evil man in himself, however well he served the divine purpose.[7] Even if the basic assumption here were correct, one would wonder if there are not exceptions to the rule, seeing that Tamburlaine is fully conscious of his divine mission and dedicates himself to it with religious fervour. But one has only to look at the source material behind the play to see that the assumption is incorrect.[8] There is no hint there of possible damnation; in fact the Scourge of God idea is used to *protect* Tamburlaine's claim to greatness.

Moreover, Marlowe's handling of Tamburlaine's relationship with Mohammedanism and Christianity serves to develop the favourable implications of the Scourge role. The Turks and their allies are characterised as proud and pitiless heathens who revel in the destruction of Christians and are dedicated to the conquest of Christendom. In both parts of the play much is made of the fact that Tamburlaine's attack on the Turkish empire cuts short the Turks' advance into Europe. But Tamburlaine is not simply the unwitting saviour of Christians, any more than he is the unwitting Scourge of God. He shows a special compassion for Christian captives in Islamic countries and makes a point of liberating them wherever he goes. Consistent with this attitude is the fact that he comes to renounce his faith in 'holy Mohamet' and to declare that his only allegiance is to a transcendent God:

> There is a God, full of revenging wrath,
> From whom the thunder and the lightning breaks,
> Whose scourge I am, and him will I obey.
>
> (Pt II, v.i.181–3)

It would have been too obvious a violation of historical fact to convert Tamburlaine to Christianity; but Marlowe seems to hint that he is moving in that direction before he dies.

It has, however, been argued that Tamburlaine's expression of contempt for Mohammed after the sack of Babylon is an act of blasphemy which ensures his damnation (since he dies shortly afterwards). It has also been said that his religious sentiments, such as they are, are repugnant to Christianity, his God being a God of vindictive justice and not of mercy.

The first of these arguments shows a strange insensitivity to the significance of Mohammedanism within the play and in the context of Christian Europe of the sixteenth century. Both arguments, too, reflect an imperfect knowledge or recollection of those parts of the Bible which deal with the visitation of God's wrath on the heathen persecutors of the true faith. But this raises the larger and more important point that Marlowe exploited his audience's knowledge of the Bible in such a way that Tamburlaine would seem to them to have fulfilled his preordained role with breathtaking exactness.

What might first be noted is the insistence of the Old Testament prophets that the descent of God's wrath on the heathen tyrant who persecutes the faithful is inevitable: 'The Lord of hostes hath sworn, saying, as I have proposed, so shall it come to pass . . . the Lord of hosts hath determined it, and who shall disannul it?'[9] Here of course is an attitude and an idiom with which Tamburlaine is wonderfully in tune: granted his belief that he is the instrument of this Lord of hosts, his claim that '*will* and *shall* best fitteth Tamburlaine' seems inarguable. Moreover, the punishment of the persecuting tyrant is prophesied in the New Testament – the Book of Revelation – as well as in the Old, and the vindictiveness of Tamburlaine's God is just as apparent in the first as in the second. 'Rewarde her [i.e. Babylon] even as she hath rewarded you, and give her double according to her workes', says the Christian God of the gentle apostle (Revelation 18:6), sharpening up the demand of Jeremiah (1:29): 'Call up the archers against Babel: al ye that bend the bowe, beseige it rounde about: let none thereof escape . . . according to all she hath done, do unto her.' But of particular interest to the student of *Tamburlaine* are two basic ingredients in the symbolism of biblical prophecy relating to the punishment of the heathen: the metaphors of the bridle and the whip (or rod), signifying the constraint and punishment which God will impose on the heathen tyrant by means of his chosen Scourge, and the image of Babylon itself. The fall of Babylon is the great refrain of the Old Testament prophets, and it constitutes the climax of Revelation. Babylon is the type of pride and tyranny, but it is identified above all else with idolatry, spiritual whoredom: this is what makes it so hateful, and this too is why the false prophet who deceived the people is taken out after its fall and cast alive into a lake of fire burning with brimstone (Revelation 19:20). It is with this imagery, typology, and emotional attitude in mind that we should consider the climax of Tamburlaine's career and the unfavourable interpretations that have been put upon it. In the last scene of Part II, Act IV, Tamburlaine comes on stage cracking a whip and riding a chariot pulled by four heathen kings '*with bits in their mouths*' (s. d.), and later exits with the exultant cry, 'To Babylon, my lords, to Babylon!' He then sacks the city, has its governor shot to death on the city walls by his archers, renounces and reviles Mohammed, burns the Koran and 'all the heaps of superstitious books' in the city, and proclaims his faith in a transcendent God 'full of revenging wrath'. Seeing and hearing all this, Elizabethans well-versed in the Bible would hardly have thought of Tamburlaine as a damnable embodiment of ruthlessness and blasphemy. They are more likely to have fully endorsed his conduct and been thrilled by the fitness of word, action, and image to his predestined role.

III

Marlowe's use of biblical tradition and the Scourge of God paradigm serves, then, to endow Tamburlaine's career with spiritual grandeur and moral justification. But there are paradigm figures from classical tradition who also illuminate his character and call for careful scrutiny. Allusions to the Titans and to Phaeton – types of futile rebellion and overweening ambition – have been interpreted as signs that Marlowe implicitly condemns Tamburlaine and sees his career as a failure.[10] But the contexts in which these allusions occur offer little support for such interpretations. For example, the first speech which associates Tamburlaine with the Titans also associates him – more directly – with Jove, against whom the Titans rebelled unsuccessfully (Pt I, II.iii.19, 21). Similarly, the first allusion to Phaeton involves only an oblique connection with Tamburlaine and is juxtaposed with a resonant identification of Tamburlaine with the sun – whose chariot Phaeton failed to control (3.ii.36–52). Moreover, Zabina's strained attempt in the following speech to identify her gloomy and defeated husband with 'the sun-bright palaces' (l. 62) confirms just how the Phaeton–Apollo analogy should be applied in the context. Undoubtedly there is a degree of rhetorical uncertainty in such passages; but it is intentional, part of Marlowe's endeavour to involve us in an exercise of stylistic judgement which is also an exercise in moral evaluation.[11] This strategy is even more apparent on the two occasions when Bajazeth, with his wife's support, identifies himself with Hercules, and Tamburlaine with the monsters destroyed by the great hero. Simply to know that Tamburlaine defeats Bajazeth is to perceive that the Turkish Emperor and his wife have committed a grave error in rhetorical decorum, one which shows that their view of reality is upside down. There is an ironic and typically Marlovian caveat here for those who bring stock responses to a revolutionary exercise in heroic drama.[12]

Of all the figures from classical myth who serve to tell us what Tamburlaine is and is not the most important by far is Mars.[13] The epithet which is applied to him most often, and which undoubtedly fits him best, is 'martial'; there are also many references to the god of war, as well as several passages which invoke the Mars–Venus myth. The imaginative effect of the allusions to Mars and Venus is greatly extended by the play's rich complex of astrological thought and expression, all tending to connect if not to identify the 'aspect' and 'influence' of the leading characters with that of planetary divinities. Indeed, the whole imaginative design of the play – Parts I and II – is firmly tied to the Mars–Venus myth.[14]

The centrality of this myth is an indication that Marlowe is attending very closely here to heroic relationships as well as to heroic singularity (it is also an echo of the sources' emphasis on Tamburlaine as a figure of strength through unity). Tamburlaine is presented as a hero whose unique greatness lies in the possession of fundamental yet contrary attributes wrought to an extreme pitch in himself and in his relationships with others, and held together for the most part in a dazzling contrapuntal harmony which echoes the concordant discord of the universe. To put this in structural terms, Part I is a heroic play where greatness is achieved through a rare binding of opposites; Part II is a tragic drama where untimely death and the impoverishment of the human stage follow from a partial fracturing of that bond.

Tamburlaine's 'majesty' and 'resolution' alike suggest that his greatness is founded on contrarious unity. 'His lofty brows in folds do figure death, / And in their smoothness amity and life' (Pt I, II.i.21–2), while his speech postulates a marriage of persuasion and conquest, the arts of peace and of war. His resolution too is a union of what in the Marlowe world are usually found to be opposites – words and deeds. Both majesty and resolution are conspicuous in Tamburlaine's famous practice of the three colours. Although it is modelled on the revelation of the divine wrath at the opening of the Seven Seals in Revelation (6:1–5),[15] this practice shows in fact that the essential components of Tamburlaine's nature are wrath *and* love; it is thus a perfect ritual of self-definition. Those enemies who respond to the white or 'gentle flags of amity' (Pt I, IV.ii.112), accepting him as the man of natural superiority that he manifestly is, are assured that he will act as 'a loving conqueror' (V.i.23); those who wait until the red and black flags appear are promised partial and total destruction respectively. Tamburlaine's fidelity to the terms of this convenant shows that he can be as pitiless to the subjects of the unwise as to the unwise themselves. But it also shows that he is a creature of bonds in the full sense, one who limits his actions to a code of 'martial justice' (Pt II, IV.i.94) and who at the same time would resolve conquest into friendship.

Tamburlaine's relationship with Zenocrate, the play's Venus figure, is the summation of all his creative relationships. Although pallid in itself, her character is of fundamental importance to an understanding of his nature and fate. This is emphasised by means of construction, staging, stage imagery, and verbal imagery, as well as by his own declarations and the motivation of the action. Thus in each part he makes his first appearance in her company (conversing on matters amorous and martial). Part I ends with her coronation by him and his friends, an act which fulfils a promise made to her in their first dialogue. Part II ends with his dying request that her embalmed body be placed at his side, and so with their joint burial and, by implication, their eternal union (see II.iv.132–4). In the imagery Tamburlaine is regularly identified with fire and Zenocrate with water. This reflects their dominant psychological characteristics (anger and gentleness, cruelty and pity) and their status as incarnations of Mars and Venus. But it also invokes the whole idea of a life-giving union of contraries which the Mars–Venus–Harmonia myth had come to symbolise.[16]

Tamburlaine himself declares his dependence on Zenocrate when, in their first encounter, he consecrates all his 'martial prizes' to her, asserting that her person is 'more worth to Tamburlaine / Than the possession of the Persian crown, / Which gracious stars have promis'd at my birth' (Pt I, I.ii.90–2, 102). This claim is not to be taken as a mere show of eloquence. It implies his recognition that her gracious aspect and influence are as necessary as the stars to the fulfilment of his heroic destiny: that their encounter is analogous to what happened at the moment of his birth when 'Heaven did afford a gracious aspect, / And join'd those stars that shall be opposite / Even till the dissolution of the world' (Pt II, III.v.80–2). In practical terms her influence on him is twofold: she inspires his martial strivings, yet moderates them; adds more courage to his conquering mind, but calms the fury of his sword (Pt I, V.i.437, 513). And of the two kinds of influence the second is the more important, since its presence accounts for the nature of the denouement in Part I and its absence for the catastrophe in Part II.[17]

As is regularly observed, the only inner conflict Tamburlaine experiences is when Zenocrate pleads with him to restrain his fury against Damascus and make his victory against her father a 'gentle' one (Pt I, V.i.396). An important clue to the significance of this incident is the almost simultaneous pleading of the tearful virgins of Damascus. Their complete failure to 'qualify' his 'hot extremes' (l. 46) not only provides a perfect example of his strict fidelity to the code of martial justice; it also serves as a foil to his eventual surrender to the tears of Zenocrate on her father's behalf. Sent to him by a foolishly obstinate governor who should have acted when Mars and Venus were in conjunction (that is, when 'the gentle flags of amity' were displayed by the invincible conqueror), the virgins are treated here as poor substitutes for 'the love of Venus' when she seeks to pacify 'the angry god of arms' (ll. 122–5). By contrast, Tamburlaine confesses that Zenocrate's 'flowing eyes' lay 'more seige unto my soul / Than all my army to Damascus walls', and accepts that she 'deserves a conquest over every heart' (ll. 139–56, 208). In thus granting her the role of 'Conquering Venus',[18] he is not being inconsistent. His surrender is the assertion of another part of his own nature and does not undo a sworn commitment. Since he has refused to spare Damascus, he can claim that 'the god of war resigns his room to me' even when he is in the act of sparing the Soldan; and at the same time Zenocrate can refer (with an apt blend of ambiguity and paradox) to 'my conquering love' (ll. 440, 448). The destruction of Damascus and the enlarging of the Soldan imply a perfect balance and fusion of opposites and are appropriately followed by the crowning of Zenocrate and the promise of a wedding in which armour will be cast off. Some have argued, though, that Marlowe sets up an ironic contrast in this extraordinary last scene of Part I between Tamburlaine's noble rhetoric and the stage spectacle of background corpses.[19] But if the stage spectacle is viewed *in toto* it will be found to combine with the language (as one expects in good dramaturgy). The bodies of the defeated enemies, the crowning of the three faithful lieutenants by Tamburlaine and of Zenocrate by all four, the reconciliation of Tamburlaine with his former enemy the Soldan, and Zenocrate's formal acceptance of the marriage proposal: these are all part of a complex ritual which expresses in bold imaginative form the resolution of strife into peace, of wrath into love. This is the complex dialectic referred to in the last lines of *Timon of Athens*: 'Make war breed peace, make peace stint war, make each / Prescribe to other, as each other's leech.' In Marlowe's play, it is a dialectic which properly comprehends irony; but this is the irony of life itself, not a criticism of Tamburlaine.

More important even than the resurgence of the Turk, the death of Zenocrate is the crucial event of Part II. The loss of one who 'temper'd every soul with lively heat' (Pt II, II.iv.10) generates in Tamburlaine a mood of impotent rage and releases 'the fiery element' in his nature (l. 59) to an unparalleled extent; he thus becomes fatally 'distemper'd' with the same kind of fiery 'fit' that destroyed her (l. 40; v.ii.216; iii.79–95). The death of Zenocrate, therefore, and not the denunciation of Mohammed, as some have suggested, is the chief cause of his death.[20] But the final unbinding of almost all his martial fire – it is still checked to some extent by other relationships – has another effect as well: it makes him pursue with single-minded ferocity the task of burning out all 'earthly dregs' (III.ii.8). It is thus a means whereby he accomplishes the greatest of his achievements – the defeat of the Turk and all his allies – and the symbolic completion of his apocalyptic destiny: the sack of 'the whore of Babylon' and the burning of the heathen books.

The nature of Tamburlaine's bond with his followers provides clear evidence that in this play love is not viewed simply in its sexual and aesthetic aspects but stands for the binding force in nature. Tamburlaine claims that he values the meanest of his followers more than all the wealth of India; and, although the common soldier is not given a voice in the action, this claim must be accepted. It is substantiated primarily by the nature of his relationship with the representative Usumcasane, Techelles, and Theridamas. These three acknowledge that his pre-eminence among men is as natural as that of fire among the elements (Pt II, V.iii.251); yet he addresses them only in such terms as 'loving friends', and whether he is absent or present they describe themselves simply and proudly as 'the friends of Tamburlaine'. Moreover, they are genuinely involved in his most important military decisions; indeed, he himself acknowledges his dependence on them, stresses that his glories are theirs too, and is quick to reward them with crowns as promised.[21] Throughout both parts of the play this ideal relationship is pointedly contrasted with the self-interested and either fractious or falsely harmonious relationships which prevail among the opposing forces.

Marlowe alerts us to the importance and significance of Tamburlaine's bond with his followers in the second and arguably most illuminating scene in Part I. After the opening spectacle of a discordant and decaying nation, where social and natural hierarchies are completely at variance, we are shown the emergence of a new society in a stable, dynamic, and natural order. It is here that the Scythian shepherd consecrates himself to the captive princess who will soon yearn to 'unite' herself to his 'life and soul' (III.ii.23), and it is here that Theridamas, the enemy-turned-friend, joins Usumcasane, Techelles, and Tamburlaine to form a quartet of unshakable martial amity. The symbolic significance of the number four (the number of the elements, of natural unity and of amity) is fully deployed in this scene when Tamburlaine solemnly binds himself to his three followers, swearing that his heart will be combined with theirs until their bodies turn to elements (ll. 232–48).[22] We must infer from this promise and its fulfilment (as from much else in the play) that Tamburlaine's famous reference to 'Nature that fram'd us of four elements, / Warring within our breasts for regiment' (II.vii.18–19) should not be torn from its context and presented as an epitome of his world view. He and all his friends are well aware that when 'Nature . . . gave eternal chaos form' (Pt II, III.iv.75–6) she based that form on the dynamic interaction of striving and reciprocity.[23]

Tamburlaine's character is further defined by his relationship with his three sons (again, the number is significant: there are only two sons in the sources). It is here perhaps that he seems to expose himself most completely to the charge of unbridled will and passion. Marlowe undoubtedly provokes his audience to make this charge, but he also makes it a very difficult one to sustain in relation to the imaginative context and the given frame of reference. The captive kings may thunder our real-life verdict that Tamburlaine's killing of Calyphas is 'barbarous damned tyranny' (Pt II, IV.i.137); but they are not objective voices, and Calyphas is a contemptible character. Moreover, Tamburlaine defends his action in a thoroughly consistent manner. Marlowe too has laid the groundwork for this defence in the scene at the beginning of Part II where Tamburlaine, accompanied by Zenocrate and the three sons, makes his first stage appearance. In his opening speech Tamburlaine expresses the fear that their sons' 'looks are amorous, / Not martial', and that an imbalance in the elements in their bodies may have given them a temperament lacking in martial fire (I.iii.21–4). The truth is, however, that Amyras and Celebinus do have 'their conquering father's heart' (l. 36) (showing in the battle against the Turk that their love of him and of war function in unison): it is Calyphas alone who weakens the bond of unity. His ridiculous display of cowardice, sloth, and sensuality during the battle perfectly exemplifies a second meaning traditionally found in the mythical union of Mars and Venus – that is, the ludicrous and unseemly nature of man's subjection to woman, or of Valour to Pleasure; in iconography, this was imaged in the spectacle of little cupids playing with the god's armour while he sleeps with Venus – it is what Tamburlaine has in mind when he broods on 'thoughts effeminate and faint' in the soliloquy prompted by Zenocrate's tearful appeals for peace in Part I (V.i.177). Moreover, Calyphas's gleeful anticipation of a wrestling-match with the captive whores not only convicts him of gross sensuality: it makes him spiritually identifiable with the opposition (even his name has a Turkish ring: compare 'Calymath'). Tamburlaine's argument, then, that the death of this 'fainting' and 'effeminate brat' is 'war's justice', demanded both by nature (fire must consume 'the massy dregs of earth, / The scum and tartar of the elements') and by God (who expects him to destroy what He abhors) is thoroughly convincing in its context (Pt II, IV.i.121–4, 145–62).

The discovery of Calyphas's 'abortive' nature occasions in Tamburlaine an outburst against Heaven of a kind paralleled in his response to the death of Zenocrate and later at the approach of his own death. Unlike the irreverence in many of his more boastful allusions to Heaven (the irreverence of a super-confident divine minion), these blasphemous outbursts would seem to give substance to Cosroe's claim that ' he opposeth him against the gods' (Pt I, II.vi.39). However, they are dramatically 'placed' as temporary overflowings of those very qualities of love and wrath which have equipped him for his divine mission. The second and third too are followed by clear declarations of his acceptance of the limits imposed on him by natural and divine law. In fact at the end he shows that he has finally learned from Zenocrate that the royal way to die is to accept death calmly as the law of 'enforc'd and necessary change' (Pt II, II.iv.46). To her sons she had said, 'In death resemble me, / And in your lives your father's excellency' (ll. 75–6). But, just as the hero of *Antony and Cleopatra* models himself at the end on Eros and (he believes) on Cleopatra, so it is Tamburlaine alone who patterns himself on the dying Zenocrate. Having raged blasphemously against the inevitable (the Senecan Hercules should be remembered here[24]), he comes to acknowledge that it is 'in vain' to 'rail against those powers / That mean t' invest me in a higher throne'; and then, echoing Zenocrate (whose hearse he immediately calls for), he advises his grieving sons to 'nobly admit . . . necessity' (v.iii.120–1, 201). His relationship with the divine has thus been another manifestation of concordant discord, an often tense but always genuine union of will and fate. And, at the end here, it is a relationship which is purified of all discord.

We may say, then, that *Tamburlaine the Great* marks the beginning of Renaissance tragedy for two reasons: because its hero's 'woeful change' and 'timeless death' (Pt II, V.iii.181, 252) are causally related to the strife of opposites (within and without); and because his noble end spiritually renews the marriage of contraries on which his greatness was built: he imitates Zenocrate, he is spiritually and eternally united with her, his will and the divine will are one. Nevertheless, the tragic content of the play is superficially developed. Tamburlaine changes fatally in that the fiery element in his nature takes almost complete possession of his physical and emotional constitution, yet this change brings with it no terrible mistake, no pitiable self-betrayal (as does the comparable change in Othello and Antony). His bond with the woman whose gentleness and beauty tempered his martial violence is broken only in a physical sense, and his friends are constant to the end: he does not experience the agony of betrayal (real or imagined) 'there, where I have garner'd up my heart'. Like Hamlet, he is born to set right a degenerate world, but not one which has changed so insidiously that the forms of love and peace remain while violent egoism mines unseen. Although he can baffle and polarise observers (on and off stage) by his astonishing combination of antithetical extremes in character, he himself remains unconfused, knowing who he is, who his enemies are, and what he must do: ultimately, he is more heroic than tragic. Having said this, however, we must also acknowledge that Shakespeare's two great tragedies of martial love would not exist as we know them were it not for this play. Nor would his one exercise in heroic history, *Henry V*.

IV

Although *Tamburlaine* does not show Marlowe's full potential as a tragedian or even as a dramatist, it is a more satisfying accomplishment than any of the plays which follow it in the canon.[25] *The Massacre at Paris* has survived in a version which leaves it unworthy of critical attention, *The Jew of Malta* and *Doctor Faustus* are notoriously uneven, and *Edward II*, although impressive in many ways, lacks both poetic intensity and the appeal which comes from a dominant character. Yet the total achievement of these last three plays is very great. An outstanding feature of the achievement is Marlowe's experimentalism, his refusal to repeat himself: none of the plays written after *Tamburlaine* seems predictable in retrospect.

Least predictable of all, perhaps, is *The Jew of Malta*. There are some resemblances between Barabas and Tamburlaine, but they are very slight; as a personification of avarice who dedicates himself with spiteful enthusiasm to a series of villainous intrigues, Barabas could hardly be more unlike Tamburlaine in fundamentals. There are outstanding differences in method and style too. Whereas in *Tamburlaine the Great* there is a conspicuous preponderance of speech and spectacle over action, the *The Jew* there is very little spectacle, and after the first act, where speech and action are finely balanced, action soon preponderates to the extent that the inner life of the principal character is forgotten,[26] so that potential tragedy becomes melodrama and comedy farce. What makes the play more than a mere theatrical success (which it undoubtedly is), and reflects Marlowe's commitment to his subject, is the coherence and consistency of its satiric attack on a society which is formally dedicated to religious values but in reality to materialism and self-interest.[27]

The play has no cosmological framework built on elemental imagery, but what it loses thus in terms of universal implication is to some extent compensated by the symbolic character of its setting. Malta is a microcosm of the world viewed from the religious perspective, a place where Christian and non-Christian coexist in a perpetual struggle for supremacy. Like *Othello, the Moor of Venice*, the title of the play is a paradoxical one which prepares us for contrariety. Given the status of the Jews as the people who rejected Christ in favour of Barabbas (i.e. in favour of worldly value: thus the choice was construed by Christian theologians[28]), and given too the reputation of Malta as a heroic outpost of Christian civilisation, an Elizabethan audience might have expected to see a play in which spiritual opposites are clearly distinguished and hierarchically ordered. Superficially, this is what is offered, since at the end the Christians triumph over Jew and Turk, secure in their belief that they are the favourites of God. But the ending is savagely ironic and the whole effect of the play is to show that Christian and non-Christian are morally indistinguishable.[29]

This conception is brilliantly disclosed in the opening encounter between Barabas and Fernese, the governor of the island. It emerges here that, instead of accepting a do-or-die struggle with militant heathenism, the famous Knights of Malta have struck a bargain with the Turks, agreeing to pay them an annual tribute in return for the freedom of their island. In politic fashion, the Turks have allowed the tribute to remain unpaid for ten years, so that they are now in a position to appropriate the impoverished and feckless island (I.i.179–84). There is a hint here of the kind of treacherous devil pact that will form the basis of *Doctor Faustus*, and it is a hint which Marlowe expands with wonderful tact and cunning. Calling upon Barabas to surrender all his possessions so that the island can be saved, Fernese quotes almost verbatim the passage in the Gospel according to John where Caiphas justifies the crucifixion of Christ and the choice of Barabbas:

> No, Jew, we take particularly thine
> To save the ruin of a multitude.
> And better one want for the common good,
> Than many perish for a private man.
>
> (I.ii.95–8)

The purpose of the ironic parallel is not just to establish that Fernese's conduct is utterly un-Christian and that he is quite ignorant of that fact. It has the further effect of putting Barabas – anti-Christ, the son of Satan himself: so his name was interpreted[30] – in the place of Christ. Barabas is being called upon to redeem the islanders from the penalty of bondage which they have incurred by their failure to respect a covenant, just as Christ redeems all men from that bondage to the Law which is the necessary result of their sinfulness. Barabas's angry response – 'Corpo di

Dio' (l. 90) – to Fernese's proposal clarifies his ironic identification with the figure of the sacrificial Redeemer. Moreover, the plot returns him in extravagant fashion to this role in the last act. There he volunteers – though by no means unselfishly – to effect a 'dissolution of the slavish bands' (V.ii.75) into which the faithless Christians have eventually fallen, and does so at the price of his life, the Christians betraying their saviour in order to make doubly sure of the freedom he has won for them from the Turk. Of course, the irony of Barabas as redeemer does not carry any suggestion that he is the one good man among a pack of damnable hypocrites. It simply confirms the utterly misleading nature of categorical distinctions in this diminished model of the civilised world. Barabas has an impressive gift for exposing the unconscious hypocrisy with which the Christians conceal the moral and spiritual confusion in which they live: 'Your extreme right does me exceeding wrong. / But take it to you in the devil's name [i.e. not in God's name]!' (I.ii.152–3). But his insight into the sins of others does not alter the fact that he himself participates in what he condemns: 'This is the life we Jews are us'd to lead; / And reason too, for Christians do the like' (V.ii.114–15). With the exception of his daughter Abigail, everyone who lives on or comes to the island is in a condition of spiritual bondage: as with the Turkish captives for sale in the market, 'Every one's price is written on his back' (II.iii.3).

But Barabas certainly stands out from the crowd and is in every sense the play's protagonist. The plot is continuously propelled by his cunning and violent response to calamity. Moreover, his wit, his energy, his resourcefulness, and his resolution in the face of the worst his enemies can offer all combine to secure for him a large measure of our respect and sympathy. The conscious skill, too, with which he approaches the art of dissembling must have endeared him to an Elizabethan audience, for Marlowe exploits this as a counterblast to the Puritan claim that all dramatic impersonation is the devil's art. When Barabas advises his daughter to assume a 'precise' manner in order to be accepted as a convertite, and when he speaks of the Christians as mere 'professors' of a faith they do not practise (I.ii.281–90), his diction would have suggested to Marlowe's audience that the most accomplished practitioners of the devil's art were those same sober Reformers who wanted to close the theatres. On the other hand, Barabas does not use his own histrionic art for any just or unselfish purpose. Thanks to the hypocrisy and treachery of the Christians, he comes to a terrible end in a Treacherous Entertainment which is even more barbarous than Hieronimo's; but the entertainment is entirely of his own devising and was meant by him for the unsuspecting Turks. Barabas's art is unmistakably demonic.

There are signs in the first act that Marlowe might have intended to write a play with a heroic rather than a villainous protagonist – the tragedy of an amoral but enormously gifted and successful individual who is corrupted and destroyed by rank injustice and personal betrayal. This hypothesis, however, is weakened by the prologue, where 'Machevell' informs us that Barabas got his wealth by using Machiavellian methods, and by the Jew's own account of his extravagantly villainous past (II.iii.172ff.). Barabas does degenerate in the course of the action, but it is not so much his character that degenerates as the playwright's handling of it. Dramatically speaking, the man who in the first act unfolds his dreams of vast wealth in colourful soliloquy, and who responds with impassioned and intelligent protest to cynical injustice, is not the same man as the one who without hesitation or compunction poisons his only daughter – and a whole convent to boot – because she becomes a nun. It will not do to dismiss critical complaints about the handling of this transformation by saying that naturalistic criteria are out of place in dealing with a character who so obviously descends from the medieval Vice. After all, it is the dramatist who has created the expectation that this character will react in a recognisably human manner to crisis and misfortune. However, the effect of inconsistency need not necessarily be put down to collaborative authorship or textual corruption; and certainly it is not due to a radical change in authorial purpose. Although its imaginative realisation leaves much to be desired, the conception of Barabas's character is consistent from start to finish. That consistency, as I hope to show, is part of a remarkably coherent pattern of ideas which informs the whole play, bringing every aspect of it into a significant unity.

V

From the beginning Barabas is presented in an ironic light. Although expert in diagnosing the 'unseen hypocrisy' (I.ii.290) of others, he too acts in contradiction to his professed beliefs and ideals without even knowing it. He aligns himself proudly with Old Testament figures such as Job and Abraham, yet his conduct is grossly at variance with these models: his reaction to the loss of his possessions is not Job-like patience but wild vengeance; and, whereas Abraham was prepared to sacrifice his child out of love and obedience towards God, Barabas kills his out of anger and hatred.[31] A third biblical model is invoked when Mathias, Abigail's fiancé, asks Barabas to 'remember' the 'comment [i.e. commentary] on the Maccabees' which he promised him (II.ii.152, 158), a request which echoes the words of Barabas's Jewish friend, 'remember Job' (I.ii.179). The point of the allusion is that the First Book of Maccabees–one of the Old Testament apocryphal books, and very popular in the sixteenth century–glorifies the conduct of Matathias (*sic*) and his sons in refusing to make any covenant or agreement with the heathens around them and in repudiating all those Jews who so betray the covenant of their fathers (1:12; 2:20–7; etc.). Barabas, of course, has quite forgotten the Maccabees, the utility of making convenants with gentile and heathen being a working principle with him. The engagement of his daughter to Mathias is the first such covenant in the play; the last–with Fernese–is what undoes him.

One part of the Book of Job which seems to have been very much in Marlowe's mind when he was writing this play is the passage in which Job justifies the conduct of his past life. Never, he claims, did he refuse alms to the poor, never did he curse his enemy and rejoice in his destruction, never did he make gold his hope or say to the wedge of gold, 'Thou art my confidence', never did he deny the God above by pride in his worldly prosperity (31:16–27; Geneva version and gloss). G. K. Hunter has quoted most of these verses and remarked correctly that 'the actions which Job denies are precisely those that Barabas rejoices in'.[32] I would suggest that Marlowe detected in this passage the sum of virtue as defined by Christian theology–faith, hope, and charity; and further–whether stimulated by this passage or not–that he found in the three theological virtues a convenient and familiar scheme for structuring and clarifying his imaginative definition of a vicious world in which everyone lays claim to virtue. In conjunction with their synonyms and antonyms, the words 'faith', 'hope', and 'charity' permeate the whole play, so that the most melodramatic and farcical incidents are brought into a meaningful relationship with the most serious to become, if not the appropriate embodiment, at least the vehicles of a considered view of life. *The Jew of Malta, Edward II*, and even *Doctor Faustus* are not notably rich in verbal imagery and are certainly devoid of the complex image clusters to be found in Kyd and Shakespeare. But patterns of verbal iteration and variation are an important feature of Marlowe's art in these three plays. The key terms in each play often blend effectively with verbal imagery or work in conjunction with stage image and spectacle. What is most characteristic of Marlowe's method, however, is that two or three of the key words will suddenly combine in a single sentence, or will form into thick constellations of synonym and antonym in particular scenes, so that we are regularly assimilating variant epitomes of the play's essential concerns.[33]

The Jew of Malta reflects an obsession with religious identities and distinctions. Christian and Jew are alike convinced that their own faith is true and beneficial, the other's false and pernicious. To Barabas, Christianity is heresy and all Christians are damned (I.ii.342, 357); he can 'see no fruits in all their faith, / But malice, falsehood, and excessive pride' (I.i.115–16). Bitter experience too has taught him exactly what they think of his religion, so that, when he pretends to Friar Jacomo that he has seen the error of his ways and wants to be christened, he knows exactly what to say. Claiming that to be a Jew is to be lost, he goes on to characterise Judaism as a faith which is founded on lovelessness and can lead only to the despair of eternal bondage: 'I have been zealous in the Jewish faith, / Hardhearted to the poor, a covetous wretch, / That would for lucre's sake have sold my soul' (IV.i.51–7).

Faith, hope, and charity all have twin dimensions of meaning in the play, referring to man's relationship with his fellows (or simply the world) as well as with God. The natural and the supernatural dimensions of faith are linked by the concept of promise or convenant. Of the various convenants which govern man's relationship with God in the Old Testament, Barabas remembers only one, the promise made by God to Abraham: 'These are the blessings promis'd to the Jews, / And herein was old Abram's happiness' (I.i.103–4; cf. II.iii.47). Christian theologians argued that this promise was transferred by default to the followers of Christ and that no Jew could lay claim to it; and it has been suggested that Marlowe implicitly criticises Barabas in the light of this doctrine.[34] But there is no hint of such a doctrine in the play, and in fact the criticism he does make is in a way much more radical: that is, Barabas is shown to betray the promise from a purely Jewish standpoint by replacing the idea of a great expanding family (Genesis 17) with that of a bursting treasure vault designed for one greedy little man – 'infinite riches in a little room' (I.i.37). Moreover, because of his boundless hatred of Fernese, Barabas embarks on a course of action so savage that it drives his only daughter into a convent. His old jest – delightful to the groundlings – about the inclination of nuns to 'increase and multiply' when the friars are about comes home to roost here: for, although the groundlings would have liked the jest, a convent was to the average Elizabethan Protestant a place of sterility, a rejection of God's promise of fruitful multiplication. Barabas's subsequent murder of Abigail (and all the nuns) because she sought in this way to escape 'The fatal labyrinth of misbelief' (III.iii.64) merely confirms the significance of what he has already done. Dramatically, it is quite unnecessary. His indictment of her as 'false, credulous, inconstant', and his simultaneous adoption of the heathen slave Ithamore as his only heir ('O trusty Ithamore'), would have been enough to round off the episode in a manner at once fantastic and expressive (III.iv.27, 41–2). With the poisoning of a whole convent the taste of the groundlings gets out of hand.

Barabas construes Abigail's conversion as a betrayal not of Yahweh but of himself: 'she . . . varies from me in belief' (III.iv.10). Betrayal of man by man – the breaking of promises, treaties, and troth-plights – is perhaps the central fact of human experience in this play. Machiavelli's notorious advice to princes that promises should not be kept if they prove inexpedient is here endorsed at every level of human relations. Worse than Machiavelli, however, Barabas and his enemies ground their faithlessness in their religious faith, finding theological justification for every treacherous act. Defending the double troth-plight by means of which he inveigles Mathias and Lodowick into mutual slaughter, Barabas says to Abigail,

> It's no sin to deceive a Christian;
> For they themselves hold it a principle,
> Faith is not to be kept with heretics:
> But all are heretics that are not Jews.
> This follows well . . . .
>
> (II.iii.308–11)

Whether this is conscious or unconscious hypocrisy one cannot say. Nor could one say for certain whether the decision of Fernese to break the treaty with Calymath has anything at all to do with the fact that Calymath is the leader of 'barbarous mis-believing Turks' (II.ii.46), although Fernese indicates it has. Faithlessness has so penetrated human psychology here that words – 'good words' (IV.iii.25; V.ii.58), 'fair words' (IV.i.125): the phrases are laden with contempt – can mean anything or nothing. Men's minds are undiscoverable.

Hope is an expectation of happiness based on faith, so that to be without faith, or to misapply it, is to end in despair. This is an experience which threatens everyone in the play, but it constitutes the story of Barabas. His great opening soliloquy is not only an expression of faith in the 'miracle' (I.i.13) of material wealth, but also an outpouring of hope: 'I hope my ships . . . Are gotten up by Nilus' winding banks' (ll. 41–3). His faith in the capacity of his ships to negotiate the winding ways of the world is immediately rewarded by the arrival of the captain of his well-named *Speranza*. However, the ensuing dialogue contains omens of things to come. 'I hope our credit in the customhouse / Will serve as well as I were present', he remarks (ll. 58–9); but apparently it has not so served. Moreover, explains the captain, his argosy has not returned and 'the seamen wonder'd how you durst with so much wealth / Trust such a craz'd vessel' (ll. 79–80). The conclusion towards which these omens point is Barabas's final tumble into the burning cauldron symbolising Hell, having been betrayed by Fernese ('This truce we have is but in hope of gold' – II.ii.25) and by his own desperate trust in the strength of mutual promises grounded solely on the principle of self-interest and material gain.

Had he understood God's promise aright, Barabas would have known that 'the gentle Abigail' was his only source of hope. He seems to come near to appreciating this in the great night scene where he waits for her to retrieve the money he has hidden in their now confiscated home. When she eventually appears above at the window, as if in answer to his prayer for divine aid, he speaks of 'my soul's sole hope' (II.i.29). The thought occurs that he might be referring to his 'sole daughter' (I.i.136); but when she throws down the bags of treasure he embraces them like long-lost children and utters that famous cry in which his characteristic confusion of true and false value is wonderfully crystallised: 'O girl! O gold! O beauty! O my bliss!' (II.i.53).

Both Mathias and Lodowick enthusiastically nominate Abigail as the sole object of their hope. Whether she would have proved their salvation, however, is doubtful, for Marlowe quietly insinuates that they are attracted not only by her virtue and beauty but also by the fact that she is 'the rich Jew's daughter' (I.i.361, 377; II.iii.290). So when the newly betrothed Lodowick cries joyfully, 'Now have I that for which my soul hath long'd' (l. 315), we cannot be sure what he means: 'The meaning', as Ithamore would say, 'has a meaning' (IV.iv.75). Anyhow his cry is immediately undercut by Barabas's lethal aside: 'So have I not; but yet I hope I shall' (II.iii.316). The Jew's hope is now to get revenge on Fernese by having his son killed in a duel over Abigail.

By disposing not only of Lodowick but also of Mathias, whom Abigail truly loves, Barabas keeps a promise with himself: 'she holds him dear; / But I am sworn to frustrate both their hopes' (II.iii.141). This perverse fidelity alienates Abigail and leads to his formal recognition of Ithamore as the new source of hope, for it is he who will satisfy his desire for revenge against daughter and nuns:

> My trusty servant, nay, my second self;
> For now I have no hope but even in thee,
> And on that hope my happiness is built.
> (III.iv.14–16)

What Barabas means and Ithamore understands by this declaration are quite different, so that Ithamore's hopes too are due for frustration.

Concerning the slave's prompt display of filial love and obedience, Barabas wisely remarks to himself, 'Thus every villain ambles after wealth, / Although he ne'er be richer than in hope' (ll. 51–2). So, even when he allows his plot to advance into the most sensational melodrama, Marlowe is keeping a firm hold on his thematic pattern. And setting an example too for Jacobean dramatists: Ithamore is the remote ancestor of tool villains such as Flamineo and Bosola, both 'fed worse than hoping Tantalus' by their unscrupulous masters.

The foundation of faith and the true object of hope is, of course, love. The play abounds in spontaneous and informal declarations of both love and hate. There are formal modes of expression, too, and when these occur we find the key terms entwined with emblematic action and spectacle. For love there is blessing, troth-plight, and the friendly 'entertainment' or 'welcome' (these two words are used almost synonymously with 'love' and must be counted among the key terms). The only formal expression of hatred is the curse; but this emotion finds formal expression of a kind in speeches of bitter and elaborate mockery and in the vengeful perversion of troth-plight and welcome. The curse is a perversion of the blessing, as even Ithamore perceives (III.iv.103).

Barabas and the Christians coexist in a relationship of mutual hatred for which they find sanction in the teachings of their religion. However, no Christian actually admits to hating Barabas: he is simply told that Jews are 'infidels' who 'stand accursed in the sight of heaven' and whose lives are in consequence 'hateful' (I.ii.63–5). And when Christians afflict him without mercy they do so with the purported intention of chastising and converting him – as he sarcastically observes, 'in catechizing sort', out 'of mere charity and Christian ruth' (II.iii.71–3). With characteristic indelicacy, Ithamore voices the relevant Christian principle when he justifies blackmailing his master–father: 'To undo a Jew is charity, and not sin' (IV.iv.76).

Barabas's religious justification for hating Christians is that they are a 'swine-eating... Unchosen nation, never circumcis'd' (II.iii.7–8). He adduces no biblical evidence of a divine malediction upon them, but his first and last reaction to their 'unrelenting flinty hearts' (I.ii.140) is to call down 'the curse of heaven, / Earth's barrenness and all men's hatred' upon their heads (ll. 162–3; v.v.91). Indeed, he has reconstituted Judaism into a barren and despairing religion of personal hatred. When the alms plate for Christian beggars comes round the synagogue, 'Even for charity I may spit into 't', 'Hoping to see them starve' (II.iii.26–30). When he curses Abigail and adopts Ithamore, he instructs him from his own tablets of stone: 'First be thou void of... Compassion, love, vain hope... Be mov'd at nothing, see thou pity none, / But to thyself smile when Christians moan' (ll. 167–70). His life story as told to Ithamore is one fantastic tale of limitless hatred for Christians (ll. 172–98); and it is on such hatred that his relationship with the Turkish slave is founded: 'We hate Christians both' (l. 212). Barabas's hatred is consuming, intense, desperately human. It gives him a terrible energy. And when set beside the contemptuous, impersonal hatred of Fernese and his followers it is positively attractive. Yet it is a hell on earth, a burning cauldron.

Barabas is indifferent to Christian ruthlessness and hatred so long as it does not affect his wealth. In fact he accepts it as the necessary consequence of being rich: 'Rather had I, a Jew, be hated thus, / Than pitied in a Christian poverty' (I.i.113–14). For him wealth and love are one, and his anguish at the loss of Abigail ('she loves me not' – III.iv.11) is really the distress of a man who has been robbed: after all, he has just been referring to her as his diamond. His final and fatal decision to make a covenant of friendship with Fernese and the Christians after the Turk has installed him as governor of the island is not prompted by any new realisation that he is truly poor without love (as Harry Levin has suggested[35]). It stems rather from his awareness that he will be hated so much now by the Christians that his life will be in danger; and it conforms to his lifelong principle that 'he from whom my most advantage comes, / Shall be my friend' (V.ii.30–3, 112–13). It distorts the whole mode of the play to suggest that Barabas is a tragic character capable of education through suffering. To the end he is simply a grotesque personification of greed and of the negative impulses it generates in the self and in others.

Yet Barabas is an integral part of the society which condemns, isolates, and uses him. The perversions of welcome and troth-plight which he devises when he sets out to dispose of Lodowick, Mathias, Friars Barnadine and Jacomo, and finally Calymath are all mirrored, for example, in the dealings of the prostitute Bellamira with Ithamore: 'welcome sweet love', ''Tis not thy money but thyself I weigh', 'I'll pledge thee, love', 'I'll marry thee'. Bellamira of the lovely look and the moneyed love and the fleeting friends is in turn a reflection of the whole society which she serves in her fashion: it is farcically appropriate that in the course of her professional activities she should uncover Barabas's anti-Christian crimes and so give Fernese the rare pleasure of condemning him justly as well as legally. Every character and incident in this strange play contributes to an intellectually coherent if imaginatively uneven vision of life.

VI

Like *The Jew of Malta, Edward II* ends with the restoration of order after a period of violent instability. But, whereas the return to power of Fernese offers no hope of a better future, the accession of the youthful Edward III heralds a genuine renewal. To dismiss the last scene of this historical tragedy as 'a formal coda' with 'no organic relation to the action it concludes' is a serious mistake.[36] Marlowe accepts the historical fact that Edward III was to prove a strong and humane king who united the country behind him and restored its lost prestige.[37] More than that, he makes the new king's immediate and future success intelligible in the light of those same ideas which he has brought to bear on the fall of Edward II and Mortimer, the two men whose self-assertion and mutual strife brought chaos to England.

In this last scene the newly crowned Edward III is carefully presented as a ruler who manages to discriminate between creative and destructive love and to strike a balance in his actions between tenderness and strength, pity and stern justice, Venus and Mars. In some respects he is the antithesis of his father and his father's enemy. Essentially, however, he is a mean figure between the two, a harmonious partnership of contrary attributes which have developed separately and to the point of destructive extremity in each of them, so that love became the source of dissension and hatred, and martial courage of ruthless tyranny. The young King here overcomes a double threat to the exercise of his royal justice posed on the one hand by the menacing personality of Mortimer and on the other by his mother's specious appeals for love and pity. Furthermore, Edward acquires the resolution necessary for this conquest primarily from his stricken love for his dead father.

Marlowe, however, does not allow the emergence of this prototypal Henry V to blur or conflict with the horrors that have preceded; indeed, his tragic ending is managed with singular skill. The final stage image which he contrives is noteworthy: the young King exits in tears, leading the funeral procession behind his father's hearse; but on the hearse sits the head of Mortimer, which he sternly demanded and placed there himself. It is a complex image, consoling and terrible, and it must be apprehended in its entirety. Behind it, as behind the play as a whole, lies the traditional view of nature as a dynamic process which makes life at its best a temporary union of warring opposites. There are no overt references to this cosmological frame of reference, but it is implicit throughout in construction, characterisation, tone, and style. Thus, although *Edward II* is undoubtedly a tragedy with a limited imaginative range (we are never made to feel that the protagonist's fate is affected by the ever-moving spheres of heaven or the mysterious operations of divine providence[38]), it is by no means without metaphysical resonance and universal implication. It is the tragedy of a weak and unheroic king which offers an appropriately diminished image of 'Chaos come again'. As in the tragic environment of Renaissance drama generally, extremism, violent change, and total confusion are the essential conditions of life in its intense but confined playworld.

Marlowe's construction is as expressive as it is symmetrical. The play opens with a young King Edward who is delighted at the death of his father, indirectly does violence to his funeral rites, and is totally at odds with those who honour his memory; and it ends with another King Edward whose feelings and actions are exactly the opposite. This embracing pattern of antithetical contrast and extreme change is continually evident in the development of the action. The struggle between the royal and the baronial factions which constitutes the plot is a restless up-and-down movement in which each party repeatedly gains and loses the position of ascendancy. The elaborate reconciliation which takes place at the end of Act I is only an apparent break in this pattern since it is simply a tactical move on the part of the barons which gives them the advantage, and it is quickly followed by the old dissensions. This hectic rhythm in the action corresponds with the emotional tone of the play. Focused mainly in the volatile character of the King, the tone is determined by a feverish interplay of jubilation and grief, deep satisfaction and raging frustration.

At first glance this whole design suggests an adaptation of the medieval tragedy of Fortune, with the goddess's famous machine suitably accelerated to ensure theatrical success for the old narrative model. There are several references to Fortune, and there is one conventional declamation on her inevitable treachery against those who reach the pinnacle of power. But these are insignificant: the idea of fatal mischance is as remote from the shaping of events as is that of fatal pre-ordination. Marlowe's refusal to admit to his play these two classic expressions of the sense of mystery in man's encounter with suffering and evil may reflect his determination to respect the historical past and endow it with a vivid actuality. Certainly it restricts the imaginative perspective of the play. But it is responsible too for much of the play's special and welcome concentration on human nature as such. Edward asks, 'how fortunes' that Gaveston did not return?, to be answered, 'Some treason or some villainy was the cause' (III.ii.113–4). To be exact, Gaveston was murdered *en route* to his royal lover and his last farewell because one of his captors broke his word on the assumption that Edward and Gaveston would do the same. Decisively, Marlowe here transfers the treacheries of Fortune to inconstant man himself. Looking at history's record of blasted hopes and miserable suffering, he intimates that most of it stems from man's own nature: from the impassioned will which rejects the limits and constraints of mutuality or turns the protective aspect of mutuality into an excuse for tyranny. His irony plays sharply on the perennial inclination of the individual to find the cause of calamity in other men or in abstract forces.

The primary source of chaos in Edward's life and realm is his passionate love of Gaveston and later of Spencer. Remarkably for the period, there is no suggestion that homosexual love is in itself wicked or unnatural. Edward's extra-marital affairs are shown to be morally wrong because they are pursued beyond all reason, involve a total confusion of value, and serve to undermine every other bond of importance in his life. His reign is implicitly likened to a Saturnalian riot, a period when the pleasure principle is supreme, a mock king is elected, authority is derided, and inversion and indecorum are the norm. The comparison is unmistakable in the first scene. Gaveston enters as a self-conscious entertainer who promises to 'draw the pliant King which way I please' (I.i.53). The King then allows himself to be overruled by his proud and disrespectful barons (although promising in an aside, 'In spite of them / I'll have my will' – ll. 77–8). Later Edward and Gaveston are left alone with the Bishop of Coventry to re-enact the game of the Boy Bishop.[39] Licensed by the King to deal with his old enemy as he pleases ('use him as thou wilt' – l. 195), Gaveston tears the Bishop's funeral vestments, casts him into the channel or open sewer, and finally sends him off to prison. He himself is then given the bishopric of Coventry, having already been named Lord High Chamberlain, Secretary to the State and King, Earl of Cornwall, King and Lord of Man.

The extreme incongruity of the titles conferred on Gaveston is crucial. Edward is a Lord of Misrule in whose kingdom the base are ennobled and the noble mocked and degraded. Although none of his favourites is without redeeming qualities, they are quite unworthy of the great honours heaped upon them and achieve eminence solely because of Edward's pathetic dependence on their affection. 'It is our pleasure; we will have it so' (I.iv.9; cf. III.ii.174–5) is the only defence he can offer for his method of distributing honours. But his wilful pursuit of pleasure makes him confuse the serious and the trivial as well as the worthy and the unworthy, so that an event such as the Scottish invasion of England is dismissed as 'a trifle' that must not be allowed to interfere with the shows and triumphs prepared for Gaveston's delectation (II.ii.10; cf. III.ii.66). In fact 'matters of . . . weight' (II.ii.8; III.ii.69, 74) are always military matters concerning the defence of his realm and of its honour, while the matters to which they are made subordinate are always his amorous preoccupations. Thus Edward's inability to distinguish between the grave and the trivial is symptomatic of a fundamental flaw in contrarious unity, the unity symbolised in the Mars–Venus myth. Most of the personal and socio-political disorders of the play relate to this flaw. Edward's love of his favourites is so excessive that it turns the love which should unite him and his barons, as it united them and his father, into violent mutual hatred. It turns his gentle wife into an Amazonian virago who takes up arms against him (see IV.iv.1–14). And it disgraces and effeminises the identity of a warrior nation. On the one occasion Edward turns out to meet the Scots in person, he and his friends march not in armour but in garish robes bedaubed with 'women's favours' (II.ii.183–6). Worse still, his one success on the field is a battle fought against his own subjects in revenge for the killing of his lover, an act of 'desperate and unnatural resolution' (III.iii.32).

Edward's shortcomings as a king all crystallise in his total lack of true resolution. In a kingdom where psychological and moral stability are hard to find, he stands out as the essence of change. To each of the crises which confront him he reacts in basically the same way: with a show of defiant and unyielding resistance (usually couched in bombastic terms) followed by an immediate climb-down into passive acceptance and pleading complaint. In the supreme test of final defeat and death, this want of 'princely resolution' (IV.v.8) is thrown into sharp relief. His friends Spencer and Baldock, like his enemies Warwick and Lancaster (and like Mortimer later), confront the worst with dry-eyed Stoicism; indeed Baldock, the Oxford scholar and sometime tutor, lessons Edward most eloquently in word and deed on the princely virtue. There are signs at the end that the lesson may have had its effect, for when Edward recognises that Lightborn has been sent to kill him he asks to see the stroke before it is delivered so that his mind will be 'more steadfast'. But, if we begin to anticipate the final reassertion of a royal identity, we are disappointed: within seconds Edward is offering Lightborn a jewel in the vain hope that 'this gift will change thy mind' (V.v.77, 87).

The treatment meted out to Edward in prison is pitiless in the extreme, and the manner of his killing – with a red-hot spit thrust up his anus – incomparably barbarous.[40] We are distanced to some extent from his sufferings, however, by his insistence that he is guiltless (V.i.73, 122), by his unfailing flow of self-pity, and by his general lack of constancy. The obviously retributive pattern in his maltreatment contributes to the same effect. The burning spit may seem too monstrous to be associated with any conception of justice; but comparable horrors were commonplace in pictorial and written descriptions of Hell, Lightborn's name is an obvious anglicisation of Lucifer, and Christians did believe that Hell was part of eternal law. Edward's 'tatter'd robes' (V.v.66), too, and his immersion in the sewage waters of the castle, recall the revenge which he and Gaveston exacted on the Bishop of Coventry. Similarly his laments about his wife's heartless indifference to his plight recall his pitiless treatment of her in her moment of greatest misery.[41]

Yet our feelings towards Edward are extraordinarily fluid and mixed: we ourselves are compelled by the dramatist to participate in the attitudinal uncertainties of the playworld.[42] There is the obvious point that the parallels between Edward's punishments and his sins leave us with a ghastly sense of disproportion (though this may be much more pronounced for us than it was for an audience accustomed to an extremely vindictive penal system). Moreover, although Edward's weakness in adversity has helped Marlowe to expose once more the irrationality of a political system which gives kingship to men without a trace of majesty, Edward himself is so obviously devoid of 'princely resolution' from the start, and so easily gives up his pretensions to it, that it has virtually ceased to be a criterion by which we respond to him as an individual. Indeed, his very inability to maintain some kind of equilibrium is, we sense, an affliction in itself. Again, Lightborn's exhibition of demonic resolution in the performance of his task ('Art thou as resolute as thou wert?' asks Mortimer needlessly – V.iv.22) makes the timorous pleadings of his victim almost attractively human. We are drawn to the imprisoned Edward, too, by his evident (though somewhat uncharacteristic) concern for the fate of his son under the 'protectorship' of Mortimer. More important, however, is Marlowe's almost surreptitious revelation that Edward does have his own kind of constancy, a form of heroism that no chronicles and no *speculum principis* would acknowledge. He may have surrendered abjectly to his councillors' demand for Gaveston's exile, but his love for him and later for Spencer is never affected by censure or separation. And, although in prison he recognises that his friendships have been his undoing, he does not regret or repudiate them, no more than did the dead friends. In fact, as he waits for the end he sees himself and his friends as united in a generous communion of sacrificial love:

> O Gaveston, it is for thee that I am wrong'd!
> For me, both thou and both the Spencers died;
> And for your sakes, a thousand wrongs I'll take.
> The Spencers' ghosts, wherever they remain,
> Wish well to mine; then tush, for them I'll die.
>
> (V.iii.41–5)

Although Edward begs and bribes for life when the time comes, the positive effect of these lines is not wholly undone. Indeed, looking back on the play from the standpoint of this speech, one might reasonably conjecture that Marlowe's willingness to dress his protagonist in the robes of weakness and contempt was essentially a device, whether conscious or unconscious, to allow him to affirm the value of homosexual love without outraging conventional morality.

Viewed in conjunction with the inconstancies of those who turn against him, Edward's chronic instability can seem a kind of innocence. In the course of the play Mortimer changes from a hothead obsessed with England's honour and well-being into a ruthless Machiavel whose only thought is personal power, while the Queen is transformed from a loving and long-suffering wife into a contented adulteress who endorses the brutal treatment of her imprisoned husband and even suggests his murder. Although these changes seem overdone, they are broadly intelligible.[43] Moreover, Marlowe prepares the ground for them with great care in the splendid scene at the start of the play where Isabella persuades Council to revoke its decision to banish Gaveston. No decision could be more binding than this, and no revocation could do less credit to royal councillors. Mortimer has already recalled that he, his father, and Lancaster swore to the dying Edward I that they would never allow Gaveston to return to England. That vow is renewed and given the seal of civil and ecclesiastical law when the whole Council, led by the Archbishop of Canterbury, meets at the New Temple to sign the form of Gaveston's exile. The irrevocable nature of this decree, too, is solemnly affirmed by the prelate when Edward desperately tries to have it changed: 'Nothing shall alter us; / We are resolv'd' (I.iv.74). Yet the ink is hardly dry on the document they have all been so impatient to sign ('Quick, quick, my lord' – l. 4) when the lords agree to Gaveston's return.

The dramatic focus in this whole turnabout rests on Mortimer and Isabella. The Queen takes Mortimer aside from the others to plead, in her own interest, for the repeal of the decree. That she should pick on him indicates that he is the one most likely to resist such a proposal; this point is enforced by the comments of the other 'resolute' (I.iv.231) lords as they watch the conversation at a distance and register their amazement at what they begin to infer from facial expressions:

> PEMBROKE. Fear not, the Queen's words cannot alter him.
> WARWICK. No? Do but mark how earnestly she pleads.
> LANCASTER. And see how coldly his looks make denial.
> WARWICK. She smiles! Now for the life of me his mind is chang'd!
>
> (ll. 233–6)

Rejoining his friends, Mortimer argues that Gaveston is more dangerous abroad than in England, where he can be quietly disposed of in due time by 'some base slave' (l. 265) suborned for the purpose. The Queen herself says nothing to the lords on the matter; but she is standing beside Mortimer as he speaks (l. 250) and we must presume that it was she who hit upon the idea–'not thought upon' before (l. 273)–that has such a transforming effect on everyone. Undoubtedly she is a sensitive, long-suffering wife, genuinely in love with her husband; but she is not the 'saint' that Pembroke (l. 190)–and many a reader who does not visualise the action–takes her to be at this point. It seems clear that she is the kind of woman who, if pushed hard enough, would be prepared to suggest the murder of her faithless husband so long as her own hands remain clean. And Mortimer, the chivalrous knight to whom oaths mean nothing, and who would stoop to the basest treachery against a man he loathes: such a character seems capable of anything. In fact the last-act partnership in crime between Isabella and Mortimer is essentially a repetition of their collusion at the New Temple: the difference is that a base fellow is promptly suborned to do the foul deed, a devil who seems to have been waiting for his call from the start: 'Lightborn, come forth' (v.iv.21).

Of course we cannot know for certain what the saint-like Isabella says to Mortimer in I.iv or how far she is on the way at that point to becoming a fiend-like queen. This is characteristic of Marlowe's remarkably restrained and subtle insistence throughout the play on the multiplying uncertainties of a world whose denizens are always changing. 'You know my mind', says Mortimer to his father (l. 423); but father does not, and neither does Mortimer himself. No one here can claim knowledge of self or anyone else. The mist of uncertainty descends on personal identity, on human relationships, and on the moral reasoning or self-justification which the problem of conflicting desires and loyalties continually provokes. It infects logic and language, gestures and manners, so that sophistry and self-contradiction abound, while titles, possessive adjectives, and terms and gestures of approval and disapproval move indiscriminately from one referent to another.[44]

The root of the problem is the King's desire–a genuinely tragic one in itself–to obliterate the difference between himself and Piers Gaveston:

> Kiss not my hand,
> Embrace me Gaveston as I do thee:
> Why shouldst thou kneel? Know'st thou not who I am?
> Thy friend, thy self, another Gaveston!
>
> (I.i.139–42)

'Thy friend, thy self': logically, the question soon arises as to who is mine and who thine. The King's cousin, Lady Margaret de Clare, rushes to meet 'my lord', 'my sweet Gaveston' (II.ii.59, 63; cf. l. 68), to whom the King has conveniently affianced her; but when Gaveston steps ashore in the next scene it is Edward who greets him with 'My Gaveston' and Edward who is addressed as 'Sweet lord' (II.ii.50, 59). Who in fact is going to be married with such triumph and jubilation? Could this reunion with Gaveston be the 'second marriage' to which Edward delightedly referred when his estranged wife secured for him the repeal of Gaveston's sentence (I.iv.335)? It is Gaveston who speaks of separation from Edward as 'divorce', and not Isabella; and it is she whom Edward calls a 'fawning French strumpet', and not Gaveston who stands beside him (II.v.3–4; I.iv.146). But, although Edward is undoubtedly Gaveston's, is Gaveston Edward's? Spencer's revelation to Baldock about his own relationship with Gaveston combines a nice distinction with a provocative ambiguity: he intends to be Gaveston's 'companion' at court, not his 'follower' – 'for he loves me well, / And would have once preferr'd me to the King' (II.ii.12–14). Lady Margaret's innocent hope that 'all things' will 'sort out' (II.i.79) evaporates in this mist. So too does the double hope expressed in Edward's ambiguous reference to the arranged marriage which brings Gaveston so very near to him: 'I have made him sure / Unto our cousin' (I.iv.377–8). No matter how close, no relationship here is sure (i.e. secure), and so no one can be sure (i.e. certain) about it.

Edward surrenders himself to his beloved both as ruler and as lover: 'Receive my seal; / Save or condemn, and in our name command / Whatso thy mind affects or fancy likes' (I.i.167–9). Thus political relationships and identities are just as confused and uncertain as sexual ones. Anyone here might be king for a little while. 'Were I a king . . . ', says Gaveston (I.iv.27), 'Were I King Edward, England's sovereign . . . ', says Spencer (III.ii.10); and each proceeds to act as if he were. The uncertainty about who is king becomes poignant in the abdication scene: 'Let me be king till night', pleads Edward (V.i.59); but in the scene where his son is crowned in his stead this uncertainty explodes upon the stage. Performed on Mortimer's instructions while Edward is still alive, the coronation ceremony is crudely interrupted by soldiers who have apprehended Kent, Edward's brother, and accuse him of having tried to 'take the King [i.e. Edward II] away perforce' (V.iv.83). Mortimer proceeds to act as if he himself had just been crowned and condemns Kent to instant execution, undeterred by Kent's bitter question: 'Art thou king? . . . Either my brother or his son is king' (ll. 102, 105).

Like 'king', the words 'traitor' and 'rebel' are adrift: since a king may be a no-king, a true subject may be a traitor or a rebel. Edward's early question, 'Where's the traitor?' (II.ii.80), echoes throughout the play. Kent calls

Mortimer a 'Base traitor' (V.iv.89) but himself is called the same by Edward, Mortimer, and the Queen, and he is executed as such: he has changed sides from Edward to Mortimer and back again to Edward, and yet no one is less deserving of that name and fate. Old Spencer, a relic from the past, angrily offers his captors a definition of the word 'rebel': 'Rebel is he who fights against his prince' (IV.v.80). But it does not remove the opprobrious name or save him from the block; lexical debate is idle talk to the new men: 'Take him away, he prates' (l. 82).

There is right and wrong on both sides, but each side continually endeavours to make its own wrong right. When Mortimer begins to argue for the repeal of Gaveston's sentence, Lancaster accuses him of wilfully attempting to make white black and dark night day, adding that 'In no respect can contraries be true' (I.iv.249, 247). But he tacitly withdraws these remarks when Mortimer explains that they can suborn some base slave to do a deed that will be chronicled as a 'brave attempt' to purge the realm of a plague (ll. 265–70). There are premonitions of Brutus here, but Mortimer's moral confusion is neither tragic nor idiosyncratic; it is part of a collective disease. Edward claims that his only fault has been too much mildness, yet he is prepared to 'Make England's civil towns huge heaps of stones' (III.iii.30; cf. I.i.151) for the sake of his minion. All those who oppose him – lords and bishops, the Queen and Kent – insist that their only thought is 'England's good' (V.i.38) when in fact their motivation is contaminated in varying degrees by wounded pride and self-interest. Everyone identifies himself with 'my country's cause' (III.i.10) and finds 'the cause' of discord and disaster in someone else or in 'Base Fortune' (II.ii.223; iii.7; v.10, V.vi.59). Pouncing righteously on 'the cause' and on causes is universal practice. The play generates a sense of moral vertigo which is at its most acute when the two armies confront each other and raise the same battle cry: 'St George for England / And the barons' right', 'St George for England and King Edward's right' (III.iii.33–5).

VII

Edward II has often been criticised for its relative drabness of style. But there is more to its verbal style than meets the eye, and much in its non-verbal style that compensates for its figurative austerity. Marlowe's word-patterning is particularly effective here as an instrument of emphasis and unity. The dialogue is periodically flooded with terms whose literal, etymological, or associative meaning suggests the high and the low, ascent and descent.[45] Memorably encapsulated in oxymora such as 'high disgrace' and 'imperial grooms', these terms serve to reinforce impressions of sudden and extreme change, of nobility and ignobility confused, of contemptuous pride. Even more important perhaps is the sweet–bitter antithesis. The word 'sweet' occurs more than forty times, and, although 'bitter' and its synonyms occur much less often, the concept itself is always in one's mind. 'Sweet' is used primarily as a term of endearment or affectionate approval and so is always on the lips of Edward and Gaveston; but almost everyone uses it sometime when speaking to or about someone else. Like the noble titles which Edward distributes so lavishly, it is obviously debased by overuse and misapplication; indeed, we sometimes sense that it has become almost indistinguishable from its antonym. Thus, when Edward hears that the barons have killed his 'sweet minion', he instantly retaliates by transferring Gaveston's titles and epithet to someone else:

> Spencer, sweet Spencer, I adopt thee here,
> And merely of our love we do create thee
> Earl of Gloucester and Lord Chamberlain,
> Despite of times, despite of enemies.
>
> (III.ii.144–6)

The transfer of Isabella's affections and of Kent's allegiance from Edward to Mortimer is similarly sealed by means of the key epithet (V.ii.15; IV.i.10), and similarly inspired by bitterness.

When directly applied to Mortimer at the beginning of the last act, the word 'sweet' seems totally corrupted. Yet almost simultaneously it is fittingly applied and begins to recover its lost value. The Queen's 'Sweet son, come hither, I must talk with thee' (V.ii.85; cf. iv.110; vi.33, 35) echoes Gaveston's opening response to Edward's amorous call: 'Sweet prince, I come' (I.i.60); yet this and all other such echoes imply that a sickly world is dying and a sweet and wholesome one is being reborn. But not just yet: the Queen's studied sweetness to her son in the last act is part of her dissembling style and constitutes a grave danger to him. Because Edward II loved 'sweet speeches' (I.i.55) and surrounded himself with flatterers, the speech style of his court split into two extreme modes, vituperation and 'speaking fair' (I.iv.63, 183) – the second being often a politic substitute for the first. Thus, even while Isabella is plying the prince with sweet words designed to ensure that he will ignore what is done to his father, Edward's gaolers are obeying Mortimer's instructions to 'speak curstly' and 'amplify his grief with bitter words' (V.ii.64, 66). But the young prince negotiates nicely between the two extremes. He is undaunted by Mortimer's scornful defiance, and resists his mother's sentimental appeals; he condemns the one sternly but without bitter amplification, dismisses the other firmly yet gently; and in his final speech he offers both the traitor's head and his own tears to his 'Sweet father' (v.vi.99). He is a just but truly amiable king, one who distinguishes yet unites opposites: a figure of stability who will contain the tides of change even in the King's English.

Although the play is short on figurative language, some critics have noticed a number of apt allusions to metamorphic myths.[46] By far the most important of these is the allusion to Proteus, for it is the key to a network of sea and water symbolism. This symbolism has gone entirely unnoticed, largely I suspect because it operates far more on the literal than on the figurative level of expression. No fewer than six scenes are located beside sea or river, and four of them open with characters ending or beginning a voyage; other voyages to and from England are mentioned in the dialogue, and there is a good deal of seemingly non-significant and merely practical talk about favourable and unfavourable winds. This sense of moving water and of moving by water ends with the image of Edward standing knee-deep in the filthy sink to which all the channels of the castle run, then brought forward to be murdered, dressed in 'tatter'd robes', dripping and slimy.

Like Proteus, water signifies change, passion, limitlessness, Chaos. It is Edward's beginning and his end. In the first scene, limitless delight comes to him from the sea in the person of Gaveston, the Italianate Frenchman who plays on his longing for 'pleasing shows' (I.i.55) as well as 'sweet speeches'. To this Proteus (I.iv.410–13), London is attractive only as an extension of his natural element, a place which 'harbours him I hold so dear'; otherwise he despises it (I.i.12–13). Edward too would willingly let 'the sea o'erwhelm my land' (l. 151) rather than be separated from his Proteus. A fitting retribution falls upon their hubris, for, while they are revelling at Teignmouth after their 'second marriage', Mortimer scales the walls of the harbour town, declaring grimly (II.iii.21–3) that his ancestors got their name on the shore of the Dead Sea (*de mortuo mari*); and, although Gaveston takes flight by sea, his native element does not save him. Later, 'awkward winds and sore tempests (IV.vi.34) blow Edward, Spencer, and Baldock off course on their flight to Ireland. They end up at Bristol, *en route* for 'Charon's shore' (l. 89), Edward by way of the foul sink and channels beneath Killingworth Castle. The channel image is important: foul though they may be, channels are signs of an attempt to govern the boundless element.

It was because of his fantastic mode of dress that Gaveston was identified by Mortimer as another Proteus. There are several vivid descriptions of dress in the play. Although obviously symbolic, they are not supported elsewhere by metaphors: they are, in fact, minor elements in a powerful symbolic strategy which is primarily visual and non-verbal. Dress is used as another sign of a nation divided into two extreme groups: on the one hand, the Italianate–French group with their 'gaudy silk' and 'rich embroidery' (I.iv.346); on the other, the native English – the three poor men (I.i.22–46) no less than the chauvinist peers – with their plain, colourless, and perhaps even puritanical dress (see II.i.44–9; V.iv.59) that brings giggles of mockery from high, royal windows (I.iv.415–17). Other sartorial contrasts focus the imagination on the inhumanities of a rapidly distintegrating social order. The 'sacred garments' (I.ii.35) which Gaveston rends and consigns to the channel in the first scene are presumably black, since the Bishop is on his way to celebrate the exequies which the two bright young men have forgotten. Black too, we must presume, is the attire of Lady Margaret when she receives the news of Gaveston's impending return and jubilantly prepares to meet and marry him: for her father has just died (II.i.2; ii.258). Mortimer's attack during the wedding-revels is not staged, but when the royal party enters in disarray from their 'sport' (II.iii.25) we should expect a stark contrast between their festive attire and their emotional condition: 'the knell of Gaveston' the bridegroom has already rung aloud, 'continual mourning' has begun (ll. 25–6; II.iv.25). The end product of this kind of confusion is the image of the King in tattered and dripping robes. It is an image of great expressiveness. 'Tell Isabel the Queen I look'd not thus / When for her sake I ran at tilt in France', says Edward (V.v.67–8); but our own memories might also tell us that he looked not thus when he rushed to share the kingdom with his friend on the day of his father's burial. At any rate the play's final stage image is designed to herald the end of such confusion: before following his father's hearse in tears, the young King sends for his funeral robes and dons them forthwith.

If our only acquaintance with this play is as readers, we must respond to it with our aural and visual imaginations alert. We must see the clashing colours, hear the winds and waters, catch the incessant drumming in the words on antithetical ideas and feelings. Although no modern production seems to have done it full justice, those who have seen the performance with Ian McKellen in the title role know that it is a coherent, intense, and swiftly moving play with fluctuating rhythms and emotional revolutions that anticipate *Antony and Cleopatra*. Of course its hero is without greatness and there is no hint that angry or envious gods are in the least interested in what he does. But if tragedy is an experience of chaos, as Eric Bentley has said, then *Edward II* deserves to be classed as such. It must be added, too, that Marlowe has envisioned chaos in terms of the thought patterns of his time. The bitter violence which engulfs England's 'sweet' king is evidence of the chaos inherent in a cosmos that rests precariously on the limitation, the distinction, and the concord of striving opposites.

VIII

Unlike Edward II, Faustus is a man of great natural endowments. At the beginning of the play he is already an intellectual hero who has established his pre-eminence in divinity ('the queen of the sciences') and in every other branch of lawful knowledge as well. After he signs the bond with Lucifer, too, he becomes the wonder of the secular world, renowned for his magical feats and for his knowledge of astronomy. Yet the total effect of the play is such that his claim to greatness seems almost as invalid as Edward's claim to the majesty he has inherited from his father. The immediate source of this impression lies in the differences between what Faustus was and aspired to be and what he becomes, differences which are extreme even by Renaissance standards of antithetical contrast in characterisation. Its ultimate source is Marlowe's unrelenting sense of human limitations and of the folly of seeking to deny them. Of course, attempts have regularly been made to see Faustus's revolt against the laws of the universe as a testament to the greatness of the human spirit. But there is not much in the text to justify such an approach. In this play the author of *Tamburlaine the Great* seems to be saying – with a certain masochistic relish – that man's notion of his own greatness is the most insidious of all illusions, a fatal trap. Thus no tragic hero of note is so thoroughly human – so unheroic, in fact – as Doctor Faustus.

And yet his tragedy is as momentous and moving as that of any fallen giant. For Faustus is religious man, a creature whose soul is so precious in itself that the powers of Heaven and Hell are responsive to its every movement. Moreover, the reality of eternal damnation, which presses in upon the action in the first, second, and last acts, gives to the folly of Faustus an aspect at once terrifying and inexplicable. Furthermore, since Faustus (unlike Barabas and Edward) is not identified with his false choice from the start, and agonises to the end on the possibility of undoing it, the play communicates a poignant sense of what might have been, a feeling of infinite loss and regret: 'Cut is the branch that might have grown full straight . . . .'

Thus Marlowe's sense of the tragic finds its purest and most intense expression in *Doctor Faustus*. As it has come down to us, however, and possibly even as it was first written, the play is a sadly uneven affair. In editions based mainly on the B-text and divided into acts, the bulk of the material in the third and fourth acts is on a completely different level of achievement from the rest of the play. In these scenes Faustus puts to use the magical powers for which he has bartered his soul, making himself invisible and reducing the Pope's banquet to a shambles, entertaining the German Emperor and the Duke and Duchess of Vanholt with visions, castles in the air, and the gift of midwinter grapes, amusing his great patrons by casting spells on knights, servants, and peasants whose antics have annoyed him. These scenes have undoubtedly a collective significance within Marlowe's broad conception of Faustus's tragedy, for they illustrate the ironic aptness to himself of the words which the doctor addresses to the infatuated Emperor: 'My gracious lord, you do forget yourself; / These are but shadows, not substantial' IV.i.98–9). Indeed, each episode has particular significance of a kind, since every character whom Faustus deals with in the course of his magical career is a separate reflection of some aspect of himself, whether it be his 'curiosity' and longing for novelties, or his vulnerability to deceit, or his arrogant self-assertion.[47] Nevertheless the stylistc flatness and coarse horseplay which characterise most of the middle stylistic flatness and coarse horseplay which characterise most of the middle scenes are such as to suspend and almost destroy our interest in Faustus as

Despite its notably episodic construction, the play does have a structural pattern to which the middle scenes, and particularly the Roman escapade, are meaningfully accommodated. It is a pattern of ascent and decline with strong suggestions of ironic circularity. In a spiritual sense, Faustus declines from the moment he rejects the redemptive message of the Bible and turns to 'heavenly' necromancy, but in a worldly sense he moves upward and reaches the pinnacle of his career at Rome.[48] The Roman visit coincides with the completion of his aerial journey to explore the secrets of astronomy and geography, and it shows him triumphing over the world's supreme embodiment of religious and secular authority just when he is about to celebrate victory over a rival. Appropriately, the visit is placed at the approximate centre of the play.

In bald summary, Faustus's antics at Rome are merely childish; they would seem utterly implausible too were it not for the fact that Marlowe has already given his hero a touch of teasing, puerile jocularity. However, the ritual organisation of the two scenes shows that Faustus's merry tricks have been shaped into actions of central significance. Impersonating two cardinals, Faustus and his familiar secure the release of Bruno, the antipope elected by the German Emperor; they then make themsleves invisible and play such tricks on the Pope and his guests that the triumphal banquet breaks up 'in most admir'd disorder'. The initial effect of all this on an Elizabethan audience woud have been to make Faustus an eminently sympathetic figure, since it shows him acting as a champion of the oppressed against a pope who conforms perfectly to the papal stereotype of Protestant prejudice – a monster of pride who would subject all men to his will. But it would have been clear to the reasonably thoughtful too that the Pope is a mirror image of the theologian who set out to become a demi-god and claimed that 'The Emperor shall not live but by my leave' (I.iii.110). Moreover, the 'redemption' of Bruno from bondage simply lets loose upon the world another pope, and one whose claim Faustus himself will soon endorse. Thus the humiliation of 'this proud Pope' (III.i.77) in the midst of his victorious celebration, like the image of Bruno in chains, is but a premonition of what will happen to Faustus. Even the prank of snatching the Pope's cup from his lips will be echoed at the end when Faustus sees Christ's blood streaming in the firmament and longs in vain for one drop to save his soul.

Ideas of ascent and descent are scattered everywhere in the diction and imagery of the papal scenes and of the chorus which introduces them. They combine with the stage action – as they will at the end of the play (V.ii.1–19, 99–139) – to impress on the imagination the inevitable fall of those who seek to 'scale Olympus top' (Chorus I.4). There are also images of circular motion and containing circularity which suggest that Marlowe's structural model is not Fortune's wheel but the clock, and beyond that the heavenly bodies in their daily, monthly, and annual rotations. In other words, the structure invokes the idea of time as the law of regulated movement within a confined space (see especially ll. 11–12), a law which indicts all those who seek to escape from creatural limitations. Mounted on a dragon's back, Faustus views the stars and planets in order 'to find the secrets of astronomy / Graven in the book of Jove's high firmament' (ll. 2–3); but he overlooks what everyone in the Renaissance saw as the chief purpose or end of all such study, the understanding of time.[49] Thus he is deaf to the implications of Mephostophilis's punning remark that the planets or 'erring [i.e. wandering] stars' have 'all one motion' and 'move from east to west in four and twenty hours upon the poles of the world' (II.ii.44–6). He is deaf too to the significance of Mephostophilis's description of the Ponte Angelo as protected by cannons 'that match the number of the days contain'd / Within the compass of one complete year' (III.i.43–4), and sees nothing suggestive in the fact that the height of his triumphs coincides with the mid-point of the natural year, St Peter's Day or 29 June (Chorus I.24; III.i.54, 199).[50] It will be observed of course that these allusions to the encompassing order of time connect the middle of the play with the end. As has often been noted, all the intensity of the great final scenes, and especially of the last soliloquy, derives from Faustus's perception of eternal law at work in the inexorable movement of time: despite his desperate attempts to alter their motions, the ever-moving spheres of heaven will not stand still, the sun will not rise before its appointed hour, the clock strikes at midnight.[51] This assertion of time's order is given extra force by the fact that Faustus's period of very limited freedom coincides numerically with the hours of 'a natural day' (II.ii.52; V.ii.133).

IX

Some of Faustus's early speeches express the excitement of intellectual inquiry at its highest level; in addition, the narrative speeches reporting his cosmograpical investigations convey a feeling of extraordinary accomplishment. But Marlowe's irony is so sustained as to rule out the possibility of arguing that he endorses Faustus's act of rebellion or finds much to admire in it. To give due weight to this irony, however, is to run the risk of presenting Faustus as an unsympathetic figure who invites from the audience an attitude of detached and complacent judgement. This would certainly be wrong, for, while the irony does make us share in Mephostophilis's view that here is a man whose mind is destined to be changed by experience (II.i.127), it also awakens in us a compassionate awareness that the wisdom which comes from experience often comes too late to save mortals from the consequences of self-deception and folly. Moreover, nothing that Faustus does alienates him from us as a human being. His rebellion involves no crime against his own kind; he is a good friend; he is without cruelty and injustice. The God, too, against whom he rebels is utterly remote and impersonal: not the friendly master betrayed by Peter and Judas, not even the Old Testament patriarch who makes generous covenants with his chosen people and faithful sons. In other words, Faustus is 'one of us' in a way that few tragic heroes are: although greatly gifted and recognisably individual, he is also Mankind or Everyman. This impression is substantiated not only by the play's morality pattern but also by its numerous echoes of the primal Fall. Imprinted on its diction and imagery, and forming the basis of its principal ironies, is the serpent's offer of fruit which was 'pleasant to the eyes' and good to taste, as well as his assurance that our first parents' eyes would be opened and that they would become as gods (Genesis 3:5–6, Geneva version). I would suggest therefore that Faustus's fundamental and inalienable humanity provides the perspective from which we should consider the play's intensely ironic vision.

What the irony establishes with absolute clarity is that Faustus has an astounding capacity for turning reality upside down in the effort to make it conform to his 'ambitious longings' and 'fantasies'. These can all be reduced to two delusions, the more important of which is his belief that magic will make him god-like. As soon as he takes his first step to 'get a deity' (I.i.61), the names of the pagan gods being to enter the dialogue. Of these, Faustus's true connection is with 'bright Lucifer' (II.i.155), at once stellar god and fallen angel; but the divinity with whom he would most wish to link himself is Jove. Like Jove, Faustus the magician is good-natured, magnanimous, fond of 'pleasure and . . . dalliance', and much given to metamorphosis. But of all the Jovian attributes it is supreme power that attracts Faustus most: the Bad Angel's encouraging words, 'Be thou on earth as Jove is in the sky, / Lord and commander of these elements' (I.i.74–5), are well chosen. For Faustus rejects the lawful sciences because he finds them fit only for the base and the servile, and he is drawn to magic because he believes it will place at his disposal a host of 'servile spirits' who will perform his every wish (ll. 36, 95, 106). When the moment comes for signing the deed, Mephostophilis extravagantly encourages this hope: 'I will be thy slave and wait on thee' (II.i.46). But, once the deed is signed, the illusory nature of Faustus's divine authority and the devil's obedience is revealed with remarkable speed. Mephostophilis refuses to grant his first request and to answer his first question. Moreover, Faustus's threat to repent brings him face to face with a terrifying Lucifer who commands him to behave like 'an obedient servant' (II.ii.100): which he promptly does. His reaction to Lucifer, too, is predictive of his relations with earthly rulers. They applaud his exploits and make large promises of honour and reward, but these promises are not kept. And his dream of acting as their overlord is quietly relinquished: he kneels and kisses the Emperor's hand (IV.ii.20), promises to lay his life at the feet of the Emperor's 'pope' (IV.i.64), and is touchingly eager to answer a call for entertainment from even a duke and his wife.

What Faustus becomes with the aid of demons is not a god but a man who is allowed to play at being a god; at the tail-end of his theological career he describes himself as 'a divine in show' (I.i.3), and that in a sense is what he remains. He is told that 'The miracles that magic will perform' will make him more renowned than Apollo himself (ll. 134–41). But, whenever the word 'perform' is used in the sense of 'to do' or 'carry out', there is always a covert pun which reminds us that his godlike power, and Mephostophilis's air of servile obedience, have no more reality than what we ourselves 'see perform'd' (Chorus II.17) on stage before us.[52] Fundamental to the meaning and method of the play is the old theological argument that magic, drama, and pagan mythology are all closely related instruments in Satan's endeavour to pervert mankind from the contemplation of unchanging truths as embodied in the Christian faith and the Bible. The gods of the pagans, explained the Fathers of the Church, were either ordinary men or magicians, and the miracles ascribed to them were simply fictions imagined by poets or devil-assisted illusions. The survival of their cults, too, depended greatly on the shows and plays in which their deeds were celebrated. Gods and magicians (it was said) were forever altering their own appearance or that of others for cruel and deceptive purposes, just as in the theatre men masqueraded as gods in stories about lust and violence, thus giving divine sanction to immorality. All such metamorphoses were thoroughly typical products of Satan, the father of lies, whose chief mode of deception was to approach men in the guise of a heavenly spirit.[53]

This theological tradition is lightly implicated in *Edward II*: Gaveston–Proteus is the tempting spirit who plays on the King's weakness for 'pleasing shows', promising in the first scene to dramatise for his delight a suitably tailored version of the myth of Diana and Actaeon. But in the tragedy of a lapsed theologian who literally espouses magic and demonism the tradition is understandably exploited to the full. Faustus shows a distinct fondness for the poetry of Ovid and 'blind Homer' (Augustine would have liked the pun), but the fictions which engage him most are dramatic. There are many shows in the play, and they all have the one purpose of distracting Faustus from thoughts of his final end: 'Talk not of Paradise or Creation, but mark the show', says Lucifer pertinently (II.ii.107). One distinction can, however, be made. Prior to his Roman visit, Faustus is merely a spectator at shows presented for his delight by Mephostophilis and Lucifer. But before his journeys begin he is given the book which teaches the art of transformation, so that when he arrives at Rome he becomes, and remains thereafter, an active participant in the art of histrionic illusion: 'Then in this show let me an actor be, / That this proud Pope may Faustus' cunning see' (III.i.76–7). None of these shows is without some sharply ironic reminder of the realities they are helping him to forget. His punishment of Benvolio–Actaeon, for example ('And I'll play Diana, and send you horns presently' – IV.i.97), like his humiliation of the Pope, anticipates his own end: he too will be punished for wilful unbelief by an angry god. The most illuminating of all his shows, however, is the vision of Helen of Troy, whose beauty so enchants his senses that he longs to re-enact the *Iliad* with himself as hero: 'I will be Paris, and for love of thee / Instead of Troy shall Wittenberg be sack'd' (V.i.104–5). Faustus's rhapsodic address to Helen is perhaps the most characteristic expression of Marlowe's genius, being a perfect fusion of the hyperbolic (or lyrical) and the ironic (or dramatic) modes. It communicates an intense perception of great beauty, yet every line confirms that 'heavenly Hellen' (l. 91 – the old spelling, with its hint of a paradoxical pun, is worth noting) is simply a demon in disguise, a succubus whose lips 'suck forth' (l. 100) the soul of Faustus and lead it to the flames of Hell. The speech looks back to his early jest that he 'confounds Hell in Elysium' (I.iii.59) and forward to the Bad Angel's grim promise: 'Then wilt thou tumble in confusion' – where 'confusion' means 'damnation' (V.ii.125)[54].

Looked at from the point of view of ethical psychology, Faustus's addiction to shows reflects the demons' endeavour to subdue his understanding and will by stimulating a desire for sensual and above all visual delights. Looked at from a biblical standpoint, it simply confirms his essential humanity, his weakness for what is 'pleasant to the eyes' (Genesis 3:6). References to the eye are very frequent in the play: in fact it has an extensive visual vocabulary whose collective sense is that Faustus is blinded to the nature of reality by his love of 'pleasant sights' (IV.vi.2) and his corresponding dislike of what 'seems harsh, unpleasant' or 'ugly' (I.i.107; iii.24; V.i.47). The devils pander to this weakness at all times. When he asks for a wife he is promised instead a courtesan 'whom thine eye shall like' (II.i.151); when he embarks on his global tour he is shown a multitude of buildings 'fair and gorgeous to the eye' (III.i.10; cf. ll. 32, 75); and when he asks for Helen the request is 'perform'd in twinkling of an eye' (V.i.95). But this addiction to what is superficially and changeably beautiful at the expense of what is essentially and permanently so rebounds on him with terrible irony before his death. Here indeed the serpent's promise that 'your eyes shall be opened' is fulfilled, for Faustus is compelled to look at the frightful realities he must now embrace (no longer clad in the Luciferian beauty of a thousand stars) and at the beautiful reality he has lost forever. The process begins with Mephostophilis's reminder of the fatal misreading which made the Bible seem 'hard' and unattractive and necromantic books seem 'heavenly' (I.i.38–53). Punning sardonically, a triumphant Mephostophilis reveals,

> 'Twas *I* that, when thou were't i' the way to heaven,
> *Damm'd* up thy *passage*; when thou took'st the book
> To view the scriptures, then *I* turn'd the leaves
> And led thine *eye*.
>
> (v.ii.86–9; italics added)

The Good Angel then (to the accompaniment of solemn music) shows Faustus the throne of 'resplendent glory' and 'Pleasures unspeakable' that would have been his if he had 'affected sweet divinity' (ll. 100–7); after which the Bad Angel insists that he contemplate each of the ghastly sights inside Hell Mouth: 'Now, Faustus, let thine eyes with horror stare / Into that vast perpetual torture house . . . .' The Bad Angel's promise that he will later 'see / Ten thousand tortures that more horrid be' extracts from Faustus a cry of ocular anguish: 'O, I have seen enough to torture me.' This anguish threads the great soliloquy which follows and dominates its climax. In the darkness, Faustus charges 'Fair nature's eye' to shine, but it will not; he can 'See, see. . . . And see' not only Christ's blood streaming in the firmament, but also God's 'ireful brows', and he cannot hide from that look; and he dies uttering impotent cries for Heaven and Hell to change their visage, horror written on his own face: 'My God, my God! Look not so fierce on me. . . . Ugly hell, gape not!' With the allusions to time, the ocular motif helps to place beyond doubt the argument that the last scenes are no magnificent appendage but 'grow integrally out of the play';[55] they are intimately connected not only with the first two acts but also with the middle scenes of travel, farce, and showmanship, where 'things fair and gorgeous to the eye' are mixed with the merry tricks of optical illusion.

Faustus's divinity, then, is mere show and pastime, something that comes and goes in the twinkling of an eye. The other great delusion of which he is the ironic victim anticipates to a degree the characterisation of Satan in the first book of *Paradise Lost*: it is the belief that rebellion against God, the denial of ultimate reality, is heroic. He and Mephostophilis speak of 'manly fortitude' and 'courage', but as always in Marlowe the term consistently used to designate heroism is 'resolution'. Faustus is formally acquainted at the outset with the need for resolution when Valdes warns him that 'The miracles that magic will perform' will materialise only 'If learned Faustus will be resolute' (I.i.31). Since he proceeds so vigorously with the conjuration rites, it would seem that he does possess the kind of resolution Valdes has in mind. Yet his response to Valdes's warning – 'as resolute am I in this / As thou to live' – and the way in which he has to prompt himself when the crucial moment arrives – 'Then fear not, Faustus, to be resolute / And try the utmost magic can perform' (I.iii.14–15) – suggest that this resolution has no assured basis in his character but is really a role assumed to meet the demands of a 'desperate enterprise' (I.i.79). The suggestion is confirmed by the fact that 'desperate resolution' is precisely what brings about the final humiliation of his pretentious *alter ego*, Benvolio:

> If you will aid me in this enterprise,
> Then draw your weapons and be resolute;
> If not, depart: here will Benvolio die,
> But Faustus' death shall quit my infamy.
>   (IV.ii.10–13)

The parallel is nicely secured by Benvolio's use of the assertive 'will' and 'shall'. Sure signs of the resolute style ('For *will* and *shall* best fitteth Tamburlaine'), these are heard at their most impressive in the speech where Faustus projects himself into the role of Homeric hero: 'Here will I dwell.... I will be Paris ... Instead of Troy shall Wittenberg be sack'd ... I will combat with weak Menelaus.... I will wound Achilles in the heel ... none but thou shalt be my paramour' (v.i.102–16).

Fundamental to Faustus's conception to himself as a heroic indivi-dualist is the belief that he will uncover truths hidden from the rest of mankind: at his command, servile spirits will 'resolve' enigma and mystery. Marlowe's use of the word in this sense is adroitly managed in such a way that the sense of heroic determination is simultaneously implied: Faustus imagines, and then performs, the part of an imperious interrogator who will not be side-tracked from his quest for truth:

> Shall I make spirits fetch me what I please,
> Resolve me of all ambiguities,
> Perform what desperate enterprise I will?
>   (I.i.77–9)

> ... meet me in my study at midnight,
> And then resolve me of thy master's mind.
>   (I.iii.99–100)

> Resolve me then in this one question.
>   (II.ii.63)

The truth, of course, is that the spirits resolve nothing of importance: after the pact has been signed, Mephostophilis refuses to answer pertinent questions and helps to develop Faustus's natural penchant for ambiguity and contradiction. One of the most revealing manifestations of this tendency occurs just after he has begun to have second thoughts about the value of his contract with Hell. When he says, 'I will renounce this magic and repent' (II.ii.11), the style itself intimates just how his resolution might be truly put to the test. But Faustus, afraid of God's wrath and even more of the devil's threats, fails the test. In so doing, however, he protects his self-image by inverting the sense of 'resolution': to retreat is to advance, to quail before the devils is to be steadfast: 'Now go not backward; no Faustus, be resolute; / Why waver'st thou?' (II.i.6–7); 'Why should I die then, or basely despair? / I am resolv'd, Faustus shall not repent' (II.ii.31–2).[56]

Faustus's confused understanding of himself and his desperate enterprise is finely underscored by Marlowe's ironic recognition that in one of its senses the word 'resolution' is synonymous with its antonym. It may signify fixity and persistence, but it also denotes disintegration, the breaking-up of something into parts. Marlowe begins to hint at this contradiction in the scene where Faustus formally makes Lucifer his ally and God his enemy. Urging himself to 'be resolute' (II.i.6), Faustus declares that the love of Belzebub is 'fix'd' in him, and then signs the pact; at the same time Mephostophilis fetches fire to 'dissolve' the divinely congealed blood that warns Faustus to desist, and is soon admitting that 'when all the world dissolves . . . every creature shall be purified' and 'All places shall be hell that is not heaven' (ll. 63, 123–5). Combined with the imagery of congealed and melting blood (an echo perhaps of the waxen, Icarian wings: Chorus I.21), the diction here intimates that resolute Faustus is now married to the spirit of change and dissolution. This idea soon gives rise to one of the play's most important symbols. For from now on all Faustus's resolves to repent will be instantly undone by the devil's threat to tear him in pieces (II.ii.81; v.i.74; ii.65; cf. I.iv.19; IV.ii.42–91; iv.31); and of course – as anticipated in the comic scenes – the symbol acquires a horribly literal status at the end when his body is discovered 'All torn asunder' by the demons whom he served (V.iii.7–8). Yet the final irony is not that Faustus's desperate resolution has proved to be a guarantee of violent dissolution. It is that he dies longing in vain for the dissolution of his soul. In his last soliloquy he imagines first that the resolution of his body into its elemental components would save him from the horrors that begin at midnight. But he quickly recalls that the meaning of Hell is the indissoluble nature of the soul: only the souls of beasts are 'soon dissolv'd in elements' (V.ii.172).

Faustus's failure to match his heroic self-conception is driven home with grim insistence at the end of the play. His last submission to the threat of dismemberment is sharply contrasted with the defiant response of the Old Man to the same threat. This contrast is given additional force by the Old Man's re-entry in the middle of the Helen speech precisely when Faustus is declaring that he will combat with 'weak Menelaus' and wound Achilles in the heel. Singularly unheroic too is his spiteful request that the Old Man should be tormented for trying to dissuade him from his vow and so exposing him to the wrath of Mephostophilis. Most eloquent of all, however, is the manner of his death, carried screaming to Hell by a demon whom he once lectured on the need for 'manly fortitude'.

X

But although the irony of retributive justice descends with singular force on Faustus at the end, no audience can share in the feeling of mocking aloofness which that irony undoubtedly engenders. Such feelings are assigned to the devils, who enter above as lofty spectators, eager to 'mark . . . how he doth demean himself' (v.ii.10) in his last desperate efforts to escape reality, and who then despatch the Bad Angel to spell out the poetic justice of everything that awaits him. Although we have been shocked by his reaction to the Old Man's kindness, we identify with Faustus entirely in the last act, seeing in him a fellow human being who has been called upon to pay a terrible price for the longings and fantasies that plague mankind. We are drawn to him by his generosity to Wagner, by his concern for his friends' welfare, by his honest acceptance of responsibility for what is about to happen, and above all by the imaginative intensity with which he voices his apprehension of eternal loss and pain. Moreover, our awareness of the great gulf between his heroic self-conception and his actual behaviour has long since been complicated by a recognition that his failure to defy the devils and turn to God is essentially a symptom of his loss of faith. If he truly believed that God's love and mercy were still available to him, then, like the Old Man, he would have little difficulty in triumphing over the devils. Theologically speaking his despair is sinful, the other side of his presumption;[57] but witnessed on stage as an existential fact it registers as a kind of torment, something pitiful, terrifying, mysterious. Thus Faustus's lack of resolution takes us to the very heart of his tragedy.

Whether Faustus can be saved after he has signed the deed is a question which often divides critics. On the one hand, it is argued that if he were damned from this point then all his subsequent actions would have no real significance: the rest of the play would be not so much dramatic as elegiac or clinical. But (it is added) the words of the Good Angel and of the Old Man, as well as the determined efforts of the devils to ensure that he does not repent, prove that the deed is not really binding and that redemption is still possible.[58] On the other hand, it has been noted that the various assurances of divine mercy are qualified if not ambiguous. Much has been made of the fact that, when Faustus utters his first prayer for help (II.ii.83–4), the prayer is answered by the immediate appearance of Lucifer,

Belzebub, and Mephostophilis.[59] However, although this is a powerfully ironic reversal,[60] I doubt if it can be confidently construed as a sign that God has abandoned Faustus: it might more reasonably be taken as a test of his faith and resolution, identical to the experience of the Old Man in Act V (whom neither Christ nor his angels intervene to save). More important altogether are the 'ifs' and 'mights' which hedge about the various assurances that it is never too late to repent. Particularly ominous is the Old Man's 'Yet, yet, thou hast an amiable soul, / If sin by custom grow not into nature' (V.i.41–2). What the Old Man refers to in his conditional clause is what Faustus remembers best from his theology: that the sinful heart can become so hardened – or God can so harden it – that a genuine repentance becomes impossible. And that, Faustus believes, is what has happened to him (II.ii.18). Moreover, his strange inability to accomplish the true repentance he so obviously desires ('I do repent, and yet I do despair' – V.i.69) would almost certainly have raised in the minds of an Elizabethan audience the possibility that he was predestined for damnation: that all his sins of presumption, sensuality, and despair are simply the acting-out of God's inscrutable decree that he belongs with Judas and his like.[61] Some critics have gone so far as to suggest that that indeed is how the play should be read.[62]

Yet to maintain either that it is never too late for Faustus to repent, or that he is a lost soul before the clock strikes (whether because he has signed the deed or because he has been predestined for Hell), is in effect to contract the imaginative horizons of the tragedy. Almost from the start, uncertainty is deliberately presented as an essential fact of the tragic experience dealt with: 'I fear me nothing will reclaim him now', says the First Scholar, and the Second replies, 'Yet let us see what we can do' (I.ii.30–1). This uncertainty is the basis of dramatic suspense, it is the primary source of Faustus's suffering, and it is Marlowe's response to the metaphysical paradox of fate and freedom. Marlowe does not resolve this paradox: like the best tragedians, he dramatises it.[63] The nearest we can get to abstracting a resolution from the play is to say that once the deed has been signed – once, as in most tragedy, the crucial choice or error has been made – the consequences add up to a situation which so narrows the range of freedom as to constitute a kind of fate. Or, to put it in terms of the deed: the power conferred upon the demons by this agreement is an illusion; but human nature being what it is, the illusion easily becomes reality – simply to believe that the deed is binding is to make it so.

The major impression left by *Doctor Faustus* is that of a 'distressed soul'. The phrase is recurrent and haunts the memory, all the more so when its full meaning is perceived. Always used punningly, the epithet links up with two other key puns: that on 'resolve', and that on 'deed' (all Faustus's 'proud audacious deeds' are deeds in two senses of the word, since they all tie him more closely to Lucifer). For 'distressed' means not only 'afflicted' but also 'torn asunder' (Latin *distringere*) and 'bound', 'held captive'. Thus 'Faustus' distressed soul' is a phrase which epitomises the whole tragedy. It evokes the spiritual disunity, guilt, constraint, and anguish that constitute the condition of human bondage.[64]

XI

We are perhaps cursed in knowing what we do about Marlowe's life (short, brilliant, violent) and personality (tempestuous, enigmatic). For almost inevitably we are inclined to read his plays not as separate texts for performance on a stage but as interrelated clues to the nature and development of one man's mind. In the process, we are apt to underplay the variety and adventurousness of his dramatic endeavours, the extent to which he anticipated and promoted different lines of development in that very comprehensive compartment of the drama to which the name of tragedy was given. *Tamburlaine*, as we have noted, provided a model for the tragedy of martial love as found in *Othello* and *Antony and Cleopatra*. *Edward II*, by contrast, is a tragedy of irresolution and effeminacy which connects with *Richard II* and even, perhaps, with *Hamlet*. More important, it is tragedy with a strongly social and realistic perspective in which the flaws of the protagonist are integral to a picture of mankind as ignoble, self-absorbed, wilful, and unstable: tragedy of a kind perfected by Middleton. The Jacobean marriage of satiric comedy and tragic melodrama begins with *The Jew of Malta*, a play which is no less difficult to classify than *The Revenger's Tragedy*; Barabas too is the first of many stage villains whose articulacy and insight into the characters of those who condemn and exploit them has such an unsettling effect on our conditioned responses to moral issues. *Doctor Faustus* is one of the most poignant as well as the first of those tragedies in which an impassioned revolt against some constricting relationship becomes the passport to servitude and degradation.

The restless nature of Marlowe's genius, and perhaps too the circumstances governing the conditions of his work and the transmission of his texts, have left serious flaws in much of what he has given us. What remains surprising, however, is the very high degree of imaginative coherence and intellectual control which is evident in the plays considered here. They are plays which deserve the compliment of scrupulous analysis and will no doubt continue to surprise us by the eloquence of their general design and the aptness and subtlety of their local detail.

The analyses offered here have helped to expose certain common characteristics of Marlowe's art: an extremist inclination which is closely related to a tendency to think in opposites; an insistently ironic cast of mind which comes to take an almost brutal delight in deflating those heroic conceptions which the same mind generates so easily; a fascination with cruelty which is cunningly contained within justifying frameworks, theological, philosophical, historical; a limited reserve of compassion that makes the tragic intensity of *Doctor Faustus* all the more impressive; an energetic variability of mind that works against continuity in attitude and mode of expression – and makes it unwise of the critic to set any limits to what Marlowe might have accomplished had he lived. But, if there is one general conclusion to which the foregoing analyses should lead, it is the unique, self-contained nature of each of the plays.

4 Cyril Tourneur(?):
The Revenger's Tragedy

I

Fifty years after its anonymous publication in 1607, *The Revenger's Tragedy* (c. 1605) was ascribed to Cyril Tourneur, author of *The Atheist's Tragedy* (c. 1609). The correctness of this attribution has, however, been challenged, strong arguments being advanced for ascribing the play to Thomas Middleton. But there is not enough external evidence to put this claim beyond reasonable doubt; nor is there sufficient internal evidence to overcome the scepticism of those who find it hard to associate the hectic moralising of the play with so cool and detached a dramatic moralist as Middleton. On the other hand, to study *The Revenger's Tragedy* in conjunction with *The Atheist's Tragedy* is a largely wasteful exercise. The second play is strikingly inferior to the first; and, although it demonstrates that 'patience is the honest man's revenge' (V.ii.275), so that the two plays can be conveniently examined as complementary explorations of the same theme, the fact remains that there are other plays with which *The Revenger's Tragedy* can be more profitably compared.

Like Hieronimo, Vindice is morally transformed by his quest for wild justice, does violence to the tongue and all it represents, and displays a fiendishly jocular delight in the execution of his murderous plots. So prominent is this jocular vein in the play as a whole that tragic violence is frequently presented in the spirit of farce, a mixture which recalls *The Jew of Malta*. Like Barabas, too, but even more like Malevole in Marston's *The Malcontent* (c. 1602), Vindice is a scorching satirist of the corrupt society within which he intrigues; indeed, like the hero of Marston's *Antonio's Revenge* (c. 1599), he is a self-conscious purger of society, a kind of savage and demented reformer. Other important aspects of *The Revenger's Tragedy* could be ascribed to the influence of these two plays: the setting of a sin-ridden Italian court, the hero's adoption of the role of melancholy malcontent, the heavy emphasis on hypocrisy and disguising, the use of a masque as the basis of the Treacherous Entertainment, the depiction of the court as a place of impudence as well as hypocrisy. There are parallels with Jonson's *Volpone* too: most of the characters are two-dimensional figures with descriptive names, their liveliness being subordinated to the demands of a thematic structure which satirically unfolds the evils of a whole society, and to the twists of a labyrinthine plot which mirrors a universal perversion of human relationships. *Hamlet*, with its disillusioned hero fascinated by what disgusts him, and *King Lear*, with its powerful sense of human bestiality, have also been cited as influences;[1] and to these one might add (for reasons indicated below), *Titus Andronicus*, *Othello*, and possibly even *Macbeth*.

The Revenger's Tragedy, in short, is a chamber of literary echoes. Yet its individuality is not in question and is indeed so striking that T. S. Eliot was prompted to see the play as spiritual autobiography in dramatic form, its characters as projections 'from the poet's inner world of nightmare, some horror beyond words'.[2] This individuality of impact derives from the play's speed, from its emotional narrowness and intensity, and above all, perhaps, from its grotesque humour. The hectic jocularity of the unhinged revenger has been extended to the whole play and blended with the humour of Death, the grinning 'antic' who always has the last laugh on human folly (*Richard II*, III.iii.160–70).

This macabre humour is medieval in origin and religious in character; it was stylised in the Middle Ages in the Dance of Death theme, of which there are clear echoes in Vindice's use of skull and dance in the execution of revenge.[3] The humour of *The Revenger's Tragedy* is thus integral to a vision of reality in which the government of the universe is taken as understood by everyone. There are no complaints here about Fortune, Fate, or the inscrutable workings of divine providence. Evil is not a mystery but a gross and grotesque fact of human experience; in the play's bitterly eloquent hero, it inspires savage indignation and sardonic contempt rather than personal anguish and metaphysical questioning. The play therefore is not a tragedy in the sense that *The Spanish Tragedy*, *Doctor Faustus*, or *Hamlet* is; rather it is a tragical satire which has been strongly coloured by some of the more gloomy and bizarre aspects of Christian thought and sentiment.[4]

II

The structure of the play, like that of *The Spanish Tragedy*, has been found seriously defective when examined in the light of an abstract model of 'the revenge play'. But, when considered in relation to its own thematic preoccupations and characteristic theatrical effects, the structure, if less than perfect, seems well crafted. There are two climactic moments of violence in the action: the murder of the Duke by Vindice and his brother Hippolito at the end of Act III, and the murder of the Duke's four sons (together with three courtiers) in the Treacherous Entertainment at the end. If the author were following the example of *Hamlet*, *Hoffman*, or *Antonio's Revenge*, Vindice's revenge on the Duke for the deaths of his mistress and father would obviously be delayed until the last act. However, the two violent climaxes are causally connected and bear witness to an expanding pattern of interactive evils. The plotting which puts Vindice in a position to strike against the Duke incidentally provides him with a double motive for later killing his heir, Lussurioso. Finding employment at court in the guise of Piato the pander, Vindice is required by Lussurioso to procure his own sister and persuade his mother to act as bawd in the affair. As a result of his desperate effort to deflect Lussurioso from Castiza, Lussurioso is temporarily imprisoned, turns against Piato, and then hires Vindice – as Vindice – to kill Piato, thus giving Vindice a second reason for wanting to kill him. The imprisonment of Lussurioso, too, interlocks with the episode of Junior Brother, and both serve, along with the episodic seduction of Spurio by his stepmother the Duchess, to fuel the mutual rivalries and hatreds of the Duke's sons. These in turn compel the action towards the bloodbath of the final scene, where Vindice's killing of the doomed Lussurioso has the appearance of an intrusion in a family affair.

Fredson Bowers objected that Vindice has no clear-cut enemy and that 'the maze of intrigue and counter-intrigue serves in the light of cold analysis virtually to obscure the plot', creating an effect of great confusion.[5] It is certainly true that Vindice seems for a while to forget his intention to kill the Duke, becoming wholly caught up in the general excitement of erotic and vengeful intrigue that prevails in the palace; but that is a significant fact about the effects on his nature of his chosen course of action. So too the essential irrelevance of his contribution to the Treacherous Entertainment is a comment on his implicit assumption that 'the almighty patience' needs him to accomplish justice and purge the realm. Moreover, the general effect of a confusing maze is surely calculated, a sign that action is being moulded as an image of theme: the curse of 'confusion, / Death and disgrace' (I.ii.195–6) which is put at the outset on the Duke and his family, the frequent punning on 'amazement', and the constant description of corrupt characters as monstrous and unnatural combine to suggest that entrapment in a deadly labyrinth is a fate that threatens everyone. There are other signs, too, of careful structuring. The ironic reversals which are an outstanding feature of the action highlight the blind conceit of knavish villains and the self-destructive nature of evil.[6] The use of parallelism in the action not only contributes to the sense of unity but also serves to contradict Vindice's assumption that he has nothing in common with those he satirises and punishes,[7] and so enforces the central theme of uncertain and lost identity.

III

The thematic structure of the play, and ultimately its characterisation and general style, are powerfully affected by three large concepts to which explicit allusion is regularly made: time, grace, and language. In brief, the play exhibits a thoroughly corrupt society in which men waste and abuse time, pretend to grace but forfeit it entirely, and are betrayed to death and damnation by their smooth tongues and their essential contempt for the word.

The time theme is related to Vindice's emphasis, as satiric moralist, on the transience of the flesh and its pleasures, an emphasis which has been traced to the *contemptus mundi* motif of religious literature and art.[8] But time is no mere synonym for mortality and decay here, nor is it assumed that man's best response to it is simply one of pious resignation. As is apparent when the Duke's death is announced and the court offers words of both condolence and encouragement to his heir, time is officially understood by the inhabitants of this play-world as a normative principle inherent in the order of nature, and one to which the joys as well as the sorrows of life can be referred: it is right for the Duke's son to 'shine in tears, like the sun in April', but it is also right for others to recall that 'sorrows must run their circles into joys' and to wish him a long and happy reign ending with 'natural death . . . three-score years a-coming' (V.i.150; iii.30–1). Elsewhere in the play there are clear signs of an awareness that choosing the opportune or fitting moment is crucial to success in human affairs, that happiness in both this and the next life is dependent on the right use of time, and that the key question to ask about any man is, 'How does he apply his hours?' (IV.i.44).

But of course this is all mere lip-service to the great law implanted in nature by 'the divine patience'. The whole endeavour here is to 'be a man o' th' time' (I.i.94); and to be that is to act instantly on one's desires, surrendering to the violence of joy and the joy of violence (III.v.27). In the triple sense of speed, vehemence, and lawless brutality, violence is the play's outstanding concern; it is also the source of its much-noted intensity. There are some contemptuous references to 'slack' and 'sluggy' men, but the only person to whom these epithets could apply is the old Duke, and to him only in his connubial and sometimes his legal responsibilities: otherwise he is the 'sudden' Duke (IV.i.84; cf. II.i.60). But not only is violence shared by young and old alike; it is also a common element in all the prevailing moral vices. It is evident in the ambitious, who cannot wait for the burial of the dead before celebrating the acquisition of new honours ('Prepare for revels' – V.i.164); or who seek to accelerate the process of hereditary succession by getting the law to dispose of the heir-apparent with 'extemporal' justice ('Excellent! Then am I heir – duke in a minute!' – III.i.13; cf. vi.8). It affects the avaricious, driven as they are with 'golden spurs' in 'a false gallop' towards moral ruin (II.ii.45–6). And it is particularly noticeable in the lustful. Always on the alert for sexual opportunities ('I do embrace this season for the fittest / To taste of that young lady' – l. 154), and tormented with impatience when pleasure is delayed ('this night I'll visit her, and till then 'tis / A year in my desires' – ll. 87–8), they beget children 'in haste' who are by this 'one false minute disinherited' (II.ii.126; I.ii.168). But violence is most conspicuous of course in the vengeful (and at this court everyone is vengeful):

> Good, happy, swift; there's gunpowder i' th' court,
> Wild-fire at midnight. In this heedless fury
> He may show violence to cross himself;
> I'll follow the event.

> (II.ii.171–4)

Here then is a nightmare world in which the natural cycle of time, with its ceremonial pace and clear distinctions, is utterly ignored. Past, present, and future are made one in the hunt for instant gratification, the joy of the 'bewitching minute' (III.v.75). The day is permanently 'out o' th' socket' because life has become an endless night of revels where torchlight makes 'an artificial noon' (II.iii.45; I.iv.27): even when pleasure is assigned to the hours of daylight it is deliberately located in 'an unsunn'd lodge, / Wherein 'tis night at noon' (III.v.18–19). Natural death in old age is unknown: to die is to be 'sped' (IV.i.67; V.iii.52) by someone else, to 'sigh blood' in the midst of all one's joys (V.ii.21–2). Personal identities, basic human relationships, and (if Vindice is to be believed) the whole pattern of society are caught up in a whirl of vertiginous change. It's a wise child now that knows her mother, and a wise father that knows his son (II.i.167; II.iii.83). Farmers' sons have become courtiers, noblemen have beggared themselves, and the great hereditary estates of the realm have been turned into jewels and dresses for the 'short-liv'd' beauties and pleasures of the court (I.iii.49–53; II.i.214–26; III.v.74). The entire nation, it would seem, has been corrupted by the court's contempt for the values and norms of a stable, agrarian, sunlit society. Fitly, it is governed by an old man whose youthful lusts are a perversion of time's natural order: 'Age hot is like a monster to be seen; / My hairs are white, and yet my sins are green' (II.iii.131–2).

No one, however, is more thoroughly identified with the spirit of violence than the protagonist. With almost demonic patience, Vindice has waited nine years to get into the court and avenge himself on the Duke, and when the opportunity arises he seizes it with alacrity: disguising himself as Piato ('I'll quickly turn into another' – I.i.134), he announces to his mother and sister that he intends 'speedy travel' into 'unknown lands' (l. 117; II.ii.44). Perhaps he has suffered from the fears and hesitations of the melancholic man (see I.i.119–20); but he differs from Hieronimo, Brutus, and Hamlet in that he is never shown hesitating at the thought of violence. He may moralise on the madness of those sensualists who will squander their patrimony and risk the gallows 'For the poor benefit of a bewitching minute' (III.v.75) in a woman's arms; but when he cries out, 'So, so, / Now nine years vengeance crowd into a minute' (ll. 122–3), it is apparent that he too is bewitched by the intensities of the moment. The gratification of vengeful desire – the sighing of blood – brings him a kind of erotic ecstasy and makes him one with his lustful victims. No one else in the major tragedies of the period goes to such extremes or takes such delight in the doing of violence on an enemy.

T. S. Eliot has remarked on the 'suddenness' and 'explosiveness' of *The Revenger's Tragedy* and observed that verse rhythm, imagery, and diction are all directed to the creation of these effects.[9] This art of dramatic violence, as we may call it, is perfected in those speeches and scenes where Vindice acts as pander or *agent provocateur*. Vindice intimates there that all things are caught up in the excitement of rapid motion, engenders in his listener an urgent desire to become part of it, and uses words with a stabbing economy, a perfection of perverse timing, that instantly translates speech into action – 'This night, this hour – / This minute, now –' (II.ii.160–1). There are suggestions of this superb art in *Othello*;[10] essentially, however, it is unique.

IV

Since respect for time was held to be a prerequisite for decorum in word and deed, and since 'grace' was an accepted synonym for 'decorum', time and grace are intimately connected in the thematic structure of *The Revenger's Tragedy*. Grace, however, means much more than decorum; it was a richly complex concept – or set of concepts – in this period. In general, grace is what makes the individual pleasing in the eyes of God or of man. In particular, it is favourable regard, the bounty or forgiveness which cannot be expected as of right: what fallen men hope for from God and needy or erring subjects from rulers and the ruling class. It is also the act of acknowledging what is so given (gratitude is gracious). Grace too is a sense of propriety and of shame. It inheres (as seemliness or decorum) in behaviour which harmonises with the variable requirements of circumstance and, more importantly, with the individual's nature and place in the scheme of things – with his humanity, sex, age, personal ties and social responsibilities. It is honour itself, a name reserved for kings and dukes; and it can be used even as a synonym for 'God'. In the major plays of this period, the Reformation stress on the importance of divine grace in the destiny of man does not have the effect of devaluing the characteristically Renaissance regard for natural grace. Rather, the theological and the secular emphases seem to reinforce each other, so that divine grace is given a rich actuality and natural grace acquires spiritual and sacred resonance (as in the idea of kingship); while the term itself becomes an index of supreme value. When an antithesis arises in the plays, it is not between supernatural and natural grace, but between grace and the absence of all redeeming qualities, or between true and 'affected grace' (*The Malcontent*, III.iii.35).

Influenced by *The Malcontent* and perhaps also by *Macbeth*, the author of *The Revenger's Tragedy* presents the degeneration of the individual and of society as a fall from grace in every sense of the word.[11] Naturally and supernaturally, this play-world has the mark of damnation on it: it is disgusting, deformed, monstrous, demonic; what grace it does possess is simply the mask that covers a hideous reality – the painting of 'Grace the bawd' (I.iii.16) or the deceits of a 'white devil' (III.v.147).

Affected grace is associated mainly with the Duke and his son-and-heir, and displayed on those ceremonial or ritual occasions when grace is most expected. The Duke opens the trial of Junior Brother for rape with a speech of 'confirm'd gravity' whose fitness to time and person is duly applauded by the First Judge (I.ii.11–12). He is later moved to a gracious act of mercy when two kneeling nobles plead on behalf of the imprisoned Lussurioso, an act which is crowned with an appropriately gracious response: 'We owe your grace much thanks, and he much duty' (II.iii.123). Lussurioso flourishes the gracious style as early as the trial when he intervenes to rebuke the flippancy of Junior Brother: 'O do not jest thy doom . . . play not with thy death' (I.ii.49, 53). But it is when his father's death is made public – when he himself is now 'my lord's grace'

(V.i.151) – that his affectation of confirmed gravity is most conspicuous: he refuses to contemplate new honours for the time being and declares that he will speak only of 'Sepulchres, and mighty emperors' bones' (l. 144). Of course, the sole effect of these gracious and graceful performances is to magnify the disgraceful nature of the situation and of what follows in each case. His Grace allows the Duchess to silence the judges, calls the trial to an abrupt halt, and takes his leave on the pretext that 'More serious business calls upon our hours' (I.ii.93); and, having forgiven Lussurioso's 'trespass', he privately admits that that is simply the decorum of moral chaos: 'It well becomes that judge to nod at crimes, / That does commit greater himself and lives' (II.iii.124–5). Lussurioso's rebuke of his rapist brother is followed in the next scene by his plan to seduce Castiza and 'cozen her of all grace' (I.iii.112); and, after his solemn talk about mourning, he promptly accedes to his courtiers' request – while 'old dad's' corpse is still on stage – that revelling should begin. Vindice's elaborate comparison of night, which cloaks the activities of the vicious, with heraldic trappings hired to advertise the vaunted gentility of a dead man and his family and then torn down in the morning, is obviously of central significance: 'thou hang'st fitly / To grace those sins that have no grace at all' (II.ii.134–5). The graces of this royal family are as transient as they are false.

Most of the evils which cannot be masked from view are defined as negations of grace. There is disgrace, either as ignominy or as loss of favour. Disgrace of the first kind is associated mainly with sexual vice. Junior Brother's rape of Antonio's wife, the Duchess's incestuous affair with Spurio, Gratiana's attempt to prostitute her daughter, the discovery of the Duke's body in the greasy doublet of his own pander – these all provoke the same kind of refrain: 'Shame heap'd on shame! / O our disgrace!' (IV.iii.13).[12] Disgrace as loss of favour points mainly to disorders in justice. Whereas Vindice's father was put in 'disgrace' by the Duke and so 'died / Of discontent, the noble man's consumption' (I.i.125–7), discontents 'Disgrac'd in former times' are sought out by the heir-apparent and offered money and office in return for base service (I.i.77–8; IV.i.47–53).

There is also impudence. Although they can act out the appropriate response to disgraceful conduct, the Duke and his family are essentially shameless: 'blushes dwell i' th' country', 'Impudence' is the 'goddess of the palace' (I.iii.5–6). Courtly impudence in its most extreme form is exhibited by Junior Brother and the Duchess during the trial and its aftermath. Junior jokes when questioned about the impulse to commit rape; he jokes too at his brother's rebuke and even at the state of his own soul: 'I thank you, troth; good admonitions, faith, / If I'd the grace now to make use of them' (I.ii.54–5). Nor does imprisonment and the scaffold sober him up.

Like the gulled Pedringano in *The Spanish Tragedy*, he is persuaded to expect a pardon and urged to 'be merry' (l. 89) until it arrives. Although the old episode has been skilfully altered to fit its new context, its original significance remains: this is the mirth of 'a wretch so impudent' that he has become careless of his own damnation; it is the sign of 'monstrous times' when grave crime is 'set so light' (*Spanish Tragedy*, III.vi.34, 89–90). The Duchess, by contrast, has none of her son's mirth, and none of his immature, narcissistic delight in his own outrageousness. Her Grace's stream of insolent interruptions during the trial, her blunt sexual overtures to Spurio immediately afterward, and her impatience with his show of deference and embarrassment, all reflect a contempt for law, morality, and the decencies of social intercourse that has long since ceased to be conscious of its own outrageousness. There is infinite boredom in her dry insistence that 'ceremony has made many fools' (*Revenger's Tragedy*, I.ii.122).

Neither disgrace nor impudence but self-loss is the gravest symptom of the general fall from grace. Of the many expressions of doubt about one's own or someone else's identity in the play, perhaps the most revealing is that of Ambitioso and Supervacuo, whose promise to be gracious to compliant officers 'if we live to be' is preceded by the mock-virtuous admission that they are 'unnaturally employ'd / In such an unkind office, fitter far / For enemies than brothers' (III.iii.25, 5–7). What is continually implied elsewhere is here made explicit: self-loss and uncertain identity are the consequences of betraying some fundamental 'natural loyalty' (II.iii.24).

No one's self-loss comes in for more comment that does that of Gratiana. Partly this is because she is a respectable woman who agrees to prostitute her own daughter, but mainly it is because she is the mother of a fiercely sententious moralist. Her conduct fills Vindice with outraged amazement; it prompts him to wonder 'Whether I'm myself, or no', whether she really is his mother, and if so whether there can be any hope for fallen man: 'Who shall be sav'd when mothers have no grace?' (IV.iv.8–26). Gratiana's name advertises the fact that she is a figure of central significance in the play. Her importance, however, is established not so much by what she says and does as by the effect she has on Vindice. As we listen to his merciless indictment of her disgraceful, unmotherly conduct, we feel compelled to ask: What is his state of grace? Is he himself or no? To consider these questions is to get to the heart of 'the revenger's tragedy'.

The link between Vindice's character and the theme of grace is forged initially from his preoccupation with the niceties of poetic justice. Like many another descendant of Hieronimo, he is determined that the process of making the punishment fit the crime will be liberally 'graced' in every respect (*Spanish Tragedy*, IV.i.50, 62, 82, 154): it will be like a play which shows meticulous respect for the decorum of person, place, time, and action. Vindice strikes this artistic attitude from the moment he is told he must play the part of court pander: 'I have a habit that will fit it quaintly' (*Revenger's Tragedy*, I.i.102). By the time he comes to murder the Duke, too, he is filled with boundless pride and delight in the exquisite propriety of all his arrangements. He has chosen a 'darken'd blushless angle' for the palsied lusts of 'his impudent grace', a 'bony lady' for an 'old surfeiter', a skull which is 'no useless property' in the 'tragic business' but will 'bear a part / E'en in its own revenge'; and he has determined that the villain will die kissing the poisoned mouth of a woman whom he had poisoned for refusing to gratify his lust: time, place, person, and action are all 'fit' (III.v.13–102). Nor does Vindice relax his attention to the graces of art when he comes to murder Lussurioso. That 'my lord's grace' should die watching a masque is, of course, a perfect conceit in itself, but Vindice insists on a perfect performance as well. The costumes in which he and his companions impersonate the official masquers resemble the original 'E'en to an undistinguish'd hair almost', the dance is to be done according to 'the true form', and the swords are to be drawn out 'handsomely' – i.e. gracefully, becomingly (V.ii.17–21). The satiric Vindice mocked the worldling's belief that vice is acceptable if carried off with style: 'Disgrace? a poor thin shell; / 'Tis the best grace to do it well' (III.v.46–7). But by the time he comes to execute justice it is very apparent that he himself has been seduced by this belief. He too participates in the masquerade of grace.

Vindice's fanatical attention to the decorum of his tragic business exaggerates the effect of his compulsive excursions into wild comedy. A comic spirit, of course, is generically proper to a revenger who has something of the Vice and the antic Death in his make-up; and sardonic wit is in keeping with the character of a melancholy satirist who is unusually sensitive to the madness of the world about him.[13] Vindice's humour, however, is presented within an implied framework of psychological, aesthetic, and ethical norms which define most of it as a symptom of confusion and self-loss. It is the emotional chaos of a man suffering from melancholy adust: 'every serious thing for a time, is turned into a jest, & tragedies into comedies, and lamentations into gigges and daunces'.[14] It is the error of a playwright who should know that 'sententious tragedy' requires a confirmed gravity of style.[15] And it is the impudence of a professional moralist who now has 'no conscience' (V.iii.108).

Unlike Hieronimo, and to a far greater degree than Hamlet, Vindice has been shocked and transformed before the action of the play begins: 'My life's unnatural to me, e'en compell'd / As if I liv'd now when I should be dead' (I.i.120–1). Thus his antic disposition is evident from the start: his 'be merry, merry', addressed to the skull of his beloved at the end of his opening soliloquy, is almost a formal indication to the audience to expect an exceptional degree of black humour. This humour ripples through the speeches in which he combines pretended approval with sardonic mockery of the worst vices of the time. It bursts into the open when he prepares the unsuspecting Hippolito to meet the 'delicious' lady he has chosen as bait for his victim the Duke; and it reaches a pitch of sustained, gleeful intensity in the scenes where he is hired to kill himself. Although necessarily muted in the last scenes (where the playwright himself accepts the need for a predominantly grave tone), it by no means vanishes. It finds an outlet in his mocking asides at the expense of the nobleman who is foolish enough to tell the truth and get himself hanged (for Vindice's crime). Finally it modulates into a tone of droll impudence when Vindice, carried away by artistic pride, and confident of a pardon, reveals to Antonio that it was he and Hippolito who killed the old Duke: "twas somewhat witty carried, though we say it. 'Twas we two murder'd him. . . . nay, 'twas well manag'd' (v.iii.97–100).

One important effect of Vindice's mirth is that it relates him to Junior Brother, who cheeked his judge, joked at death, expected a pardon (grace), and died impenitent. The rapist provides himself with an epitaph which could serve Vindice just as well: 'My fault was sweet sport' (III.v.80). But Vindice's jocularity links him also with Ambitioso, Lussurioso, and Supervacuo. Although greatly inferior to him as plotters, they too are given to ecstatic outbursts of glee when their 'rare' devices seem to 'fall out so fit. / So happily' (III.iii.29–30). At such moments, scenic juxtaposition and cunningly placed verbal echoes make us feel that Vindice and Hippolito resemble the opposition 'E'en to an undistinguish'd hair almost'.

The three roles which Vindice adopts to further his plots objectify his condition of self-loss:[16] the significance of these disguises is pinpointed in a remark made by Hippolito in the brief interval between the first and the second: 'So, so, all's as it should be, y'are yourself' (IV.ii.1). The final disguise – as reveller – is an ironic index of total transformation, masques and revels having always been a prime target for Vindice's moral rage. Neither of the other two roles is alien to his inclinations, however: that of melancholy malcontent simply exaggerates what he has already become, and that of pander serves to endorse his boundless contempt for women.

Of the three roles, the last is by far the most important. For, if a single tragic error can be imputed to Vindice, it is not his decision to undertake private justice but his attempt to corrupt his sister and mother at the behest of Lussurioso. The specious reasoning with which he seeks to justify this undertaking to his own conscience represents a somewhat clumsy and unsatisfactory attempt on the part of the playwright to give plausibility to an extraordinary turn in the plot. But it is also indicative of the fact that Vindice is succumbing to the spirit of a world whose perverse, oxymoronic confusion he himself habitually condemns. He and his brother, he says, are 'innocent villains' (I.iii.170). The attempt on his mother and sister is not a betrayal but a test of their 'faith' (l. 178). Not to go through with it would make him untrue to the oath sworn to Lussurioso and blister his soul with perjury (II.ii.37–9). The true nature of the promise to Lussurioso, however, is indicated by the implied comparison with a devil compact and the references to Piato as a witch (I.iii.84–7, 111; V.iii.118). The manner in which Vindice seeks to dignify fidelity to his black promise is no less ironic than Faustus's; but there is a difference between the two exercises in self-deception which is very relevant here. Whereas Faustus saw such fidelity as heroic resolution (fit for a man who 'will be Paris'), Vindice construes it as a form of noble self-restraint (fit for a severe moralist): 'I . . . will . . . forget my nature, / As if no part of me were 'kin to them' (I.iii.180–3). The phrasing disqualifies the note of self-regard; its irony anticipates Lussurioso's later remark to Vindice (as Vindice) that the villain Piato 'hath disgrac'd you much' (IV.ii.124).

The irony which reveals the depth of Vindice's self-deception is at its most acute in the scene where he sets about conjuring 'that base devil out of our mother' (IV.ii.226). So vehement are his denunciations of Gratiana's fall that we instinctively credit him with the complete moral integrity which his stance assumes and are inclined to attend only to the wickedness of his mother. But the phrasing of the dialogue sets up a contrary view and prompts us to recognise that this is a situation where preacher and sinner could well change places handy-dandy. He too is an arch 'dissembler', has 'uncivilly forgot' himself, and acted in a shameful, unnatural, monstrous fashion (IV.iv.3–18). If her conduct has not been 'motherly' (l. 92), his has been anything but filial and brotherly. He more than she should be kneeling in tears to plead for 'kind' forgiveness and to promise: 'to myself I'll prove more true' (l. 37). Vindice unwittingly plumbs the depths of his own psychology here when he apologises to Hippolito for temporarily forgetting the business of revenge: 'Joy's a subtle elf: / I think man's happiest when he forgets himself' (ll. 83–4).

Of course Vindice does show some clear signs of revulsion when he is tempting his mother and sister; and he is genuinely delighted when Castiza proves constant and his mother repents. But the image of a noble self which we see in flashes is not restored in the end; unlike his mother, he is not redeemed. After Lussurioso's death he re-enacts the 'exorcism' scene in gross form, playing the part of an indignant judge in a transparent attempt to shift guilt from himself to another: 'Confess, thou murderous and unhallow'd man' (V.iii.64). And, although he does reveal that it was he who murdered the old Duke, he does so with pride rather than contrition. His wry remark, '''Tis time to die, when we are ourselves our foes' (l. 110) is very apt, but not in the sense that he intends: he simply means that those who reveal their own crimes must face the consequences. We must distinguish this sentence from the expression of humble self-recognition which redeems a later changeling of the tragic stage: '''Tis time to die when 'tis a shame to live'.[17]

That Vindice should be condemned to death by a friend, and die unregenerate, is consistent with the coldly ironic vision which informs the entire play. But the extent of the play's pessimism may, however, have been exaggerated, and certainly the suggestion that it voices a Calvinist view of nature and grace is incorrect.[18] After all, Castiza proves a 'most constant sister' (II.i.45) in scenes which vigorously stamp her character on the play; Gratiana's repentance is an authentic ritual of regeneration; and we hear of other women – martyrs to virtue – in whose natural modesty 'the flush of grace' shone gloriously (I.iii.14; iv.6–9). Despite all the emphasis on human corruption and corruptibility, there is no suggestion that human nature is inherently depraved. Brother kills brother, fathers sleep with their sons' wives, wives seduce their husbands' sons, mothers prostitute their daughters, old men fornicate, and young moralists swoon in ecstasies of sadism. But the play tirelessly insists that this is all a monstrous perversion of nature; the theological position is put clearly by Hippolito: 'how far beyond nature 'tis, / Though . . . many . . . do't (IV.iv.40–1). The ending of the play, too, may be less bleak than is often assumed. If we take the last three scenes as a whole, we can detect a pointed contrast between Lussurioso, the short-lived successor of the old Duke, and Antonio, the nobleman who succeeds him in turn. Lussurioso responds with thinly disguised satisfaction to the suggestion of flatterers ('My gracious lord, please you prepare for pleasure'), utters a hypocritical prayer that he will fit his new role and title ('Then heavens give me grace to be so'), and then inaugurates another reign of demonic revelry. Antonio, however, is unmoved by the ingratiating words of Vindice and Hippolito ('''Twas all done for your grace's good') and condemns them instantly to death for a self-confessed crime; he then attends to the 'tragic bodies', leads off the funeral procession, and ends with a prayer which befits the 'heavy season': 'Pray heaven their blood may wash away all treason'. Thus, unlike his predecessors, Antonio knows what ' is fittest for a duke' and is 'gracefully establish'd' (V.iii.36, 29). However, although the contrast between himself and Lussurioso is obviously intentional, he is undeniably a slight character; he is also old, childless, and without anyone of integrity to lean on. The suggestion of renewal has been half-heartedly advanced, and may well have been only an afterthought.[19]

V

One of the neater ironies of the last act is that Vindice is betrayed to the scaffold by that nimble-tongued loquacity which he so despised in others. He cannot leave his witty murder of the Duke to sleep 'in tongueless brass' (V.iii.113), but must boast it to the world. Thus the terrible – and terribly funny – jibe which he whispers in the ear of the dying Lussurioso follows him to the grave: 'Now thou'lt not prate on't, 'twas / Vindice murder'd thee ... Tell nobody' (V.iii.78–9).

The Revenger's Tragedy belongs with *Titus Andronicus*, *Hamlet*, and *Othello* as a play which follows *The Spanish Tragedy* in making the abuse of speech a major cause and symptom of degenerative change in the individual and society.[20] It takes for granted the belief that the true function of the word is to secure the bonds of society as embodied in marriage and law and proceeds to show a world in which the characteristic action of the tongue is to 'ravish', 'sting', 'poison', 'strike', 'overthrow'.[21] The *dramatis personae* are endowed with a high degree of linguistic consciousness. They seem much concerned with names, titles, and epithets; with truth in speech (the oath 'in faith' occurs over forty times); with good sentencing (both moral–rhetorical and judicial); and with the art of pleading or persuasion. In this realm, however, good names are accorded mainly to the wicked (such as 'Grace the bawd') and even 'foul incest' is called 'but a venial sin' (I.ii.171). Flattery and lies are the common currency of conversation at court. Judicial sentences, if not aborted by interference or 'knavish exposition', are abrupt and irrational: 'this iron-age' can fall 'with a word' on those who displease the great (IV.i.33–5). Aphoristic sentences, although abundant, and ostentatiously fulfilling a neo-classical requirement for the right tragic style, contribute ultimately to the impression of sham and cynicism: we sense a huge gulf between words and deeds, between understood moral norms and actual practice,[22] between a proper gravity of attitude and the Vice-like flippancy which habitually displaces it. And, of the nine or ten occasions when the art of persuasion is practised, on all but two of them it is used to subvert moral and civil law. As this dramatist and his audience understood it, rhetoric was the art of moving and so of changing. From the secular standpoint, its proper function was to convert barbarism to civility, and, from the religious, to convert sinners to the Word. Here it is primarily an art which serves to change everyone for the worse: it is the 'nimble' and 'quick' agent of violent passion (IV.ii.46; iv.34), the instrument for cozening the unwary of all grace. The speech theme, therefore, may be viewed as the linking element in the play's thematic structure; at any rate, its effect on characterisation and on the conduct of the principal scenes is profound.

The importance of speech to the play's meaning and method is registered in the first two scenes. In I.i, the dialogue between Vindice and his family, and the reported dialogues between Hippolito and his master and Gratiana and her husband, posit a contrast between speech which is 'direct and true' (l. 114) and uttered with a seriousness appropriate to the issue, and speech which either conceals thought altogether or is playfully evasive and equivocal. The disorders in language and relationships defined by this contrast are greatly magnified in I.ii. This has a two-part structure, each part dominated by the impudent and voluble tongue of the Duchess. In the first part, her Grace pleads to the Duke for mercy on behalf of her rapist son (who answers questions and rebuke with jests); failing to get any response whatever from her husband, she then uses her own loquacity to stop the judge in mid-sentence (grammatically as well as judicially). In the second part, when she is alone with the bastard, she proceeds to get revenge on the silent Duke ('one of his single / Words would quite have freed my youngest, dearest son' – ll. 102–3) by persuading Spurio that he too has a grievance against 'his wither'd grace' (l. 97) and convincing him that incest would be no more than justice.

The Duchess's persuasions to grace, lust, and revenge are echoed throughout the play in comparable endeavours by Vindice, Gratiana, Ambitioso and Supervacuo, the two anonymous nobles, and Lussurioso. The universality of such endeavour creates a context in which Vindice figures simultaneously as 'a man o' th' time' (I.i.94) and the natural master of his environment. Although drama provides the comprehensive symbol for his manipulative skills, he is in fact more of an orator than an actor–playwright. For him, to change roles is primarily to 'change tongue': as court pimp he will speak saucy and familiar, as melancholy malcontent he will employ a countrified formality (I.iii.37–46; IV.ii.26, 41–6). His histrionic art is essentially an elaboration of his rhetorical genius.[23]

In Vindice's mind, speech is life itself. This conviction is symbolically expressed in the revenge he executes on the Duke: his father's disgrace 'made him die speechless' (III.v.173), so he compels the Duke to witness the incestuous embraces of his wife and son in speechless horror, his tongue poisoned and pinned down by the dagger that soon ends his life (in mid-sentence).[24] The essence of Vindice's fall, however, is not that he puts the tongues of his enemies 'out of office' so violently but that he is seduced by the power of his own: the denomination of Piato as a witch is rooted in a favourite Renaissance metaphor, 'the witchcraft of the tongue'. When Lussurioso asks him to 'bewitch' the ears of a certain young lady with his 'smooth enchanting tongue' (I.iii.111-12), the enthusiasm in his voluble response is so perfectly dissembled that it is also sincere. The wording and the incompleteness of the response (for his master has to cut him short) certainly suggest that this is where his fall begins:

> You have gi'en it the tang, i'faith, my lord.
> Make known the lady to me, and my brain
> Shall swell with strange invention; I will move it
> Till I expire with speaking, and drop down
> Without a word to save me; but I'll work –
>   (ll. 118–22)

Moreover, although he is delighted to discover that 'it is not in the power of words to taint' his 'most constant sister' (II.i.45, 49), there is a trace of real disappointment in his report of partial failure to Lussurioso, and of real vanity in his claim that the words he used would have changed many a right good woman into white money (II.ii.28). Of course, the powerful speeches in which he converts the mother he has so impressively perverted show (as she remarks) that he can plead as persuasively against as for the devil (IV.iv.88). However, the ironies of the scene not only make him the victim of his own sententious indictments; they also hint that the sheer pleasure of orating is what matters to him. Once he gets the tang, pleading for and against the motion can be all one to him; the means and not the end is what absorbs him wholly. Thus the humble and urgently compassionate speeches in which his mother seeks to dissuade Castiza from the path of vice (which she pretends she will follow) provide the only instance in the play of rhetorical art serving its highest end. All else is grossly or subtly perverted.

The almost complete perversion of Vindice's sententious and eloquent self is established in the last act. He who once praised his sister for her just and unequivocal verdict on a self-confessed criminal ('Sister, y' have sentenc'd most direct and true; / The law's a woman, and would she were you' – I.i.114–15), now mocks the innocent courtier who speaks truthfully, and applauds the ruler who condemns him to death without a trial: 'You've sentenc'd well' (V.i.130). He who once used his fiery eloquence to make his mother confess and repent now goes through an impudent charade of moral outrage and legal interrogation in order to shift suspicion from himself to another: 'Law you now, sir; – / O marble impudence! will you confess now?' (V.iii.69–70). Finally, when his long tongue has betrayed him, he recalls the saying of a courtier to the effect that 'time / Will make the murderer bring forth himself' (ll. 116–17; cf. V.i.166–7) and jocularly refers to it as 'a knavish sentence'. It is, of course, the most revered and confirmedly grave sentence in the whole dictionary of dramatic aphorisms.[25]

VI

This double allusion to Time as the author of truth and right is a reminder that Time did not need Vindice's helping hand and tongue at all: the ducal family was already on the way to self-destruction. Yet it must be acknowledged that Vindice is always hero as well as villain and that much of the pride in his final, laconic speech seems right when heard in performance. For Vindice does supervise the purgation of an infected realm, and the wickedness of his chief victims is so absolute that we rejoice in their destruction. His moral passion too, though tainted, is genuine. Indeed, the intensity and vividness of his verbal attacks on corruption, the energy with which he performs his self-appointed task as purger, and the absence of any really challenging antagonist give him an almost magnetic authority on stage.

It is impossible, however, to accord him the status of a tragic character, even though we can see in him the tragic pattern of psychic confusion and self-loss. This is not because he fails to achieve self-knowledge or 'recognition'. Rather it is because (and these two reasons are connected) he amuses himself and us so much, and seems incapable of suffering and inner conflict. It is not the dramatist's intention that Vindice's response to the evils of the world should awaken our compassion: the murder of his betrothed and the virtual murder of his father are quite deliberately placed in a distant past, and his anger is cleansed of all grief and pain; nor is there any poignant contrast between his actual inhumanity and a rich humanity he should be capable of. In fact the corruption of Vindice is presented with the same satiric detachment as are all the other transformations in the metamorphic world he combats. What distinguishes him is that his involvement in the universal process of degenerative change is vastly more interesting than anyone else's. Although his lack of inner conflict makes him an essentially simple character, the almost continual confusion in his make-up of reformer and anarchist, preacher and voyeur, embodies strange and disturbing insights into human nature. The other characters are two-dimensional figures in a morality structure, but Vindice lends substance to Lussurioso's ignorantly-wise sentence: "tis the deepest art to study man' (II.ii.3).

What gives the play its distinction, however, is not the character of its protagonist but its own intense and dynamic unity. The major themes entwine one with the other in a sinuous partnership and combine in turn with characterisation, symbolism, verse, and the shape and tempo of the action in the expression of a single vision. Vindice's unique character is a function of his opposition to and his participation in the 'violence', the impudence, the false graces, the perversions, the confusion, and the volubility that make up the imagined universe to which he belongs.

5 John Webster

Webster, said Eliot, was much possessed by death and saw the skull beneath the skin. The remark has obvious truth, but it would fit the author of *The Revenger's Tragedy* much more exactly than Webster himself; for Webster's two great tragedies show less concern with death – in the sense of mortality and decay – than they do with the art of noble dying. More than any of his predecessors, Webster finds that the heroism which redeems nature from its frailties and vices is the constancy with which a violent end is accepted. Everything else in the lives of his principal characters seems preparatory to this final test; in it, they are brought to accept the huge burden of pain, frustration, and mystery which is life itself.

Those who die nobly in Webster's plays are not the 'great men' – the princes of state and church – who hold the destinies of all in their hands; they are the women and the malcontent intellectuals whom they use, abuse, and despise. Webster seems to find in the feudal system a demonic travesty of natural and divine order. To look up the ladder of degree for models and direction is to follow the road to moral ruin; yet to be one's own example in defiance of the great is a form of suicide.

Concentration of all power in the hands of a few individuals who use law as the instrument of their own diseased will is the primary fact of socio-political experience in *The White Devil* and *The Duchess of Malfi*. 'The oppressor's will' invades the emotional and spiritual life of all men and women, so that violent death becomes – for those who see clearly – a generous manumission. Tyranny, in fact, is so ubiquitous and active that the metaphoric conception of life as a condition of bondage becomes a major symbol with a basis in literal reality.

Disunity and secrecy are among the chief characteristics of life in the realm of tyranny as imagined by Webster. Although society may be committed to the show of unity, the root relationships of man and wife and master and servant are in ruins. Those relationships which are officially acceptable are sterile and unbalanced; those which promise something better are furtive and treacherous. Extensive and idiosyncratic use is made of the Mars – Venus – Harmonia myth in *The White Devil*, giving us a bitter echo of the glories of *Tamburlaine*, *Othello*, and *Antony and Cleopatra*. But a mythical model which comes more naturally to Webster in his investigation of human relationships, and is common to both *The White Devil* and *The Duchess of Malfi*, is the bond or deed of gift between demon and bewitched mortal. His is a world of 'black deeds' (a favourite pun): of dark, conspiratorial acts and commitments which give no lasting satisfaction to the rebellious spirit but quickly confine it to a hell on earth reverberant with the laughter of mockery. It is an outstanding peculiarity of Webster's 'dark deed' – especially in *The White Devil* – that each party to the contract is the other's enticing demon, each the other's victim. From every point of view, relationships are treacherous.

Webster's most comprehensive symbol, however, is not the demonic deed but the Italian setting. This is Italy as filtered through the lens of English Protestantism: a sophisticated land of squabbling, would-be-autonomous princes who cannot escape the sinister overlordship of the Pope and his cardinals; a modern Babylon where rites and ceremonies have become the vehicle for boundless will and pride. With Webster, the myth of Italy – a compound image of religious and secular villainy – is exploited on the stage in its totality for the first time. Given his attachment to the symbolism of demonic deeds, however, Webster's use of the religious side of the Italian myth is understandable, for to the Protestant imagination the Pope and his prelates strongly resembled those familiar spirits who bewitch the unwary with false promises and an empty show of power – Marlowe himself had said as much in the middle scenes of *Doctor Faustus*.

As Webster sees it, tyranny not only reduces society to a shifting agglomeration of secret and deathly relationships; it also divides the individual within himself. Survival means self-betrayal, deceit, the playing of roles 'Much 'gainst mine own good nature'. This kind of psychic disunity is common, of course, to most of the tragedies we have met so far; but it is much more widespread here, and it is greatly intensified by the burden of guilty secrets which most of Webster's characters seem to carry (sometimes half-consciously). For us, getting to know such characters is a slow and erratic business, full of guesswork, and always, we feel, incomplete. The good can astonish us by their sudden descent into baseness of one form or other; the wicked by ghostly stirrings of conscience, compassion, or magnanimity in the ashes of a long-dead self. The most representative inhabitant of this world is the criminal mal-content, twisting between angry self-justification and a bitter recognition that his soul has become a black charnel.

The 'maze' or 'mist' which Webster's characters inhabit is projected by most of them onto the universe.[1] When they look up to Heaven they 'confound / Knowledge with knowledge'; when they contemplate the voyage of death, they go they 'know not whither'; they believe their fate is written in the stars but are convinced there are no spectacles which would help them to read the script.

But these powerful impressions of disintegration, doubt, and doom do not account for the total effect of Webster's tragedies; were that the case, the plays would not be so compelling as they are (nor have given rise to such varying interpretations). Both plays exhibit a retributive pattern which, although not always complete in every respect, goes well beyond what most providentialists would have expected to find in the workings of history.[2] There are delicate yet potent hints (in *The Duchess of Malfi*) of a natural process, at once cyclical and dialectical, whereby the ruins of the present become the fortifications and monuments of the future: in personal terms, those who are destroyed by tyranny but triumph over it spiritually provide inspiration and guidance for those who remember them. There is evidence too in both plays that suffering is not meaningless but brings both self-knowledge and moments of self-expression and communion which are qualitatively finer than anything experienced in times of justice and peace. Cosmic optimism and cosmic pessimism, providentialism and acci-dentalism, free will and determinism: these are all accommodated within the infinitely receding horizons of Webster's metaphysics.

Webster's psychological, moral, and metaphysical subtleties are bound up with the more idiosyncratic features of his construction and style. Construction is notably episodic and very dependent on parallelism for its sense of unity. Webster's use of parallelism differs from that of his contemporaries by its abundance, its delicacy, and its often unsettling effect. Actions and speeches are echoed with strange precision long after the event; what was mere pretence, appearance, or jest becomes reality – or vice versa; the parallel may be such that we cannot easily perceive whether it stresses essential difference or essential sameness. This structural technique creates the impression of a mysterious ironic order within which all is unstable, mutable, unclear. In language there is the quick succession of different styles, the long speeches where every sentence seems a fresh start, the compound sentence without conjunction or subordination. This discontinuous, paratactic method of composition used to be attributed to stylistic gaucherie and, in particular, to undue reliance upon passages culled from other authors. Although its occasional and sometimes gross crudities of effect cannot be denied, it is rightly acknowledged nowadays to be one of Webster's greatest strengths as a dramatic poet. Particularly on stage, it induces a sense of energetic restlessness. It leaves us acutely conscious of the need to reconcile sharply different perspectives on a subject and to supply connections and explanations – whether logical or psychological – for ourselves. And it can inspire a terrible wonder: 'Cover her face: mine eyes dazzle: she died young.'

Another striking aspect of Webster's tragic art is its very high proportion of ritual and ceremonial action.[3] This peculiarity reflects his fondness for static and emblematic images, a tendency to atomise narrative and focus sharply on the patterned significance of the scene. Conjoined as it is with so much violence in language and action, it suggests a quest for striking contrasts and contradictions. In particular, Webster's ceremonialism reveals an obsession with the glittering façade which corrupt power uses to cloak and justify its actions. But it is, of course, a logical consequence of his basic symbolism, Rome, witchcraft, and devilry being all associated with the wilful perversion of divinely prescribed rites. Of Renaissance tragedy in general it may be said that it is a form of ritualised violence much concerned with the violation of ritual; but of no one tragedian is this more true than of Webster himself.

II

The title of *The White Devil* (1612) offers a very exact clue to the nature of its vision and form: in construction, characterisation, and style, it is oxymoronic through and through.[4] In the organisation of his heavily loaded narrative, Webster traces a double pattern of rise-and-fall which demonstrates the incapacity of the principal characters to perceive that the way up, as they have chosen it, is also the way down. The 'most happy union'effected by the pandering Flamineo between his sister and the great duke Bracciano in I.ii seems to bring to all three the happiness they desire; and in Act II that happiness is secured by the removal of the lovers' inconvenient spouses, murdered so cunningly that guilt cannot be legally established. Happiness, however, is undone in Act III when Vittoria is tried for adultery by an ecclesiastical court and confined for life to a 'house of convertites' or penitent whores. This cycle repeats itself more swiftly in Acts IV and V. Bracciano's clandestine visit to the house of convertites parallels his nocturnal rendezvous with Vittoria in I.ii, with the difference that he now offers her the title of duchess and escape to the safety of his own city of Padua. The marriage, however, is a trap laid by Francisco, brother of Bracciano's murdered wife, and the entertainments arranged to grace the wedding provide Francisco with the opportunity for bringing the most happy union to a sudden and horrific end. Webster reinforces and complicates the ironic effect of this design by counterpointing the fortunes of Vittoria and Flamineo with those of Lodovico, the villainous nobleman elected by Francisco as the instrument of their fate: as they rise prosperously 'above law and above scandal', he falls; as they fall, he rises.

This overall pattern of contrarious exchange is continuously apparent at local level in the sequencing and structure of individual scenes.[5] In conjunction with characterisation and style, it creates a sense of chaos so extreme that it can only be called demonic. The play's key words are the synonyms 'turn' and 'convert'. Almost everyone turns, returns, and turns again until they are all, like Marcello, 'turn'd to earth'. Spiritual conversion – a turning from evil to good, from worldliness to religion, from heathenism to Christianity – is a recurrent motif. But all formal declarations of repentance and conversion serve only to conceal or facilitate yet another turn to the bad and are in marked contrast to the authentic regenerations of the last scene. The repentance–conversion motif is, of course, ironically appropriate to the setting. Rome itself is a great House of Convertites where sin wears the garb of rectitude; a historic birthplace of civil and religious order, it is a 'city . . . in a great confusion' which really 'deserves to be call'd Barbary' (IV.ii.204, 212).

The barbarising of Rome and of Romans is rooted in the unleashing of violent passions. Taking the word 'violence' in the simple sense of aggressive fury and force, one could say that this is easily the most violent play of the period. It presents seven killings together with one attempted murder and one wounding. There are scenes of physical assault which include kicking, striking on the face, and stamping on a fallen body. Pistols are fired off twice. In the dialogue there are vituperative exchanges packed with the imagery of warfare, mutilation, and storms. And there is continuous reference to the Furies: 'turning Fury' – a recurring phrase – is the one transformation to which everyone is liable. Indeed, Webster comes as near as is aesthetically possible to producing a play of mere and absolute violence; this he does by ensuring that everything representative of the non-violent is either violence disguised (the quiet of the Trojan horse – IV.ii.200) or doomed to be transformed by the prevailing spirit.

So the confusion of appearance and reality posited by the play's title and fundamental to its whole conception of character and action is not simply a confusion of good and evil, sin 'candied o'er' with the show of grace and virtue.[6] More than anything else, it is a confusion of the universal contraries of Strife and Love. The first is associated in the language of the play with 'division' and all that is 'violent', 'passionate', 'rough', 'loud', 'uncivil', 'wild', 'raging', 'sharp'; the second with 'union' and whatsoever is 'sweet', 'gentle', 'mild', 'peaceful', 'soft', 'tame', 'calm', 'quiet' – the binary vocabulary is extensive and repetitive. Although the two halves of this conceptual antithesis tend on the whole to be identifiable with good and evil, the identification is neither necessary nor stable. Like Kyd, Marlowe, and Shakespeare, Webster assumes that controlled Strife is valorous manhood itself, and that uncontrolled Love means effeminacy, inaction, division: the twin guiding norm is interdependence and distinction, oneness in difference, bonds (ties) and bounds (limits), complementary opposition. The precise nature of this dialectic is indicated with obvious care on a number of occasions, but most notably when the gentle Isabella pleads with her brutally offensive husband not to frustrate the reconciliation she has been trying to effect between them:

> these your frowns
> Show in a helmet lovely, but on me,
> In such a peaceful interview methinks
> They are too too roughly knit.
>   (II.i.168–71)

The last phrase here is doubly oxymoronic: knots are bonds, yet a knitting of the brow spells wrath and division; and rough bonds are a contradiction in terms. Isabella's punning oxymoron pinpoints the threat to harmonious unity posed by a violence which in itself is neither unattractive nor incompatible with love and unity.

Sentences such as these, however, are merely refractions from the Mars–Venus–Harmonia myth, the chief means by which Webster indicates the relationship of his action to the universal dialectic of *discordia concors*.[7] Although there is not a single reference to Mars or Venus, the shaping-effect of their myth on the narrative is unmistakable. From a few hints in the source material, Webster develops for the story of love-and-revenge a background of secular and religious war – 'just' war against both pirates and infidels (compare Shakespeare's amplification of Cinthio's grimly domestic tale in the writing of *Othello*). The martial context is echoed in the play's metaphoric patterns and also in emblematic imagery and pageantry: this culminates in the appearance in armour of Bracciano and his guests to celebrate his marriage with a bout of chivalrous duelling at the barriers – a crowning pageant of Mars and Venus. The love theme too is expanded in ways which are consonant with but not identical to earlier uses of the myth in tragedy. Love is taken in its widest sense as the principle of unity, the binding force. As well as sexual relations, it comprehends kinship, friendship, hospitality, repentance and forgiveness, compassion, 'Christian charity', the Christian religion itself: in short, it signifies 'atonement' (at-one-ment):

> Now you and I are friends sir, we'll shake hands,
> In a friend's grave, together, a fit place,
> Being the emblem of soft peace t'atone our hatred.
> (III.ii.295–7)

The fullest formal expression of love occurs in two rites: the rite of welcome (the play begins and ends with violated hospitality and as in many other plays of the period the word 'welcome' echoes ominously throughout); and the rite of extreme Unction (the final act of kindness, the ultimate reconciliation).

For a number of reasons, it is very important that we should sense the submerged but potent presence of the Mars–Venus myth. It is a source of significant unity in a play whose characteristic effect is one of dense fragmentation and diffusion. It serves to universalise the significance of a uniquely corrupt world which could well be taken as having no reference beyond its own horrendous self. It is closely bound up, too, with Webster's crucial interest in distinguishing between false and true heroism – between Machiavellian violence and martial courage in the first place, and between the mere show and the reality of 'bravery' in the second (as in Chapman's *Bussy D'Ambois*, there is a continuous if covert play on the two meanings of this word). Finally, the myth and its concomitant dialectic function as an instrument of intellectual control over the ambiguous and blurred effects for which the play is notorious: these are not to be judged as evidence of authorial inconsistency or uncertainty. Webster's characters compound confusion with confusion for two reasons. In the first place, they disguise their evil motives or actions behind a show of good. In the second, what is evil in them is not essentially or permanently separated from what is good: the show of virtue may have an authentic element, and the virtuous mask may imperceptibly become the true face (just as the true face of good may in time become a mask for evil). Given Webster's premise about the contrarious constitution of human nature, confusion and error are to be expected; but the premise itself is grounded on a coherent view of universal nature.

To a large extent, confusion (both as error and disaster) stems from the fact that Strife and Love overrun their prescribed limits, so that Strife takes the form of love, friendship, effeminacy, and sensuality, and Love becomes violent, aggressive, cruel – 'personates' masculine virtue and vice (III.ii.136).[8] Much of this is symbolised in the marriage entertainment at which Bracciano is murdered by his chief guest. The function of the barrier (bar) in the chosen form of entertainment is to ensure that knightly exercise does not become mere violence; it is a limit which acknowledges that the rivals are also friends. Thus, when Bracciano is overcome by the poison placed in his beaver by Francisco, and Flamineo cries out, 'Remove the bar: here's unfortunate revels' (V.iii.8), the meaning of Bracciano's fate becomes instantly clear. It has in fact been available to us since I.ii, when his pander jested cynically about the 'paltry enclosures' of marriage and mockingly advised Camillo that the best way to ensure his wife's rebellion would be to restrict her freedom: 'bar your wife of her entertainment' (ll. 89, 95). Webster's point, of course, is that to remove the bar is to turn the two dimensions of chivalry – love and challenge – into something very different, and so put an end to all revels and entertainments.[9]

From the point of view of plot, Bracciano is the play's hero. There are some signs too that he is a tragic hero in the mould of Shakespeare's Antony, for he is a princely leader who risks everything for the woman he loves and dies with her name on his lips. Initially too it seems as if his passion for her has made him eloquent, humble, tender, and protective: a martial man overcome by the spirit of gentleness and peace: 'Your best of rest' are his first words. However, while he is no hypocrite in the role of chivalrous lover, it is a 'character' which quickly 'escapes' him (the phrase, an important one, is Vittoria's). For in the same scene where he appears in this guise (I.ii), he is also presented as the 'adulterous duke' who has gained access to his lady by means of a pander's 'trick . . . to divide' her from her husband (ll. 36, 284). The 'two fair cushions' provided for him and Vittoria to sit on were accepted emblems of lechery and sloth in iconographic tradition.[10] His promise that government, dukedom, wife, children, and friends will not 'divide' him from her is a solemn commitment to wholesale disunity. And the abrupt intervention of Cornelia to condemn the meeting turns him instantly from a gallant lover to a furious tyrant bent on murder – one who has the impudence to make Cornelia the 'Uncharit-able . . . cause of all ensuing harm' (ll. 304–7; cf. l. 270).

Bracciano's martial character is very much to the fore in the next scene, where Isabella makes her painstaking attempt at a family reconciliation. Her husband and brother are quick to engage in a battle of words which hotly promises conflict on the field (II.i.73–9). But Bracciano's heroic threats sound bombastic; and when his wife is temporarily left alone with him, without the protection of Francisco and the Cardinal, he becomes a coarse and brutal bully. The worst aspect of his behaviour here (anticipated in his parting fling at Cornelia) is his willingness to let Isabella assume all responsibility for the oath of divorce which he himself solemnly proclaims at the height of his fury. For the sake of preserving peace between two kingdoms, and because Bracciano is not the fearless fellow he wishes to be, Isabella acts out before her brother and the Cardinal the part of an angry, divisive woman – a role utterly foreign to her nature:

> ISABELLA O that I were a man, or that I had the power
> To execute my apprehended wishes,
> I could whip some with scorpions.
> FRANCISCO What? turn'd Fury?
> ISABELLA To dig the strumpets eyes out. . . .
>
> (ll. 243–7)

A similar pattern is evident in Bracciano's behaviour at the trial of Vittoria, and it results in a similar inversion of the natural order. His bustling intrusion upon the court proceedings promises something heroic, but in effect he is no more than a temporary observer of a painful situation for which he himself is primarily responsible. Instead of rescuing the woman he promised to protect from law and scandal, he contents himself with a few impudent remarks and loud threats and then leaves as abruptly as he came; the Cardinal sums up his performance when he says to Vittoria, 'Your champion's gone' (III.ii.180). This 'amorous gallant' leaves his lady to fend for herself when danger arrives: she must 'personate masculine virtue' and be Perseus to her own Andromeda (ll. 134–6).

Bracciano's next scene (IV.ii) shows the two poles of his nature in their most extreme and unbalanced form. Tricked by Francisco into jealous rage, he threatens to kick the unmoved Flamineo ('Do you brave?') and swears he will cut his 'whore' into atomies; yet this mood turns swiftly to one of idolatrous sexual surrender when Vittoria shrewdly abandons angry self-defence and throws herself in tears upon her bed. This surrender is his undoing, for it leads to the marriage proposal; thus the note of peaceful and harmonious union on which the violent scene ends is thoroughly ominous: 'Couple together with as deep a silence / As did the Grecians in their wooden horse.' (ll. 199–200).

The treacherous manner in which Bracciano is defeated at the barriers – the poisoned helmet, the terrible pain, and the consequent madness – was surely intended to recall the poisoned shirt of Nessus and the death of Hercules, most famous of all martial heroes. Again, however, the model functions ironically. For this piece of treachery matches the manner in which Bracciano had his wife disposed of. Moreover, although he yearns for 'soft natural death . . . joint twin / To sweetest slumber' (V.iii.29–30), he dies raving and terrified, convinced that he will be forgotten on earth and damned hereafter: there is nothing in his death of that spiritual calm, that transcendence of rage and pain which the assurance of lasting fame brings to the dying Hercules.[11] Yet one must not conclude that Bracciano has been a man of straw: that role has been reserved for Camillo, the comical and impotent cuckold 'turn'd soldier' by the 'scorn'd purpose' of his relatives. Although it finds expression only in furious execration, vindictive sentences, and hireling murders, Bracciano's violence is present to us on stage as an awesome reality. The chivalrous 'bravery' to which he is addicted not only tells us that his claim to being a great man is spurious but also suggests that it need not have been so. Bracciano is not a tragic character, yet there is some sense of tragic waste in his turbulent life and death.

Francisco, Duke of Florence, is no less overtly identified with martial bravery than Bracciano. Because of Bracciano's amorous distractions, it is he who has to provide the young Giovanni with his first suit of armour, catechise him in the art of war, and generally serve as the boy's 'pattern' of manhood (II.i.100–8). It is, however, the boy who points, albeit unwittingly, to the chief flaw in his uncle's 'bravery'. It is not simply that his 'noble revenge' against Bracciano is covert and sadistic – a fact which he himself passingly regrets:

> And yet methinks that this revenge is poor,
> Because it steals upon him like a thief, –
> To have ta'en him by the casque in a pitch'd field,
> Led him to Florence!
>
> (V.i.79–82)

The main flaw in his martial bravery is that he leads his troops from behind, a practice which the noble boy rejects: 'If I live / I'll charge the French foe in the very front / Of all my troops . . . not bid my soldiers up and follow / But bid them follow me' (II.i.121–5). Repaying Bracciano, Flamineo, and Vittoria for the death of his sister, Francisco does not administer the poison or deliver the blow himself, but works by meticulous, remote control. So perfect indeed is his control over his instruments of violence that Lodovico, who began by repudiating the cynicism of great men, goes serenely to rack and scaffold, wholly committed to the notion, fed to him assiduously by Francisco, that the black deeds he was paid to perform constitute a glorious enterprise that will bring deathless fame to all those involved. Lodovico's end, which effectively closes the tragedy, is a perfect parody of the Herculean death. Its author however, is not present to applaud it: he has dropped the disguise of 'brave Mulinassar' and vanished.

Francisco's violence is masked not only by martial bravery but also by the spirit of atonement, repentance, and charity. He arranges Camillo's commission so that 'his wish'd absence will give violent way / To Duke Bracciano's lust' (II.i.375–6) and has Lodovico recalled from exile to act as a revenger: nevertheless he joins with the Cardinal in the pretence of assisting Isabella's attempt to effect a reconciliation with Bracciano and reform his behaviour; he even makes friends with Bracciano in this scene and rebukes his sister for her apparent failure to 'Grow to a reconcilement'. After Isabella has been murdered, he is even more careful to cultivate a peace-loving image, assuring the Cardinal that despite his wrongs he has abjured 'the horrid lust of war' and 'turn'd all marble'. This note of Christian idealism is even incorporated in the charade of martial heroism which cloaks the murders of the last act. Mulinassar is a 'brave soldier' of 'iron days', but he is also – like Othello – a christianised Moor who has done 'honourable service 'gainst the Turk'. His two companions – Lodovico and Gasparo in disguise – have undergone an even more thorough conversion; having renounced the court and fought against the enemies of Christ, they are now on their way back to join the strictest of Franciscan orders, the Capuchins; and it is in the habit of these charitable friars that they come to strangle Bracciano (his Last Rites) and stab Vittoria, Flamineo, and Zanche to death.

Although no warrior, the Cardinal too is part of the general confusion of strife and love (or peace). The studied homily in which he ostensibly attempts to reform Bracciano and 'end the difference' (II.i.96) between him and Isabella makes apt points. But its combination of unctuousness and bluntness seems designed only – like 'the soft down / Of an insatiate bed' (ll. 31–2) – to arouse violent passion (which it does); far more important, however, he himself is already involved with Francisco in the vengeful plot to give Bracciano's lust its violent way. At the trial of Vittoria his earlier criticism of the two angry brothers-in-law for failing to 'word it' within 'a milder limit' (l. 80) rebounds ironically upon him when he slips abruptly from the role of ecclesiastical judge into that of a prosecuting lawyer who hurls bitter abuse at the defendant ('poor charity' is 'seldom found in scarlet', remarks Vittoria). His behaviour after he becomes Pope is extremely puzzling, for it is then that he seeks to prevent Francisco from pursuing revenge for the deaths of Camillo and Isabella. Perhaps he is satisfied with the sentence of banishment and excommunication on the escaped sinners and is now bent on acting like a true embodiment of Christianity. Or perhaps the explanation for his apparent change lies in the significance of his Black Book. Has he compiled it because he is 'a worthy member of the state', anxious to protect it by the discovery of crime (IV.i.69–71), or is it an instrument in the pursuit of revenges even more Machiavellian than those of Florence? Constrained perhaps by history (which records that Cardinal Montalto became a fairly respectable pope), Webster leaves the question open. But it is hard to forget the sententious comment to which Florence is inspired by the Black Book: 'Divinity, wrested by some factious bloods, / Draws swords, swells battles, and o'erthrows all good' (ll. 96–7).

The only important character in the play who makes no pretence to nobility of motive or conduct is Flamineo. As pander and hit-man, he personifies the prevailing spirit of division and violence. He procures his sister, murders his brother and brother-in-law, arranges the poisoning of his lady, disowns his mother and effectively drives her mad, and is about to kill his sister and mistress when the 'Franciscans' intervene to kill all three. Flamineo's sins all proceed from his cheerful commitment to the Machiavel's principle of self-advancement at any price. Quite deliberately, he has rejected the soldier's career and its code of simple honesty (chosen by his brother) for the plain reason that they are very unprofitable: great men are far more inclined to pay their all-purpose secretaries than their brave captains (III.i.36–63; v.i.116, 133–42).

Flamineo's cold-blooded killing of 'the virtuous Marcello' might well make him seem the most villainous character in the play. Yet this is not the case, for Webster shows that the younger brother's end, and the consequent madness of Cornelia, are really a kind of self-destruction. Marcello and his mother fiercely condemned Vittoria's adultery and Flamineo's 'policy'; but, when Isabella and Camillo are disposed of and Bracciano proposes marriage, they ask no questions and quietly move from Francisco's court to Bracciano's. At Padua, the moral fervour with which they condemned Vittoria's relationship with Bracciano finds a new object in Flamineo's relationship with the black Zanche; but now their criticisms smack of hypocrisy and their verbal energy has become physical. Cornelia strikes Zanche, Marcello kicks her and threatens to cut her throat. Finally he asks an upstart lord (his 'noble friend') to bear the sword of challenge to his brother (now his 'opposite' – v.ii.2). This gesture marks the complete 'conversion' of virtuous mother and son; with symbolic propriety, Marcello is killed with his own sword.

Although treacherous and violent, and capable of specious self-justification (I.i.315–54), Flamineo has a degree of moral honesty which helps to distinguish him from almost everyone else. But the important distinction is his courage. He becomes the enthusiastic spokesman for

'Mulinassar's' martial reputation simply because Mulinassar voices so well that very contempt which he himself feels daily for the great men and the courtiers who are Colossuses in the chamber and pigmies in the field. Twice before the last scene his courage is shown in action against men who presume to despise him: against an indignant Count Lodovico ('That e'er I should be forc'd to right myself, / Upon a pandar' – III.iii.126–7); and against a fuming Bracciano ('In you pandar! . . . do you brave? do you stand me?' – IV.ii.49–51). The Count and the Duke both remember their humiliation when they are in a position to retaliate unopposed: petty vindictiveness which merely confirms Flamineo's exposure of their spurious valour. Lodovico's retaliation is, of course, Flamineo's death blow; and it is his reception of that blow which establishes his perfect valour. But Flamineo's death cannot be considered in isolation from that of his sister and black mistress; for his death and theirs are a union in noble courage which allows them to transcend the base, divided world of 'great men'.

A useful little key to the character of Vittoria is the pompous lawyer's reference to her as a 'diversivolent woman' (III.ii.28) – where the nonce word means 'desiring strife'. The phrase is appropriate not only in the sense that she provokes violence and division, but also in the higher sense that her relationship with Bracciano could or should be a union of Venus and Mars. That certainly is how the pair see their 'most blessed union' in I.ii. Avoiding the conventional 'cruelty' of the courtly mistress, Vittoria responds to his appeal for pity and is greeted as 'a sweet physician'; and, when she in turn tells him of her distress, he responds in kind: 'Sweetly shall I interpret this your dream' (ll. 209, 259). In the dream, which she recounts with lilting feminine hesitancy, Vittoria is presented as a sad, prayerful figure, Bracciano as 'harmless', Isabella as a 'fell Duchess', and Camillo as a brute who joins this 'Fury' in verbal and physical attack on the two lovers – until a timely whirlwind removes them to the 'base shallow grave that was their due'. The dream, of course, functions as a perfect inversion of the relevant mythical relationship. Venus here is not pacifying Mars or inspiring him to chivalrous exploits; she is a Fury in disguise who is whipping him on to murder his 'sweetest duchess' (IV.ii.99) and her own harmless husband.

At the trial, Vittoria's white devilry reveals the same ingredients as here. She appeals to her 'modesty' and 'womanhood', protests that beauty, gay clothes, and a merry heart are 'All the poor crimes' she is guilty of, and assures her judge that her presence will make the house of convertites 'honester . . . and more peaceable' than a cardinal's soul. But when the sentence is delivered, she tells the Cardinal–judge to drown in his own spittle and cries, 'A rape, a rape!'; as the Cardinal remarks, 'She's turn'd Fury' (III.ii.273–8). What characterises her total performance here, however, is neither false gentleness nor mere fury but a controlled anger which is indistinguishable from great courage. She 'outbraves' (l. 74) every accusation with cool disdain and impudent lies, and turns defence into attack with justifiable criticisms of legal and ecclesiastical impropriety. This is 'adulterate' virtue (I.i.51), and it may even be mere 'bravery' rather than the real thing; but it commands respect in its context, and it is an excellent rehearsal for her confrontation with death.

Vittoria oscillates between a violent kind of courage and a show of female gentleness in dealing with Bracciano's jealous rage and Flamineo's menacing proposal of the suicide pact. In the first of these scenes (as already noted), gentleness prevails; in the second, violence: as she and Zanche stamp wildly on the fallen Flamineo, they become comically identifiable with 'the infernal Furies' to whose care they consign his soul (v.vi.136). One purpose of this amazing scene is to anticipate in jest the role which Flamineo will soon play in earnest, that of instructor and 'pattern' in the art of dying. The role is proposed as part of the women's evasive tactics: 'Gentle madam / Seem to consent, only persuade him teach / The way to death' (ll. 72–4). Flamineo accepts the role with mock enthusiasm ('Thou dost instruct me nobly'), delivers his protracted farewell to the world with Stoic flair, and 'dies' urging imitation: 'as you are noble / Perform your vows and bravely follow me.'

The speed with which the tables are turned on the triumphant Flamineo with the arrival of the 'Franciscans' heightens the effect of his laconic Stoicism when the 'violent death' he has extolled to Vittoria and Zanche looks him in the face: 'Fate's a spaniel. We cannot beat it from us.' This contrasts with the reaction of Vittoria: still trying to avoid the inevitable, she pleads for 'gentle pity' from her stony captors. Attention is then focused once more on Flamineo as he responds to the gloating of those who have him completely in their power:

> LODOVICO. Sirrah you once did strike me, – I'll strike you
> Into the centre.
> FLAMINEO. Thou'lt do it like a hangman; a base hangman;
> Not like a noble fellow, for thou seest
> I cannot strike again.
> LODOVICO. Dost laugh?
> FLAMINEO. Would'st have me die, as I was born, in whining?
> GASPARO. Recommend yourself to heaven.
> FLAMINEO. No I will carry mine own commendations thither.

LODOVICO. O could I kill you forty times a day
    And use't four years together; 'twere too little:
    Nought grieves but that you are too few to feed
    The famine of our vengeance. What dost think on?
FLAMINEO. Nothing; of nothing: leave thy idle questions –
    I am i' th' way to study a long silence,
    To prate were idle, – I remember nothing.
    There's nothing of so infinite vexation
    As man's own thoughts.

(V.vi.190–206)

This is no ordinary exchange of words. It is a duel in which the captive strips the captor of all vestige of triumph and quite undoes his assumption – signalled in the contemptuous 'Sirrah' – that nobility is a function of class. Flamineo's noble example here has its effect on his sister, who is now inspired to 'welcome death / As princes do some great ambassadors' and to deny her killers their claim even to basic manliness: ''Twas a manly blow – / The next thou giv'st, murder some sucking infant, / And then thou wilt be famous.' This in turn has a profound effect on Flamineo, turning contempt into admiration and furious hatred into love: 'Thou art a noble sister – / I love thee now . . .'. Zanche too is affected by the example of both, so that her 'unalter'd complexion' alters the application of Francisco's mocking oxymoron: 'O noble wench' (V.iii.258). That the black servant should die constantly with the lover and mistress she fully intended to betray does not diminish the nobility of their end (as some have suggested). It stresses the power of Flamineo's noble instruction and enhances the sense of unity in a divided world. And it helps to set up a firm contrast with what follows. When Count Lodovico says to his companions – as they are seized by Giovanni and the guards – 'Why then let's constantly die all together, / And having finish'd this most noble deed, / Defy the worst of fate', we are in a position to distinguish between true nobility (bravery, love, unity) and false.

III

A notable element in the heroic achievement of Flamineo and Vittoria is the way they make 'fear . . . convert to laughter' (V.ii.8–9). Exceptional in that it wins from us an unequivocally sympathetic and approving response, their laughter in the face of death is otherwise typical of its environment. For this is a tragedy which accommodates the comic spirit to a remarkable degree and at the deepest level. J. R. Mulryne has pertinently remarked that Webster's humour in *The White Devil* 'sets at a distance the anarchy it embodies and yet in some way intensifies it'.[12] One could go further and claim that it intensifies the impression of anarchy precisely because it is conceived as a major symptom of that anarchy. Since demonism provides the play with its controlling metaphor (most of the characters are seen by others as cunning devils), a vein of cruel and mocking humour was perhaps to be expected. What is remarkable, however, is the thoroughness with which this humour has been subordinated to the contrarious design of the whole. Laughter here invariably seeks to degrade or displace its natural opposite, gravity and grief. It may command our partial assent by virtue of its attachment to a justifiably satiric attitude or a fitting retribution, but we are never in doubt about its essentially anarchic character. It is an instrument of malice and aggressive self-assertion; it creates division and confusion.

In his preface to the play, and later in the text itself, Webster acknowledges the disorderly implications of tragic laughter and even hints at an affinity between the confusions of his tragic art and those of the shoddy world which he himself as playwright has to cope with. Had he been writing for a 'full and understanding auditory' instead of 'the uncapable multitude', then he would readily have produced a sententious tragedy 'observing all critical laws, as height of style, and gravity of person'; instead, he is forced to accept that the 'weighty business' of his tragedy 'must have some idle mirth in't, / Else it will never pass' (IV.i.119–20). Given the undoubted sincerity with which he hankered after the neo-classical purities of Chapman and Jonson, Webster's whole-heartedness and skill in pursuing the mixed mode is somewhat surprising. He leaves us in no doubt, however, that the artistic fusion which he himself accomplishes mirrors a confusion of opposites and that the laughter we are allowed to indulge in is at worst Satanic and at best Democritean. Invoked in the second line of the play, Democritus was well known as a perfect type of the melancholy man; so distressed was he by the disorders of the world that he laughed continually, even at tragic spectacles. Thus Democritean laughter signifies an invasion of the human psyche by the world's chaos; it is a loss of emotional equilibrium and moral discrimination.

The quality and direction of the play's humour are exactly unfolded in the opening scene. Gasparo and Antonelli here respond to the sentence of banishment on their friend Lodovico with a combination of grief and gravity which seems entirely appropriate to the occasion. In reality, however, they view the sentence as casually as they do the 'violent sins' which provoked it (they expect to get him a quick reprieve), so that the role of grieving, sententious friends is one they are playing with lightly concealed mirth. They even go so far as to tease the disgruntled Lodovico with allusions to fair-weather acquaintances who now 'Laugh at your misery', 'Jest upon you, / And say you were begotten in an earthquake' (I.i.24–7).

Being directed at whatsoever is most serious and painful in life, the play's humour finds its most characteristic expression in those scenes where the rites of the dying and the dead are made the object of derision. The first scene of this kind discloses with singular exactness its relation to the general design of violent contrariety: in the dumb show which reveals to Bracciano the process of his wife's murder, Isabella's body is *'convey'd out solemnly'*, with *'sorrow expressed in Giovanni and in Count Lodovico'* – but the murderers *'depart laughing'* (II.ii.23, s. d.) and the bereaved husband responds with cheerful satisfaction: 'Excellent, then she's dead.' The representative nature of these scenes of funeral mirth is apparent from the fact that most of the other comic exchanges seem to echo or pre-echo them. For example, the jesting reaction of Gasparo and Antonelli to the 'violent sins' and severe punishment of Lodovico anticipates the demonic mockery with which Gasparo and Lodovico administer their 'last rites' to the dying Bracciano; so too Bracciano's jocular explanation to the court for his attentiveness to the widowed Vittoria ('Why my charity, my charity . . .') is heard again when Vittoria, about to be widowed a second time, is asked by the 'friars' to leave the chamber 'for charity, / For Christian charity' (V.iii.172–3).

Although all the major characters mock what is grave or painful, in Flamineo this is a habitual tendency. His humour, of course, is inseparable from the qualities which make him so attractive on stage: his love of play-acting, his contempt for fraudulence, his sense of the absurd, his resilience. But it also identifies him as the impresario of chaos. He it is who orchestrates the mirth which surrounds the misery and death of his mistress. After her death, too, he scorns to 'counterfeit a whining passion' and opts instead for a feigned garb of mirth / To gull suspicion' (IV.i.30–1; ii.304). The melancholy pact which he makes with Lodovico mocks not only a fashionable pose but also Lodovico's probably genuine mourning for 'The deceas'd duchess' (III.iii.61). And his suicide pact with Vittoria inveigles her into frantic derision of his own supposed death agonies: a performance which he thoroughly enjoys.

Twice in the last act, however, Flamineo's anarchic wit is eclipsed by a funeral gravity which it sets out to undo. The mourning Giovanni – in happier times a 'witty prince' (II.i.137) – refuses to 'be merry' at his impudent behest and asserts his new authority by ordering the jester's

ejection from all the places that 'owe him reverence' (V.iv.12, 34). The mad
Cornelia's gravely beautiful lament for Marcello, which Flamineo dismisses in advance as 'superstitious howling', affects him so deeply that he is
overcome for a time by melancholy feelings of guilt and remorse. His awed
exclamation to Bracciano's ghost – a product of this melancholy – exactly
defines the nature of the two reversals which have befallen him: 'What a
mockery hath death made of thee? / Thou look'st sad' (ll. 125–6).

In addition to showing that Flamineo too is subject to the prevailing
retributive pattern of laughter converted to fear, these incidents serve to
give him some claim to our compassion; beyond that, they sharpen the
heroic effect of his laughter in the face of his own death. Moreover, the
confrontation with Giovanni is a meeting of opposites which helps to
consolidate the prince's own role as a norm figure. In a morally rudderless
and emotionally confused society, Giovanni provides a model of noble
living not only by his determination to lead his men from the front but also
by the marriage of love and duty shown in his mourning for his mother and
later his father. Appearing in black, he dominates the conclusion of the
trial scene; his lament for his mother, and his poignant recollections of her
private griefs (once the subject of 'excellent laughter' – II.i.276), move even
Francisco to tears: the episode is designed to suggest that this is a prince
whom the world should 'imitate . . . in virtue' as well as in the colour of his
garments (III.ii.310–12). The same idea is advanced when Bracciano's
death agony begins and the boy's cry of grief counterpoints that of
Vittoria – 'O my lov'd lord' (V.iii.7):

> GIOVANNI. O my most lov'd father!
> BRACCIANO. Remove the boy away, –
>   Where's this good woman? had I infinite worlds
>   They were too little for thee. Must I leave thee?
>   (ll. 15–18)

Bracciano's action postulates a tragic rejection of true love in favour of a
doubtful or false one (cf. 'Remove the bar' – l. 8), a point which is
confirmed by the subsequent contrast between a Giovanni whose grief is
unassailable and a Vittoria whose 'mourning' withers before Flamineo's
mockery.

It is commonly held that the hopeful note at the end of this tragedy is
extremely muted if not illusory. Giovanni, it is pointed out, is a mere boy
who, according to Flamineo, 'hath his uncle's villainous look already'
(V.iv.30); and, although Francisco's henchmen taste the prince's justice, the
great Machiavel himself remains untouched. However, the circumstances

in which Flamineo's sour comment is made (he has just been ejected from court for his impudent mirth) suggest that the opposite view of Giovanni, expressed by Gasparo in the opening line of the same scene, is the correct one: this generation has never seen 'a sweeter prince'. The more 'capable' among Webster's audience and readers would have known that the Duke of Bracciano's son grew into a fine young prince who was received with honour by Queen Elizabeth when he visited London in 1601;[13] and believed, too, that his uncle, Francesco de Medici, met an appropriate end – murder by poisoning – a few years after the death of Vittoria.[14] Much as in *Edward II*, then, the characterisation of the 'sweet prince' – witty and grave, loving and courageous – as a norm by which the moral and emotional chaos of his father's and uncle's world is understood and judged conforms to historical fact. More important, however, it is very carefully integrated to the design of the whole play.

However, one must not overemphasise the gradual emergence of Giovanni as an ethical model. It is primarily in the deaths of Flamineo and Vittoria – their union in courage and love – that the positive aspect of the tragedy finds expression. Webster perhaps has strained too hard to produce a fraternal version of the union-in-death achieved by Antony and Cleopatra: Flamineo's murderous hatred of Vittoria prior to the end seems very contrived, a mere device to justify the obligatory reconciliation (why should she wish to deny him his overdue wages?). Yet Webster's care to make their death a union of courage and love, a reconciliation of opposites, accords with the direction of his thinking in the play as a whole. It is a mode of thinking which calls in question the view that in this play he fails to penetrate 'the surface violence or anarchy of life to illumine the underlying pattern and meaning of man's fate'.[15]

IV

Webster's choice of a woman as the protagonist for each of his two major tragedies reflects his intense concentration on mankind as the helpless victim of oppression and on its capacity for unexpected extremes of heroism. This twin preoccupation is noticeably more acute in *The Duchess of Malfi* (c. 1614). Vittoria is just barely the principal character in *The White Devil* (the play's title might plausibly be referred to the prevailing spirit of her world rather than to herself in particular). But the Duchess, although she dies in the fourth act, is the animating spirit of the action throughout. Moreover, one whole act is given to her death, and she dies with a nobility which is matched by no one else in the play. She is unique in her suffering and her heroism.

Because she is noble by nature as well as by birth and marriage (she is warm-hearted, gay, courageous, and wholly without malice), the cruel death which she suffers at the instigation of her evil brothers evokes an extreme sense of pity and waste. The question arises, however, as to whether she is simply the innocent victim of an external evil, a heroine of high melodrama rather than tragedy,[16] or whether some culpable error or weakness on her part activates the evil forces which threaten her. To put the question more concretely: Is she utterly different from her brothers, or has she something in her noble nature which relates them to her as members of the same tragic family, victims of the one curse? It is of course a notoriously divisive question and has to be approached warily. The view to be argued here is that Webster does indeed assign to the Duchess a touch of culpable frailty, although in an exceptionally oblique and compassionate manner.

An instructive approach to the Duchess's tragic flaw, as well as to the meaning of the play as a whole, is by way of Webster's somewhat eccentric structure. The problem of the protagonist's death occurring in Act IV is solved much in the manner of *Julius Caesar*:[17] everything that happens in the last act is a working out of the consequences of her murder, while the echo scene – a quasi-ghost scene – keeps her memory alive and intimates that her spirit will triumph over those who sought to destroy it.

The echo scene (V.iii) is unashamedly (and beautifully) theatrical; but it has been carefully anticipated and in fact is but one of many signs of an intense interest in the effect of echo. In this tragedy, echo (the word itself occurs several times outside the echo scene) is Webster's delicate technique of repetition and parallelism become subject and theme; it is an integral part of his whole vision of reality. In general, it stands for memory and the relationship between present and past, and so has psychological, ethical, and metaphysical implications. There is the impersonal past of history, imaged in reverend monuments and the ruins of cities and civilisations: this tells the reflective that it is impossible to escape necessity, that with prudence it may be possible to postpone the inevitable end ('the dead stones seem to . . . give you good counsel'), and that death and life, destruction and creation are interdependent ('this fortification / Grew from the ruins of an ancient abbey'). There is also the vital, personal past of human ties, whether in the aspect of admiration and love ('still methinks the duchess / Haunts me') or of obligation ('I do haunt you still . . . I have done you / Better service than to be slighted thus'). There is too the personal past of misdeeds that will not die, being part of a universal process of cause and effect that brings the retributions of the present ('O Justice! / I suffer now for what hath former been'). The past is urgent reality, an organic part of the present and the future; it is a being, sometimes ghostly and sometimes very substantial, that says, 'Let me quicken your memory....' It may be forgotten or ignored, but it will not go away.

Looked at more closely, the theme of memory and the living past emerges as a common strand running through most of the play's themes and motifs. It inheres in the following:

(a) *The theme of providence* (human and divine, but mainly human).
The root sense of 'providence' is 'seeing ahead', but for a full definition of the term as understood by Webster's contemporaries we could turn to a passage at the beginning of Ralegh's *History of the World* (1614):

> Now Providence ... is an intellectual knowledge, both fore-seeing, caring for, and ordering all things, and doth not onely behold all past, all present, and all to come, but is the cause of their so being, which Prescience ... is not: and therefore Providence by the Philosophers (saith St Augustine) is diuided into Memory, Knowledge, and care: Memory of the past, knowledge of the present, and care of the future: and we ourselues account such a man for prouident, as, remembering things past, and obseruing things present, can by iudgement, and comparing the one with the other, prouide for the future, and times succeeding.[18]

It is from just this perspective that Webster begins his investigation into a tragic episode from the history of the royal house of Arragon and Castile. Newly returned from France, Antonio explains that its 'judicious king' keeps both state and people in 'a fix'd order' by acting on the advice of 'a most provident Council, who dare freely / Inform him the corruption of the times' as well as what he 'ought to foresee'; the King believes that when ruling thus he is acting in harmony with divine providence – his 'blessed government' (as Antonio terms it) and 'His Master's masterpiece' are one (I.i.5–22). Antonio does not specify the importance of memory in this ideal mode of government, but, since his own memory of his stay in France is still so very much alive in his outlook and 'habit' (l. 3), we are necessarily conscious of it. The providence theme keeps recurring in the play, and on a number of occasions is advanced quite explicitly. This explicitness becomes dramatic irony when the Duchess, rejecting the good counsel of Cariola, and following the advice of Bosola, proclaims, 'Prepare us instantly for our departure: / Past sorrows, let us moderately lament them, / For those to come, seek wisely to prevent them' (III.ii.320–2; cf. v.iii.30–1).

(b) *The theme of time.* Time is set in specific antithesis to Chaos and identified with the still-shining stars and the 'smiling seasons of the year' (IV.i.97–100). It dictates 'the art of patience' ('take time for't') and is ominously invoked as a retributive possibility when violence of any kind is in the ascendant: 'give your foster-daughters good counsel; tell them that the devil takes delight to hang at a woman's girdle, like a false rusty watch, that she cannot discern how the time passes' (II.ii.24–7). But time is also seen at one point as the medium through which divine providence operates in a benignly corrective manner to bring good out of evil, order out of chaos:

> Heaven hath a hand in't; but no otherwise
> Than as some curious artist takes in sunder
> A clock or watch when it is out of frame,
> To bring't in better order.
>
> (III.v.62–5)

(c) *Madness.* There are two degrees of madness: the clinical insanity of Ferdinand (in Act V) and the Bedlam dancers, and the temporary loss of rational control and judgement suffered by those swayed by strong passion, whether wrath ('Are you stark mad?'), or sexual desire ('A fearful madness'), or ambition ('a great man's madness'). Pertinent here is Bosola's point that madness means loss of memory (V.ii.290–2).

(d) *Identity and constancy.* As usual in Renaissance drama, these two concerns are closely related and fundamental to the playwright's thinking about the nature of tragic fall and recovery. The subplot brings them to attention with noticeable overtness. Julia tells the Cardinal that if he is true to himself he will share his secret with one he has loved 'These many winters ', and that if he were constant he would remember the fine things he said 'when you woo'd me first' (V.ii.239; II.iv.38). Since he knows that Julia protests her love just as loudly to her husband as to him, and since he believes that no woman is 'fixed' and 'constant', the Cardinal finds these exhortations amusingly meaningless; in his view, the governing norm in relations between men and women should be an unreflecting, animal deter-mination to satisfy the desire of the moment (ll. 10–30).

Webster's use of such interconnected ideas as discrimination, decorum, and the ethical model should perhaps be viewed as an extension of the identity–constancy theme. It is indicated on several occasions that those who are to be an 'example to the rest o' th' court' should be careful to express and sustain important differences in their outward behaviour. The travelled Antonio, for example, remembers that 'the distinction . . . show'd reverently' in those countries where courtiers remained unhatted – despite the coldness of the climate – in the presence of the prince; he resists the Duchess's (perhaps teasing) suggestion that such customs are ceremonies which have nothing to do with duty (II.i.120–8). Conversely, however, it is taken as wisdom for princes and subjects alike to remember that at root – historically and pyschologically – we are all the same:

> say you were lineally descended from King Pepin, or he himself, what of this? search the heads of the greatest rivers in the world, you shall find them but bubbles of water. Some would think the souls of princes were brought forth by some more weighty cause than those of meaner persons – they are deceived, there's the same hand to them; the like passions sway them . . . .   (ll. 96–104)

(e) *Fame*. The true test of fame (also 'honour', 'reputation') is to live in men's memory after death. Those whose 'greatness was only outward' are 'laid by, and never thought of', frozen footprints that vanish in the sun. But those who achieve 'Integrity of life' (the phrase means moral rectitude, but has connotations of unity, coherence of word and deed, duty and conduct) are crowned 'nobly, beyond death' and become types of greatness for posterity (V.v.42ff.). The Elizabethans, it must be stressed, had a special dread of being forgotten after death.[19] This was reflected in the sumptuousness of their funerals and funerary art; and it left its mark on the drama. After *Richard III* and *Edward II*, disrespect for the rites (rights) of the dead becomes a common symptom of serious socio-political disorder. After *Hamlet*, too ('I have some rites of memory in this kingdom'), and with Webster in particular, the brevity of the widow's tears is a favourite variation on the theme of woman's inconstancy. We might dismiss Flamineo's words on this topic as a piece of conventional railing:

> O men
> That lie upon your death-beds, and are haunted
> With howling wives, n'er trust them, – they'll re-marry
> Ere the worm pierce your winding-sheet: ere the spider
> Make a thin curtain for your epitaphs.
> (*White Devil*, V.vi.154–8)

Yet these words have an impressive poetic intensity. Moreover, they voice a fear which must have gnawed at the soul of Bracciano. When the jeering 'Franciscans' tell him, 'thou shalt be . . . forgotten / Before thy funeral sermon', a cry is uttered which seems to rise from the depths of Hell: 'Vittoria? Vittoria!' (V.iii.164–6). Webster returns (compulsively, it would seem) to this subject in the first scene of *The Duchess of Malfi*, where he dramatises a stark contrast between Antonio's view of the widowed Duchess's behaviour and that shared by her brothers. For Antonio it is exemplary, 'divine'. For them, the lavish revels now ending at her court are proof that she is just another 'lusty widow'; they receive with open scepticism her protestation that she will never remarry: 'So most widows say: / But commonly that motion lasts no longer / Than the turning of an hour-glass – the funeral sermon / And it, end both together' (I.i.190–204, 301–5). This antithesis clung to Webster's memory, for he reworked it in his characters of 'A vertuous widow' and 'An ordinarie Widow'. The first 'thinkes shee hath traveld all the world in one man; the rest of the time she directs to heaven'; she has laid her husband's body 'in the worthiest monument that can be . . . buried it in her owne heart'. The second 'is like the Herald Hearse-cloath; she serves to many funerals, with a very little alteration; and the end of her teares beginnes in a husbande'.[20]

(f) *Ceremony*. Like the echo, this is an aspect of meaning and form which Webster names quite often. It is also the most conspicuous element in the play's network of echoes; this is because rites and ceremonies, as Hooker recalled, are the chief means by which we relate the present to the past[21] – without Ceremony, remarks Chapman, memory dies (*Hero and Leander*, III.121). What is echoed most insistently in the play is the moment when the widowed Duchess throws aside 'all vain ceremony', marries her unprepared steward in a secret exchange of vows (a version of the legally acceptable contract *per verba de presenti*), and says defiantly, ''tis the church / That must but echo this' (I.i.456, 492–3). This tragic choice is heard again when the Duchess tries to dispense with the custom of removing the hat in the presence of the prince (''Tis ceremony more than duty' – II.i.122); when she and the Cardinal converge at the shrine of Loretto, she to 'feign a pilgrimage' (III.ii.207), he to 'resign his cardinal's hat' in favour of the sword – the Second Pilgrim expects 'A noble ceremony', but the event ends in a manner which bespeaks its true nature, with the Cardinal tearing his sister's wedding-ring from her finger 'with such violence' (III.iv.4–7, 36). The tragic choice is echoed too when the Duchess denounces Ferdinand for calling her children by Antonio bastards (he has, of course, no real evidence that she is married): 'You violate a sacrament o' th' church / Shall make you howl in hell for't' (IV.i.39–40); when Ferdinand tells Bosola that the 'bloody sentence' they have executed on her is utterly indefensible in that it was carried out without reference to 'any ceremonial form of law' (IV.ii.299–300); and, lastly, when a ruined church echoes to the sound of the dead Duchess's voice warning her second husband to beware of the 'league / Of amity and love' (III.v.42–3) which her brothers proffered while she was alive and the Cardinal has invoked yet again.

Analysing the play's structure and thematic content in these terms, we begin to see that the Duchess is initially tainted by the world she inhabits; that the norms it violates and the retributive action of Time have a significant bearing on her own tragic choice. After she is dead, of course, both Ferdinand and Bosola describe her as innocent. This is glaringly true in the sense that there was no justification whatever for what they did to her. It does not mean, however, that the act which set her tragedy in motion had nothing to do with moral frailty, deviation from an ethical ideal. She is a woman infinitely more sinned against than sinning, but sinning in some sense none the less; her 'most vulturous eating' of the fruit offered to her (devil-like) by Bosola restrospectively confirms the impression that the wooing-and-wedding of the previous scene re-enacted the Fall. In broad terms, the nature of her fall is a loss of constancy. This entails deafness to the past, blindness to the future (others' as well as her own), unreason ('our violent passions', 'a fearful madness'), and disdain for the ceremonial order which protects the individual and society from the tyrannies of sudden impulse and blind will.[22] Her brothers, of course, are guilty of the same faults to a heinous degree. The crucial point, however, is that we cannot fully appreciate the Duchess's moral triumph unless we see that it is a triumph over that part of her nature which relates her to them spiritually (and to other characters such as the Old Woman, who will not have women's 'frailties' abused – II.ii.14). To adapt the sentiments of Cleopatra, her greatest predecessor among tragic heroines, her brothers are the opposites to which her noble nature is bound, the baser elements she leaves to earth in the process of becoming a monument of transcendent worth.

Unlike Cleopatra's 'marble constancy', the Duchess's is not of the Roman and pagan kind. When she protests that she will 'revive / The rare and almost dead example / Of a loving wife' by emulating Portia (wife of the Stoic Brutus and daughter of Cato, the Stoic 'saint'), she is filled of course with suicidal despair; her salvation lies in accepting the reproof, 'O fie: remember / You are a Christian' (IV.i.72–5). Much of the originality in Webster's presentation of her response to misery and death derives from the fact that it incorporates Neo-Stoic as distinct from Stoic attitudes.[23] It is close in spirit to the writings of Justus Lipsius (*Of Constancie*, trs. 1594) and Guillaume Du Vair (*The Moral Philosophie of the Stoicks*, trs. 1598),

where Stoic fatalism is made compatible with Christian providentialism
and the pride associated with the typical Stoic of old is abjured. Christian
Stoics 'both allowe fate or destinie, and also ioyne handes with libertie or
freedome of will', for they hold that fate is what is determined by God's will
and that God's will requires men to 'use deliberation and choice'. They
hold too that constancy precludes 'pride and vainglory': this is so because
constancy is founded on 'right reason', and that consists of 'a true sense
and judgement of things human *and diuine*' (the italicised words being a
Christian addition to the old definition). In fact, for the Neo-Stoic,
constancy is a synthesis of two great Christian virtues, patience and
humility ('lowliness of mind').[24] No dramatist could be more free from
doctrinal exactitudes than Webster; but, as we shall see, he appears to have
made a very conscious commitment to this form of Stoicism with a view to
creating a new kind of tragic heroine.

Our interest in the Duchess is first kindled by Antonio's enthusiastic
description of her character in a speech which, for all its air of breathless
hyperbole, merits close attention. She is, he insists, utterly different from
the Cardinal (who, among his other crimes, sought to become pope by
bestowing bribes and ignoring 'the primitive decency' or ancient decorum
of the Church) and from Ferdinand (a tyrant possessed of 'a most perverse,
and turbulent nature'). She is quite without pride ('vain-glory'), and has 'so
divine a continence / As cuts off all lascivious and vain hope' in those who
are enchanted by her speech and countenance. Her days are so virtuous
that her nights and even her sleeps are more in heaven than other ladies'
shrifts. Such is her worth that '*She stains the time past, lights the time to
come*' (I.i.163–209; emphasis added).

Here then is an image of spiritualised constancy, a true 'vertuous
widow': one who has been liberated from the vanity of human wishes by
her husband's death and from the turbulence of the flesh by her
contemplation of what lies beyond. However, it is a portrait not of what the
Duchess is, but of what she becomes after she has been shown the waxen
effigies of her second husband and their children '*as if . . . dead*' (IV.i, s. d.).
The rest of this long scene (Act I) provides an ironic commentary on the
inaccuracy of Antonio's panegyric and has the final effect of endowing its
resonant last line with a strange ambiguity.[25] For, immediately that line is
uttered, Cariola conveys a terse message to Antonio, 'You must attend my
lady, in the gallery, / Some half an hour hence'; and the consequence of
that command is that the steward is wooed, wedded, and bedded by his
heavenly-chaste lady within 'the turning of an hour-glass'. That these
extremes are managed without any sense of the grotesque or the gross is
due to the delicate graduations of Webster's stagecraft and dialogue, a

delicacy which is one with the Duchess's winning grace. But the irony which points to discrepancies between the Duchess's conduct and relevant ethical ideals is as potent as it is delicate. After Cariola delivers her message, our attention is moved to the Duchess and Ferdinand, who has a request to make before he departs: would she bestow upon Bosola – 'One that was in the galleys . . . A worthy fellow' – the post of provisorship of the horse? She grants the request instantly, adding 'Yes, I know him. . . . Your knowledge of him / Commends him and prefers him.' What has happened, of course, is that the Duchess's preoccupation with Antonio – her eyes should be straying in his direction while Ferdinand talks – has fatally neutralised her 'memory of the past, knowledge of the present, and care of the future'; for her choice of Bosola as a man of worth, as if his 'notorious' (1. 71) past has never existed, is her first blind step on the road to disaster.

The ghost of another past, together with the whole notion of what befits a prince in terms of memory, care, and foresight, keeps intruding unnoticed when Antonio is being chosen as the man of complete worth and offered the lordship of a wealthy mine (I.i.428–35):

> It's fit, like thrifty husbands, we
> Inquire what's laid up for tomorrow . . . .
> I am making my will (as 'tis fit princes should,
> In perfect memory) . . . .
> They say 'tis very sovereign – 'twas my wedding ring,
> And I did vow never to part with it,
> But to my second husband.
>
> (ll. 377–407)

The last phrase, of course, falsifies the past (unless human nature has changed drastically since the seventeenth century): so that, when the Duchess slips the ring on to her steward's finger and asks, 'Is it fit?' (instead of 'Does it fit?'), we should see that the odd usage has a dramatic purpose. Its insinuation is accented when the Duchess seeks to overcome Antonio's diffidence by reminding him that she is flesh and blood and 'not the figure cut in alabaster / Kneels at my husband's tomb', and he responds with words that might once have been hers: 'Truth speak for me: / I will be the constant sanctuary / Of your good name' (ll. 459–61). Of the many other details in the dialogue which suggest a critical as well as an ominous view of what is happening, perhaps the most eloquent is the Duchess's identification of herself as Antonio's Lady Fortune, a lady noted for her inconstancy as well as her blindness.

That this scene of love and marriage is radiant with a strangely beautiful and tender joy is incontestably obvious. Most of the subtlety of Webster's art, however, has gone into concealing and hinting that though the union is right in some senses it is wrong in others. It is not what one expects from a great lady who should be the constant sanctuary of her husband's good name as well as a model of providence and stability in the eyes of her subjects. It is inescapably tied to secrecy, scheming, and lies ('we'll only lie . . . and plot . . . '). It will make the Duchess the object of scandalous jokes at her own court, and give her the grossest of names among the common people; and it will damage Antonio's reputation as a man of impeccable honesty (III.i.24–30). It has been fuelled by violence in the sense of haste and blind passion, and it is clearly headed for violence of another kind: its 'speed' is not 'good', Time will collect and not scatter the tempest (I.i.358, 471). Lastly, it has been marred by hints of ambition and bribery, and carried out with undue disdain for 'the primitive decency of the church'[26].

One conclusion, therefore, which can be drawn from the first act is that the distinction between the Duchess and her wilful, turbulent, scheming, and unpredictable brothers is not yet absolute. But yet another conclusion is that her fate is unequivocally tragic. It is so not only because her 'woman's fault' (IV.ii.426) is combined with noble qualities which make her pre-eminent in her own world. It is tragic too because Webster's compassionate imagination has fully exposed the dilemma which lurks in the doctrine of original sin – that is, the Church's teaching on what happened to mankind once 'that first good deed began i' th' world, / After man's creation, the sacrament of marriage' (I.i.385–6), ran into trouble. In the Christian dispensation, men and women are born under laws which require them to be what – given the demands of their fallen human nature – they can only become in death: unchanging examples, alabaster images.[27]

After the secret wedding, the experiences of the Duchess fall roughly into two phases: in the first (Acts II and III), she tries to avoid, by deception and flight, the cruel fate she has set in motion; in the second (Act IV), she moves painfully towards a perfect acceptance of that fate. There is some overlapping. When she turns in horror to find Ferdinand and not Antonio standing behind her in their bedroom, she knows that her happiness is at an end; later she will panic, abandon her kingdom, and divide her family in order to escape the worst, but here she accepts it instantly: ''Tis welcome: / For know, whether I am doom'd to live or die, / I can do both like a prince.' And, when the enraged Ferdinand says, 'Do not speak', she answers with exquisite disdain, 'No sir: / I will plant my soul in my ears to hear you'

(III.ii.69–76). This anticipates the innate nobility she will display at the beginning of her captivity: 'a behaviour so noble / As gives a majesty to adversity' (IV.i.5–6). But it represents only a stage in her progress towards perfection and contains something of her unregenerate self. Two words used by Bosola in the prison scenes aptly define the process of change she is yet to undergo: 'mortification' and 'fortification'. Mortification does not mean 'the state of torpor and insensibility preceding death' (as the Revels editor [p. 136], in an uncharacteristic slip, suggests): it is a religious term which signifies a disciplined dying to the body that gives strength to the soul, a spiritual activity specifically associated with the virtues of patience and humility. It is only by mortification that the Duchess will be fortified to endure the 'perfect trial of . . . constancy' (V.ii.256) that Ferdinand (now Scourge of God and Job's adversary) has in store for her. The tragedy had begun to assume this religious dimension towards the end of Act III when she railed against having to endure tyranny 'like to a slave-born Russian', but immediately – as if in response to Antonio's words about providence and patience – continued, 'And yet, O Heaven, thy heavy hand is in't. . . . naught made me e'er / Go right but heaven's scourge-stick' (III.v.60–81).

Passion, despair, and pride are the forms of human weakness which the Duchess has to overcome in her imprisonment. First there is the emotional longing that made her rebel against the constraints of widowhood and political responsibility: 'this restraint / (Like English mastiffs, that grow fierce with tying) / Makes her too passionately apprehend / Those pleasures she's kept from' (IV.i.12–15). This is quickly succeeded by the combination of hatred and despair which issues in fierce curses against her brothers and against creation itself: she wants killing and nothingess 'with speed' (l. 110). But Bosola's mocking exclamations, 'O fie! despair? remember / You are a Christian', and, 'O, uncharitable', seem to have an effect, for in the next scene she can report 'a miracle': 'Necessity makes me suffer constantly, / And custom makes it easy' (IV.ii.29–30). Later too she will have so much 'obedience in my blood', and so much charity, as to wish her brothers well and forgive her executioners (ll. 169–70, 207).

But first and last there is pride. At the beginning, 'her melancholy seems to be fortify'd / With a strange disdain' (IV.i.11–12), and it is to this disdain Bosola directs most of his attention after she has survived the torment of waxen effigies and dancing madmen. Her question, 'dost know me? . . . Who am I?' (IV.ii.121–3), initiates a catechetical investigation of the self in which there is no place for such an attitude. Taking his position on the Christian–Platonic notion of the body as the prison-house of the soul, Bosola offers the perfect rationale for total mortification: 'what's this flesh? a little crudded milk, fantastical puff-paste; our bodies are weaker than those paper prisons boys use to keep flies in; more contemptible, since ours is to preserve earth-worms'. And when she resists this denial of all self-regard based on corporeal values ('Am not I thy duchess?'), he answers drily that being a duchess simply means that she is even more troubled by passion than a milkmaid (his words about her unquiet slumbers echo Antonio's praise of the Duchess whose sleeps were more in Heaven than other ladies' shrifts). But still she resists the drift of his argument, and in doing so utters her most famous words: 'I am Duchess of Malfi still.' These words do not mark the high point of her triumph over adversity, as is often held;[28] they constitute a sign of perfect constancy in the pagan and not the Christian sense. The total context implies that they are flawed with the kind of pride which blinds the mind to the true nature of reality and is incompatible with 'right reason' and humility – on which, in the Christian Stoic's definition, true constancy is based. Thus Bosola informs the Duchess that it is precisely this pride of rank which makes her the victim of passion and illusion: 'That makes thy sleeps so broken: / *Glories, like glow-worms afar off shine bright, / But look'd to near, have neither heat, nor light.*' And the Duchess wryly accepts his unflattering truth: 'Thou art very plain.'

She is now ready for the violent death her brothers have prepared for her. Rejecting the proud, upright stance of the Herculean hero and heroine (this is very pointed), she goes on her knees to meet the end:

> heaven-gates are not so highly arch'd
> As princes' palaces, they that enter there
> Must go upon their knees. – [*Kneels.*] Come violent death,
> Serve for mandragora to make me sleep!

With modest humour, she acknowledges and 'put[s] off' her 'last woman's fault': she calls it tediousness, but we might remember the enchanting 'eloquence' (rich in equivocation, riddles, and dreams) that stirred her steward's blood and awakened in him 'a saucy and ambitious devil'. Her last words and gestures are very plain; she dies like a Christian prince, and not 'in the high Roman fashion'. So dying, she creates a constant sanctuary for her own good name. Thomas Middleton was thinking of this when he praised the achievement of her creator:

> Thy monument is rais'd in thy life-time;
> And 'tis most just; for every worthy man
> Is his own marble, and his merit can
> Cut him to any figure and express

More art than Death's cathedral palaces,
Where royal ashes keep their court. Thy note
Be ever plainness, 'tis the richest coat:
Thy epitaph only the title be –
Write, 'Duchess' . . . .[29]

V

It is essential to Webster's conception of the Duchess's character and tragedy that her second husband is not a person of commanding interest. Antonio is a good and gifted man and a loving husband, but he is not the 'complete man' of unchallengeable worth that the Duchess proclaims him to be in the wooing-scene. The fact that he is not is one reason why she falls so helplessly into the snare laid for her by her brothers.

The meaning of Antonio's personal tragedy lies to some extent in the contrast between his sincere devotion to courtly order and decorum and the devious improprieties into which he falls. Once married, he keeps up the appearance of 'A very formal Frenchman' and a 'precise fellow', but in a sense (as his wife jocularly remarks) he is a Lord of Misrule. Since he is deeply unhappy about all the subterfuge into which he has been drawn, we cannot but pity him. But it is the Duchess we pity when we observe his conduct during and after Ferdinand's electrifying appearance in her chamber. Pistol in hand, Antonio stands outside while Ferdinand utters his terrible threats; he enters when the Duke departs but only to accuse the faithful Cariola of treachery and to indulge in wishful heroics: 'I would this terrible thing would come again . . . .'[30] There is a touch of this weakness when he leaves for Padua on the Duchess's instructions. He does not protest that he will stay by her to the end, but says obediently, 'You counsel safely.' Always he is the steward. Thus the essence of his (small-scale) tragedy is that he is not 'Duke of Malfi'; he has greatness thrust upon him and cannot cope with it.

Unlike Ferdinand and Bosola, Antonio disappears from the play for the whole of Act IV. He returns buoyed up with the 'hope of reconcilement / To the Arragonian brethren' (V.i.1); deaf to the provident voices of Delio and the echo (V.iii.), he is still, as in the beginning, the victim of 'vain hope' (I.i.200). But he finds comfort in reckless fatalism as well as facile optimism: 'impossible / To fly your fate', 'Lose all, or nothing', 'Necessity compels me'. This combination of attitudes suggest both irrationality and instability and contrasts strongly with the image of perfect constancy left by the Duchess. And the contrast deepens. Although he contemns

Fortune and speaks of 'our noble sufferings', he dies in despair, describing himself as a miserable creature. He is deeply pitiable in his death to be sure: his 'I would not now / Wish my wounds balm'd, nor heal'd, for I have no use / To put my life to' (on hearing that his wife and children have been murdered) is the most poignant utterance in English drama outside of Shakespeare (v.iv.62–4). But nothing he says or does at the end prompts admiration. Antonio of the last act, then, is largely a retrospective comment on the Duchess: both on what she was when she thought him a complete·man and what she showed herself capable of when put to the ultimate test.

It is sometimes said that the major character in the play is Bosola. This view is understandable, for Bosola is the primary agent in the plot, the instrument of revenge both against and for the Duchess. But there are deeper reasons for his strong hold on the imagination, reasons connected with the fact that conflict and change are the essence of drama. In the first place, Bosola is a deeply divided character. He is a criminal with a conscience who derives no satisfaction (not even aesthetic) from the villainy to which he is driven by economic necessity; a corrupt idealist whose bitter railing against human nature and society cannot hide his fundamental dissatisfaction with himself. In addition, Bosola undergoes a profound spiritual crisis and change, being so affected by the conduct of the imprisoned Duchess, and by the Duke's cynical refusal to pay him for his 'black deed', that he bitterly repents his action and determines to do something of worth. To speak of his change, however, is to acknowledge that the impact he makes on the play is dependent on the character of the Duchess. Much of the play's fascination, and certainly much of Bosola's, turns on the relationship between these two characters. It is a complex one in which Bosola shifts from the role of spy, hunter, tormentor, and executioner to that of mentor, comforter, and finally disciple. The change is not depicted naturalistically, of course, but the role of comforter suggests its basis in psychological realism. Bosola begins in the prison scenes as a Job's comforter (borrowings from the Book of Job have been found in the Duchess's speeches), but, as admiration eclipses mockery and pity detachment, the instinct to turn false to true comfort imperceptibly and naturally asserts itself; so that, before he knows it, Bosola has changed sides spiritually.

The 'comfort' theme is continuous in the play, being essential to Webster's conception of Antonio, Bosola, and the Duchess. There is an implicit contrast between true and false comfort; the latter is Webster's version of the Stoic and Neo-Stoic False Goods, which, with False Evils, 'do greatlie disquiete the life of man' and 'assaulte this castle of Constancie in us'.[31] Although strikingly different in most respects, Antonio ('vain hope') and Bosola ('worse than hoping Tantalus' – I.i.57) are both alike in that they are initially 'lur'd' (l. 231) into a relationship which promises to make Fortune smile on them. But simultaneously the Duchess is lured into employing Ferdinand's spy, and the spy soon turns his professional relationship with her into one of confidentiality by an extravagant eulogy of Antonio's worth; although there is a hint of mockery in it, the eulogy falls sweetly on the Duchess's ear: 'I taste comfort in this friendly speech' (III.ii.299). The same blend of mockery and friendly concern is evident at first during the imprisonment scenes: 'All comfort to your grace!', 'Come, be of comfort, I will save your life.... Now, by my life, I pity you' (IV.i.18, 86–8). Yet, when he reminds her in the same mocking or half-mocking tones that despair and hatred are un-Christian, he is moving in the direction of true comfort; and by the end of IV.i he assures Ferdinand that if he is compelled to return to her 'The business shall be comfort' (l. 137).

Returning, he enacts the charitable ritual of the common bellman, sent on the night before their execution to the condemned prisoners at Newgate 'to put them in minde of their mortalitie', 'awake their sleepie senses from securitie', and so 'saue their soules from perishing'.[32] His one theme now is the delusory nature of material and earthly values; so that when she says, just before death, 'Now I am well awake' (IV.ii.224), it is clear that he has given her true comfort. But the point for emphasis here is that he too is liberated from false comforts. Denied 'the reward due to my service', and overawed by her noble constancy, he renounces his 'sweet and golden dream' and 'vain hopes'; had he to do it again, he would not change his 'peace of conscience / For all the wealth of Europe' (ll. 294, 324, 337–41). Thus in the final act his state of mind is antithetical to that of Antonio, who is deluded by his 'hope of pardon' until virtually his last moment (V.iv.45). Bosola is deflected from his intention to do 'somewhat ... Worth my dejection' (IV.ii.374–5) neither by the Cardinal's promise of great good fortune ('O, the fortune of your master here, the prince, / Dejects you – but be you of happy comfort ... I'd make you what you would be' – V.ii.113–17), nor by the fickle Julia's offer of her favours ('Kill my longing', 'I'll be your maintenance' – ll. 161, 211). He merely pretends to accept each offer and in this way is able to establish the Cardinal's guilt, get the master key to his lodgings, and perform his one worthy action: 'Revenge, for the Duchess of Malfi' (V.v.81).

But Bosola is not presented in an ideal light at the end. The mood of pity and contrition which came upon him when he kissed the dead Duchess does not persist. He kills an innocent servant with ruthless pragmatism.

And, because he kills Antonio in the dark (whom he meant to save), he dies in despair, believing that 'We are only like dead walls ... That ruin'd, yields no echo', and that the world is a deep pit of darkness where 'womanish and fearful mankind live' (V.v.97–102). Some would say that Bosola here becomes spokesman for the play's general meaning; but Webster has so phrased these despairing utterances that they are automatically invalidated by the dramatic context. The spirit of a fearless woman has echoed through the last act (and not least in Bosola's words and deeds); and it is heard in the concluding speech, where Delio speaks about making noble use of a 'great ruin' and about a noble fame which crowns the end.

But Bosola dies like a man, having shown great constancy of purpose ('There sits in thy face some great determination' – V.v.9). By contrast, the great Cardinal, who always 'seems fearless' (V.iii.336), dies 'like a leveret', howling for mercy and then for help: no different in the end from the waiting-woman Cariola. And the Duke, driven insane with rage and remorse, dies imagining himself a horse: 'Give me some wet hay, I am broken-winded'. Thus the deaths of all the principal characters suggests something like a scale of human quality, with Christian constancy at the top, pagan constancy and despairing acceptance below it, and at the bottom a non-human irrationality and terror. The effect of this scale is to assist in the general differentiation of character and to reassert in the last act the spiritual pre-eminence of the dead Duchess.[33] If we feel that in the last act Webster has moved on to tell us what man and the universe are really like, and that somehow the death of the Duchess is irrelevant here, then we have been less than sensitive to his insistent pursuit of reverent distinctions (as well as irreverent comparisons). The play is a whole and is greater and wiser than any of its parts.

VI

Webster relies more than any other dramatist on the use of imagery and symbolism for his effects of unity, intensity and magnitude. The martial imagery in *The White Devil* has shown that his images are particularly effective when they are seen to emerge from some mythical paradigm to which the whole action is related. In *The Duchess*, three classical myths combine to give substance and grandeur to such key ideas as oppression, irrationality, uncertainty, and degenerative change. Although potent in their imaginative effects, they are deployed with more than the usual Websterian reticence, probably because poetic and dramatic tradition had already rendered them very familiar to his contemporaries.[34]

The myth which contributes most to *The Duchess* suggests a universal model for its tragic world, and at the same time provides an imaginative matrix for its animal imagery. The most important animal image, it seems agreed, is that of the wolf.[35] Ferdinand's lycanthropia gives to this image the kind of literal foundation which pertains to the most effective imagistic clusters in drama: he may not be a wolf, but his conviction that he is one is real enough, and in a good production his appearance, utterance, and movement would progressively endorse this belief.

There are early hints of Ferdinand's fifth-act 'transformation', as when Bosola, philosophising on mankind's moral and physical deformities, refers to such diseases as 'the most ulcerous wolf and swinish measle' (II.i.54); or when the Cardinal, listening in amazement to his brother's howls of cruel rage, reminds him how 'deform'd' and 'beastly' man is when he succumbs to passion (II.v.57). But by far the most powerful premonition occurs in the bedroom scene (III.ii). Here the play's major transformation in outward fortunes – the eclipse of the Duchess's secret happiness – combines with a powerfully suggested transformation of the human image to give us an unforgettable realisation of the idea of swift and terrible change which lies at the heart of Renaissance tragedy. A characteristically oblique clue to Webster's conception of Ferdinand in this scene is furnished by Antonio's light-hearted ramblings on love, marriage, and the 'transshaping' of mythical maidens. He names three such maidens: Daphne, Syrinx, and Anaxarete – the second, fourth, and last persons to be transformed in Ovid's *Metamorphoses* (I and XIV). But we are soon to perceive that the transformation which Webster has in mind is the first and most terrible in Ovid's great poem. Quietly deserted by Antonio and Cariola, the Duchess chatters on about her hair turning grey, and then looks round to find Ferdinand standing behind her. He offers her a poniard ('Die then, quickly!'), proclaims that he 'could change / Eyes with a basilisk', and rants about 'the howling of a wolf'; he ceases to be recognisably human and is remembered afterwards as 'this apparition . . . this terrible thing' (III.ii.71–146). He has become one here with Lycaon, the world's first tyrant, whose name (meaning 'wolf') was descriptive of his nature and fate. Lycaon was the presiding spirit of the Age of Iron, a time when treachery, greed, and violence took the place of truth and loyalty, all natural affection died, and the Maiden Justice fled the earth. The worst of his crimes was a banquet at which he served his guests with human flesh, and for this Jove's wrath descended on him:

Lycaon fled terrified until he reached the safety of the silent countryside. There he uttered howling noises, and his attempts to speak were all in vain. His clothes changed into bristling hairs, his arms to legs, and he became a wolf. His savage nature showed in his rabid jaws, and he now directed against the flocks his innate lust for killing. He had a mania, even yet, for shedding blood. But though he was a wolf, he retained some traces of his original shape. The greyness of his hair was the same, his face showed the same violence, his eyes gleamed as before, and he presented the same picture of ferocity.[36]

The parallel between Ferdinand and Lycaon rests not only on the wolf imagery and the lycanthropy; there is also his repeated and explicit identification with tyranny (for Bosola he becomes simply 'the cruel tyrant' – IV.ii.372), and the presentation of the Duchess, Antonio, and their children as helpless, innocent victims of a relentless ferocity: Ferdinand and his brother hunt them down like 'most cruel biters' who are never satisfied when they have 'some . . . blood' (V.ii.341–2).[37] Other dramatists had likened the tragic world to the Iron Age; but only Webster sought to consolidate the comparison between general conditions by making his principal villain an unmistakable counterpart to the one character in myth who personified the spirit of that dark phase in the cyclic history of mankind.

Another tyrant of myth who is shadowed in the figure of Ferdinand is Atreus, the protagonist of Seneca's *Thyestes*. Atreus differs from Lycaon in that his cruelty is the expression of a furious personal hatred. This passion is caused by the wrongs (sexual betrayal and theft) done to him by his brother Thyestes: but it is so far in excess of its immediate cause that its original cause – a curse on the house of Tantalus – alone makes sense of it. As presented by Seneca, the revenge of Atreus has three elements: a treacherous reconciliation, a ritual killing, and a celebratory banquet. Atreus pretends to have buried all hatred and invites Thyestes to return with his children to the kingdom to make 'a league' of 'love and faith'.[38] Secretly, he kills the children in a madly punctilious parody of the religious rites of sacrifice. Then at the end of the banquet celebrating their reconciliation he informs his brother that he has eaten the flesh of his own children. Atreus does not kill Thyestes and did not want to : his whole aim has been to inflict unbearable mental pain.

Largely because of Kyd's Treacherous Entertainment, Atreus had already left a deep mark on Renaissance tragedy. But Webster returns to Kyd's part source (Seneca's *Medea* was another inspiration for that symbolic scene) and exploits the dramatised myth in ways which are new as well as old. The specific links and echoes add up to a fairly substantial parallel. There is the early reference to 'hoping Tantalus' (*Duchess of Malfi*,

I.i.57), the first character to speak in *Thyestes* and, in a sense, the prime mover of its action. There is Ferdinand's conviction that his sister's 'madness' is a curse on the house of Arragon and Castile for some sin. There is his longing to 'boil their bastard to a cullis, / And give't his lecherous father, to renew / The sin of his back' (*Duchess of Malfi*, II.v.71–3). There is the repeated offer of a 'noble and free league / Of amity and love', which the Duchess comes to treat as a cruel mockery but which leads Antonio to his doom. Lastly, the spirit of Atreus takes possession of the stage when Ferdinand puts a dead man's hand in his sister's ('I come to seal my peace with you'), shows her the bodies of Antonio and their children 'fram'd in wax', and treats her to a hideous parody of the ritual entertainments (masque, giving of gifts, epithalamic song) which were her due but were necessarily absent from her secret wedding.[39] Here, revenge as mental torment and the ritualising of mad violence are brought to their ultimate point of refinement.

Ferdinand's nature is not simply a combination of tyrannic cruelty and vindictive hatred. There is (as many have suggested) a strong hint of perverse attraction to the sister he torments, so that he often speaks in the anguished tones of a jealous or deserted husband. Of course we cannot know for certain whether his references to family honour, the distasteful nature of second marriages, and his hope of gaining 'An infinite mass of treasure' from his sister had she remained a widow are simply rationalisations of an incestuous jealousy he cannot bring himself to acknowledge; but it is a reasonable conjecture. It remains a conjecture, however: or rather a secret, lodged at the heart of the play.[40] And in that respect it is characteristic, for essential to the whole vision of this tragedy is the idea that the turbulent heart of man, and the society spun from his passions, is a dark maze full of secrets, some of them monstrous and all dangerous. For this reason, Webster plays quiet variations on the mythic theme of the labyrinth, the artful construct designed to conceal from the world the monstrous offspring – half-beast, half-man – of an extravagant passion.

The theme is introduced when the Duchess confides her 'secret' (I.i.350, 352) to Cariola, hides her behind the arras, and utters those words which anticipate the whole tragedy: 'wish me good speed / For I am going into a wilderness, / Where I shall find nor path, nor friendly clew / To be my guide' (ll. 358–61). There is a delicate pun here on 'clew' which marries instantly with verbal image and stage action to evoke the mythic symbol; for 'clew' ('clue') has come to signify a principle or fact that serves as a guide solely because it was a clew or ball of thread which enabled Theseus to defeat the labyrinth (after killing the monster). The relevance of the symbol springs to attention later in the scene when Cariola emerges from behind the arras and the steward, astonished to discover that he is already married to his lady, is told by her, 'Be not amaz'd, this woman's of my counsel' (i.e. 'shares my secret, and both acts as a legal witness and gives legal advice with me').[41] For the time being, Antonio's wonderment is delighted; but it acquires a dark colouring when he begins to perceive that the old-world map he has relied on so confidently cannot save him from 'this terrible thing': 'I am lost in amazement: I know not what to think on't' (II.i.173).

With the desperate stratagems practised by the Duchess and Antonio to conceal her childbearing from the world, the imagery of lock and key emerges as a symbolic equivalent to that of maze and clue. A palace theft is abruptly proclaimed, every officer is locked in his chamber, his chest is locked too, and both keys are sent to the Duchess's bedchamber; at the same time, the court gates and the postern gates are 'shut up', while the park gate is locked and the key surrendered by Forobosco (II.ii.27ff.). Devices such as these have kept even the trusted Delio in the dark for at least nine months: 'And so long since married? / You amaze me' (II.i.71–2). And even he has to accept a common fate: 'Let me seal your lips forever' (l. 73), says Antonio.

Simultaneous with Bosola's discovery of the Duchess's secret is the gradual but imperfect revelation of Ferdinand's. Bosola is pointing us in the right direction when he meditates:

> What thing is in this outward form of man
> To be belov'd? we account it ominous
> If nature do produce a colt, or lamb,
> A fawn, or goat, in any limb resembling
> A man; and fly from't as *a prodigy*.
> Man stands amaz'd to see his deformity
> In any other creature but himself.
> But in our own flesh . . . .
>
> (II.i.45–52; emphasis added)

Bosola himself, however, does not pursue this line of thought in the direction of Ferdinand's motives. It is only the Cardinal who attempts a diagnosis of what he senses is a 'prodigy' ('something amazing, out of the course of nature') (II.v.2), but all he can think of is 'intemperate anger'. This diagnosis so completely ignores the obsessively sexual streak in Ferdinand's howling about his sister –

> Methinks I see her laughing –
> Excellent hyena! – talk to me somewhat, quickly,
> Or my imagination will carry me
> To see her, in the shameful act of sin.
>
> (ll. 38–41)

– that we feel compelled to find our own explanation.

The main source of dramatic conflict in the last act is the Cardinal's attempt to conceal his secrets, and Bosola's – aided at first by Julia, his Ariadne – to discover them. Julia's death by poisoning is an exemplum on the evils of secrecy: 'think what danger 'tis / To receive a prince's secrets' (v.ii.259–60); but so too is the Cardinal's own death. Fearful lest his crucial role in the Duchess's murder will emerge in Ferdinand's ravings, and hoping to hide Julia's body until morning, he locks himself in his chamber, ordering that no one should attempt to enter under any circumstances; thus 'confin'd', he ensures that rescue cannot come to him in his hour of need: 'I am lost!' (v.v.17, 23).

Having uncovered the Cardinal's secret and secured from him the master key to his lodgings, Bosola is able to kill him and his brother; so that in the end the base intelligencer becomes a kind of Theseus. He is, however, a Theseus *manqué*, since he kills the very man he hoped to save and is killed himself by the lycanthrope – all 'In a mist, I know not how' (v.v.94). Bosola defeats and is defeated by the monstrous maze; but then that is the fate of the hero in a number of Renaissance tragedies.

VII

It has become an axiom of criticism that Webster's imagination dwells on the experience of chaos with an intensity unequalled by any other dramatist of the period. Nowadays, too, most critics would reject the view that Webster himself is an artistic victim of the experience which haunts him. But just how much of an underlying unity is to be found in his two major tragedies, and of what kind it is, is an issue on which critics differ substantially. What I hope to have shown is that the pattern is more defined in *The White Devil* than in *The Duchess of Malfi*, and that in both plays it is metaphysical as well as moral. In *The White Devil* the pattern is that of the contrarious cosmos, here fulfilling its inbuilt threat of a return to total strife and confusion. In *The Duchess of Malfi* it is the pattern of time, which is the contrarious universe in its non-spatial dimension: past and present and present and future are a unity which is visible and audible to human providence and divine, invisible and inaudible to tragic individuals who live 'violently' in the present.

To recognise these shadowy patterns is not to find the experience of the plays any the less terrifying: it is to become even more conscious of disintegration and confusion. But at the same time it is to suspect that the plays are not expressions of metaphysical despair. Further, it is to find special significance in the heroic process of self-definition, the move through suffering and death towards 'constancy' and 'integrity': towards constancy, which means standing together as well as enduring; and integrity, which means wholeness, unity. It is through constancy and integrity that women and men are remembered; and that, in a world of time and change, is almost everything.

6   Thomas Middleton

I

Middleton's two best tragedies, *The Changeling* (1622) and *Women Beware Women* (c. 1621–5), are domestic, unheroic, low-toned. They reveal an intense fascination with the process of evil working quietly, and with devastating effect, in prosaic people in everyday situations and settings. Although they are profoundly sociological in their orientation, their conception of society is simple – a group of individuals knit together by the bonds of family and neighbourhood. The evil which corrodes those bonds is not something which can be traced to the vices of the great and the abuses of political power. Rather, Middleton's world is a moral democracy where ruler and subject, master and servant, parent and child, and male and female are all marked in varying degrees with the same flaw: a blind determination to get their own way.

Like Webster and Ford, Middleton locates the tragic experience mainly in women. That is not because he is interested in miracles of constancy or the condition of humankind as victim; nor is it due to his obviously sensitive awareness of the woman's plight in the practice of made marriages. The main reason, I suspect, is that he wishes to emphasise the extraordinary speed with which the process of spiritual degeneration can take place and is able to do that most plausibly in relation to young women who have led sheltered lives, are inexperienced in the ways of the world, and lacking in the self-knowledge and prudence which such experience brings. But that is to say also that the youth of his tragic heroines is almost as important as their sex: theirs is the tragedy of characters who begin to mature only after they have become corrupted.[1]

What firmly identifies Middleton's wilful and gullible protagonists with the adult world, and gives them their enduring fascination, is a capacity for self-deception which quickly dispels their sense of guilt. Their moral identity continues to assert itself after their fall in sincere self-justification, in forthright denunciations of others, and in a fastidious regard for the appearance of moral rectitude. They continue to exist for the most part in a state of profound moral confusion until catastrophe compels them to acknowledge what they have managed to suppress.[2] This spectacle of corruption drawing sustenance from morality on a casual, day-to-day basis is presented by Middleton with passionless objectivity; it is as horrifying in its way as the nightmare enormities of *The Revenger's Tragedy* and *The White Devil*.

Middleton's immense skill in delineating complex psychological processes, his grasp of the conditioning effects of social background, and his preference for irony and plainness over hyperbole and rhetorical amplification combine to make him the most naturalistic of Renaissance tragedians. The naturalistic effect of the two plays is enhanced by the absence of any sense of circumambient mystery about the confines of his prosaic world.[3] There are no sceptics or atheists here, just sinners and villains skilled in forgetting or perverting moral and religious codes which they are not inclined to question. Nevertheless Middleton's investigation of the growth and effects of evil is unobtrusively conducted within a metaphysical framework which invests it with gravity and magnitude.[4] To begin with, there is an abiding recollection of the primal Fall, not only as an archetype of all tragic transformations but also as a cause and guarantee of continuing corruption; for Middleton, as for many of his contemporaries, that hereditary corruption is to be seen most often and most poignantly in sexual relations.[5] Both tragedies, too, incorporate the Faustian pattern of bond-breaking followed by a state of spiritual bondage, and are in tune with the religious outlook of Marlowe's tragedy to the extent that the entrapment and loss of a soul is deemed an event which needs no political framework to endow it with momentousness.

In both tragedies, moreover, the marriage bond symbolises the harmony of opposites on which the order of nature rests; a mysterious phenomenon, that harmony is dictated by 'Providence' and is the basis for the Eden-like happiness attainable by man and wife (*Women Beware Women*, II.ii.177–83). Such happiness, however, is elusive and mostly illusory in these tragedies; they figure a world of opposites conjoined in deadly mixtures, without balance, violently, confusedly. In the *Entertainment* which Middleton wrote with Dekker in 1604 celebrating the reign of James 'the Peacemaker', Middleton explains that before the King's accession all classes in England 'mov'd opposite to *nature* and peace'; then, emblematically, he depicts the peaceful order of James's realm as a coming together of the (personified) Four Elements, these having abandoned their '*natural* desire / To combat each with other'.[6] This puts explicitly what is everywhere implicit in the tragedies: that in the world of time it is as natural to divide and destroy as it is to unite and create. Middleton's primary concern as tragedian, of course, is with the first impulse; but he does not reduce human nature to that one impulse (as Hobbes will soon do); in fact he is obsessed with the way in which the second impulse can conceal, be confused with, even beget the first.

Like the 'dissolute rout' of 'abusive villains' who perform the anti-masque in his *Inner Temple Masque* (1619), most of the characters in Middleton's tragedies heap scorn 'upon the reverend form and face of Time'.[7] More than in any other non-Shakespearean tragedy, wrongful or mistaken action is represented in these plays as a violation of the natural order in the guise of Time. And when retribution occurs, as it does with sonorous inevitability, we are in no doubt that the victims are being 'struck' (the pun is Middleton's) by Time's hand.[8] But, as in *Faustus* and *Macbeth*, the orders of time and eternity are related; it is assumed that happiness in the next as well as in this life is dependent on the right use of time. Thus disrespect for Time is a sacrilege for which the ultimate penalty can be damnation.

All Middleton's emphasis, however, is on the social implications of untimely action. Time (as the equivalent of Ceremony) requires that the coming-together of human beings be neither forced nor merely impulsive; it seeks to ensure that the urge to unite does not produce a situation in which the urge to strive, dominate, and confound is let loose. But the tempo of human intercourse in Middleton's tragic world is hectic, so that the rites both of hospitality and of marriage are continually being abused and perverted. That world has its own recognisable dynamics, dictated by a staccato succession of comings and goings, meetings and partings, welcomes and farewells. So swiftly do strangers become friends, lovers, and spouses, and so swiftly do friends, lovers, and spouses become strangers and enemies, that the space between two human beings can seem at one moment absurdly small and negotiable, and then as wide and treacherous as No Man's Land. Here, the friendly greeting can be an omen of the end.

II

Middleton wrote *The Changeling* in collaboration with William Rowley. It is agreed that Rowley was responsible for the comic subplot and also the first and last scenes of the play. The numerous parallels between the two plots, and the general absence of inconsistency in detail, show that the collaboration was an unusually close one.[9] Critics have linked the play with *Doctor Faustus* (as a 'tragedy of damnation'),[10] with Beaumont and Fletcher's *The Maid's Tragedy* (as an ironic inversion of Petrarchan romanticism), and with *Romeo and Juliet* (as a mocking variation on the theme of a star-crossed love).[11] I should like to suggest, however, that its main link is with *A Midsummer Night's Dream*. This connection will seem less surprising and devoid of potential significance if it is remembered that Shakespeare's vision of a contrarious, unstable, confusing world is embodied in that early comedy with the formal exactness of a masque (or masque-and-antimasque). In its conceptual patterning, its imagery and symbolism, and its general sense of the anarchic violence which surrounds the matrimonial order of society, it comes nearer to Shakespeare's tragedies than any other of his happy comedies. The antithetical construction of its play-world is rich with significance. There is Athens, governed by Theseus and Hippolyta, the Amazon queen whom Theseus wooed with his sword: it represents the order which results from the differentiation and union of once-warring opposites ('an union in partition'); beyond that, it stands for reason, law, civility. And there is the forest outside Athens where quarrelling fairies play havoc with the fruitful marriage of the four elements, and coarse plebeians rehearse their formless comical tragedy: it stands for irrationality, confusion, nature in the raw. Between these two worlds there is an exchange of traffic which blurs their antithetical relationship. Four courtly lovers enter the wood and are soon caught up in a merry-go-round of transferred loyalties which results in conspicuously 'ungentle' and even violent behaviour. The plebeians take their play to court for the wedding-celebrations, where their gentle concern for the ladies' feelings, and their somewhat ungentle reception, emphasise the fact that the formal confusion of their play is less inappropriate at court than the newly-weds imagine.

Fundamental to the play is the idea of change and inconstancy, embodied mainly in the turbulent relationships of the four friends-and-lovers; we never see the 'changeling child' to whom Oberon and Titania refer, but the susceptibility of the two men to Puck's (= Cupid's) tricks is such that all four lovers could be so described. Key symbols for the darkly confusing nature of love's changefulness are the 'wandering wood' itself, the mythical labyrinth (conquered originally by Theseus), and the moon. The experience of love in the wood is in every sense 'amazing' (see II.i.99–100; III.ii.220, 344; IV.i.143); moreover, its darkest potential is comically disclosed in the passion conceived by the fairy queen for *Bully* Bottom, the ass-headed 'monster' who recalls Pasiphae's bull (and the Minotaur too). The moon stands for love's madness – or total irrationality – as well as its mutability; there is an etymological quibble on 'lunatic' (from Latin *luna*, the moon) which alludes to the belief that lunar influence is a cause of madness.

All of this – down to the names of Oberon and Titania and the quibble on 'lunacy'[12] – is remembered in *The Changeling*. Its play-world too is antithetically constructed. The action of the main plot takes place in Vermandero's castle, that of the subplot in Alibius's asylum: the first connotes stability, constancy, civility, the second irrationality, caprice, deformity.[13] Between these worlds also there is a two-way movement which calls in question their antithetical relationship. Two gentlemen in the service of Vermandero, infatuated by Alibius's wife, enter the asylum disguised as fool and madman; they assure her that their folly and madness are merely apparent, but she teaches them that this is a delusion. Alibius on the other hand has been invited to present an entertainment at the castle as part of the festivities for the wedding of Vermandero's daughter, Beatrice-Joanna. The dance of madmen and fools which he has rehearsed – 'they imitate the beasts and birds, / Singing, or howling, braying, barking; all / As their wild fancies prompt 'em' (III.iii.196–8) – should function as an antimasque at the wedding, an image of the discord and confusion to which the harmonious order of marriage (symbolised in a masque) stands opposed. But the 'antimasque' is a true reflection of the castle wedding, it being a union where the bride is 'all deform'd' and the bridal sheets are 'shrouds / For murdered carcasses' (V.iii.77–84). Alibius's desire that his performers should avoid 'rough behaviours' such as would 'Affright the ladies' (IV.iii.59–60) is even more ironic here than Bottom's concern for the sensibilities of Amazonian Hippolita and vixenish Hermia.

As the title of the tragedy indicates, its theme too is change, 'the transforming power of love'.[14] The eponymous changeling – according to the list of *dramatis personae* – is Franciscus, the counterfeit madman. But, because the word 'changeling' had several meanings – 'a fickle or inconstant person'; 'a person ... put in exchange for another'; 'a child secretly substituted for another in infancy'; 'a "child on a sudden much changed from itself"'; 'a half-witted person'[15] – the title is applicable to most of the principal characters. But the supreme changeling, of course, is Vermandero's daughter, a child on a sudden much changed from herself.

As in *A Midsummer Night's Dream*, love's changefulness begets amazement and a monstrous union. Hiring De Flores to murder her fiancé so that she can marry her latest 'saint', the beautiful Beatrice-Joanna finds herself 'in a labyrinth' (III.iv.71) of cross-purposes and compulsive sexuality where the hideous, 'dog-faced' servant takes first her body and later her heart.[16] And, when the truth is discovered by her father and husband, they are filled with horrified bewilderment, 'lost' (V.iii.81). Is this the child of Vermandero's noble blood or a changeling substitute? Which is Beatrice and which Joanna? – 'A thousand enemies enter'd my citadel / Could not amaze like this: Joanna! Beatrice! Joanna!' (ll. 147–8). By contrast, the constant Isabella of the subplot is unamazed (III.iii.117) by the folly and madness of her disguised admirers and even acts as their Ariadne:

> Stand up thou son of Cretan Dedalus,
> And let us tread the lower labyrinth,
> Come, I'll lead you to the clue.
>
> (IV.iii.106–8).

It is clear then that Middleton and Rowley found in *A Midsummer Night's Dream* the idea for a binary structure which would allow their quite different talents to work separately but in unison, a structure too which threw into sharp relief some of the most fundamental ideas in the tradition of tragedy that began with Kyd and Marlowe. Their play, it might be said, dramatises the tragic potentialities of Theseus's court, and does so in such a manner as to endorse the suggestion of one critic that Shakespeare wrote *A Midsummer Night's Dream* with more than a backward glance at *The Spanish Tragedy*.[17]

III

Although *The Changeling* is very much the tragedy of Beatrice-Joanna, the meaning of her tragedy lies in her relationship with De Flores. It is a relationship depicted with startling realism, yet it is profoundly symbolical too, an image of the complex structure of the human psyche and its potentialities for good and evil. Middleton grasps the simple symbolism offered by his source in the name of De Flores and quietly extends it to the full. De Flores is the man destined to deflower Beatrice in every sense of the word, robbing her not only of her virginity but also of her moral and aesthetic sense, her very soul. As the imagery constantly reminds us, he is a poison which infects her whole nature, making every reference to her 'sweetness' a hideous irony.

From the start their relationship is one of opposites. She is the lady of the castle, beautiful, fastidious, admired; although a gentleman by birth, he has been 'thrust . . . out to servitude' by 'hard fate' (II.i.48), is gross in mind and speech, and physically repellent. Beatrice's consuming hatred for him, however, is the chief sign of their contrariety. The brutal rudeness with which this self-consciously polite young lady habitually reacts to his presence is evidence of her wilful, spoilt-child psychology. But it is also symptomatic – one might say symbolic – of a deep instinct which tells her that De Flores, with his lust-marked face, is her moral opposite, and that the distance between them must be maintained at all costs.[18] This idea is overtly dramatised in the analogous relationship between Tomazo de Piracquo and De Flores. At first Tomazo accepts De Flores on the basis of friendly trust. But later 'instinct . . . of a subtler strain' (V.ii.40) tells him of 'a contrariety in nature / Betwixt that face and me' and turns what De Flores thought would be a friendly meeting into an abrupt and violent parting – he is dismissed as if he carried the plague: 'Dost offer to come near and breathe upon me? (*Strikes him*)' (ll. 13–26). This is at once preparation and elucidation for Beatrice's dying words to her father:

> O come not near me, sir, I shall defile you:
> I am that of your blood was taken from you
> For your better health; look no more upon't,
> But cast it to the ground regardlessly:
> Let the common sewer take it from distinction.
>
> (V.iii.149–53)

De Flores – who kills her when she makes a desperate and dishonest effort to disown him morally – is the common sewer in which Beatrice loses her 'distinction'.

To say that Beatrice and De Flores are opposites is not, then, to imply (as one critic has insisted it must) that her tragedy is that of an ingenuous girl overcome by a masterful villain with whom she has no real affinity.[19] It is to suggest rather that De Flores (who has himself been changed by hard fate and self-indulgence) represents a polarity within her own nature; just as his foul face images his own corrupted nature, so that corrupted nature represents what Beatrice of the opening scene is capable of becoming – a creature in whom reason and will are wholly subservient to appetite and the senses. In fact, when she decides to change her 'first love' and 'saint' for the next gentleman to charm her eye (I.i.155; III.iv.143), she takes the first step on that downward path without any encouragement from De Flores. He himself points out that she had committed whoredom in her heart before she employed him; unlike Alsemero (and many a critic) he will not accept her belated claim that the betrothal to Alonzo de Piracquo was arranged by her father without regard for her wishes. Indeed, that first 'giddy turning' (as she herself describes it) is just what encourages De Flores in his seemingly preposterous belief that the loveliest of women can be induced to find satisfaction in 'swine-deformity' and that his day with Beatrice will come (I.i.156; II.i.43).

Behind this brilliant drama of psychic contraries is adumbrated an ideal of opposites in harmony, of things clearly distinguished and fittingly related. There is frequent allusion to hierarchical structures of opposition such as Creator and creature, king and subject, parent and child, master or mistress and servant (where 'servant' can mean lover as well as employee), reason (judgement) and passion (appetite, the senses). Alsemero and Beatrice antiphonally invoke all of these in a delicate exchange during the first scene, as if in token of their wish to ensure that all oppositions will be resolved in their relationship (I.i.78–83). Far more important, however, is the structure of harmonious relationships known as decorum – fitness of action to the circumstances of person, time, place, and purpose.[20] In the form of one or more of the circumstances, the notion of decorum is invoked throughout both plots with astonishing frequency. Place and time are the circumstances most often referred to, but each of these serves easily as a shorthand for others as well. Place signifies not only physical location (the castle, the bridal bed, the different positions in the games of 'We Three' and 'Barley-brake') but also social status or office, and in that sense necessarily implies person too. Time is more significant, partly because of its importance in the metaphysic of tragedy, but partly too because of its special status in the doctrine of decorum, where 'seasonable' conduct is usually thought of as conduct proper in every respect (agreeable to all the circumstances). The function of all the allusions to decorum, of course, is to denote an ideal of civilised and gracious behaviour with which the castle is to be identified. Its leading role in the thematic structure is emphasised by the opening speech, and in a manner which gives it the most far-reaching implications. Alsemero, who is twice hailed at the castle as the 'complete gentleman' (title of a treatise on manners and morals which appeared in the same year as *The Changeling*[21]), here relates the proprieties of social encounter and courtship to the larger decorums of religion and the providential order:

> 'Twas in the temple where I first beheld her,
> And now again the same; what omen yet
> Follows of that? None but imaginary;
> Why should my hopes and fate be timorous?
> The place is holy, so is my intent:
> I love her beauties to the holy purpose,
> And that, methinks, admits comparison
> With man's first creation, the place blest,
> And is his right home back, if he achieve it.
> The church hath first begun our interview
> And that's the place must join us into one,
> So there's beginning and perfection too.

Her mother being dead, it is perhaps natural that Beatrice should see herself as the voice and custodian of decorum at the castle. With characteristic irony, however, Middleton makes this trait increasingly conspicuous the further she departs from her 'honourable self' (IV.i.95); thus decorum becomes the mask which enables her to conceal from herself and others the transformation which has taken place in her. Typically, she instructs others on propriety while she herself is in the process of subverting it, sometimes in the most radical fashion. Securing a welcome at the castle for a total stranger, and a postponement of her wedding (due in a week), she half-jokingly admonishes her impetuous ('violent') father for wishing her to bid an unceremonious farewell to an old friend – her virginity (I.i.190–7). Arrangements for clandestine meetings in the castle with her father's unexpected guest are all set down on paper with explicit guidance on 'Fitness of time and place' (II.i.4); and, because the complete gentleman is duly responsive to these instructions, he is warmly praised by her well-drilled servant, acting as go-between: 'The place is my charge, you have kept your hour, / And the reward of a just meeting bless you' (II.ii.1–2). But Alsemero is gently rebuked by Beatrice during one of these just meetings both for his impetuosity and for his choice of an office that would not befit him: volunteering to get rid of Alonzo in an 'honourable' duel, he is told that 'Blood guiltiness becomes a fouler visage' and that 'The present times are not so sure of our side / As those hereafter may be' (ll. 40, 49–50). This anticipates Beatrice's reaction to De Flores's offer to kill Alonzo, and Diaphanta's to take her place in the bridal bed (so as to conceal her loss of virginity from Alsemero): each offer is accepted, but both servants are criticised for undue enthusiasm – they are 'too violent to mean faithfully', 'too quick' (ll. 118, 102; IV.i.93).

It was an axiom that knowledge of what is appropriate in particular circumstances requires an experienced discretion, a fine discrimination. Thus Beatrice prides herself on her ability to 'make choice with judgement' (II.i.6–15). Her choices are always of persons to serve her in a particular role or place; but the timing of the choice and task is crucial. What springs to attention in these choices is her blind opportunism and her serene belief that she has a perfect sense of good timing. Her choice of Alsemero occurs in an aside during their third meeting and a week before her wedding is due: 'This man was meant for me; that he should come / So near his time, and miss it!' (I.i.85–6; cf. III.iv.10–11). Her choice of De Flores to kill Alonzo is made in one of those sudden, all-consuming 'nows' which disclose her astounding obliviousness to temporal continuity in the sense of consequences: 'And now I think on one . . . the ugliest creature / Creation fram'd for some use' (II.ii.41–4). The choice seems doubly wonderful to her in that it will rid her of 'two inveterate loathings at one time' (l. 145) – De Flores, she assumes, will pocket his gold and leave her father's service (it will be noted that the word 'inveterate' adds a special twist to the irony of the remark). The choice of Diaphanta to take 'the bride's place' is yet another brainchild of the dislocated present in which she lives: 'Seeing that wench now, / A trick comes in my mind' (IV.i.125, 53–4). Once made, this choice is followed by more than the usual show of discretion. Apart from being rebuked for her quickness, Diaphanta is subjected to the virginity test to ensure that she is a fit replacement for her lady's 'honourable self', and is then instructed on the proper carriage of the business: 'About midnight / You must not fail to steal forth gently, / That I may use the place' (ll. 95, 122–4).

What emerges from all this is that the proper Beatrice does exactly the opposite of what is required in decorum: she makes person, time, and place fit her purposed action, and not the reverse. It is beautifully ironical therefore that she should choose in De Flores a man who cannot be pushed from his chosen position and who is vastly her superior in bending circumstances to his will. Although thrust out by hard fate into servitude, and made ugly by the effects of his lust, he does not despair. He fixes his desires on Beatrice, 'frames ways ... To come into her sight', and will endure all storms before he will 'part' from her (II.i.29–30, 51). His patience seems to be rewarded when (after her first brainwave) she calls, 'Come hither; nearer, man!', touches his face, and speaks in amorous accents (II.ii.78ff.). Although he seriously misreads her purpose, he is right in judging this to be an opportunity, and he is determined not to waste it: 'I was blest / To light upon this minute; I'll make use on't.' So that, when she begins to sigh and hint, he makes the task of proposing murder very easy, falling on his knees in the posture of a chivalrous servant–lover prepared for any undertaking. She has always detested his forwardness (compare her response to his 'officious forwardness' in stooping to lift her glove at I.i.228), but now she promises him a rich reward for being so 'forward' in 'service dangerous' (II.ii.131). However, he has already gone much further ahead in time, and come much closer in person, than she imagines. His hungry opportunism has met and outstripped hers, contracting all of the future into the 'now' of fulfilled desire: her fiancé is 'no more', and the act of stabbing is coincident in his mind with the sexual thrust that will undo her endlessly: 'the thought ravishes ... I thirst for him. ... Methinks I feel her in mine arms already ... praising this bad face' (ll. 134–49).

De Flores's next encounter – with a friendly Alonzo, asking to be shown the castle – is another opportunity keenly appreciated (II.ii.156ff.). He arranges to meet his victim after dinner, leads him to a casement with a good view ('There you may dwell awhile'), calmly draws his sword, and then deposits the body in a vault which 'serves to good use now' (III.ii.14, 20). The sparkle of a ring on the corpse (a gift from Beatrice) offers a last challenge to his opportunism: 'well found, / This will approve the work'. The ring 'will not part in death', so he takes the 'speedy course' of removing finger and all. Its reluctance to part is, of course, an omen that the bond between present and past cannot easily be broken; but from the point of view of his own economy, De Flores has managed time, person, and place superbly.

His second encounter with Beatrice is perhaps the most admired scene in Renaissance tragedy outside Shakespeare. Many have felt that it exists in splendid isolation from the rest of the play; others have argued that it is closely linked in conception with what has gone before. My own analysis reinforces the second view and suggests in addition that the scene draws much of its strength and significance from a conceptual pattern which extends throughout the whole play, main plot and subplot. The scene is essentially a clash of wills and expectations, with De Flores confident that the meeting will end in physical union, Beatrice assuming that it will seal the parting she has long hoped for, and each character seeking to impose on the other his and her own conception of place and person. De Flores proudly introduces himself as the omnicompetent servant–lover of her heart's desire: 'All things are answerable ['suitable, fitting, proper, becoming' – *OED*, s. v. 'answerable', sense 2], time, circumstance, / Your wishes, and my service' (III.iv.22). When it dawns on him that he has not come into his lady's favour at all, and that gold is to be his only reward, it is as if hard fate has thrust him out to servitude a second time; he is filled with an indignant sense of moral and social displacement: 'Do you place me in the rank of verminous fellows, / To destroy things for wages?' (ll. 64–5). On the other hand, Beatrice's failure to grasp his meaning, and her perception that he will not easily be dislodged, suddenly make her feel quite lost: 'I'm in a labyrinth; / What will content him? I would fain be rid of him.' But this is nothing to her profound sense of disorientation when his meaning becomes clear; desperately, she tries to reassert their respective socio-moral positions: 'Think but upon the distance that creation / Set 'twixt thy blood and mine, and keep thee there.' But she has shattered that unity of moral and social categories postulated by the terms 'noble' and 'base', and De Flores ruthlessly explains the consequences. To 'fly' to her birth is to abandon her true rank; she is 'the deed's creature' and must settle her in what the act has made her – his partner in a marriage of like and lost souls: 'Nor is it fit we two, engag'd so jointly, / Should part and live asunder.' Triumphant Lord of Misrule, demonic anarchist, De Flores has bent person, time, and place to his own determined purpose; he is Beatrice's evil and eminently appropriate fate, the decorum of poetic justice in person. When Beatrice slips trembling and astonished into his arms, and is escorted off stage, one can believe in the existence of a hell on earth. It is a place of degradation and servitude where the only voice that is heard is the voice that says, 'y'are no more now ... peace and innocency has turn'd you out, / And made you one with me' (ll. 135–40).

IV

It is sometimes argued that the essence of Beatrice's tragedy lies in the first three acts. Certainly what gives the play its distinction is the sustained power and intensity of the scenes where Beatrice moves swiftly and blindly into the clutches of De Flores. But the ironic process of transformation and retribution which constitutes her tragedy as conceived by Middleton is by no means complete at this point. She still believes (and De Flores does not discourage her in this) that she can find happiness with Alsemero: her punishment will be complete when she sees him recoil from her love in horror and describe her as 'all deform'd'. Moreover, she becomes dependent on De Flores in a way that changes the whole nature of her feelings for him, so that her spiritual transformation acquires a startling completeness. It is with these two aspects of the tragedy that I shall now concern myself.

The spiritual distance between the moment when Beatrice surrenders passively to the villain she loathes and the moment when she tells him spontaneously, 'I'm forc'd to love thee now' (V.i.47 – where 'forc'd' means its opposite), is enormous. Typically, however, Middleton delineates the change, and makes it fully intelligible, within the space of ninety lines. The scene is one of high tension in which Beatrice calls upon De Flores to save her from the potentially disastrous consequences of Diaphanta's tardiness. De Flores revels in the challenge, his cool resourcefulness contrasting finely with Beatrice's mounting desperation. With dawn approaching, and Diaphanta still in the bride's place, he decides to set fire to the waiting-woman's chamber in order to 'force a rising' and get her to 'hasten towards her lodging'; there he will be ready with a fowling-piece, partly to scour the chimney, but mainly to kill Diaphanta while the household is in an uproar ('The deed shall find its time'). Meanwhile Beatrice is to wait for the opportunity to join Alsemero ('Watch you your minute'). The plan works so well that Beatrice is gathered into the arms of Alsemero as 'all sweetness' and De Flores is praised by her father as the perfect servant. It is this capacity to make things seem as they ought, even when living madly from moment to moment, that changes Beatrice's feelings for De Flores: his reassuring 'There, 'tis proper now' is rewarded instantly by her, 'I'm forc'd to love thee now' (ll. 46–7).

It is when her precious mask of propriety has been torn from her by Alsemero ('you fall down / Beneath all grace and goodness' – V.iii.45–6) that Beatrice, in a paradox typical of tragic endings, exhibits a true sense of decorum, seems to rise in grace. As we have seen, she acknowledges that she has lost distinction in the common sewer, and would not have her father come near her for fear of infection; she also asks forgiveness from all, perceives the relationship between past, present, and future ('my loathing / Was prophet to the rest, but ne'er believ'd'), and sees the fitness of her untimely death: ''Tis time to die, when 'tis a shame to live' (ll. 156–7, 179). Theological rigorists might damn her (and there have been some such among the critics); but it hardly seems Christian to damn someone who has confessed her sin and begged forgiveness. Secularly speaking, at any rate, Beatrice is redeemed, dies as she ought.

Despite the triumphant replacement and disposal of Diaphanta, and the successful feigning in Act IV of a suitable response to Alsemero's virginity test ('handsomely', keeping 'both the time and method' – ii.138, 148), the dominant impression created by the last two acts is of an inescapable retribution closing in upon Beatrice. She is 'fearfully distress'd' (IV.i.2, 10) throughout both acts; and, although she is conscious only of being 'distress'd' by the possibility that Alsemero will discover her loss of virginity, rather than by the consequences of murder, the Marlovian pun on that word is an omen that her plight is very much graver than she imagines.[22] From the beginning of Act IV, there is a strong sense that the whole natural order (of person, place, and time) will reassert itself and that Time will fulfil its appointed task of bringing forth truth and justice. The ghost which comes between De Flores and the daystar, and the clock which strikes one, two, and three while a distressed Beatrice waits for Diaphanta to emerge from the bridal chamber, are potent signs that this is so (v.i.1–68). But Time's action is carefully defined in terms of plot and characterisation as well.

Beatrice's deeds prompt two quite independent lines of inquiry. One of these, involving her father and Tomazo, is contaminated by haste and bad judgement and might well have ended in the deaths of two innocent men. Reluctantly, Vermandero accepts the force of Tomazo's argument that 'the hasty tie / Of this snatch'd marriage' makes Alonzo's disappearance from the castle smack of murder; and he accepts too that 'This is the place must yield account for him' (IV.ii.18–22). His suspicions fall on Franciscus and

Antonio: since they disappeared from the castle ten days earlier – the time of Alonzo's arrival and disappearance – 'The time accuses 'em', and he gives orders for them to be pursued 'suddenly' and with 'wing'd warrants for the purpose' (ll. 9–15). When the suspects have been apprehended, however, Vermandero's commendable speed gives way to that impetuosity ('violence') which prompted him to rush the first wedding and to sanction its hasty alternative. Without interrogating them, and with no other evidence than that they left the castle in disguise ten days earlier, he decides that Antonio and Franciscus are guilty; proudly, he hands them over to a Tomazo who by now has an eagerness to kill which momentarily allies him with his brother's murderer: 'Time's too precious / To run in waste now. . . . I thirst for 'em' (v.ii.49–85).

What prevents this grim miscarriage of justice is the investigation conducted by Alsemero and Jasperino into Beatrice's relationship with De Flores. Vermandero and Tomazo think they have 'suspicion near as proof itself', but these two discover 'proof / Beyond suspicion' (v.iii.123–5) by proceeding both promptly and patiently from the start. When his friend tactfully relays his news about Beatrice's secret meetings with De Flores, Alsemero is astonished and will not believe the worst; unlike Alonzo in a similar situation, however, he is not so blinded by love as to reject a prudent warning out of hand (II.i.124–55), but applies the virginity test learned from his *Book of Experiments, Call'd Secrets of Nature* – and, of course, is fooled. Later in the day, however, he and Jasperino observe 'Enough for deep suspicion', and his friend wisely leaves him alone to interrogate the suspect and 'seek out truth' (v.iii.3, 36). Dialogue, soliloquy, and action here constitute a marvel of eloquent, dramatic compression: they align the whole play with Sidney's conception of tragedy as a form which 'openeth the greatest wounds, and showeth forth the ulcers that are covered with tissue';[23] and they greatly extend that conception by relating the unfolding catastrophe to a natural order – now a fatal order – where union and division, meeting and parting, are subject to a law of fit relationships in time, person, and place:

> JASPERINO. Touch it home then: 'tis not a shallow probe
> Can search this ulcer soundly, I fear you'll find it
> Full of corruption; 'tis fit I leave you;
> She meets you opportunely from that walk:
> She took the back door at his parting with her.
>
> *Exit* JASPERINO.

ALSEMERO. Did my fate wait for this unhappy stroke
    At my first sight of woman? – She's here.

Enter BEATRICE.

BEATRICE. Alsemero!
ALSEMERO.   How do you!
BEATRICE.   How do I?
    Alas! How do you? You look not well.

                                        (ll. 7–15)

Alsemero's development in the last two acts into a model of judgement
and justice is unexpected. Moreover, in the final scene his attitude of
unsullied innocence and righteous indignation seems unwarranted;
certainly it is much less attractive to us than the dying candour of Beatrice,
even the unrepentant pride of De Flores. But it is unlikely that any ironic
effect was intended. His character (that of a deluded idealist who has had to
confront grim facts) is basically consistent; it has been developed in this
manner so as to give firm expression to the retributive element in the
thematic pattern.

                                    V

In arguing for the influence of *A Midsummer Night's Dream* on *The
Changeling*, I indicated that the relationship between the two plots of the
tragedy is something like an inverted hierarchy of opposites, a structural
image of confusion. I should now like to show just how thoroughly that
structural conception has affected both plots by examining the way in
which the subplot deals with the theme of decorum in place, person, and
time.

Despite all its lunacy, folly, and deformity, this Bedlam is essentially a
well-ordered place where discretion and propriety prevail. No one is fooled
here into taking gentle birth or a fine exterior as guarantees of decent
conduct. Forward fellows are repulsed, upstarts put down, violence is
cooled. Folly and even madness are cured. Much of this is due to the good
sense and the constancy of Isabella, but credit also is due to Alibius and his
servant Lollio. Despite their undoubted zaniness, these two run the asylum
on admirable lines, a basic regard for person, time, and place being built
into their daily procedures. Each new arrival is allocated a 'sweet lodging'
and then questioned by Lollio (a wise fool) in order to decide 'what form to

place him in' (I.ii.116, 148). Those with promise are tutored and 'raised to the higher degrees of discretion' (l. 118). Fools and madmen are kept in separate wards, and Alibius and Lollio divide their duties accordingly: Lollio's 'place' or 'charge' is with the fools, Alibius's with the madmen. There is no clock in the asylum, but the day is divided by meals, and mealtime is signalled by the hungry cries of the patients. To these signals the doctor and his man are always properly responsive: 'You may hear what time of day it is, the chimes of Bedlam goes. . . . their hour's come, they must be fed . . . . Go to your charge, Lollio, I'll to mine' (ll. 199–209).

This comical system of order and propriety is threatened by the departure of Alibius (his name, from the Latin *alibi*, signifies 'in another place') and by the intrusion of Antonio and Franciscus; and it is saved by Isabella's judgement and constancy. In ordinary circumstances, Lollio would be capable of protecting Isabella from the attentions of forward inmates with a sharp word and a wave of the whip: 'Not too near; you see your danger' (III.iii.53). But he is now the victim of his master's faulty judgement. Alibius distrusts Isabella and is fearful lest she be 'taken in another man's corn . . . in another place' (l. 10); yet he trusts Lollio completely, leaving him to watch both Isabella and the madmen in addition to the fools: 'Supply my place' (I.ii.40). Running desperately from one ward to the other, poor Lollio is unable to keep Isabella's two admirers from 'thrusting' at her; and he is soon tempted by their example to 'put in' for the 'first place' himself, using blackmail to strengthen his plea (IV.iii.38). Instantly put down, he is happy to resume his proper role and to help his mistress cure her two admirers.

Lollio's relationship with Isabella is neatly parallel and antithetical to that of De Flores with Beatrice. Antonio and Franciscus are analogous to Alonzo and Alsemero, but they are also representative of what is wrong with the castle in general and Beatrice in particular. This is suggested by the symbolism of dress and by two epithets which are repeatedly but doubtfully attached to them – 'handsome' and 'proper' (each of which signifies both 'good-looking' and 'becoming, appropriate'). Although they are disguised as fool and madman, the two gentlemen are 'Of stature and proportion very comely' (I.ii.55) and can reproduce under the threat of the whip something resembling the behaviour of 'a proper gentleman' (III.iii.60). But each is no more than 'a proper / Body . . . without brains to guide it', and so each fails Lollio's simple test: 'let me see how handsomely you behave yourself' (ll. 23–4, 37): as soon as he is alone with Isabella, each resorts to the desperate 'now' of the seducing opportunist (ll. 79, 116). Thus, although they both insist that their 'unbecoming', 'unhandsome' exterior hides a true lover, a proper gentleman,[24] Isabella tartly rejects the claim: 'keep / Your habit, it becomes you well enough' (l. 142; cf. IV.iii.142). Isabella in fact is the only one who ever, in a strict sense, appears improperly clad in Bedlam, and then only in the interest of reason, truth, and propriety. In order to get rid of Antonio and at the same time make him realise that the beauty he foolishly ascribed to her was merely apparent, she dons the attire of 'a wild unshapen antic' and dances madly before him: 'You a quick-sighted lover? Come not near me!' (IV.iii.125, 133). Here, of course, she contrasts with Beatrice, who uses a mask of spotless virtue and propriety to blind her lover (V.iii.3, 42-8).

We may conclude, then, that the partnership which Middleton and Rowley achieved in *The Changeling* is astonishingly close. From start to finish, the play is ordered by a relatively complex pattern of ideas on which there was complete mutual understanding. It is a tragedy of spiritual transformation in which the heroine becomes her own opposite. The second self, however, is a polarity in her own nature, and it is embodied externally in the hated servant who becomes her lover and master. This duality in the self and in the relationship of heroine and villain has a universal significance which is figured in the antithetical but confused relationship between castle and Bedlam. The confusion which results when identities are lost and opposites change place is expressed continuously in terms of decorum, a state of order and propriety which can be detected in Bedlam but survives only as a mask for folly and madness at the castle.

Except, however, in the first and in parts of the last scene, the partnership between the two dramatists is conceptual and structural rather than imaginative. The different elements do not 'concord and sympathise' and 'grow together' (I.ii.21-2) in a true artistic union, for the simple reason that both the comic and the antimasque elements of the subplot are pedestrian: there is a qualitative discontinuity between the two plots which keeps forcing itself upon our attention. Yet it should be emphasised that the philosophical grasp of the dramatists never falters and that in consequence there is more to admire in all parts of the play than is generally suspected.

VI

Women Beware Women offers a more comprehensive picture of moral degeneration than *The Changeling*; it is a less thrilling play, but ultimately it is a more subtle and satisfying one. It has two closely connected tragic plots, used to give the impression of a society affected at every level by basically the same corruptions. There are clownish characters in the secondary plot, but the comic element does not clearly differentiate the two plots and their respective milieus; rather, there is a scale of folly cutting across both plots, marked by urbane wit at one end and by gross buffoonery at the other, with a good deal of the fatuous in between. This mixing of the tragic and the comic is largely a consequence of Middleton's long saturation in the mode of satiric comedy; it is offered without any sign of literary embarrassment, no attempt being made to endow the generic confusion with metadramatic significance. The effect of the comic–satiric element is to put the stamp of ordinariness on evil and to sustain in the audience a mood of ironic detachment from the misfortunes of the principal characters.[25]

Each plot deals with a precipitate and unbalanced marriage which rapidly collapses into adultery. In other respects, however, the marriages are strongly contrasted. One is a runaway, secret marriage between a factor or merchant's agent and the daughter of wealthy parents; the other is between a rich but stupid heir and an intelligent, well-bred girl chosen for him by agreement between her father and his guardian. One union is romantic, the other mercenary; one does injustice to the bride's parents, the other to the bride. This polarised design is not intended simply for the purposes of balance and completeness. It incorporates a point of view, a suggestion that the 'fit match' (I.ii.21) is one which strikes a mean, avoids extremes, and is founded on the 'consent' (I.i.49) of all parties concerned (where 'consent' also means 'concent', harmony).

An outstanding feature of *Women Beware Women* is the extent to which the rites of hospitality figure in the action and are either directly or indirectly entwined with those of courtship and marriage. The play exhibits in classic form a favourite constructional formula of the Renaissance tragedian, having three great ritual scenes which stand out vividly from the rest of the action.[26] One is the chess scene (the game being a prelude to supper), where a neighbourly visit is contrived for the purpose of seducing the newly-wed Bianca. Another is the banquet where Bianca is introduced to society as the Duke's mistress, and Isabella, her counterpart in the other plot, is put on display for the benefit of her intended husband. The third is the masque celebrating the marriage of Bianca and the Duke – a Treacherous Entertainment which brings destruction to a society whose evils it mirrors comprehensively. But Middleton's interest in entertainment is not confined to the great set scenes shaped for symbolic purposes. For him entertainment is hospitality and neighbourliness, part of the fabric of everyday social life. Virtually every scene dramatises a welcoming or a farewell, so that the rituals of hospitality invade language itself, providing metaphors for all forms of human interaction and every psychological posture. The final effect is a thorough blending of hospitable, familial, and matrimonial concerns calculated to show a society whose binding principles are being undone at every point and at every moment of the day.[27]

The tragic process is considerably more sordid in *Women Beware Women* than in *The Changeling*, for lust is more predominant and is compounded with avarice as well.[28] As many have observed, this combination of evils, seen as gnawing at the roots of society, recalls the pattern of Middleton's city comedies. But the comparison can easily become a critical distraction, for this is a play of unique range and suggestiveness: every fresh encounter with the text seems to yield something new and exciting, and no one formulation of its thematic concerns ever seems quite adequate. To characterise it, for example, as a tragedy about the destructive effects of lust and greed is to leave out of account the crucial role played by the fascinating Livia in the downfall of Bianca. In search of a more comprehensive formulation, we might say that the source of evil is a form of self-assertion which is revealed in acquisitiveness, a desire to dispossess and outwit others, and in social manipulation generally. But if we speak of self-assertion we must come down to Middleton's own word and acknowledge that the source of all evil is to be found in something as simple as the will:

> a wife knows she must have, nay, and will,
> Will, Mother, if she be not a fool born;
> And report went of me, that I could wrangle
> For what I wanted when I was two years old,
> And by that copy, this land still I hold.
> You hear me, Mother.
>
> (III.i.55–60)

But, if it is typical of Middleton to trace all complexities back to a radical simplicity, making us feel that we have returned to the bedrock realities of human nature and experience, it is equally characteristic of him to move us in the other direction. Continually, he invests the familiar and the simple (for which his domestic material is a kind of sustained metaphor) with an air of elusive complexity, a recalcitrance to all univocal definition. So, if we decide that this is a tragedy about the destructive effects of self-will (the egoistic, anti-social impulse), and reconsider it accordingly, we soon recognise that it is also about the destructive effects of kindness, compassion, conviviality (the altruistic, social impulse) – and, further, about the disasters that can occur when the two tendencies form an unholy alliance, or become genuinely confused.

The main reason for the elusive complexity and comprehensiveness of *Women Beware Women* is the extent to which it is embedded in dualist habits of thought and expression: in this respect the play surpasses all other tragedies of the period. One manifestation of its dualist temper is the incessant but essentially unobtrusive punning.[29] Coextensive with this is the insistently ironic mode of expression: whole sentences assume the character of a pun and function with single words as instruments of the double vision. Then there are the paradoxes and oxymora, some of them overt, but most of them as quick and unobtrusive as the puns. Most significant of all, however, are the contrarious groupings of concept, word, and image. Like the puns and paradoxes, these too are devoid of formal emphasis, the opposite members of each group rarely being seen in conjunction. They are at once complicated and reinforced by means of polysemy and synonymy. Since the various meanings of a word in a particular group are liable to be played on, since each member of an antithesis is usually supported by a wide range of synonymous terms, and since there is no such thing as a perfect synonym, the outline of the antithesis forming in the mind is constantly changing. Evaluative or ethical priority, too, can switch from one opposite to the other: this may be effected simply by context (as in the sweet/bitter antithesis), or it may be signalled by a covert pun (as in mean/rich). The total effect of these polarities, and of the manner in which they are communicated, is of natural binary structures – psychological, ethical, social – forever in process of being undone: quietly, invisibly, treacherously. In Middleton's terms, 'Creation' slides into 'confusion'; and that is the first step towards – in fact, also means – 'destruction', 'ruin'.

If the play could be said to have one binding theme, it is doubleness-and-confusion (doubleness being the beginning of confusion). Doubleness is duality without unity, and so connotes division, contradiction, deception; but, as in *Macbeth* ('Double, double, toil and trouble'), it also carries suggestions of excess, of wanting more than is allowed by the natural order. Where all unity is held to be binary and quadruple at root, and where unity is the supreme good, it follows that doubleness is evil itself. It is identified as such when the seducing Duke – in a scene which clearly echoes the primal Fall – assures Bianca that in addition to a husband ('That's a single comfort') a wife needs 'a friend', and Bianca replies, 'That's a double mischief / Or else there's no religion' (II.ii.346–8). Thus the supreme villain of the play, the woman of whom all women must beware (for womankind, as the paradoxical title tells us, is no longer one), is duality personified. The bewitching (II.i.232–3) Livia is Middleton's equivalent of Spenser's witch Duessa, the beguiling creature dedicated to frustrating the marriage of Una

(True Religion) and the Red Cross Knight (Holiness) and replacing it with an adulterate facsimile (*Faerie Queene*, I).[30] In Middleton's play, Livia and her vicious associates completely confound the simple and the innocent with their double talk and their hypocritical shows. However, they owe much of their success to the fact that their victims are already divided within and have begun the process of confounding themselves.

I shall attempt to elucidate the experiences and meanings embodied in the play, and to demonstrate its singular subtlety and range, by examining its interrelated dualisms in a roughly logical sequence. This method has the obvious disadvantage of precluding any extended analysis of character; but, in relation to a play where the interaction of characters is of much greater interest than character itself, and where there is no dominant individual, that may not be a serious drawback. The method also runs the risk of giving a fragmented picture of a very coherent play. I would hope, however, that any such impression will be offset by my concluding analysis of the chess scene and the marriage masque, the play's major turning-point and its catastrophe: all of the major dualisms are brought together in those emblematic scenes in eloquently comprehensive commentaries on the total dramatic context.

Because there is so much semantic overlapping between the various dualisms, any attempt to classify them is necessarily somewhat arbitrary. However, I shall distinguish between three groups, the first of which bears on the essential nature and functioning of the given play-world. In a philosophical sense, the most important dualism in this group is that of peace and strife.[31] Its key expression occurs in Isabella's despairing reflection, as she contemplates enforced marriage to a fool, that the contradictions attendant on the marriage bond are sometimes resolved by 'honesty and love' into a condition of Edenic joy, much as 'Providence, that has made ev'ry poison / Good for some use . . . sets four warring elements / At peace in man', making 'a harmony / In things that are most strange to human reason' (I.ii.177–82). Leantio offers a neat account of the ethical basis of this marital harmony when he delivers the following homily to his overaffectionate wife:

> love that's wanton must be ruled awhile
> By that that's careful, or else all goes to ruin:
> As fitting is a government in love
> As in a kingdom; where all's mere lust
> 'Tis like an insurrection in the people,
> That raised in self-will wars against all reason.

> But love that is respective for increase
> Is like a good king that keeps all in peace.
>
> (I.iii.41–8)

Since Leantio is 'the poor thief' who stole Bianca from her rich home, the effect of this speech is deeply ironic. And the irony is characteristic, for throughout the play love is pursued in a manner which can only beget strife, yet is understood as a quest for peace. Leantio and Bianca discount the 'storms' and 'furies' which must erupt in Venice after their escape and expect to find 'a shelter' for their 'quiet innocent loves', a 'temple' of 'peace' and 'content', in his mother's simple home (I.i.50–3, 127–30). The Duke is prepared to rape Bianca if she resists his persuasion to love, and yet 'peace' is his great theme: 'Let storms come when they list, they find thee sheltered . . . Put trust in our love for the managing / Of all to thy heart's peace' (II.ii.383–6). And, if Bianca yields because she has no alternative, she yields also because his tyrannous lust is genuinely confused with a desire for the contentment of true union, and because she herself is attracted by the promise of a peaceful, sheltered love: she is ruined because she is confounded. After her fall, that temple of peace which she sought with Leantio instantly becomes a place of discord. The quiet bride turns strident, and Leantio, overwhelmed by the sudden transformation, inverts his original view of marriage: 'What a peace / Has he that never marries. . . . what a quietness . . .' (III.ii.199–205). The storms that rack his breast compound longing and regret, love and hate, and culminate in furious threats of revenge which disturb the peace of Bianca's lodgings at court. She complains to the Duke ('I love peace, sir') and is reassured by him in a characteristically sinister confusion of primal contraries: 'Do not vex your mind, prithee to bed, go, / All shall be well and quiet' (IV.i.124–5). All shall be quiet, that is, when Leantio has been disposed of by an infuriated Hippolito: the plan is fully formed in the Duke's mind as he speaks. But the troublesome Leantio is murdered partly because he has become the lover of Hippolito's sister Livia, who has soothingly offered him the means to excite envy in his 'enemy' (i.e. Bianca) without fear of consequences: 'shalt not spend a care for't . . . / Nor break a sleep; unless love's music waked thee, / No storm of fortune should' (III.iii.301–6). The killing of Leantio is the logical consequence of the way in which everyone has misconstrued the conditions for true peace. And it sparks off the bloodbath which, in the final scene, all but destroys 'the general peace of Florence' (V.ii.199).

'All shall be well and quiet.' Only a dramatist obsessed with the nuances of everyday speech and what it can tell us about the strangeness of the commonplace would engage in so much manipulation of the terms 'well', 'good', and 'ill'. In comparative and superlative forms, and supported by numerous synonyms, these words flow through the dialogue in such abundance that their distinctive meanings are all but obliterated:[32] indeed, the word 'good' becomes a kind of definite article for everything.[33] All this is dramatically apt, for most of the characters spend their lives making wrong right and right wrong: sometimes consciously, often unconsciously, and sometimes – it seems – both. We are introduced to the practice in the opening scene with Leantio's account of his marriage. In eloping with Bianca he was guilty of 'theft' and 'sin'; but, because of her 'hidden virtues', and because he married her, it is 'the best piece of theft ever committed', 'never to be repented', 'noble', something to 'glory in' (I.i.35–43, 55). Far from being affected by his mother's suggestions of 'blame' and 'wrong [to] such perfection', he criticises her in terms which exaggerate his own confusion: 'old people ... strive to mar good sport, because they are perfect'; they 'talk of nothing but defects, / Because they grow so full of 'em themselves' (ll. 103–4, 123–4). Bianca makes her own little contribution with the charming admission that Leantio did not – as she first claimed – neglect to give her a welcoming kiss: 'Now I remember well. I have done thee wrong' (l. 145). In fact her memory of such rights and wrongs does not serve her well here (as we shall shortly emphasise).

But in the art of making ill seem well Leantio and Bianca are as yet novices beside the lady whom we meet in the next scene. A perfectly humanised descendant of the Vice, Livia of the smooth and witty tongue can make the language of goodness do wonders in the service of sin. She gently rebukes her brother for allowing his eye to 'Dwell evilly' on his niece; but, when it becomes clear that he is deeply in love, she quickly shifts her ground and promises to get him what he wants, declaring affectionately, and in a paradox whose terrible truth she can hardly be aware of, 'Beshrew [curse] you, would I loved you not so well' (II.i.9, 63).[34] Her device is to free Isabella from the fear of incest by declaring her illegitimate, blackening her mother's name with a tale of adultery, and assuring her that this 'secret' will 'take no wrong' if it is 'Made good by oath' between them (l. 157). Isabella is thus encouraged to 'make shift' with marriage to a fool by taking a genuine lover: 'the best wits will do't' (l. 115). A measure of Livia's success is the promptness with which 'the virtuous Isabella' (l. 58) adopts her idiom, ''Twould be ill', she tells Hippolito, if her marriage to the Ward did not go forward; she has no objection now to being married to a fool – for her purposes, 'the worse the better'; although she and Hippolito will not 'fare well' every day, they will have at least one 'good bit' weekly (ll. 206–23).

Livia's seduction of the deserted Leantio follows a somewhat similar pattern. She descends upon him in his misery with an offer of 'good counsel' which is gratefully accepted: 'It never could come better' (III.iii.24). Her first point is that he should promptly 'make away all ... good thoughts' about his wife because – and this is a secret which it would be 'sin' not to reveal to him – 'most assuredly she is a strumpet' (ll. 274–9). Her next point is a cunningly confused appeal to his acquisitiveness and his moral self-regard – his love of goods and good. He was 'too good and pitiful' to marry a girl who brought him no dowry; his life with her would have been one of miserable penury; what he needs is a lady who – 'Thanks to blessedness' – is able to 'reward good things ... and bears a conscience to't' (ll. 289–300, 351). Given the circumstances, he is morally free to accept this offer: 'You do well I warrant you, fear it not sir; / Join but your own good will to't' (ll. 352–3). Having succumbed, Leantio – like Isabella – gives a vivid exhibition of Livia's art, more startling than anything he was capable of before. Visiting Bianca to excite her envy and denounce her immorality, he tells her she is a 'court saint' devoid of all 'charity' and tied to a 'devil'. His own partner is a 'beauteous benefactor' rich in 'the good works of love' (IV.i.68–79); in other words, she has turned him into a factor who 'does well' (Latin *bene facere*, do well).

Along with the rhetorical art of making ill sound well, there is the commercial art of putting imperfect or bad goods on display in the best light. Again (and appropriately) this begins with the young commercial agent. He may talk about his wife's 'hidden virtues', but he wants his mother to concentrate only on her physical appearance and to view her as a beautiful object: 'Look on her well, she's mine. Look on her better' (I.i.40). The banquet scene is a sustained exhibition of this kind, with the difference that the goods are now seriously defective. Isabella's father proudly arranges for her 'good parts' (i.e. her singing and dancing) to be made public for the benefit of the Ward, and a doting Duke presents Bianca to society as a creature 'of purpose sent into the world to show / Perfection once in a woman' (III.iii.5, 23–4). Counterpointed by the appropriate antonyms, and by situational and verbal irony, the word 'good' (including 'well', 'better', and 'best') occurs no less than twenty-eight times in this scene; nowhere else are we so firmly directed to the misuse of morally approving terms and to the general confusion of good and ill. The scene is given a grotesque coda in the incident where the Ward and Sordido subject Isabella to a private inspection to see if she has any hidden 'faults' (III.iv.26–30); they conclude that all is 'good', 'well', 'right'.

Almost everything that relates to peace and strife and good and ill finds expression in *welcomes* and *farewells*: dramatically and symbolically, this is the major dualism. Middleton's constant playing with the root forms and meanings of the two words – 'come', 'fare' (i.e. 'go' or 'the food provided'), and 'well' – not only links them with the other two dualisms; it also stresses their own mutual affinities as well as their radical distinction, and so points to an area of potential confusion. The society depicted is one which puts pressure on the individual to 'come', 'stay', be ever more 'near'; it discourages partings and is unceremonious with farewells. The effect of this ethos, however, is not to enhance unity; it is to ignore limits, distinctions, and timely progressions in an emotional prodigality that quickly turns peace to strife. So it is obvious that not all comings are well, and that to be happy in life (to fare well) it may often be necessary to refuse good cheer and bid a firm farewell.

The importance of farewells to the welfare of the individual and the community is dramatised openly in the second and third scenes and hinted at in the first. Making little of the delighted welcome which his mother gives him, Leantio devotes all his efforts in the opening scene to securing the same for his bride: 'Go, pray salute her, bid her welcome cheerfully' (I.i.110). In the circumstances it is not easy for the Mother to do as she is bid. There is a great social distance between this elegant young lady and herself, she has arrived unannounced, and she has come to stay permanently. Moreover she has left 'rage' and 'heavy hearts' (III.iii.50, 96) behind her. Bianca's gracious attempt to smooth over the situation by enthusiastically embracing the humble conditions of her new home – 'they shall all be welcome . . . they must all be welcome and used well' (I.i.135–8) – merely serves, by its insistent inclusiveness and its added phrase, to suggest that through neglect of a precedent farewell this coming cannot be made good.

The next two scenes would encourage us to think that the crucial failure to bid farewell concerned the couple alone and not Bianca and her family and friends. In I.ii Hippolito's declaration of passion is received by his niece as an unwelcome visitor: 'ill news come towards me'. Sadly but firmly, she puts an immediate end to their friendship:

> Though my joys fare the harder, well fare [farewell to] it:
> It shall ne'er come so near mine ear again,
> Farewell all friendly solaces and discourses,
> I'll learn to live without ye, for your dangers
> Are greater than your comforts.
>
> (ll. 221–5)

I.iii is a development from the moment in I.i when Leantio turned aside from Bianca's 'dear welcome' to reflect with bitterness on the morrow, when he would have to leave her and the pleasures of love for the rest of the week. Although tempted in the morning to say, 'Farewell all business' (I.iii.16), he rises with good intentions. Bianca, however, appears at the window as he is about to leave, and almost prevents his departure: 'Come, come, pray return. / Tomorrow, adding but a little care more, / Will despatch all as well' (ll. 37–9). But it is here that Leantio delivers his little homily on the need for self-government in love, and it wins from Bianca a reluctant agreement to part: 'Since it must, farewell too' (l. 57). The scene with Bianca '*above*' at the window occurs three times in the play and is an image of great significance; among other things, it is a remembrance of the way in which she and Leantio conducted their courtship (IV.i.44–5). It tends to support one's feeling here that Bianca has called, 'Come, come, pray return', many times before, and that this is the first time Leantio has been able to resist the call. As always in tragedy, wisdom is late a-coming.

And in this tragedy (when it is not folly in disguise) it is quick to leave. With the intervention of Livia on behalf of Hippolito and the Duke, the restraint shown by Isabella, Leantio, and Bianca comes to an end. 'So lively and so cheerful' (II.ii.449), Livia is the very spirit of welcome; but her conception of 'great cheer' (III.i.5) is simply good fare, and that, in the symbolism of the play, stands for sensual gratification. Having promised to secure for Hippolito the 'pleasant fruits' of 'sensuality' (II.i.31), she sets about awakening Isabella's dormant sexual attraction to her uncle, deceives her about her parentage, and creates another version of her own hospitable self. The gravely polite young lady who bade Hippolito a lasting farewell is replaced by a cheerful woman of the world who comes 'so unexpectedly / To meet [his] desires'. Inviting him to a 'feast', she explains that prudence will later entail some economies ('She that comes once to be a housekeeper / Must not look every day to fare well, sir'); but she hopes that they will learn to 'fare with thankfulness' together (ll. 217–330).

The chess scene is Livia's triumph in the art of welcome. Everything here turns initially on the Mother's inability to resist her invitation to stay. A whole world – of class, experience, culture, and age – separates this simple woman from the fashionable Lady Livia; but Livia overwhelms her with the pretence that they are just two old neighbours ready for an evening of 'tongue discourse' together (II.ii.152). Yet another world separates the sixteen-year-old Bianca from the fifty-five-year-old Duke, but that too is presently obliterated: 'sin and I'm acquainted, / No couple greater' (ll. 440–1). Ruined in her own eyes, Bianca despairingly surrenders herself forever to 'Cupid's feast' – 'Come poison all at once' (ll. 402, 426).

The final departures of Leantio and Bianca are grim commentaries on all ill comings. Leantio's vague threat that 'a plague will come' to Bianca's 'everlasting parting' (IV.i.104, 88) is reported to the Duke; and he, having welcomed Leantio to his circle as a complaisant cuckold, now sees him as a troublesome guest who must be 'sped' on his way. So Hippolito the killer is instructed to come quickly, which he does: 'he comes; Hippolito, welcome'; and Leantio is on his way before he knows it: 'Farewell, Leantio, / This place shall never hear thee murmur more' (ll. 141, 178–9). What speeds Bianca is the 'parting kiss' (V.ii.196) which she takes from the poisoned lips of the Duke, and the poisoned cup – symbol of hospitality betrayed – which she had intended for the Cardinal. Her last speech is that of a guest who hastily departs when she discovers she has not been among friends after all: 'What make I here? These are all strangers to me, / Not known but by their malice' (ll. 206–7).

The second group of dualisms – kind/strange, sweet/bitter, and fair/ foul (or bright/dark) – is comprised of epithets which are used primarily to register feelings about characters and actions deemed welcome, good, peaceful and the reverse; as such they lie at the heart of the play's emotional life. The kind/strange antithesis has a narrow range of synonyms, but each of the key terms has a number of meanings which are fully exploited. Some of these meanings are now obsolete, but it is from them that the antithetical relationship of the two terms derives. 'Strange' means not only 'unusual', 'surprising', but also (1) 'of another country', (2) 'not of one's own kin or family', (3) 'unfriendly, not affable'. 'Kind' means not only 'friendly and affectionate', but also (1) 'natural', (2) 'native', (3) 'related by kinship'. 'Kind' is an especially complex word in that it can designate a concept – nature – which is manifestly dualist: to act 'in one's kind' towards others may be to act in a kindly or cruelly selfish manner, or both (see II.ii.417; III.iii.72). This oxymoronic pun is central. At one level, the play is about kindness to strangers; at another, it is about the cruelty of much kindness, about the unnatural love of kind, and about the strangeness of nature. Although rooted in a mundane world, it is a play which strikes a note of strangeness throughout: characters are repeatedly experiencing things which seem to them 'most strange to human reason', 'beyond compre-hension'. The root cause of their wonder is the changing nature of the contrarious world; more immediately, it is passion and its transforming power, 'amazed affection' (V.ii.77).

The play begins with a fine contrast between natural and strange kindness. On the one hand there is the Mother's spontaneous outburst of 'natural love' for Leantio (in which she relives her 'birth-joy'). On the other there are the strained mutual reactions of the two women. Carefully, the Mother offers first the kiss 'of courtesy / Which fashionable strangers pay each other / At a kind meeting', and then another 'Due to the knowledge' she now has of her 'nearness'. For her part, the fashionable stranger addresses the older woman as 'Kind Mother' and declares that 'The voice of her that bare me is not more pleasing' – indeed, 'I'll call this place the place of my birth now'. In order to be kindly, Bianca is prepared to rewrite her own biological history.

Thus the first scene prepares us gently for the various perversions of kind and kindness that dominate the two plots. These all find a focus in Livia, a woman whose exuberant kindness ('how't exceeds!') is genuine at root, yet tends always towards the instant annihilation of proper distinctions and natural rights: 'though I knew you not, / Nor ever saw you – yet humanity / Thinks every case her own' (II.ii.455, 248–50). Because of her 'kindness', the strangeness (or unkindness) inherent in Bianca's marriage comes abruptly to the surface. Once she has experienced 'great cheer at my lady's', Bianca finds her adoptive home 'the strangest house / For all defects', and says so with an unladylike harshness that astounds the Mother: "Tis the most suddenest, strangest alteration, / And the most subtlest' (III.i.516–17, 63–4). She makes her lip 'strange' to Leantio and becomes an advocate of moderate 'kindness betwixt man and wife' (III.ii.76–7). Formally completed at the banquet, when she takes her seat beside the Duke as a cynical woman of the world, her transformation registers upon the miserable Leantio as a perception that he is now a complete stranger to his adored wife; 'Canst thou forget / The dear pains my love took? . . . Canst thou forget all this?' (III.iii.252–64). The wonder and anguish he expresses in this great soliloquy – 'so new it is / To flesh and blood, so strange, so insupportable a torment' – is the emotional high point of the tragedy; but it is also coincident with a moment of maximum ethical insight. Like her family, Leantio experiences Bianca's 'strange departure' from him as if it were a sudden bereavement (ll. 315–20); and he acknowledges (what he will quickly forget) the operation of poetic justice: 'I'm rightly now oppressed; / All her friends' heavy hearts lie in my breast' (ll. 95–6).

The strangeness of kind and of kindness is at its most insidious in the relations between Livia, Hippolito, and Isabella. Initially Livia tells her brother that his 'strange affection' for their niece is 'somewhat too unkindly'; but his misery excites her sisterly affection and she decides he must be 'eased' (II.i.1, 8, 71). This decision will seem both less and more surprising if we accept the view, held by a number of critics, that there is something incestuous in her own feelings for Hippolito. Because of a simple parallel, the view appears correct to me: Isabella blushes when she hears Hippolito's declaration of desire, so does Hippolito when his sister greets him in terms of remarkable warmth (l. 55; I.ii.147). At any rate,

Livia's kindness to Hippolito becomes unnatural by virtue of the 'strange cure' it entails (II.i.50). Having slandered her own sister, this 'Kind, sweet, dear aunt' persuades Isabella to 'set by the name of niece awhile, / And bring in pity in a stranger fashion' (ll. 101, 90–1). Returning to Hippolito with Isabella in tow, she utters a triumphant little cry which crystallises brilliantly the bottomless confusion over which she reigns: 'She's thine own, go' (l. 179).

The sweet/bitter dualism is supported by a rich cluster of sensory images, olfactory and gustatory as well as auditory (the much-noted food imagery is assimilated to this dualism). It denotes a society where everyone is driven by appetite and deluded by the senses; where the acceptable manner is one of habitual and undiscriminating sweetness; and where true sweetness either turns or seems bitter, and what is apparently sweet is essentially corrupt and poisonous. This whole pattern of meaning is figured in the contrasting responses of Livia and the Cardinal to the sinful desires of their respective brothers. Seeing that her 'sweet brother' finds her 'reprehension' unpleasant, Livia drops her 'too bitter' concern for 'truth and zeal' and promises to produce such 'pleasant fruits as sensuality wishes' (II.i.22–31). But the Cardinal, knowing that there is no 'sweet ease' to wretchedness in the next life for confirmed sinners, persists in his 'reprehension' (IV.i.232). His severity, however, is moderated by tears and prompted by a compassionate desire for 'the blest fruits' of repentance (l. 254). The Duke himself recognises (for the moment only) that he is a 'sweet brother' (l. 228).

Especially important is sweetness in the sense of freshness, purity, and wholesomeness, as opposed to rankness and putridity. This is linked up with ideas of nature and artifice in tracing the simultaneous process of moral corruption and social sophistication which both heroines undergo. Returning home, Leantio anticipates a kiss 'sweet as morning dew upon a rose' and fervently contrasts the 'chaste flowers' of married love with the pleasures offered by strumpets – rotting 'carcasses' covered in paint and powder (III.ii.5–18). He does not know that Bianca has already lost her original sweetness and is demanding artificial substitutes: to begin with, perfumes for her plain bedroom, 'A silver-and-gilt [=guilt] casting bottle' (III.i.21). The Ward is similarly deluded for a time by Isabella. Although warned by 'sweet Sordido' that a sweet-kissing wench might prove diseased and rotten in bed, he detects in Isabella's kiss the 'delicious scent' of 'a comfit-maker's shop' – she'll be his 'sweetheart' (II.ii.95; III.iv.60–1, 131).

Although the official style of this society is sweet, it has in fact two other styles, the bitter–sweet and the bitter. The bitter–sweet effect is noticeable at the banquet in the cynical love song sung by Isabella, the girl with the 'sweet' voice who is betrothed to a 'rank ass' (III.iii.120; II.ii.118). This serves as a preparation for the rich tonal complexities of Leantio's moving soliloquy (later in the same scene) on the loss of Bianca. But the bitter style is more significant. It stands out against the official norm with startling clarity to make this a tragedy with a rarely bitter flavour: a cold, terse, sardonic bitterness expressed mostly in asides and short soliloquies, and rendered intense by a shocked sense of trust betrayed and affection abused. It is heard in Bianca's initial response to the treachery of Livia and Guardiano; in Livia's reaction to her brother's 'reason' for killing her lover ('The reason! That's a jest Hell falls a-laughing at' – IV.ii.63); and in Isabella's response to the discovery of her aunt's lies and continued hypocrisy ('Here's e'en a sweet amends made for a wrong. . . . All the smart's nothing' – ll. 180–3). In the end, sin embitters everyone: the cup of nectar was wormwood indeed (II.ii.476–7).

The fair/foul (or dark) dualism is distinct in that it is focused with special sharpness on Bianca.[35] Initially she is conceived by Leantio as a brilliant jewel to be hidden in some obscure place from 'fair-eyed Florence' (I.i.16–6). In the ironic progress of the action this contrast is inverted. Quick-eyed Florence catches sight of the hidden gem and appropriates it; thereafter the contrast is between outer brilliance (physical beauty, social advancement) and inner darkness or foulness (spiritual blindness and corruption). To the Duke, Bianca is 'fair', 'bright', 'glorious'; a dazzling light in a lustreless world, a precious stone due for a noble setting. To the Cardinal and Leantio, she is the 'fair', 'glistering' strumpet with the black soul, lost in darkness herself and leading others in that direction (IV.i.95, 244; ii.20). Her 'beautified body' is like 'a goodly temple / That's built on vaults where carcasses lie rotting' (III.ii.14–18).

Central to this symbolic dualism is the heroine's full name: Bianca Capelli (or Capello) in the originals, but by Middleton changed to Bianca Capella, the White or Fair Temple (here, as in *The Changeling*, 'temple' is used synonymously with 'church'). This symbolic idea is given great resonance by association with two well-known biblical passages: Christ's description of the Pharisees as 'whited Sepulchres, which indeed appeare beautifull outward' (Matthew 23:27); and Paul's injunction to avoid fornication because 'your body is the Temple of the Holy Ghost' (1 Corinthians 6:18–19; 3:16–17).[36] Like Webster's White Devil, Bianca Capella – the ruined temple of peace, the befouled temple of virtue – is a representative figure, and the symbolism of her name has wide application. It extends to Leantio, the Duke, Isabella and her family, and ultimately to the whole of society. For Leantio accepts 'goodness' in compensation for his cuckolding, becoming captain of the 'Rouans [ruins] citadel'

(III.iii.67), a gentleman in 'fair clothes' got by 'foul means' (IV.i.111); and he and the others all use the 'privileged temple' of matrimony as a 'sanctuary' for their crimes and vices (IV.iii.39–44; III.ii.165).

My third and final class of dualism is directly concerned with tragic error and, in particular, with the problem of making choices whch are morally right and conducive to happiness. First is the generic antithesis of wisdom and folly. Wisdom is shown to have been degraded to the level of worldly wisdom – 'wit', 'subtlety','art', 'craft', 'discretion'. Its function is to conceal the truth (III.ii.159) and to beguile the innocent and the inexperienced into making wrongful choices. To the wise of this world, the 'simple . . . goodness' of the innocent (I.ii.213; II.ii.306) is just as comical as the folly of the simpletons (such as Fabritio and the Ward):

> I can but smile as often as I think on't:
> How prettily the poor fool was beguiled,
> How unexpectedly; it's a witty age.
>
> (II.ii.394–6)

Middleton's point, however, is that worldy wisdom is mad folly. Almost certainly he has in mind the admonitory paradox which follows immediately upon the passage on the body as temple of the Holy Spirit in the First Epistle to the Corinthians: 'For the wisdome of this world is foolishnesse with God: for it is written, Hee catcheth the wise in their owne craftinesse' (3:119).

Livia of course is the apostle of worldly wisdom, and Isabella, Bianca, and Leantio are her converts. She persuades Isabella that 'Fools will serve to father wise men's children', and thereafter 'wit' and 'discretion' are Isabella's chief terms of reference (II.i.162, 215). At the start, Leantio sees himself as a wise and politic fellow (I.i.162; iii.28), but until he meets Livia his worldly potential is unrealised. Cunningly she leads with the proposition that 'Young gentlemen . . . love not wisely' who marry for beauty alone, and then convinces him that deserted husbands who love their pain and sickness are equally unwise (III.iii.279–80, 355). But it is in Bianca that the change from innocent simplicity to worldly wisdom is most fully delineated. The girl who is welcomed to Florence is unquestionably an innocent abroad, one whose moral goodness is fragile and imperfect but none the less genuine. Its authenticity is endorsed by the exactness with which she is identified with Eve, and by her seducer's appeal to worldly wisdom in overcoming her explicitly religious sense of morality: she should 'pluck fruit' from the 'tree that bears all women's wishes' – a duke's favour – and 'play the wise wench, and provide forever'; her own mother would commend her 'wit' if she saw her do so (II.ii.348–82). After her fall, Bianca plays the wise wench so well that she replaces Livia as the presiding genius of this 'witty age'. At the banquet, for example, her sage and jocular remarks about the wisdom shown by Florentine damsels in managing foolish husbands are publicly commended by the Duke: 'That wit deserves to be made much on' (III.iii.112–34). But her great triumph comes when she silences the Cardinal with a sermon on charity, 'the first born of religion', the virtue which 'begins the rest, / And sets them all in order' (cf. 2 Corinthians 13:13). Taking up his Pauline argument about the body as temple of the spirit, she wittily turns it against him (''Tis nothing virtue's temple to deface, / But build the ruins, there's the work of grace') and then buttresses her position by means of the most famous of all passages in the epistles to the Corinthians. Her Satanic seducer is delighted: 'I kiss thee for that spirit; thou hast praised thy wit / A modest way' (IV.iii.50–71); but her dead husband's words ring truer than ever: 'damnation has taught you that wisdom' (III.iii.134).

A corollary to the wisdom/folly dualism is that of earnest and jest, business and play. The wits are all 'wise gamesters' (III.iv.80) who treat sexual relations as a sport: Livia's chess, the Ward's cat trap, and the allusions to hot cockles, shuttle-cock, and bowls are all sexually symbolic. A consequence of this confusion of the serious and the trivial is that the playfully friendly manner of the wits conceals a brutal intent: as the Ward – who lacks 'discretion' – confesses, 'When I am in game, I am furious; came my mother's eyes in my way, I would not lose a fair end . . . . I think of nobody when I am in play, I am so earnest' (I.ii.98–102). On the other hand, avarice and ambition can turn 'wanton' sex into a 'serious', profit-making occupation: thus the words 'business', 'service', 'game', and 'sport' are all synonymous, all slang terms for copulation.[37]

Hot cockles is a form of blind-man's-buff; yet, whatever form the game takes (as the Ward implies), it is played blindly. Blindness is a familiar motif in tragic literature, but its impact on this tragedy is distinctive and very sharp.[38] Whereas blindness is usually confined to the main character in other tragedies, here it affects almost everyone. Usually too there is progress from blindness through suffering to a compensatory and ennobling recognition; but this play is remarkable for the way in which moments of understanding are followed by bitterness, evasion, and more blindness. The theme, too, is integrated to the play with exceptional thoroughness. In the first place, it is explored dualistically. Overtly and throughout, the play is concerned with seeing and looking (physical vision) as well as 'blindness' (want of intellectual or moral sense): this double emphasis generates the paradox that sight (the senses) is the cause of blindness, seeing is not seeing.[39] The theme is greatly extended too in the cognate but distinguishable theme of concealment and revelation (all revelations blind, being either false or provocative). Lastly, the metaphors of vision and blindness are richly supported by non-verbal imagery (masks, dress, lights) and by emblematic or significantly shaped action (Bianca seeing and being seen from the window '*above*', being put on display, being ordered to 'Withdraw' and 'Come forth', being taken on a sight-seeing tour of Livia's home).

Undoubtedly the theme bears most fully on 'bright Bianca'. When she comes down from Livia's gallery, the paradox of Eve's fallen condition – blinded, but with her eyes open to sin – is renewed in her: 'I' faith, I have seen that I little thought to see, / I' th' morning when I rose' (II.ii.456–7). With its faintly punning suggestion of a blown rose (her innocent kiss was 'sweet as morning dew upon a rose'), and its sense of numb shock and total disillusion, this brief utterance is unbearably poignant. But Middleton's irony does not allow Bianca to become a figure of tragic pity. From now on he contrasts her growing conviction that she sees everything with the fact that she sees nothing. Soon she is extrapolating from her own history of domestic restraint, rebellion, and worldly success the principle that young people should not be restricted since their fortunes will find them out anyhow: 'I see't in me' (IV.i.36). She 'cannot see' any charity in the Cardinal's opposition to a marriage which uses 'the immaculate robe of honour' to conceal 'leprosy and foulness': she even accuses him of attempting to 'take light / From one that sees' (IV.iii.52, 14, 17, 63–4). She spies malice behind his resigned gesture of reconciliation ('this shall not blind me' – V.ii.17), and poisons the Duke in mistake for him. The superb paradox in the Duke's dying words apply even more aptly to her than to him: 'I am lost in sight' (l. 183).

A fundamental truth to which most characters in the play blind themselves is that happiness in society depends on a balance of freedom and restraint.[40] Their self-will makes them extremists who turn rule into tyranny and freedom into licence. They thus achieve effects exactly opposite to what they intended, since one extreme naturally begets the other. Justice of the Peace Fabritio compels his daughter to marry the Ward (she 'must of force consent' – II.i.88) and so provokes a sexual rebellion that breaks all laws. Bianca escapes from a home which she claims (unconvincingly) to be too restrictive, only to find herself 'mewed up' as never before. The Duke marries Bianca in order to escape his brother's strictures, but, having to dispose of Leantio in order to do so, 'he must bind himself in chains' to sin forever (IV.iii.13). The great error lies in the assumption that all one's desires can be satisfied (I.i.126; II.ii.371;

v.ii.16). 'Content' (perhaps the chief word in the play for happiness) means 'contained', 'having ones desires bounded by what one has'.

The symbolism of ascent and descent, evident everywhere in metaphoric diction and stage movement, provides an imaginative link between the freedom/restraint dualism and that of will and chance (or fortune). As in *The Changeling*, tragic disorder is viewed hierarchically as well as contrariously: lust, greed, ambition, and pride are all expressions of the impassioned will 'rising' against reason (I.iii.45–6). Although the play catches the spirit of contemporary bourgeois competitiveness, Middleton makes it clear that this blind upward striving is a universal phenomenon and not something peculiar to his own time: it is what 'gave Lucifer / A tumbling cast' (III.ii.44–5), and it is as common in domestic and political spheres as in external nature: everyone and everything is predisposed to 'strive' for 'the upper hand' (III.iii.210–11). The Mother translates this fact into a pertinent psycho-social warning for her newly-wed son: 'ev'ry woman' expects 'maintenance fitting her birth and virtues', but 'most to go above it; not confined / By their conditions, virtue, bloods, or births, / But flowing to affections, will, and humours' (I.i.66–70). Of course, this warning is ominous only because Leantio has already gone far above himself: perhaps because in the past his 'obedience' has been as indisposed to 'give way' to a parental 'check' as it clearly is now (l. 57).

Plot and emblematic action vividly uphold the old paradox that the wilful way up is also the way down; but, despite the spectacular descents and falls of the last scene, Middleton's emphasis is on spiritual collapse rather than worldly misfortune. On 'coming down' from the gallery where she has been made 'fortunate in a duke's favour', Bianca acknowledges that she has been 'abased, and made for use' (II.ii.419, 370, 436). Kneeling to accept honours from the man who stole his stolen wife, Leantio rises a moral wreck: 'Rise now the Captain of our fort at Rouans' (III.iii.42). The depth to which husband and wife have sunk as a result of their elevation is most eloquently disclosed, perhaps, in the scene where they indulge in a ritual of mutual abuse, she from her high court window, he in his gigolo's finery (IV.i.23–111).

Those who follow the dictates of the impassioned will characteristically ascribe everything that happens – good and bad – to Fortune. The disasters of the last scene, heavily dependent as they are on accident and miscalculation, would seem to justify such an attitude; the significance of the scene, however, is that the victims of accident have exposed themselves to it by virtue of their own wilfulness. That is consistent with the rest of the play, where the accidentalist philosophy is shown to be a glib manifestation of the prevailing confusion. Livia, for example is never more enthusiastic about the blessings of Fortune and the stars than when she is wittily arranging for the desires of the impassioned will to be satisfied (II.i.59–60; III.iii.290, 359–60); again, when Bianca coldly informs the Mother that 'Fortune matched me to your son', she goes on to wrangle about what she 'must have, nay and will, / Will, Mother' (III.i.46–56). Given the endemic nature of accidentalist attitudes, it seems reasonable for Guardiano to assume that the masque murders planned by himself and Livia 'Will be laid all on Fortune, not our wills': 'will be thought / Things merely accidental – all's but chance, / Not got of their own natures' (V.i.36; IV.ii.164–6).[41] Outside of *Edward II*, no other tragedy of note is quite so insistent that Fortune is essentially a device whereby men and women absolve themselves of responsibility for the consequences of what they have willed.

However, metaphysical questions relating to human responsibility and world order are touched on far more lightly in the will/fortune theme than in two antithetical themes which are themselves complementary opposites: memory and forgetfulness, providence ('thrift', 'good husbandry', 'increase', 'fruitfulness') and improvidence ('waste', 'expense', 'ill-husbandry', 'barrenness'). These two themes are integral to the overarching themes of time and 'divine Providence' (I.i.98); as such, they afford a more synoptic view of the play than has hitherto been possible in this analysis.

It is understood that providence means acting wisely now with an eye to the future: 'let not passion waste / The goodness of thy time, and of thy fortune' (II.i.24–5). Being at once 'good husbandry' (a useful pun), 'thrift', and 'fruitfulness', it is a form of wisdom which is rooted in nature and applicable equally in marital and economic matters. Because it imitates the economy of both nature and (as the term itself implies) divine providence, it posits an ideal of timely relationships flourishing in a timeless order.

By a nice logic, the theme of memory and forgetfulness is focused initially in Bianca, that of providence and improvidence in Leantio. As befits him, the newly-wed factor is determined to 'prove an excellent husband . . . Lay in provision, follow my business roundly' (I.i.107–8). But his commitment to providence, human and divine, is mere talk, and very confused at that. His mother points out that he had difficulty in managing as a single person and will be unable to keep his dowerless lady in 'maintenance fitting her birth and dues'; to this he responds with a blustering assurance in which outright improvidence is disguised as providence, and 'divine Providence' is treated as an insurance scheme for sexually prodigal couples (ll. 61–109). There is a touch of the comic in this, and at worst it is feckless immaturity. But it marks the beginning of a tragic chain of cause and consequence, and is the first in a series of occasions when the idea of providence, human or divine or both, is wantonly perverted. There is Isabella, determined to be a thrifty 'housekeeper' in managing the pleasures of adultery – 'choice cates once a week, / Or twice at most' (II.i.217, 223–4); the serpentine Duke, urging Bianca to 'provide forever' like a wise wench (II.ii.382), or telling her to be not anxious for the morrow: 'Do not vex your mind . . . take you no care for't, / It shall be provided to your hand' (IV.i.124–7; cf. Matthew 6:34); there is worldly-wise Bianca hoping that 'poor' Isabella has 'laid in provision for her youth' since 'fools will not keep in winter' (III.iii.115–18); and middle-aged Livia encouraging Leantio to leave the ranks of young gentlemen who father beggars and waste their life away in labours (ll. 282–307). All these perversions are suddenly placed in the widest possible perspective by the figure of the Cardinal. Phrases such as Leantio's 'everlasting spendthrift' (I.iii.54) and the Duke's 'provide forever' fall into place as anticipations of his warning that man's real need is to find 'time enough to repent in' so that he will not be 'lost forever' (IV.i.186–240).

As in *The Duchess of Malfi*, memory is taken as an instrument of moral awareness. It makes actions conformable to commitments and relationships endorsed by time; and it is institutionalised in names, customs, and ritual (see *Women*, I.iii.80–99). Middleton makes his characters reflect on memory a good deal, but the salient fact about all their remembering is that they have 'the main point forgot', or are about to do so (I.ii.201). And their forgetfulness is not involuntary: it is 'an obstinate wilful forgetfulness' (l. 202).[42] Even the Mother, so needlessly apologetic about the effects of age on memory, and so exact in remembering dates and ceremonies and their significance, falls into this vice when she becomes involved in her son's marriage troubles.

Forgetfulness is evident mainly in relation to names and naming. Although Bianca is the chief victim of its destructive effects on names, the vice begins with her. Cheerfully and abruptly severing all connections with family and friend, she addresses a woman she has never seen before as 'Kind Mother', promising to 'call' her house 'the place of my birth', 'name' her ups-and-downs 'my fortunes too' (I.i.125–41) – it is here that she takes up her little teasing-game with Leantio about the rights and wrongs of remembering and forgetting. In the next such incident, the name of another absent mother is unkindly dealt with, this time by the lady who will do so much to deprive Bianca Capella of her good name and reduce her fair names to a mockery title. Livia contrives to make Isabella 'set by' 'the names of niece / And aunt' as being merely a product of 'custom'; and to do that, of course, she has to slander the 'name' and 'memory' of her own sister. In consequence, the man whom Isabella has 'all this while called uncle' can be greeted as a stranger; yet such is the confusion that Livia generates that the new language is entangled in the old: 'I pray forget not but to call me aunt still; / Take heed of that, it may be marked in time else' (II.i.89–171). Unawares, Leantio is wrestling with Livia's evil influence in the scene where he tries, unsuccessfully, to discover how the Duke got hold of Bianca's name (he is also unaware that the Duke has already got 'her good name too': he will not know that for certain until Livia informs him so) (III.ii.113–28). But he has to wrestle openly with Livia's influence at the end of the banquet, and he succumbs quickly. Filled with lust for him, Livia cannot endure his poignant memories of early love ('Canst thou forget all this?') and his tender lingering on the name 'Bianca' ('Still with her name? Will nothing wear it out?'); promptly she gets to work and convinces him that he must no longer call Bianca his wife: 'Know most assuredly she is a strumpet' (III.ii.264–309). And that (or 'whore') is how he addresses and refers to Bianca thereafter, his dying words being, 'Rise strumpet by my fall' (IV.ii.43). But she reciprocates in kind. He is no longer 'husband' or 'Leantio' but 'sir' (ironically), 'base start-up', and 'the former thing . . . to whom you gave / The captainship' (ll. 110–14). Leantio and Bianca are as good as dead well before 'forgetful fury' buries them and their 'friends' in the after-effects of 'lust and forgetfulness' (l. 175; V.ii.146): they have no past, no selfhood.

The purpose of memory and good husbandry is to accommodate the individual to time, the regulated movement of the universe symbolised by Bianca's suposedly unerring watch (she says she sets it by the sun, but her 'sun' is the Duke[43]). Forgetfulness and lack of foresight, however, are not the only ways in which Time is abused. These two defects are themselves the consequences of impatience, haste, and greedy opportunism – the usual signs of the impassioned will's demand for instant satisfaction: 'make more haste to please me' (II.ii.367). Pointers to this aspect of untimeliness are thickly distributed throughout the play; 'hasty nuptuals' (IV.ii.164) are its characteristic social manifestation.

VII

The dualist design which so strongly affects theme, symbol, language, and dramatic presentation in *Women Beware Women* reflects that fondness for significant patterning which critics have contrasted with the naturalistic bent of Middleton's genius.[44] It is in the chess scene (II.ii) and the masque scene (V.ii) that this love of significant pattern is most apparent. In accordance with Kydian precedent, these two scenes – as crisis and catastrophe – are singled out for maximum symbolic elaboration; like the Mars–Venus duet and the marriage playlet in Kyd, moreover, they are linked by causal, contrastive, and analogous relationships which confirm their fundamental position in the imaginative design of the play. All the skills which found scope in Middleton's work as City Chronologer (producing moral–allegorical pageants in which Time, Custom, and Ceremony are honoured) are exploited here not only to enhance dramatic irony but also to provide eloquent dramatic models of the surrounding play-world. I wish to conclude with a close look at these two scenes since I believe they embody Middleton's conception of what the tragedy is all about and should, in consequence, clarify and corroborate the interpretative approach I have been following.

v.ii. is the most elaborately wrought example of the Treacherous Entertainment in the whole period; but II.ii. – an evening's hospitality culminating in virtual rape – is treacherous entertainment of a kind too. In both scenes the moving spirit is the play's Duessa, and in both the informing idea is confounding doubleness. In II.ii, staging, style, and symbolism are combined superbly in the service of this idea.[45] Below, Livia engages the Mother in diversionary play, while, above, Guardiano (champion of 'ladies' rights' – l. 257) works in partnership with the Duke to 'confound' (l. 358) Bianca. At the close of the scene, Bianca's ruin is signalled by her sudden conversion to double-talk. Spiritually divided within herself, she 'hates the traitor' but 'likes the treason well' (l. 443). Divided forever from her second mother, she tells her cheerfully that she was the recipient of exceeding kindness above and that she has seen all (ll. 451, 455). Socially and spiritually linked now with Guardiano and Livia, she proceeds with them to supper expressing herself in icily ironic courtesies and devastating asides.

But split staging and equivocal language derive much of their force from the symbolism of the scene. The particular form of pre-prandial entertainment chosen by Livia to separate the Mother from her charge is beautifully apt. A game in which war is patiently acted out between friends, chess is a perfect symbol for the confusion of primal contraries which is central to the scene and the tragedy. Livia devised the evening's entertainment in order to 'work [the Duke's] peace' (II.ii.23) and also, she pretends, to enable the Mother to make amends for her purportedly unkind behaviour (ll. 224, 242). But the true nature of the occasion is better defined by Livia's jocular designation of the game as 'an old quarrel / Between us, that will never be at an end' (ll. 263–4), or by the Duke's playfully-tender and brutal attempt to silence and overcome Bianca: 'Pish, strive not sweet . . . strive not . . .' (ll. 327–9):

> The lifting of thy voice is but like one
> That does exalt his enemy, who proving high
> Lays all plots to confound him that raised him . . . .
> I should be sorry the least force should lay
> An unkind touch upon thee.
>
> (ll. 336–45)

Below, the equivocal dialogue of the gamesters keeps sharpening the point that all semblances of playful friendliness here are masks for mere violence: 'Here's a duke [i.e. rook] / Will strike a sure stroke for the game anon', 'Yes 'faith . . . H'as done me all the mischief in this game' (ll. 300–1, 415–16). Other thematic dualisms are generated by the chess scene to enhance its microcosmic status – vision/blindness, patience/haste, rise/fall, and, of course, earnest/jest. But the key dualism is that of strife and peace. The war game between friends universalises the attack on Bianca's virtue, puts it in the context of a confusing war that never ends.

V.ii is also based on an essentially oxymoronic symbol. The Stuart court masque was pre-eminently a celebration of social harmony; but the masks worn by the performers were reminders to many that the essential function of these extravagant spectacles was to conceal the realities of a faction-ridden and corrupt court. Middleton develops this contradiction with unparalleled thoroughness and places it decisively in the context of universal contrariety. As in *The Spanish Tragedy* (where Hieronimo is formally reconciled with Lorenzo before the playlet), the proper function of the entertainment as a symbol of unity is emphasised by preliminary reconciliations: Livia and Guardiano with Isabella and Hippolito ('all peace and friendship' – IV.ii.73), and the Cardinal with Bianca ('A fair noble peace' – V.ii.11) – all the wronged and 'incensed' characters pronounce themselves 'appeased', 'content to make one' (IV.ii.220, 213). The incomplete plot of the masque mirrors this pattern in a manner which stresses the need to transcend doubleness and confusion. Its heroine is a nymph who is equally in love with two admirers and eager both to appease the marriage goddess Juno and to win her pity and assistance:

> Pity this passionate conflict in my breast,
> This tedious war 'twixt two affections;
> Crown one with victory and my heart's at peace.
>
> (V.ii.87–9)

The paradigmatic nature of the nymph's situation is emphasised by the number of characters in the masque – 'only four' (l. 68) – and by a very studied use of elemental imagery.[46] One side of the stage has tapers burning on the altar of 'incensed' Juno, the other has two or more wells representing the nymph's springs of love; incense is wafted to Juno above, and she is a goddess 'wont to scorn the earth' (l. 137). The obvious prominence of fire and water among the elements accords with the fact that anger and pity are the key emotions in the masque.

The masque cannot reach unity, of course, because the enveloping situation is riddled with doubleness. The marriage it celebrates is sanctified vice, just as its marriage goddess is played by a bawd. And the precedent reconciliations between the divided actors and spectators have been entirely false: Livia's tense aside to her co-revenger Guardiano, 'Peace, I'll strive' (IV.ii.157), summarises the intentions of this pair and of Isabella and Bianca. Their 'plots to confound each other' (V.ii.151; cf. l. 143) produce a fair imitation of primal Chaos. The poisoned incense which Isabella wafts up to 'Juno' is not designed to appease her but to bring her abruptly down to earth (ll. 135–7). The pity which 'Juno' bestows is flaming gold that kills Isabella instantly, and Cupid's arrows that shoot poison 'in a wild flame' (l. 139) through the veins of Hippolito. And the wine of peace which Ganymede mistakenly gives to the Duke infects the very breath he exhales, so that his desperate wife can die with a kiss: 'wrap two spirits in one poisoned vapour' (l. 194). After this explosion there is, however, a deftly graduated change from doubleness and confusion to singleness and order. Disfigured now by poison, Bianca's fair face no longer masks her spirit: 'A blemished face best fits a leprous soul' (l. 204). And the Duke is succeeded by a 'brother of spotless honour' (IV.i.252) in whom passion does not seek to rule with reason: the Cardinal's concluding speech is pithily significant:

> Sin, what thou art these ruins show too piteously.
> Two kings on one throne cannot sit together,
> But one must needs down, for his title's wrong;
> So where lust reigns, that prince cannot reign long.

The real purpose of this change is not to assure us that all will now be well; rather it is to consolidate, through contrast, our understanding of the significant pattern of the scene and the tragedy.

The microcosmic character of the last scene is rendered complete by its element of fatal speed. Inordinate haste, of course, is as much a sign of confusion in a spatio-temporal order as the indiscriminate mixing of opposites: indeed, it seems to be a prerequisite for all bad unions in the play that they be 'joined in haste' (I.ii.60). Bianca's second marriage, unlike her first, is a sumptuously public affair, but it too is contracted 'With all speed, suddenly, as fast as cost / Can be laid on' (IV.ii.200). And the stately masque which adorns it has an undercurrent of violent impatience that quickly turns into Time's revenge on those who have abused it. Given new life by the novelty of the stage action, conventional puns on words such as 'fast', 'speed', 'dispatch', and 'quick' are plentiful, driving home the point that hasty plans and commitments are inherently insecure, deadly traps. Guardiano thinks 'all fast' in his plot, but stamps his foot too soon and is unintentionally 'dispatched' through the trap-door by the Ward, that master of cat trap (V.ii.125–6). Bianca would be 'Quickly rid' of the Cardinal and believes that her 'plot's laid surely' (ll. 19, 21); but the poison goes to the wrong brother. Livia finds that her niece – against whom she was once so quick to bestir her wits – has paid her in kind: 'My subtlety has sped, her art has quitted me' (l. 132).

In so far as these characters have any control over their last moments, they die exactly as they have lived: impatiently, hastily. Livia begs (in her last oxymoron) to be 'let down quickly' (V.ii.130). Her brother must 'run and meet death, then, / And cut off time and pain' by throwing himself on a guard's halberd (ll. 167–8). Bianca consumes what remains of the poison, threatening anyone who would 'restrain her ignorant wilful hand': 'give me way; / The plagues and pains of a lost soul upon him / That hinders me a moment' (ll. 209, 186–8). That eternal curse on the restraining moment of time tells all: it relates the scene and the tragedy to a philosophical tradition which binds past and present, present and future, and time and eternity.

Many critics have condemned the last scene as a serious lapse from psychological realism into spectacular melodrama; a few have defended it on the grounds that it is meaningfully related to the conceptual and symbolic pattern of the rest of the play.[47] I think I have shown that relationship to be more intricate and profound than has hitherto been perceived; however, although the scene does appear to me to be admirable in its way, and certainly worthy of the most serious scrutiny, I do not find it artistically satisfying. As with *The Changeling*, we are here faced with the regrettable fact that thematic and symbolic unity is no guarantee of qualitative consistency and dramatic inevitability. Each of the four murders planned for the last scene (there are three unplanned deaths) is inadequately motivated and abruptly conceived; collectively, they are totally implausible. It may be argued that the only proper response to such a scene is on the purely symbolic level: we should see it simply as a fantastic figure for the inevitable self-confounding of a wilful and duplicitous society. But it is difficult to respond in this way for the very reason that Middleton himself – in the brilliant chess scene, and indeed throughout –

has led us to assume that the most complex symbolic effects can be obtained in a naturalistic context. Nor does it help to recall that this is another version of a highly conventionalised scene in which multiple deaths are to be expected. For, in the best scenes of this kind, naturalism and symbolism are basically harmonious, the explosion of violence being not only patterned and significant, but also consistent with the atmosphere of the given play-world and with the psychology of the principal characters involved. The effect of the last scene of this tragedy, however, is to reduce a richly imaginative response to an essentially intellectual one. Characters who have almost always convinced us of their flesh-and-blood reality (engaging us in the devious workings of their mind) become characterless figures in a moral–theatrical diagram, and the awe which their ends should induce is seriously diluted. Working with Rowley, Middleton had managed to distract attention from the comparable element of contrivance at the end of *The Changeling*, mainly by concentrating on the horror of Vermandero, the tragic candour of Beatrice, and the unrepentant defiance of De Flores; here however there is no one to register an adequate response to the horrors (Hippolito's 'My great lords, we are all confounded' – l. 143 – is conceptually right but imaginatively insufficient), and there are too many deaths for any one of them to impress us deeply. Middleton, however, seems to have had difficulty in working out satisfactory conclusions to many of his plays; largely for that reason, *Women Beware Women*, like *The Changeling*, is a flawed masterpiece.[48]

VIII

If Middleton's tragedies do not ring with questions concerning the nature of the universe and the fate of mankind, it is not because his preoccupation with the psycho-social dimensions of tragedy is so intense as to preclude such questions. Rather it is because he is confident that he understands the universe sufficiently and believes that the conduct and fate of his characters are intelligible within his world view. His characters bring misery, untimely death, and even damnation upon themselves because of a striving impassioned will which destroys unity in the self, in personal relations, in the pattern of time, in the relationship between time and eternity. That, of course, is a structure of explanation for tragic calamity that has been used before; but Middleton differs from others by the quiet assurance and the completeness with which he incorporates it in the design of his tragedies.

What is really distinctive, however, in Middleton's view of the tragic is its emphasis on 'confusion'. 'Ruin' and 'destruction' follow almost entirely from the individual's capacity for making wrong seem right and evil good, both at the moment of fatal choice and in the subsequent accommodation of the moral self to an immoral course. Confusion here is not a state of extreme perturbation or an error of judgement forced upon the individual by some terrible change in the familiar world, or by some overwhelming external pressure. It is always moral error, and it proceeds from within. There are, of course, accomplished tempters and villains, but they are essentially extensions of the corruptible self, and the tricks they play are no more subtle than those which their victims play upon themselves. There is also (in *Women Beware Women*) a corrupt society, but it is made up of people who do not differ fundamentally from the tragic protagonists. Nor is there any initial sense of an overhanging fate, other than an impending outbreak of 'some hidden malady within'. Thus Middleton's tragedies generate no feelings of injustice in the order of things; if there is any injustice, it is that women and men are born with a double nature which is fearfully unstable and liable to 'confound' itself. But, unlike others before him, Middleton does not find cause for complaint in that fate. He accepts it as a fact, and contemplates it with a unique blend of detachment and awe.

Notes

1. For Senecan influence, see John W. Cunliffe, *The Influence of Seneca on Elizabethan Tragedy* (London: Macmillan, 1893); F. L. Lucas, *Seneca and Elizabethan Tragedy* (Cambridge: Cambridge University Press, 1922); T. S. Eliot, 'Shakespeare and the Stoicism of Seneca', in *Elizabethan Essays* (London: Faber, 1934) pp. 33–54; Philip Edwards, *Thomas Kyd and Early Elizabethan Tragedy*, Writers and their Work Series (London: Longmans, 1966) pp. 10–11. The importance of Senecan influence has been denied by Howard Baker in *Induction to Tragedy: A Study in Development of Form in 'Gorboduc', 'The Spanish Tragedy' and 'Titus Andronicus'* (Baton Rouge: Louisiana State University Press, 1939), and by George Hunter in 'Seneca and the Elizabethans: A Case Study in "Influence"', *ShS*, XX (1967) 17–26.

2. Sir Philip Sidney, *An Apology for Poetry*, ed. Geoffrey Shepherd (London: Nelson, 1965) p. 118.

3. John Foxe, *Actes and Monuments* (London, 1583). For a pictorial anthology of 'sundrye kindes of Tormentes' (including blinding), see pp. 794f. at the end of vol. I. A chained copy of this immensely popular work was made available in every cathedral, and regular public readings were prescribed by Church ordinance.

4. This meaning has not been recorded by the *OED*. For examples, see Chapman, *Hero and Leander*, III. 59–64, 146; Middleton and Rowley, *The Changeling*, I.i.191; *Hamlet*, V.ii.289–90.

5. *Romeo and Juliet*, II.vi.9–15; *Othello*, I.iii.341–2, II.i.219–20.

6. On the Greek attitude to change, see J. B. Bury, *The Idea of Progress* (London: Macmillan, 1932) pp. 8–19. For the persistence of this attitude in the Middle Ages and the Renaissance, see C. S. Lewis, *The Discarded Image: An Introduction to Medieval and Renaissance Literature* (Cambridge: Cambridge University Press, 1964) pp. 85, 184; Herschel Baker, *The Wars of Truth: Studies in the Decay of Humanism in the Earlier Seventeenth Century* (Cambridge, Mass.: Harvard University Press, 1952) pp. 43–78.

7. Plato, *Timaeus*, 31–2, and *The Republic*, IV.443; Ovid, *Metamorphoses*, I.5–433; Bernardus Silvestris, *Cosmographia*, trs. Winthrop Wetherbee (New York: Columbia University Press, 1973) pp. 67–75, 117–27 (I.i–ii, II.xii–xiv); Boethius, *The Consolation of Philosophy*, II, metre 8, and III, metre 9; Alain de Lille (Alanus de Insulis), *The Complaint of Nature*, trs. Douglas M. Moffatt, Yale Studies in English XXXVI (New York: Holt, 1908) p. 24 (prose III), 43–5 (prose IV), 87 (metre IX); Pierre de la Primaudaye, *The French Academie*, trs. T. Bowes *et al.* (London, 1618) pp. 523–5, 528 (II.lxiv). See also John Burnet, *Greek Philosophy: Part I: Thales to Plato* (London: Macmillan, 1920) pp. 22, 48, 61, 106; Leo Spitzer, 'Classical and

Christian Ideas of World Harmony' *Traditio*, II (1944) 409–64, III (1945) 307–64; S. K. Heninger, *Touches of Sweet Harmony: Pythagorean Cosmology and Renaissance Poetics* (San Marino, Calif.: Huntington Library, 1974) pp. 146–200, and *The Cosmographical Glass: Renaissance Diagrams of the Universe* (San Marino, Calif.: Huntington Library, 1977) chs 4–5.

8. My quoted phrase is from Marlowe, *Tamburlaine the Great*, Pt II, IV.ii.86. On hierarchical correspondence and analogy, see James E. Phillips, *The State in Shakespeare's Greek and Roman Plays* (New York: Columbia University Press, 1940) chs 4–6; E. M. W. Tillyard, *The Elizabethan World Picture* (London: Chatto, 1943) chs 4–7, and *Shakespeare's History Plays* (London: Chatto, 1944) pp. 10–17; W. R. Elton, 'Shakespeare and the Thought of his Age', in *A New Companion to Shakespeare Studies*, ed. Kenneth Muir and Samuel Schoenbaum (Cambridge: Cambridge University Press, 1971) pp. 180–8. Analogy and polarity have been usefully studied as modes of analysis in early Greek thought by G. E. R. Lloyd in his *Polarity and Analogy: Two Types of Argumentation in Early Greek Thought* (Cambridge: Cambridge University Press, 1966). On the decay of nature and the strife of the contraries, see John Norden, *Vicissitudo Rerum* (1600), Shakespeare Association Facsimile no. 4 (London: Oxford University Press, 1931), Preface, stanzas 9, 33–6, 40–6; Godfrey Goodman, *The Fall of Man* (London, 1616) pp. 34–7, 51–2, 123–5, 206.

9. See Willard Farnham, *The Medieval Heritage of Elizabethan Tragedy* (Berkeley, Calif.: University of California Press, 1936) pp. 78–9, 85; J. M. R. Margeson, *The Origins of English Tragedy* (Oxford: Clarendon Press, 1967) ch. 4.

10. See Raymond B. Waddington, '*Antony and Cleopatra*: "What Venus did to Mars"', *ShakS*, II (1966) 210–27; Robert G. Hunter, *Shakespeare and the Mystery of God's Judgements* (Athens, Ga: University of Georgia Press, 1976) pp. 137–50. (Neither critic refers to Marlowe or Kyd.) On the symbolism of the myth, see Plutarch, *Moralia*, ed. and trs. F. C. Babbitt, Loeb Classical Library (London: Heinemann, 1936) v 116–21; Natalis Comes (Conti), *Mythologiae* (1567; Hanover, 1619) p. 164. See further Edgar Wind, *Pagan Mysteries in the Renaissance*, 2nd edn (London: Faber, 1967) pp. 77–88.

11. Joel B. Altman, *The Tudor Play of Mind* (Berkeley, Calif.: University of California Press, 1978).

12. For the absurdist interpretation, see A. C. Spearing in his edn of *The Knight's Tale* (Cambridge: Cambridge University Press, 1966) pp. 78–9.

13. Apart from exercising a strong influence on *A Midsummer Night's Dream*, Chaucer's Tale was adapted twice for the stage in the sixteenth century (both plays are lost) and once in the seventeenth – as Shakespeare and Fletcher's *Two Noble Kinsmen*. See Ann Thompson, *Shakespeare's Chaucer: A Study in Literary Origins* (Liverpool: Liverpool University Press, 1978). Miss Thompson does not concern herself with the philosophical aspects of Chaucer's poem, a subject I have dealt with in a forthcoming article, 'Cosmology, Contrariety, and *The Knight's Tale*'.

14. The contrarious cast of Renaissance and especially Shakespearean drama – its 'ambivalent', 'dialectical', or 'complementary' vision – has not lacked attention. Until recently, however, this has been due more to the influence of Hegel and Nietzsche, and the effects of the New Criticism, than to any special interest in the intellectual background of the dramatists. Most critics who have investigated the dualisms of Renaissance drama have been intent on counteracting the impression, given by much historicist criticism, that the playwrights of this period obediently

endorsed all the more simplistic teachings of the time on the nature of man, society, and the universe; with a few exceptions, therefore, such critics have been non- if not anti-historical in their methodological stance. See, for example, W. B. Yeats, 'At Stratford-on-Avon' (1901), repr. in *Essays and Introductions* (London: Macmillan, 1961); G. Wilson Knight, *The Shakespearean Tempest* (London: Oxford University Press, 1932); A. P. Rossiter, 'Ambivalence: The Dialectic of the Histories' (1951), in *Angel with Horns* (London: Longmans, 1961); Eugene M. Waith, 'Marlowe and the Jades of Asia', *SEL*, v (1965) 229–45; Norman Rabkin, *Shakespeare and the Common Understanding* (New York: Free Press, 1967); Bernard McElroy, *Shakespeare's Mature Tragedies* (Princeton, NJ: Princeton University Press, 1973); Robert F. Whitman, 'The Moral Paradox of Webster's Tragedy', *PLMA*, LXC (1975) 894–903; Michael Long, *The Unnatural Scene: A Study in Shakespearean Tragedy* (London: Methuen, 1976). Shakespearean contrariety has been studied in relation to its intellectual environment by Marion Bodwell Smith, *Dualities in Shakespeare* (Toronto: University of Toronto Press, 1966); and Robert Grudin, *Mighty Opposites: Shakespeare and Renaissance Contrariety* (Berkeley, Calif.: University of California Press, 1979). Sacvan Bercovitch has related Kyd's contrarious vision to a somewhat narrowly understood Empedoclean cosmology in 'Love and Strife in *The Spanish Trgedy*', *SEL*, IX (1969) 215–19. There are also some pertinent comments on the contrarious aspect of Renaissance cosmology in Rolf Soellner, *Shakespeare's Patterns of Self-Knowledge* (Athens, Ohio: University of Ohio Press, 1972) pp. 53–8. Lastly, historical justification for dualist interpretations of Renaissance drama has been supplied in Theodore Spencer, *Shakespeare and the Nature of Man* (New York: Macmillan, 1942); Hiram C. Haydn, *The Counter-Renaissance* (New York: Scribners, 1950); Rosalie F. Colie, *Paradoxia Epidemica: The Renaissance Tradition of Paradox* (Princeton, NJ: Princeton University Press, 1966); and William F. Elton, *King Lear and the Gods* (San Marino, Calif.: Huntington Library, 1966). These critics present the period as one of intense intellectual activity when different ideas were in competition with one another and men had to learn to live with uncertainty, contradiction, and paradox.

15. De Lille, *The Complaint of Nature*, pp. 24–8 (prose III), 46–7 (metre V), 85 (prose VIII); Thomas Aquinas, *Summa Theologica*, I–II, qq. 82, 85; de la Primaudaye, *The French Academie*, pp. 418 (I.xi), 528 (I.lxv); Richard Hooker, *Of the Laws of Ecclesiastical Polity*, Everyman's Library (London: Dent, 1907; repr. 1969) I, pp. 161, 173–4; Milton, *Paradise Lost*, VII.192ff., x.640ff.; Robert Burton, *The Anatomy of Melancholy*, Everyman's Library (London: Dent, 1932) I 133–4.

16. Alwin Thaler, 'Shakespeare and Sir Thomas Browne', in *Shakespeare's Silences* (Cambridge, Mass.: Harvard University Press, 1929) pp. 97–138. For *Religio Medici*, I have used the text in Browne, *The Major Works*, ed. C. A. Patrides (Harmondsworth: Penguin, 1977). Page references to this edn henceforward appear in the text.

17. Shakespeare spells out his contrarious conception of villainy in the passage on Sinon in *The Rape of Lucrece* (ll. 1555–61):

> Such devils steal effects from lightless hell;
> For Sinon in his fire doth quake with cold,
> And in that cold hot burning fire doth dwell;
> These contraries such unity doth hold

Only to flatter fools and make them bold;
So Priam's trust false Sinon's tears doth flatter
That he finds means to burn Troy with his water.

18. See n. 108 below.

19. On the rhetoric of Milton's Satan, see J. B. Broadbent, 'Milton's Rhetoric', *MP*, LVI (1958–9) 224–42; Douglas Wortele, '"Perswasive Rhetoric": The Techniques of Milton's Archetypal Sophist', *ESC*, III (1977) 18–33. For the humanist doctrine of eloquence, see for example de la Primaudaye, *The French Academie*, pp. 53, 380–5 (I.xii, II.xiv–xv); Henry Peacham, *The Compleat Gentleman*, ed. G. S. Gordon (Oxford: Clarendon Press, 1906) p. 8.

20. 'It was noted and observed [by one of the justices at a recusant trial in 1613] that the lawe and civill policy of England, being chiefly founded uppon religion and the feare of God, doth use the religious ceremonie of an oathe not only in legall proceedings, but in other transaccions and affaires of most importance in the commonwealthe, esteeming an oathe not onely as the best touchstone of truthe in matters of controversie, but as the fastest knot of civill societie, and the firmest band to tie all men to the performance of their severall duties . . . . a greater mischiefe cannot arise then that subjectes should be perswaded that it is lawfull for them to mocke and dallie with an oathe under pretence of colour of aequivocation or mentall reservation' – *Recusant Documents from the Ellesmere Manuscripts*, ed. Antony Petti (London: Catholic Record Society, 1968) pp. 249–50 (see also p. 254). As Petti observes (p. 255), the argument that disrespect for oaths would dissolve the bands of society was first heard (from Chief Justice Coke) at the trial of Robert Southwell in 1595; it seems to have become a familiar theme. See also John Gerard, *The Autobiography of an Elizabethan*, trs. Philip Caraman (London: Longman, 1951) pp. 125–6, 269–70.

21. Marlowe, *The Jew of Malta*, I.i.131–2.

22. Marlowe, *Edward II*, V.iv.51; Webster, *The Duchess of Malfi*, V.ii.114–17; Tourneur(?), *The Revenger's Tragedy*, IV.ii.190.

23. 'Thus have the gods their justice, men their wills, / And I, by mens' wills ruled, myself renouncing, / Am by my Angel and the gods Abhorr'd' – Chapman, *The Tragedy of Caesar and Pompey*, IV.iii.1–3. Cf. *Hamlet*, V.ii.76; *Antony and Cleopatra*, III.x.19–24, xi.1–20, 51–4; Heywood, *A Woman Killed with Kindness*, vi.151; Marston, *Antonio and Mellida*, IV.i.83; Tourneur(?), *The Revenger's Tragedy*, V.iii.110; Middleton, *Women Beware Women*, V.ii.146; Ford, *'Tis Pity She's a Whore*, V.i.1–30.

24. Cf. M. C. Bradbrook, *Themes and Conventions of Elizabethan Tragedy* (Cambridge: Cambridge University Press, 1935) p. 61; Maynard Mack, 'The Jacobean Shakespeare: Some Observations on the Construction of the Tragedies', in *Jacobean Theatre*, SUAS I, ed. Bernard Harris and John Russell Brown (London: Arnold, 1960) p. 34.

25. Examples of this pattern are: Shakespeare's Titus Andronicus, Brutus, Othello, Macbeth, and Timon; Chapman's Bussy D'Ambois; Tourneur's(?) Vindice; Middleton's Bianca, Leantio, and Beatrice-Joanna.

26. Other examples of this method are Marlowe's Faustus, Shakespeare's Richard II, Hamlet, Lear, and Antony and Cleopatra. Relevant also are the characters of Andrugio and Antonio in Marston's *Antonio and Mellida* and

Antonio's Revenge, who waver between Stoic resignation and the passions of grief and wrath.

27. Cf. Hardin Craig, *The Enchanted Glass: The Elizabethan Mind in Literature* (1935; repr. Oxford: Blackwell, 1960) pp. 124 and 131. Craig notes that the dramatists found sanction for sudden changes and brilliant contrasts in characterisation in the psychologists' teaching that one emotion or passion drives out another, the substitution being immediately operative.

28. Boccaccio, *Genealogie deorum gentilium*, VI.ix, in *Opere*, X, ed. Vincenzo Romano (Bari: Laterza, 1951) p. 344. Cf. Spenser, *Faerie Queene*, III.viii.30–42.

29. Pierre Charron, *Of Wisdome*, trs. Samson Lennard (London, c.1607) p. 88. Cf. p. 101.

30. Timothy Bright, *A Treatise of Melancholie* (London, 1586) p. 98.

31. De la Primaudaye, *The French Academie*, p. 12; Thomas Wright, *The Passions of the Mind* (London, 1601) pp. 100, 303–6.

32. Robert Ornstein, *The Moral Vision of Jacobean Tragedy* (Madison: University of Wisconsin Press, 1960), p. 41.

33. Augustine, *The City of God*, XIV.x, xv, xix; Aquinas, *Summa Theologica*, I, q. 95, art. 1–2, and I–II, qq. 82, 85; de la Primaudaye, *The French Academie*, p. 458; Burton, *Anatomy of Melancholy*, I 69, 136–7.

34. In *Artificial Persons: The Function of Character in the Tragedies of Shakespeare* (Columbia, SC: University of South Carolina Press, 1974), J. Leeds Barroll contends that traditional psychology is of no use for an understanding of Shakespearean characterisation. Deviation, he believes, is Shakespeare's controlling principle; and he finds the source of this principle in transcendentalist teachings to the effect that man aspires by nature to an immaterial perfection which his fallen condition necessarily precludes. It seems logical to suppose, however, that Christian transcendentalism – in so far as it affected dramatic characterisation – could only have worked in partnership with the psychologists' emphasis on man's inherently contrarious and therefore unstable nature. Of obvious relevance here is the way in which Shakespeare's tragic heroes are overcome by their irrational, uncivilised, 'other' self in a psychomachia where melancholy or choler is often clearly in the ascendant.

35. Elmer Edgar Stoll, 'Source and Motive in *Macbeth* and *Othello*', *RES*, XIX (1943) 25–32; J. I. M. Stewart, *Character and Motive in Shakespeare: Some Recent Appraisals Examined* (London: Longman, 1949) pp. 94, 101–2.

36. On the other hand, orthodox hostility to inordinate passion does not imply disapproval of emotion as such. To go back to Augustine, only those 'perturbations' which resist reason are to be condemned; moreover, to abjure natural feeling – love, pity, sorrow, fear, and anger – is 'great stupidity of body and barbarism of mind' – *The City of God*, trs. John Healey, Everyman's Library (London: Dent, 1945) II 38 (XIV.ix). (Cf. Wright, *Passions of the Mind*, pp. 32–4.) Thus it is quite mistaken to assume that the cold malevolence of an Iago or a Goneril constitutes an implicit criticism of orthodox attitudes to reason and passion.

37. Chapman, *Byron's Conspiracy*, I.ii.27–35.

38. Robert F. Whitman, 'The Moral Paradox of Webster's Tragedy'; Michael Long, *The Unnatural Scene: A Study in Shakespearean Tragedy*. See also Northrop Frye, *Fools of Time: Studies in Shakespearian Tragedy* (Toronto: University of Toronto Press, 1967); Norman Rabkin, *Shakespeare and the Common*

Understanding, ch. 1. Nietzsche's tragic theory first enters English dramatic criticism in Yeats's seminal essay on Shakespeare, 'At Stratford-on-Avon' – see T. McAlindon, 'Yeats and the English Renaissance', *PMLA*, LXXXII (1967) 157–69. Broadly speaking, its influence has proved extremely beneficial; like other dualist approaches, it has had the effect of enhancing critical responsiveness to the complexities, ambiguities, and insinuations of the dramatic text.

39. *The Duchess of Malfi*, I.i.57; *Macbeth*, I.vii.35; *The Jew of Malta*, I.i.71.

40. Chapman, *Caesar and Pompey*, V.ii.81–2.

41. Heraclitus, *The Fragments*, trs. Charles M. Bakewell, *Source Book in Ancient Philosophy* (New York: Gordian Press, 1973) pp. 30–1. Heraclitus adds, 'Opposition brings men together, and out of discord comes the fairest harmony, and all things have their birth in strife. Men do not understand how that which is torn in different directions comes into accord with itself, – harmony in contrariety, as in the case of the bow and the lyre.'

42. Leone Ebreo, *The Philosophy of Love*, trs. F. Friedeberg-Seeley and Jean H. Barnes (London: Soncino Press, 1937) p. 125; Louis le Roy, *Of the Interchangeable Course or Variety of Things in the Whole World*, trs. Robert Ashley (London, 1594) p. 5; Norden, *Vicissitudo Rerum*, stanzas 47, 82–100; Browne, *Religio Medici*, pp. 140 ('contraries, though they destroy one another, are yet the life of one another'), 146 ('the world, whose divided Antipathies and contrary forces doe yet carry a charitable regard unto the whole by their particular discords, preserving the common harmony'), and 152 ('The greatest Balsames doe lie enveloped in the bodies of most powerful Corrosives . . . poysons containe within themselves their own Antidote'). As Robert Grudin has pointed out (*Mighty Opposites*, pp. 22–30), this Heraclitean theme was basic to Paracelsian medicine and chemistry. However, the likes of Sir Thomas Browne would have known that it was included in the Christian world view when Augustine responded to the Manichean claim that some things are naturally evil: see *The City of God*, XI.xviii.

43. I have discussed 'the art of dying' in *Shakespeare and Decorum* (London: Macmillan, 1973) pp. 22, 85–6, 139, 167ff. For an illuminating study of this aspect of Shakespearean tragedy, see Walter C. Foreman, Jr, *Music of the Close: The Final Scenes of Shakespeare's Tragedies* (Lexington, Ky: University of Kentucky Press, 1978).

44. Foxe, *Actes and Monumentes*, p. 1888.

45. In Foxe, the fortitude of the martyrs is more often referred to as 'constancy' ('godly constancy', 'Christian constancy') than as patience. See ibid., pp. 1013, 1039, 1201, 1242, 1555.

46. See *Seneca his Tenne Tragedies Translated into English*, ed. Thomas Newton (1581), Tudor Translations, 2nd ser., XII (London: Constable, 1927) II 242 ('such should our ending bee . . . / Now let mee dye a manly death, a stout and excellent, / And meet for me'), 250 ('upright and stiffe he standes, / And neither stoupes nor leans awrye'), and 241 ('What heavenly harmony is this that soundeth in myne eare?'). For the motif of the upright stance in Renaissance tragedy, see *Macbeth*, V.viii.41–3 ('In the unshrinking station where he fought . . . like a man he died'); Chapman, *Bussy D'Ambois*, V.iii.135–45 ('I am up here like a Roman statue; / I will stand till death had made me marble'), and *The Tragedy of Chabot*, V.iii.65–8, iv.155–202; *'Tis Pity She's a Whore*, V.vi.78–83. For music metaphor, see *Hamlet* V.ii.352; Chapman, *The Revenge of Bussy D'Ambois*, V.v.165–6 ('death should make / The consort sweetest'); Ford, *The Broken Heart*,

v.iii.1–94. The self-conscious decorum of the Noble Death needs no illustration; the change of mood is discussed below.

47. *Antony and Cleopatra*, V.ii.238; Webster, *The White Devil*, v.vi.245 (cf. III.ii.136). See also *The Broken Heart*, v.ii.95 ('She has a masculine spirit').

48. Theodore Spencer, *Death and Elizabethan Tragedy* (Cambridge, Mass.: Harvard University Press, 1936) pp. 178–9.

49. In *Othello* Iago's reference to the hero's collapse as 'A passion most unsuiting such a man' (IV.i.77) points the contrast. In the early tragedy, the contrast is heavily underlined, both structurally and verbally. Romeo's first reaction to bad news leads to behaviour which the Friar lengthily condemns as unbecoming in a man – both 'womanish' and bestial ('the unreasonable fury of a beast') (*Romeo and Juliet*, III.iii.109–12). His controlled reaction to the second piece of bad news is so remarkable that he can plausibly speak to the nervous servant and the furious Paris in the accents of experienced and world-weary manhood: 'Give me thy torch, boy', 'Good gentle youth, tempt not a desperate man' (v.iii.1, 59). In the end, the Friar's rebuking question, 'Art thou a man?' (III.iii.109), is triumphantly answered.

50. *The Broken Heart*, v.ii.131–2.

51. Middleton, *Women Beware Women*, v.ii.152–3.

52. Justus Lipsius, *Two Bookes of Constancie*, trs. Sir John Stradling (London, 1594) p. 9.

53. *The Duchess of Malfi*, v.ii.348–9.

54. *The Revenge of Bussy D'Ambois*, v.v.113. Cf. *Bussy D'Ambois*, v.iii.160; *Hamlet*, v.ii.321; *Othello*, v.ii.303; *King Lear*, IV.vii.71–85; *The Changeling*, v.iii.149–61, 178. Contrast *A Woman Killed with Kindness*, xvii.75–122, where the elaborate process of contrition and pardon is overtly ritual in character.

55. *Bussy D'Ambois*, v.iii.166–70; *The Tragedy of Chabot*, v.iii.147–53, 185–99.

56. Cf. *Romeo and Juliet*, v.iii.295–7.

57. *The Changeling*, v.iii.202–3. See also *Richard III*, v.v.20 ('this fair conjunction'), 31 ('By God's fair ordinance conjoin together'); *Macbeth*, v.viii.56ff.; *Timon of Athens*, v.iv.

58. Marlowe, *Doctor Faustus*, v.iii.170. In *The Vision of Tragedy* (New Haven: Yale University Press, 1959), Richard Sewall views Faustus's end as unambiguously heroic: 'He transcends the man he was. He goes out no craven sinner but violently, speaking the rage and despair of all mankind' (p. 66).

59. See, for example, Ruth Nevo, *Tragic Form in Shakespeare* (Princeton, NJ: Princeton University Press, 1972) pp. 256–7; Foreman, *Music at the Close*, pp. 3, 49. Contrast Helen Gardner, 'Milton's Satan and the Theme of Damnation in Elizabethan Tragedy', *E&S*, new ser. I (1948), repr. in *Elizabethan Drama: Modern Essays in Criticism*, ed. R. J. Kaufman (New York: Oxford University Press, 1961) p. 327.

60. Cf. Dorothea Krook, *The Elements of Tragedy* (New Haven, Conn.: Yale University Press, 1969) p. 26.

61. Montaigne, *The Essays*, trs. John Florio, Everyman's Library (London: Dent, 1910) II 271–2 (II.xii).

62. J. H. Baker, *An Introduction to English Legal History* (London: Butterworth, 1972) pp. 29ff.; W. S. Holdsworth, 'The Elizabethan Age in English Legal History and its Results', *ILR* XII (1927) 321–35.

63. A. L. Rowse, *The England of Elizabeth*, 2nd edn (London: Macmillan, 1957) p. 405.

64. Alfred Harbage, *Shakespeare and the Rival Traditions* (Bloomington and London: Indiana University Press, 1952) p. 53.

65. *The Mirror for Magistrates*, ed. Lily B. Campbell (Cambridge: Cambridge University Press, 1938) pp. 73, 266.

66. Douglas Cole, *Suffering and Evil in the Plays of Christopher Marlowe* (Princeton, NJ: Princeton University Press, 1962) pp. 70, 248; J. M. R. Margeson, *The Origins of Elizabethan Tragedy* ch. 5; Philip Edwards, *Thomas Kyd and Early Elizabethan Tragedy*, 2nd edn (London: Longman, 1970) p. 10.

67. John Calvin, *Institutes of the Christian Religion*, trs. Henry Beveridge (London: Clarke, 1949) p. 653 (IV.xx.23–31). Cf. p. 188 (I.xvii.5). See also Christopher Morris, *Political Thought in England: Tyndale to Hooker* (London: Oxford University Press, 1953) pp. 38–40, 162, 170.

68. See, for example, Kenneth Muir's comments in *Shakespeare's Tragic Sequence* (London: Hutchinson, 1970) pp. 57ff. on Eleanor Prosser, *Hamlet and Revenge* (Stanford, Calif.: Stanford University Press, 1967).

69. See R. A. Foakes, 'John Marston's Fantastical Plays: *Antonio and Mellida* and *Antonio's Revenge*', *PQ*, XLI (1962) 229–39. (Foakes's view of the Antonio plays as satiric parodies of revenge tragedy has, however, been challenged by a number of critics.)

70. Jonson, *Sejanus*, IV. 73.

71. Rolf Soellner remarks on 'the polarization of passion and patience' in Shakespeare's Jacobean tragedies and points out that in these plays and the romances patience acquires special importance as the prerequisite for self-knowledge – *Shakespeare's Patterns of Self-Knowledge*, p. 251.

72. There is a particularly illuminating account of Renaissance regard for timeliness in Edgar Wind's *Pagan Mysteries in the Renaissance*, pp. 97–112. On respect for time in the doctrine of decorum, see my *Shakespeare and Decorum*, pp. 10, 93–7, 99–103, 146–63, 166.

73. William Tyndale, *Doctrinal Treatises*, ed. Henry Walter, Parker Society Publications (Cambridge: Cambridge University Press, 1848) p. 332; Hugh Latimer, *Sermons*, ed. George Elwes Corrie, Parker Society Publications (Cambridge: Cambridge University Press, 1854) p. 300; Thomas Beard, *The Theatre of God's Judgements* (London, 1597) p. 56.

74. Plutarch, *The Morals*, trs. Philemon Holland (London, 1603) p. 542.

75. *Recusant Documents from the Ellesmere Manuscripts*, pp. 14–15, 247; Francis Bacon, *The Advancement of Learning*, VIII.iii, aphorism 94, in *The Physical and Metaphysical Works of Lord Bacon*, trs. Joseph Devey (London: Bohn, 1853) p. 365. For explanation of this aspect of legal theory and practice in sixteenth-century England, see Baker, *Introduction to English Legal Theory*, p. 60.

76. Kyd, *The Spanish Tragedy*, II.v.58. On the Time, Truth, and Justice theme, see Fritz Saxl, 'Veritas Filia Temporis', *Philosophy and History*, ed. Raymond Klibansky and H. J. Patton (Oxford: Oxford University Press, 1936) pp. 197–222; Erwin Panofsky, *Studies in Iconology: Humanistic Themes in the Art of the Renaissance* (1939; repr. New York: Harper and Row, 1972) pp. 69–93; Donald Gordon, 'Veritas Filia Temporis: Hadrianus Junius and Geoffrey Whitney', *JWCI* III (1939–40) 228–41; Guy de Tervarent, '*Veritas* and *Justitia* Triumphant', *JWCI* VII (1944) 95–101; Samuel C. Chew, *The Pilgrimage of Life* (New Haven, Conn.: Yale University Press, 1962) pp. 18–19.

77. S. K. Heninger, *The Cosmographical Glass*, p. 12.

78. See ibid., pp. 12–13, 110–15.

79. The significance of time in Shakespearean drama has been much discussed. See especially Paul A. Jorgensen, '"Redeeming Time" in Shakespeare's *Henry IV*', *TSL*, V (1960) 101–9; Inga-Stina Ewbank, 'The Triumph of Time in *The Winter's Tale*', *REL*, V (1964) 83–100; Frye, *Fools of Time*; Douglas L. Peterson, *Time, Tide, and Tempest: A Study of Shakespeare's Romances* (San Marino, Calif.: Huntington Library, 1973); G. F. Waller, *The Strong Necessity of Time: The Philosophy of Time in Shakespeare and Elizabethan Literature* (The Hague and Paris: Mouton, 1976); Wylie Sypher, *The Ethic of Time: Structures of Experience in Shakespeare* (New York: Seabury, 1976); T. McAlindon, 'The Numbering of Men and Days: Symbolic Design in *The Tragedy of Julius Caesar*', *SP* LXXXI (1984) 386–93.

80. The twenty-four years of voluptuousness and power allowed to Doctor Faustus is an obvious example. Compare *'Tis Pity She's a Whore*, where it is clear from the start that within nine months Nature will shatter the lovers' belief that they have discovered 'a paradise of joy' where 'all time' is 'struck out of number' (II.i.43, vi.66).

81. The clock is used in *Faustus, Julius Caesar, Macbeth* and *The Changeling*; possibly, too, in the first scene of *Hamlet*.

82. Shakespeare is unique in the thoroughness with which he uses night scenes as evidence of a conflict between man and Time (*Romeo and Juliet, Julius Caesar, Hamlet, Othello, Macbeth*). Only the author of *The Revenger's Tragedy* approaches him in this respect.

83. *The Spanish Tragedy*, II.vi.8, III.ii.98, ix.8–14, xiii.5–55; *The Jew of Malta*, I.ii.239–40, II.iii.374–5; *Hamlet* III.iii.73–96, IV.vii.64, 110–126, V.ii.19–47; *Othello* II.i.262–76, II.iii.358–66, III.iii.248–55, IV.i.75, 87–90, V.i.87; *The Revenger's Tragedy*, I.i.55–7, 99, II.ii.124–6, 151–74; Henry Chettle, *The Tragedy of Hoffman*, Malone Society Reprints (Oxford: Oxford University Press, 1950) ll. 1103–4; *The Changeling*, II.ii.90–1; *Women Beware Women*, II.i.104–18.

84. *Macbeth*, I.vii.51–2; *The Changeling*, I.i.191–7, II.i.4, ii.49–53; *Women Beware Women*, I.iii.27–34, III.ii.84–8, iii.314–19.

85. Two of the earliest examples of retrospective irony occur in *Titus Andronicus* and *Edward II* and are noticeably similar: Titus's fruitless appeal for pity to the tribunes in III.i, echoing Tamora's similar appeal to him in I.i; the imprisoned Edward's appeal for pity (from his wife, Mortimer, the murderers), echoing his pitiless treatment of the weeping Isabella in I.iv (ll. 145–90). (It is impossible to say which of these two plays was written first.)

86. *The Spanish Tragedy*, I.ii.189. For the traditional (Aristotelian) distinction between the two kinds of justice, see Sir Thomas Elyot, *The Book Named the Governor* (1531), ed. S. E. Lehmberg, Everyman's Library (London: Dent, 1962) pp. 159–63 (III.i–ii).

87. See Theodore Spencer, 'The Elizabethan Malcontent', *Joseph Quincy Adams Memorial Studies*, ed. J. G. McManaway, J. G. Dawson, and E. E. Willoughby (Washington, DC: Folger Library, 1948) p. 531; Bridget Gellert Lyons, *Voices of Melancholy: Studies in Literary Treaments of Melancholy in Renaissance England* (London: Routledge, 1971) pp. 17–21.

88. Jonson, *Sejanus*, III.245–6, 209, and *Catiline*, V.221.

89. Tourneur, *The Atheist's Tragedy*, IV.iii.227–32, V.ii.118–20. Cf. *Hamlet*, III.iii.57–64.

90. *Hero and Leander*, III.64 (Chapman's emphasis).

91. Several critics have already made this point in relation to *The Spanish Tragedy* (as distinct from the 'genre' as a whole). See Ejner J. Jensen, 'Kyd's *Spanish Tragedy*: The Play Explains Itself', *JEGP*, LXIV (1965) 7–8; G. K. Hunter, 'Ironies of Justice in *The Spanish Tragedy*', *RenD*, VIII (1965) 89–92.

92. 'Hymen... we will scorn thy laws' – Beaumont and Fletcher, *The Maid's Tragedy*, II.i.211–15. Tyrannic interference with marriage (whether by enforcement or prevention) is a theme which occurs in *The Spanish Tragedy, Titus Andronicus, The Jew of Malta, Romeo and Juliet, King Lear, The Atheist's Tragedy*, Marston's *The Malcontent* and his two *Antonio* plays, *The Duchess of Malfi, Women Beware Women, The Broken Heart*, and *'Tis Pity She's a Whore*. In *The White Devil*, Bracciano's unofficial divorce of his loving wife is a variation on the theme, (The identification of the political tyrant with contempt for Hymen's laws probably owes much to the popularity of the Senecan – or pseudo-Senecan – *Octavia*.)

93. See *The Spanish Tragedy*, III.xiv.95–102; *Antonio's Revenge*, III.ii.1, V.iii.1–2; *The Atheist's Tragedy*, II.iii.1–22; *Hamlet*, V.v; *The Maid's Tragedy*, II.i.41–60; *Women Beware Women*, III.iii; *The Broken Heart*, I.i, II.iii.

94. For example, Mortimer (*Edward II*), Richard III and Claudius, Mendoza (*The Malcontent*). As noted by Marston in *The Malcontent*, the classical prototype is Aegisthus (Mendoza even quotes from Seneca's *Agamemnon*: see V.iv.15).

95. *Titus Andronicus*, II.iv.26, IV.iii.4.

96. Robert Ornstein, *The Moral Vision of Jacobean Tragedy*, p. 171.

97. Alvin Kernan, '*The Henriad*: Shakespeare's Major History Plays', *YR*, LIX (1969–70) 3–32, and in *The Revels History of the Drama in English*, Vol. III: *1576–1613*, ed. J. Leeds Barroll, Alexander Leggatt, Richard Hosley and Alvin Kernan (London: Methuen, 1975) pp. 241ff. As Kernan notes, he is developing ideas suggested in C. L. Barber, *Shakespeare's Festive Comedy* (Princeton, NJ: Princeton University Press, 1959) pp. 193–5.

98. Chapman, *Hero and Leander*, III.59, 112–54.

99. *De captivitate ecclesiae Babylonica praeludium*, trs. Bertram Lee Woolf, in *The Reformation Writings of Martin Luther* (London: Lutterworth Press, 1952) I pp. 201–334; Calvin, *Institutes*, pp. 400–36 (IV.x–xi); John Bale, *The Image of Both Churches, Being an Exposition of the Most Wonderful Book of Revelation of St John the Evangelist*, in Bale, *Select Works*, ed. Henry Christmas, Publications of the Parker Society (Cambridge: Cambridge University Press, 1849) pp. 498, 517, 524–6; *Puritanism in Tudor England*, ed. H. C. Porter (London: Macmillan, 1970) pp. 20, 45, 53, 86.

100. *Titus Andronicus*, V.i.76; *The Atheist's Tragedy*, III.i.49–50.

101. The court is identified with Babylon in *The Spanish Tragedy, The Malcontent, Antonio's Revenge, The Maid's Tragedy*, and *The Revenger's Tragedy*. (In the last play, the identification is not explicit, but it is imaginatively potent none the less, the feast of Belshazzar, King of Babylon, being echoed in the Treacherous Entertainment of the final scene.)

102. *Antonio's Revenge*, II.i.107, 136–142, V.iii.130, 138.

103. For discussion of Calvinist influence in seventeenth-century tragedy, see Irving Ribner, *Jacobean Tragedy, the Quest for Moral Order* (1962; repr. London: Methuen, 1979) pp. 9, 74–5, 123–52; George C. Herndl, *The High Design: English Renaissance Tragedy and the Natural Law* (Lexington, Ky: University of Kentucky Press, 1970) pp. 116–21 and *passim*. See also (on predestination) R. G. Hunter, *Shakespeare and the Mystery of God's Judgements*.

104. For Anglican 'mediocrity' or moderation, see Hooker, *The Laws of Ecclesiastical Polity*, I, pp. 385–6, 426–7; Porter, in *Puritanism in Tudor England*, p. 17. In 'The Visible Solemnity: Ceremony and Order in Shakespeare and Hooker', *TSLL*, XII (1970–1), Eileen Z. Cohen argues that Shakespeare was influenced by Hooker in his endorsement of the moderate, Christian–humanist attitude to ceremony.

105. Mary Douglas, *Natural Symbols: Explorations in Cosmology* (London: Barrie and Rockliffe, 1970) pp. 1, 19–20.

106. Cicero, *De Officiis*, ed. and trs. W. Miller, Loeb Classical Library (London: Heinemann, 1947) p. 117; Epictetus, *The Moral Discourses*, trs. Elizabeth Carter, Everyman Library (London: Dent, 1910) p. 260.

107. Hence Perdita's pun: 'I see the play so *lies* / That I must bear a part' (*The Winter's Tale*, IV.iv.645–6).

108. Tertullian, *De spectaculis*, iv–vi, x, xvii in *Patrologia Latina*, ed. J. P. Migne (Paris: Garnier, 1844) I 709–12, 716–18, 723–5); Augustine, *The City of God*, II.viii, VI.i, xxvi, VII.xviii, VIII.xviii.

109. *The Ancrene Riwle*, ed. M. Day, Early English Text Society, original ser., no. 225 (London, 1952) pp. 99–102, 105; Walter Hilton, *The Ladder of Perfection*, trs. Leo Sherley-Price (Harmondsworth: Penguin, 1957) pp. 10–11, 170–4; *Seinte Iuliene*, ed. S. T. R. O. D'Ardenne, Early English Text Society, original ser., no. 248 (London: Oxford University Press, 1961) p. 31; Walter Map, *De nugis curialium (Courtiers' Trifles)*, trs. F. Tupper and M. B. Ogle (London: Chatto, 1924) pp. 202, 207.

110. In *The Comedy of Evil on Shakespeare's Stage* (London: Associated University Presses, 1978) chs 1–2, Charlotte Spivack offers an historical explanation for the tradition of demonic comedy which differs from my own. Developing an idea of C. S. Lewis's, she argues that this kind of comedy stems from the Christian metaphysician's conception of evil as non-being, a conception which logically reduces the threats of Satan to the level of ridiculous pretence. Like earlier scholars in the field, Professor Spivack does not take account of the fact that there are two distinguishable (though often overlapping) types of humour in medieval devilry, one emanating from and the other directed at the demon or demonic character. There is the sinister, subtle humour of the character who is credited with intelligence, success, and *de facto* power in his dealings with foolish and sinful men; and there is the simple ridiculousness of the type whose role in the given story pattern is to bear witness to the power of divine grace and of those who have recourse to it in time. The privative conception of evil probably helped to consolidate the second kind of comedy, and may in some sense account for it. But it does not account for the first kind; and it is that which bears rich fruit in non-dramatic and dramatic literature. I have distinguished and illustrated the two types of comedy in 'Comedy and Terror in Middle English Literature: The Diabolical Game', *MLR*, LX (1965) 323–32; 'Magic, Fate and Providence in Medieval Narrative and *Sir Gawain and the Green Knight*', *RES*, XVI (1965) 123–37; 'The Emergence of a Comic Type in Middle-English Narrative: The Devil and Giant as Buffoon', *Anglia*, LXXXI (1963) 365–71.

111. John Northbrooke, *A Treatise against Dicing, Dancing, Plays, and Interludes* (c. 1577), Shakespeare Society Reprint (London, 1843) pp. 85–104; Phillip Stubbes, *Anatomy of Abuses in England*, ed. Fred. J. Furnivall, New Shakespeare Society (London: Trubner, 1877–9) pp. 140–6; Beard, *The Theatre of God's Judgements*, pp. 374–6.

112. Calvin, *Institutes*, II, p. 435 (IV.x.29); see also pp. 424–5 (IV.x.15, 16).
113. *Henry VI*, Pt III, v.vii.43–4; *Richard III*, I.i.29, II.ii.39, I.ii.109.
114. See III.v.25–30, III.vi.4–8, IV.ii.200–2 etc.
115. *The Duchess of Malfi*, IV.ii.289–90. Cf. v.v.85–6, where the dying Bosola refers to himself as 'an actor in the main of all / Much 'gainst mine own good nature'. The Duchess, too, sees herself as an unwilling performer: 'I do account this world a tedious theatre, / For I do play a part in't 'gainst my will' (VI.i.84–5).
116. See, for example, Kernan, in *YR*, LIX 3–32, and *The Revels History of the Drama in English*, III 241ff.; John Holloway, *The Story of the Night: Studies in Shakespeare's Major Tragedies* (London: Routledge, 1961) pp. 26–7, 35–6, 57; Hugh P. Richmond, 'Personal Identity and Literary Personae: A Study in Historical Psychology', *PMLA*, LXXXV (1975) 209–21. Disagreement with Kernan's interpretation of the role metaphor in Shakespeare has been expressed by Philip Edwards in 'Person and Office in Shakespeare's Plays', *PBA*, LVI (1970) 93–109; he does not find in Shakespeare a 'necessary disjunction between the inner self and the public' self'.
117. *Bussy D'Ambois*, IV.i.25.
118. Montaigne, *Essays*, trs. Florio, II 14 (II.i) (Author's emphasis.)
119. In *Role Playing in Shakespeare* (Toronto: University of Toronto Press, 1978) p. 180, Thomas Van Laan notes that in Shakespeare's tragedies, by contrast with the comedies, 'losing oneself is not a necessary and ultimately beneficial stage in the progress towards final happiness. It is to lose all, to be torn loose and cast adrift in a void without dimensions ... an experience that no one can survive.'
120. *The Duchess of Malfi*, I.i.360–1; *Othello*, III.iii.375; *The Revenger's Tragedy*, II.iii.15. See also *Hamlet*, I.ii.235, II.ii.558;* *Macbeth*, II.iii.107;* *A Woman Killed with Kindness*, vi.160–1, x.57–61; *The Malcontent*, II.v.84, IV.ii.11, v.130; *Antonio's Revenge*, II.ii.202,* IV.i.202, 229; *The Revenger's Tragedy*, III.vi.62;* *The Maid's Tragedy*, II.i.200, IV.i.179–85, v.iv.117, 150; *The Duchess of Malfi*, I.i.477, II.i.50, 72, 173; *The Changeling*, III.iii.116, iv.72, IV.iii.106–9, v.iii.148; '*Tis Pity She's a Whore*, IV.i.40,* v.vi.17.* In the asterisked references, 'amaze' occurs in contextual relationship with 'confusion' (or 'confound'), meaning bewilderment, the clash of contraries, destruction. Heywood, Marston, and Middleton–Rowley explicitly invoke the myth of the labyrinth and the Minotaur in association with 'amazement'.
121. *Hamlet*, IV.v.101–2. Shakespeare is here quoting a well-known classical axiom on the foundations of language. See Quintilian, *Institutio Oratoria*, ed. and trs. H. E. Butler, Loeb Classical Library (London: Heinemann, 1949) I.vi.1. It is cited also by Ben Jonson in his *Discoveries* (*Works*, VI 622). Striking examples of antonymic nominalism will be found in *Edward II*, *Richard III*, *Richard II* (acts IV and V), *Sejanus*, and *King Lear*.
122. Plato, *Cratylus*, 439 c–d.
123. Eric Bentley, *The Life of the Drama* (1964; repr. New York: Atheneum Press, 1975) p. 286.

CHAPTER TWO. THOMAS KYD: 'THE SPANISH TRAGEDY'

1. Kyd's preoccupation with opposites has been discussed from different angles by a number of critics. See Jonas A. Barish, '*The Spanish Tragedy*, or the Pleasures and Perils of Rhetoric', in *Elizabethan Theatre*, SUAS (IX) ed. John Russell Brown

and Bernard Harris (London: Arnold, 1966) pp. 68–70; Sacvan Bercovitch, 'Love and Strife in Kyd's *Spanish Tragedy*', *SEL*, IX (1969) 215–29; Peter B. Murray, *Thomas Kyd*, Twayne's English Authors Series no. 88 (New York: Twayne, 1969) pp. 33–4 and *passim*; Roger Stilling, *Love and Death in Renaissance Tragedy* (Baton Rouge: Louisiana State University Press, 1976) pp. 26–40. My own approach is closest to that of Bercovitch, but differs from it in emphasising the importance in Kyd's design of the bond or harmony of opposites and, especially, their confusion. More generally, it differs in its assumption that most of Kyd's ideas on unity and contrariety had been available for centuries in standard teachings on the nature of the cosmos and the psycho-physical constitution of man.

2. *Romeo and Juliet*, I.iii.104. Parallels between this play and *The Spanish Tragedy* have been noted by Barish, in *Elizabethan Theatre*, SUAS IX, p. 84; Philip Edwards, *Shakespeare and the Frontiers of Art* (London: Methuen, 1968) pp. 71–2, and his *Thomas Kyd and Early Elizabethan Tragedy*, pp. 26–27, 33.

3. On the contrarious unity of the year, see above, p. 32.

4. Several critics have felt that the King's first 'device' shows partiality towards Lorenzo; on the other hand, G. K. Hunter, in 'Ironies of Justice in *The Spanish Tragedy*', *RenD*, VIII 94, finds in it a Solomon-like wisdom. I wholly agree with the second view.

5. The words 'extreme' and 'extremity' are frequently used in the play, and so too is the word 'mean'. When 'mean' is used in the sense of 'method', it is always a covert pun: this is a world in which moderate procedures are doomed to failure.

6. Peter Wilhelm Biesterfeldt, *Die dramatische Technik Thomas Kyd* (Halle/Salle: Max Niemeyr, 1936) p. 53.

7. Cf. Philip Edwards, in his edn of *The Spanish Tragedy*, pp. liv–lv. (In the line quoted, I have modified Edwards's punctuation, adding an apostrophe after 'Horatio'.)

8. For Iago's patience, see pp. 33 and 244 (n. 83).

9. See Murray, *Thomas Kyd*, pp. 34–5.

10. For its operation in later tragedies, see especially the scene of Antony's oration in *Julius Caesar*. His eyes 'red as fire with weeping', Antony skilfully turns the tearful citizens into an incendiarist mob which exits crying, 'We'll burn his body in the holy place, / And with the brands fire the traitors' houses' (III.ii.115, 255–6). This longing for 'revenge' (l. 244) has been stirred by Antony's appeal to Caesar's 'love' for them and theirs for Caesar (ll. 141, 219, 237).

11. I have capitalised Edwards's 'fury' (he gives 'a troop of Furies' at III.xiii.112, but 'deepest hell, / Where bloody furies shake their whips of steel' at I.i.64–5). This would be an entirely trivial point were it not for the fact that Kyd's mythological allusions are often quite pointed.

12. See p. 154.

13. The 'History of the Turks' contained in Foxe's *Acts and Monuments* acquainted ordinary Elizabethans with Suleiman's villainies.

14. It is often said that seventeenth-century tragedy differs from Elizabethan tragedy in that it is concerned more with the fate of society than with that of the individual. Failure to qualify this distinction by reference to *The Spanish Tragedy* may owe something to the fact that critics of Kyd's play have regularly ignored the significance of its title (though for a notable exception to the rule, see Murray, *Thomas Kyd*, pp. 64–5). A comparable Elizabethan play is *Julius Caesar*, which might more appropriately have been called *The Roman Tragedy* – 'O,

what a fall was there, my countrymen! / Then I, and you, and all of us fell down' (III.ii.190–1).

15. *The Metamorphoses of Ovid*, trs. Mary M. Innes (Harmondsworth: Penguin Books, 1955) p. 246 (x 40–7).

16. Boethius, *The Consolation of Philosophy*, III, metre xii.

17. *The XV Bookes of P. Ouidius Naso, entvtuled Metamorphoses*, trs. Arthur Golding (London, 1567) Epistle, ll. 521–6; Peacham, *The Complete Gentleman*, p. 8.

18. See Kirsty Cochrane, 'Orpheus Applied: Some Instances of his Importance in the Humanist View of Language', *RES*, XIX (1968) 1–13.

19. Although the Orphic analogy has not been noticed, the significance of language in the tragedy has come in for a good deal of discussion. See, for example, Barish, in *Elizabethan Theatre*, SUAS IX, pp. 78–81; Scott McMillin, 'The Figure of Silence in *The Spanish Tragedy*', *ELH*, XXXIX (1972) 27–48; Carol McGinnis Kay, 'Deception through Words: A Reading of *The Spanish Tragedy*', *SP*, LXXIV (1977) 20–38.

20. According to John D. Ratcliff, 'Hieronimo Explains Himself', *SP*, LIV (1957) 118, Kyd 'looked upon Hieronimo as an honorable, justified revenger'. Ronald Broude maintains that the marriage slaughter is justified because Hieronimo is acting 'both as magistrate (he is still Knight Marshall of Spain) and as revenger of blood' or kin – 'Time, Truth, and Right in *The Spanish Tragedy*', *SP*, LXVIII (1971) 141.

21. Cf. Eleanor Prosser, who finds in this declaration 'a total inversion of values' – *Hamlet and Revenge*, p. 49.

22. Fredson Bowers, in *Elizabethan Revenge Tragedy, 1587–1642* (Princeton, NJ: Princeton University Press, 1940) p. 77, and Eleanor Prosser, in *Hamlet and Revenge*, p. 50, have found transparent sophistry and logical contradiction in the '*Vindicta mihi*' soliloquy. John Ratcliffe (see n. 20) considers its reasoning perfectly coherent and acceptable. So too do Ernst Chickera in 'Divine Justice and Private Revenge in *The Spanish Tragedy*', *MLR*, LVII (1962) 231–2; David Laird, in 'Hieronimo's Dilemma', *SP*, LXII (1965) 137–46; and Ronald Broude, in *SP*, LXVIII 137–8.

23. Cf. III.ix.6–14, where Bel-imperia sees herself as a 'martyr' who must practise 'patience, and apply me to the time' – until she can accelerate the execution of 'revenge'!

24. Cf. Murray, *Thomas Kyd*, pp. 33–4.

25. For discussion of Kyd's internal drama and theatrical metaphor, see Dieter Mehl, *The Elizabethan Dumb Show: The History of a Dramatic Convention* (London: Methuen, 1965) pp. 64–70, and 'Forms and Functions of the Play within a Play', *RenD*, VIII (1965) 46–7; Ann Righter, *Shakespeare and the Idea of the Play* (London: Methuen, 1962) pp. 77–81; Edwards, *Thomas Kyd and Early Elizabethan Tragedy*, pp. 31–33; G. K. Hunter, in *RenD*, VIII 101–2; Harriet Hawkins, *Likenesses of Truth in Elizabethan and Restoration Drama* (Oxford: Clarendon Press, 1972) pp. 27–31; Murray, *Thomas Kyd*, pp. 29–30, 138–9, 143–50.

26. For an identical combination of stage symbols, image clusters, and thematic ideas, see *The Winter's Tale*.

27. See S. F. Johnson, '*The Spanish Tragedy*, or Babylon Revisited', in *Essays on Shakespeare and Elizabethan Drama*, ed. Richard Hosley (Columbia, Mo.: University of Missouri Press, 1962) pp. 24–5.

28. See *Seneca his Tenne Tragedies*, I 79–80: 'Kept is in all the order due, least such a mischiefe gret / Should not be order'd well. . . . He is himself the priest. . . . No rites were left of sacrifice undone . . . , such a cruelty / It him delights to order well.' After Kyd, the planning and execution of murderous acts is frequently attended by a tragically confused or viciously perverse sense of ritual decorum: see, for example, *Titus Andronicus*, *Julius Caesar*, *Othello*, *Catiline*, *The Revenger's Tragedy*, *The White Devil*, *Women Beware Women*.

29. The question becomes something of a refrain. See I.ii.191; iv.139–40, 172–3; II.i.110–11. Cf. I.v.1–5; III.v.16–19.

30. See above, p. 65.

31. For discussion of the comic elements in the play, see Alfred Harbage, 'Intrigue in Elizabethan Tragedy', in *Essays on Shakespeare and Elizabethan Drama*, pp. 37–44.

32. Just how prevalent and conscious is the search for meaning can be inferred from the following quotations: 'Sister, what means this melancholy walk?' (I.iv.77); 'I sound not well the mystery' (l. 139); 'I have . . . found a stratagem / To sound the bottom of this doubtful theme' (II.i.35–6); 'Why stands Horatio speechless all this while?' (II.ii.24); 'What means this unexpected miracle?' (III.ii.32); 'What means this outrage that is offer'd me?' (III.ix.1); 'Then list to me, and I'll resolve your doubt' (III.xi.12); 'What means this outrage?' (III.xii.79); 'But wherefore stands yon silly man so mute?' (III.xiii.67); 'Alas, my lord, whence springs this troubled speech?' (l. 144); 'Awake, Revenge, reveal this mystery. . . . Sufficeth me, thy meaning's understood' (III.xv.29, 36). It might also be noted that Kyd's wordplay establishes a connection between 'mean' as method, as moderation, and as significance–motive–intention; and between all of these and 'demean'. The collective sense of this linkage is dramatised when the Knight Marshall falls into incomprehensible fury in the presence of the King – 'What means this outrage? . . . I have not seen him to demean him so' (III.xii.79, 84) – and Lorenzo passes it off as a distraction resulting from 'extreme pride' (l. 86).

33. On the metadramatic and metalinguistic elements in Shakespeare's plays, see Righter, *Shakespeare and the Idea of the Play*; James L. Calderwood, *Shakespearean Metadrama: The Argument of the Play in 'Titus Andronicus', 'Love's Labour's Lost', 'Romeo and Juliet', and 'Richard II'* (Minneapolis: University of Minnesota Press, 1971), *Metadrama in Shakespeare's Henriad: 'Richard II' to 'Henry V'* (Berkeley, Calif.: University of California Press, 1979); T. McAlindon, 'Language, Style, and Meaning in *Troilus and Cressida*', PMLA, LXXXIV (1969), 'Indecorum in *Hamlet*', ShakS, V (1969) 70–96, and *Shakespeare and Decorum* (London: Macmillan, 1973); Lawrence Danson, *Tragic Alphabet: Shakespeare's Drama of Language* (New Haven, Conn.: Yale University Press, 1974); J. A. Porter, *The Drama of Speech Acts* (Berkeley, Calif.: Universit of California Press, 1979); Terence Hawkes, *Shakespeare's Talking Animals* (London: Arnold, 1973).

34. The sentence is truncated by Chiron's, 'Nay, then, I'll stop your mouth' (l. 185). Shakespeare did not forget Lorenzo's superb exit line: 'Come, stop her mouth, away with her' (II.iv.63).

35. The verb 'mean' reverberates throughout *Julius Caesar*. Act I alone yields the following instances: 'What mean'st thou by that?' (i.19); 'What means this shouting?' (ii.78), 'I know not what you mean by that' (l. 256); ''Tis Caesar that you mean, is it not, Cassius?' (iii.79), 'they say the senators to-morrow / Mean to establish Caesar as a king' (ll. 86–7). The hermeneutic complexities of this play are

exquisitely enhanced by means of number symbolism. See my article 'The Numbering of Men and Days: Symbolic Design in *The Tragedy of Julius Caesar*', *SP*, LXXXI 372–93.

36. See n. 33.

CHAPTER THREE. CHRISTOPHER MARLOWE

1. F. P. Wilson, *Marlowe and the Early Shakespeare* (Oxford: Clarendon Press, 1953) pp. 30, 48.

2. The hyperbolic aspect of Marlowe's art has been stressed by Harry Levin in *Christopher Marlowe: The Overreacher* (London: Faber, 1953) pp. 41–3, the ironic by Douglas Cole in *Suffering and Evil in the Plays of Christopher Marlowe.*

3. Wilson, *Marlowe and the Early Shakespeare*, p. 100; J. B. Steane, *Marlowe: A Critical Study* (Cambridge: Cambridge University Press, 1964) p. 85; Wilbur Sanders, *The Dramatist and the Received Idea: Studies in the Plays of Marlowe and Shakespeare* (Cambridge: Cambridge University Press, 1968) pp. 29–30, 124.

4. See *Tamburlaine the Great*, ed. Una Ellis-Fermor, 2nd edn (London: Methuen, 1951), Appendix C (pp. 287–301).

5. Sir Thomas Elyot, *The Book Named the Governor*, ed. S. E. Lehmberg, pp. 100, 102.

6. Irving Ribner, 'The Idea of History in Marlowe's *Tamburlaine*', *ELH*, XX (1953), repr. in *Elizabethan Drama: Modern Essays in Criticism*, ed. Kaufmann, pp. 81–94.

7. See especially Roy W. Battenhouse, *Marlowe's Tamburlaine: A Study in Renaissance Moral Philosophy* (Nashville, Tenn.: Vanderbilt University Press, 1941) pp. 113, 149, 257.

8. See Paul H. Kocher, *Christopher Marlowe: A Study of his Thought, Learning, and Character* (1946; repr. New York: Russell and Russell, 1962) p. 83.

9. Isaiah 14:27 (Geneva version, 1560).

10. M. M. Mahood, 'Marlowe's Heroes', repr. from *Poetry and Humanism* (London: Cape, 1950) in *Elizabethan Drama: Modern Essays in Criticism*, pp. 98–100.

11. Tamburlaine's dying speech has an extensive allusion to Phaeton which cannot be misinterpreted. Handing over authority to his son, Tamburlaine exhorts him to exercise vigilance and control and to be warned by the example of Phaeton and his foolish pride (Pt II, v.iii.228–44).

12. We must take our cue from the rhetorically alert Tamburlaine, with his droll, 'I do you honour in the simile' (Pt II, III.v.69), and his intense, 'Fair is too foul an epithet for thee' (Pt I, v.i.136).

13. It has long been assumed that the mythological character who makes most sense of Tamburlaine's amazing character is Hercules, especially as interpreted by Seneca: see Eugene M. Waith, *The Herculean Hero in Marlowe, Shakespeare, and Dryden* (London: Methuen, 1962) pp. 27–60. I would contend, however, that the essential function of the allusions to Hercules is to provide appropriate local refinements and variations on the martial paradigm.

14. For the meaning of the Mars–Venus–Harmonia myth, see pp. 7, 74. Several critics have remarked on the symbolic importance of Mars and Venus in *Tamburlaine*, but only W. L. Godschalk, in *The Marlovian World Picture* (The Hague and Paris: Mouton, 1974) pp. 110–14, has recognised that Marlowe is

employing a myth with philosophical dimensions. However, he deals briefly with this aspect of the play and argues that it supports his diabolonian view of Tamburlaine.

15. See John P. Cutts, 'The Ultimate Source of Tamburlaine's White, Red, Black, and Death?', *N&Q*, v (1958) 146–7.

16. 'Although fire and water are always opposites, none the less moist heat is the source of everything, and this discordant harmony is suited to creation' – Ovid, *Metamorphoses*, I.429–33, trs. Innes.

17. Cf. G. I. Duthie, 'The Dramatic Structure of Marlowe's *Tamburlaine the Great*', *E&S*, new ser. I (1948) 116, 124.

18. In Renaissance iconography *Venus victrix* (or *Venus armata*) is dressed in armour and represents the strength that comes from love. See Wind, *Pagan Mysteries in the Renaissance*, pp. 85–6.

19. Katherine Lever, 'The Image of Man in *Tamburlaine, Part I*', *PQ*, XXXV (1956) 426; Cole, *Suffering and Evil in the Plays of Marlowe*, pp. 102–3.

20. The presence of the three ineffectual physicians at the bedside of both Zenocrate and Tamburlaine visually enforces the connection between the two deaths.

21. See Pt I, II.v.72–86, vii.56–67, III.iii.32; Pt II, III.v.154–9.

22. The symbolic significance of four – the constitutive number in Pythagorean numerology – was common knowledge. See, for example, de la Primaudaye, *The French Academie*, pp. 726–9 (III.xxxviii). See also Plato, *Timaeus*, 31–2; Macrobius, *Commentary on the Dream of Scipio*, ed. and trs. William Harris Stahl, Records of Civilization, XLVIII (New York: Columbia University Press, 1952) pp. 98, 103–6.

23. Contrast Kocher, *Christoper Marlowe*, pp. 71–2, Cole, *Suffering and Evil in the Plays of Marlowe*, pp. 113–14, Steane, *Marlowe: A Critical Study*, pp. 64, 77–8, all of whom argue that Tamburlaine acts on the assumption that nature is a disruptive force whose only law is that of strife.

24. See above, pp. 19–20.

25. Steane, *Marlowe: A Critical Study*, p. 62.

26. M. C. Bradbrook, *Themes and Conventions of Elizabethan Tragedy*, p. 156.

27. In his valuable survey of the criticism of this play, '*The Jew of Malta* and its Critics: A Paradigm for Marlowe Studies', *PLL*, XIII (1977), Kenneth Friedenreich argues for an approach which gives proper emphasis to the play's theatrical unity and adds that too many critics have 'failed to acknowledge the wonder, the excitement, and the spectacle which Marlowe's dramaturgy . . . generates, attempting instead to unify *The Jew of Malta* superficially by uncovering some theme that expresses Marlowe's modern and ironic sensibility' (p. 355). The appeal is a reasonable one, but one must add that without intellectual force and coherence good theatre will not become good drama.

28. G. K. Hunter, 'The Theology of Marlowe's *The Jew of Malta*', *JWCI*, XVII (1964) 214.

29. Cf. Kocher, *Christopher Marlowe*, pp. 121–2; Sanders, *The Dramatist and the Received Idea*, pp. 42–3, 50.

30. G. K. Hunter, in *JWCI*, XVII 214.

31. On the Job and Abraham allusions, see ibid., pp. 217–20.

32. Ibid., p. 220.

33. I have dealt more extensively with this aspect of *Faustus* in my article, 'The

Ironic Vision: Diction and Theme in Marlowe's *Doctor Faustus'*, *RES*, XXXII (1981) 129–41.

34. G. K. Hunter, in *JWCI*, XVII 217–18.

35. Levin, *Marlowe: The Overreacher*, p. 99.

36. Sanders, *The Dramatist and the Received Idea*, p. 127. Sanders's attitude to the conclusion is tied up with his view that 'it is exceedingly difficult to get hold of the pattern in the play' – 'the shape of the dramatic movement does not in any obvious way reveal a general conception behind the plotting' (p. 122).

37. Note the reference to 'King Edward's fame' in *Henry V*, I.ii.162. Henry, by implication, is to model himself on Edward III.

38. On the absence of providentialist ideas in the play, see Irving Ribner, *The English History Play in the Age of Shakespeare* (Princeton, NJ: Princeton University Press, 1957) pp. 151–2; Sanders, *The Dramatist and the Received Idea*, pp. 121–2. Sanders notes a 'consistent subjugation of the political and the public to a narrowly conceived pattern of personal conflict' (p. 126).

39. A specifically medieval form of the Saturnalian riot which survived into the second half of the sixteenth century. See E. K. Chambers, *The Medieval Stage* (Oxford: Clarendon Press, 1903) I 336–71.

40. The manner of Edward's death was not an invention of Marlowe's but was taken from Holinshed.

41. 'Seek all the means thou canst to make him droop, / And neither give him kind word nor good look', says Mortimer to Gurney and Matrevis (v.ii.54–5); 'Speak not unto her, let her droop and pine', said Edward to Gaveston (I.iv.162).

42. Cf. Eugene M. Waith, 'Marlowe and the Jades of Asia', *SEL*, V (1965) 243–5 – an acute investigation of Marlowe's 'multiplicity of vision' and 'insistence on balancing one view against another' (p. 229).

43. Cf. Wilson, *Marlowe and the Early Shakespeare*, p. 94; Eugene M. Waith, '*Edward II*: the Shadow of Action', *TDR*, VIII (1964) 69; Steane, *Marlowe: A Critical Study*, p. 229.

44. Judith Weil has emphasised the prevalence of moral and intellectual confusion in the characters of this play: *Christopher Marlowe: Merlin's Prophet* (Cambridge: Cambridge University Press, 1977) pp. 144–6.

45. See, for example, I.i.88–160, iv.7–422, v.ii.3–54.

46. See especially Charles G. Masinton, *Christopher Marlowe's Tragic Vision* (Athens, Ohio: University of Ohio Press, 1972) pp. 90–1, 95.

47. On the sin of curiosity (both of the senses and the intellect) as defined by theologians, and its relevance to the fall of Faustus, see James Smith, 'Marlowe's *Doctor Faustus'*, *Scrutiny*, VIII (1939), repr. in *Marlowe: 'Doctor Faustus'. A Casebook*, ed. John Jump (London: Macmillan, 1969) p. 57; J. C. Maxwell, 'The Sin of Faustus', *The Wind and the Rain*, IV (1947), repr. in *'Doctor Faustus' Casebook*, pp. 91–3. For consideration of the deflationary effect of the comic scenes on Faustus's heroic aspirations, see Robert Ornstein, 'The Comic Synthesis in *Doctor Faustus'*, *ELH*, XXII (1955), repr. in *'Doctor Faustus' Casebook*, pp. 165–72; Richard Levin, *The Multiple Plot in English Renaissance Drama* (Chicago: University of Chicago Press, 1971) pp. 120–4.

48. Cf. Levin, *Marlowe: The Overreacher*, p. 146.

49. See p. 32.

50. The detail about the cannons occurs in the Faust Book; St Peter's Day is an addition.

51. Levin, *Marlowe: The Overreacher*, p. 152; Cole, *Suffering and Evil in the Plays of Marlowe*, p. 226; J. P. Brockbank, *Marlowe: Dr Faustus* (London: Edward Arnold, 1962) p. 56.

52. McAlindon, in *RES*, XXXII (1981) 129, 133. Marlowe's interest in dramatic illusion has been sensitively considered by D. J. Palmer in 'Magic and Poetry in *Doctor Faustus*', *CQ*, VI (1964), repr. in *'Doctor Faustus' Casebook*, pp. 188–203.

53. T. McAlindon, 'Classical Mythology and Christian Tradition in Marlowe's *Doctor Faustus*', *PMLA*, LXXXI (1966) 214–23.

54. There is a long line of critical commentary on the ironic subtleties of this speech; it begins with Leo Kirschbaum's 'Marlowe's *Faustus*: A Reconsideration', *RES*, XIX (1943) 225–41.

55. Cleanth Brooks, 'The Unity of Marlowe's *Doctor Faustus*', repr. from *To Nevill Coghill from Friends*, ed. J. Lawlor and W. H. Auden (1966), in *'Doctor Faustus' Casebook*, p. 220. Cf. James Smith, 'Marlowe's *Doctor Faustus*', ibid., pp. 49–50; Helen Gardner, 'Milton's Satan and the Theme of Damnation in Elizabethan tragedy', in *Elizabethan Drama: Modern Essays in Criticism*, pp. 323–4.

56. The first critic to give due emphasis to Faustus's irresolution was M. C. Bradbrook (*Themes and Conventions of Elizabethan Tragedy*, p. 150).

57. Gardner, in *Elizabethan Drama: Modern Essays in Criticism*, p. 323; Arieh Sachs, 'The Religious Despair of Doctor Faustus', *JEGP*, LXIII (1964) 625–47.

58. Brooks, in *'Doctor Faustus' Casebook*, pp. 213–14.

59. Max Bluestone, '*Libido Speculandi*: Doctrine and Dramaturgy in Contemporary Interpretations of Marlowe's *Doctor Faustus*', in *Reinterpretations of Elizabethan Drama*, ed. Norman Rabkin (New York: Columbia University Press, 1969) pp. 66–9.

60. Bradbrook, *Themes and Conventions of Elizabethan Tragedy*, p. 152.

61. 'If God foreknew that Judas would be a traitor, Judas necessarily became a traitor, and it was not in the power of Judas . . . to do differently or to change his will, though he did what he did willingly and not under compulsion, but that act of will was a work of God, which he set in motion, like everything else' – Luther, *On the Bondage of the Will*, in *Luther and Erasmus: Free Will and Salvation*, trs. and ed. E. Gordon Rupp and Philip S. Watson, Library of Christian Classics no. XVII (London: SCM Press, 1959) p. 240.

62. See Sachs, in *JEGP*, LXIII 626, 640; Sanders, *The Dramatist and the Received Idea*, pp. 228ff.

63. Cf. Nigel Alexander, 'Critical Disagreement about *Oedipus* and *Hamlet*', *ShS*, XX (1967) 36; R. G. Hunter, *Shakespeare and the Mystery of God's Judgements*, pp. 42–4, 66. Hunter's examination of *Faustus* in the light of conflicting theological attitudes to predestination, grace, and free will leads him to the conclusion that Anglican, Roman Catholic, and right-wing Calvinist would all have found their respective positions endorsed by the play: ultimately, therefore, Marlowe acknowledges the essential 'mystery of God's judgements'.

64. On the 'deed' pun, see McAlindon, in *RES*, XXXII 137–9. On 'distress', see *OED*, s.v. 'distrain', 'distress' (*sb.*, sense 3; *v.*, sense 6). Several critics have registered the importance of Faustus's sense of 'distress' (without noting its full significance). See, for example, Bradbrook, *Themes and Conventions of Elizabethan Tragedy*, p. 151.

CHAPTER FOUR. CYRIL TOURNEUR(?): 'THE REVENGER'S TRAGEDY'

1. The relationship of *The Revenger's Tragedy* to other plays of the period has been considered by Fredson Bowers in *Elizabethan Revenge Tragedy*, pp. 133–6. E. E. Stoll, *John Webster* (Boston: Mudge, 1905) p. 106, remarked that Marston and Tourneur are more alike than any other two dramatists of the period; J. W. Lever, *The Tragedy of State* (London: Methuen, 1971), has examined *Antonio's Revenge* and *The Revenger's Tragedy* in conjunction (ch. 2).

2. Eliot, 'Cyril Tourneur', *Elizabethan Essays*, p. 129.

3. L. G. Salingar, '*The Revenger's Tragedy* and the Morality Tradition', *Scrutiny*, IV (1937–8), repr. in *Elizabethan Drama: Modern Essays in Criticism*, p. 218; Samuel Schoenbaum, '*The Revenger's Tragedy*: Jacobean Dance of Death', *MLQ*, XV (1954) 201–7.

4. On the play as satire, see John Peter, *Complaint and Satire in Early English Literature* (Oxford: Clarendon Press, 1956) pp. 256–73; Alvin Kernan, *The Cankered Muse: Satire of the English Renaissance* (New Haven, Conn.: Yale University Press, 1959) pp. 221–32.

5. Bowers, *Elizabethan Revenge Tragedy*, pp. 136, 138.

6. Bradbrook, *Themes and Conventions of Elizabethan Tragedy*, pp. 165–6; Peter Lisca, '*The Revenger's Tragedy*: A Study in Irony', *PQ*, XXXIII (1959) 242–51.

7. Philip Ayres, 'Parallel Action and Reductive Techniques in *The Revenger's Tragedy*', *ELN*, VIII (1970) 103–7.

8. Ribner, *Jacobean Tragedy: The Quest for Moral Order*, pp. 76–8.

9. Eliot, *Elizabethan Essays*, pp. 122, 131. See also Foakes in his edn of *The Revenger's Tragedy*, p. xxxv.

10. Compare Iago's provocation of Brabantio: 'Even now, now, very now, an old black ram / Is tupping your white ewe' (*Othello*, I.i.89–90).

11. The interpretation of the grace theme which follows is obviously at odds with the view of Peter B. Murray, who believes that the play dramatises a distinction between human and divine grace – *A Study of Cyril Tourneur* (Philadelphia: University of Pennsylvania Press, 1964) pp. 239–40.

12. See also I.ii.1–10, 196; iv.47; IV.iv.61–7; v.i.70–1.

13. Kernan, *The Cankered Muse*, pp. 110–12; Lyons, *Voices of Melancholy: Studies in Literary Treatments of Melancholy in Renaissance England*, pp. 59–63.

14. Bright, *A Treatise of Melancholie*, p. 111.

15. 'For should a man present to such an auditory, the most sententious tragedy that ever was written, observing all the critical laws, as height of style, and gravity of person, enrich it with the most sententious *Chorus*, and, as it were life and death, in the most passionate and weighty *Nuntius*: yet after all this divine rapture . . . the breath that comes from the uncapable multitude is able to poison it' – Webster, *The White Devil*, 'To the Reader'. Like Tourneur(?), Shakespeare, and Kyd, however, Webster – in this play – turns the obligatory mixing of sententious gravity and 'discordant' laughter into a symptom of tragic reality (see pp. 167–70). This is a point which is missed by Nicholas Brooke in his attractive study *Horrid Laughter in Jacobean Tragedy* (London: Open Books, 1979). Brooke assumes that in plays such as *The Spanish Tragedy*, *The Revenger's Tragedy*, and *The White Devil* the medieval dramatic tradition of mixing violence and farce survives unmodified by humanist convictions that such mixtures should never occur in tragedy.

16. Ornstein, *The Moral Vision of Jacobean Tragedy*, p. 114. The transformation

theme (which I consider as part of the larger theme of grace) has been much discussed: see for example Salingar, in *Elizabethan Drama: Modern Essays in Criticism*, p. 214; Lisca, in *PQ*, XXXIII 245–7; Murray, *A Study of Cyril Tourneur*, pp. 193ff.; Philip Ayres, *Tourneur: 'The Revenger's Tragedy'* (London: Edward Arnold, 1977) pp. 23–4.

17. *The Changeling*, V.iii.179.

18. For the Calvinist reading, see George C. Herndl, *The High Design: English Renaissance Tragedy and the Natural Law*, pp. 218–23.

19. Interpreting Antonio as a norm figure is not without some difficulty. Since he was present at the vow of revenge sworn by Hippolito and 'certain lords' at the end of Act I, and since he condemns the brothers with the words, 'You that would murder him [i.e. the old Duke] would murder me' (v.iii.105), some critics have not unreasonably assumed that we are to see him in the end as something of a hypocrite, or at least as a cynical politician. However, the vow proposed by Hippolito was only to exact justice on Junior Brother, and only then if the law did not act (which it does, albeit accidentally). Moreover, we cannot be sure whether Antonio participates in this vow or simply stands by – beside his wife's body – as a grateful but distracted witness ('I thank you gentlemen in mine ire' – I.iv.65). His remark at the end that Vindice might murder him, too, probably implies a recognition that Vindice has become a permanent threat to all authority, 'gracefully' established or not.

20. My interpretation of the significance of language in the play coincides in some essentials with that of James L. Simmons – 'The Tongue and its Office in *The Revenger's Tragedy*', *PMLA*, XCII (1977) 56–66. What follows here, however, stems from what I have written on 'the office of the tongue' in Shakespeare's plays, especially *Richard II* and *Othello* (*Shakespeare and Decorum*, chs 2 and 4).

21. Cf. the action of the tongue in *Titus Andronicus* (above, p. 79).

22. Cf. Foakes in his edn of *The Revenger's Tragedy*, pp. xxx, xxxiv.

23. Murray (*A Study of Cyril Tourneur*, p. 237) notes pertinently that the name 'Piato' derives from the Italian for 'a plea', 'a suit in law', 'a pleading'.

24. Cf. the fate of Lavinia, violated after having her tongue cut out (in mid-sentence); and, of course, the suicide of Hieronimo after biting out his tongue (above, p. 66).

25. See above, pp. 32, 67.

CHAPTER FIVE. JOHN WEBSTER

1. M. C. Bradbrook notes in Webster 'a scepticism far deeper than that of professed rebels like Marlowe', an 'intense capacity for feeling and suffering, within a clueless intellectual maze' – 'Fate and Chance in *The Duchess of Malfi*', *MLR*, XLII (1947), repr. in *John Webster: A Critical Anthology*, ed. G. K. and S. K. Hunter (Harmondsworth: Penguin, 1969) p. 133.

2. On retribution see George Hunter, 'English Folly and Italian Vice: John Webster', in *John Webster: A Critical Anthology*, p. 262; Ralph Berry, *The Art of John Webster* (Oxford: Clarendon Press, 1972) pp. 98–106, 124–6.

3. George Hunter, in *John Webster: A Critical Anthology*, pp. 261–2; James R. Hurt, 'Inverted Rituals in Webster's *The White Devil*', *JEGP*, LXI (1962) 42–7; James L. Calderwood, '*The Duchess of Malfi*: Styles of Ceremony', *EIC*, XII (1962)

repr. in *John Webster: A Critical Anthology*, pp. 266–80; Clifford Leech, *Webster: 'The Duchess of Malfi'* (London: Arnold, 1963) pp. 61–2; Peter B. Murray, *A Study of John Webster* (The Hague and Paris: Mouton, 1969) pp. 41–2, 119, 124; Ralph Berry, 'Masques and Dumb Shows in Webster's Plays', *ETh*, VII (1980) 124–46.

4. The play's dualities have been widely discussed. See M. C. Bradbrook, *Themes and Conventions of Elizabethan Tragedy*, pp. 186–92; James Smith, 'The Tragedy of Blood', *Scrutiny*, VIII (1939), repr. in *John Webster: A Critical Anthology*, pp. 116–32; Ribner, *Jacobean Tragedy*, pp. 100–5; Hereward T. Price, 'The Function of Imagery in Webster', *PMLA*, LXII (1955) repr. in *John Webster: A Critical Anthology*, pp. 179–90; B. J. Layman, 'The Equilibrium of Opposites in *The White Devil*', *PMLA*, LXXIV (1959) 336–47. Una Ellis-Fermor, in *The Jacobean Drama* (London: Methuen, 1936) ch. 9, saw both of Webster's major tragedies as the expression of a divided mind, torn between a Machiavellian–materialist and a moral–religious view of the universe.

5. Cf. A. J. Smith, 'The Power of *The White Devil*', in *John Webster*, Mermaid Critical Commentaries, ed. Brian Morris (London: Benn, 1970) p. 84.

6. See Price, in *John Webster: A Critical Anthology*, pp. 179–60; and Ribner, in *Jacobean Tragedy*, pp. 100–5.

7. See above, p. 7.

8. Cf. p. 94 (*Tamburlaine*) and pp. 109–12 (*Edward II*).

9. Robert Ornstein remarks that 'the power of *The White Devil* is its dramatization of the isolated criminal will shattering moral restrictions' – *The Moral Vision of Jacobean Tragedy*, p. 136.

10. Erwin Panofsky, *Hercules am Scheidewege, und andere antike Bildstoffe in der deueren Kunst*, Studien der Bibliothek Warburg 5 (Leipzig, 1924) p. 97, and *Studies in Iconology: Humanistic Themes in the Art of the Renaissance*, p. 88.

11. See pp. 20, 98.

12. J. R. Mulryne, '*The White Devil* and *The Duchess of Malfi*', in *Jacobean Theatre*, SUAS I, p. 207. See also his 'Webster and the Uses of Tragicomedy', in *John Webster*, ed. Morris, pp. 133–45; Brooke, *Horrid Laughter in Jacobean Tragedy*, pp. 28–47; Jacqueline Pearson, *Tragedy and Tragicomedy in the Plays of John Webster* (Manchester: Manchester University Press, 1980) pp. 53–83. There are illuminating remarks on the humour of *The White Devil* in Berry, *The Art of John Webster*, ch. 3: 'Irony, Parody, and Caricature'.

13. M. C. Bradbrook, *John Webster: Citizen and Dramatist* (London: Weidenfeld and Nicolson, 1980) p. 121. Concerning Giovanni's role in the play, Professor Bradbrook notes that 'for a minor part it is strongly highlighted' (p. 122); but she does not attach any artistic significance to this fact.

14. In fact Francesco died from natural causes, but the popular view that he was poisoned could not be shaken.

15. Ornstein, *The Moral Vision of Jacobean Tragedy*, p. 129.

16. Robert Bechtold Heilman, *Tragedy and Melodrama: Versions of Experience* (Seattle and London: University of Washington Press, 1968) pp. 61–9; James L. Smith, *Melodrama* (London: Methuen, 1973) pp. 8–9, 62–3.

17. Murray, *A Study of John Webster*, p. 143.

18. *History of the World* I.xii; 1614 edn, p. 15. The passage in Augustine to which Ralegh refers is probably *De Trinitate*, XIX.xi.

19. Spencer, *Death and Elizabethan Tragedy*, pp. 135–6.

258 *English Renaissance Tragedy*

20. *The Complete Works of John Webster*, ed. F. L. Lucas (London: Chatto and Windus, 1927) IV 38–9.

21. 'Visible solemnity . . . the memory whereof is far more easy and durable than the memory of speech can be' – Hooker, *Laws of Ecclesiastical Polity*, Everyman edn, I 361–2 (IV.i).

22. For a similar interpretation of the significance of ceremony in this tragedy, see Calderwood, in *John Webster: A Critical Anthology*.

23. The element of Christian Stoicism has been noted in general terms by Ribner, in *Jacobean Tragedy*, p. 113, and Murray, in *A Study of John Webster*, pp. 153, 162.

24. Lipsius, *Two Bookes of Constancie*, trs. Stradling, pp. 8–9, 32–4. Cf. Guillaume Du Vair, *Moral Philosophie of the Stoicks*, trs. T. I[ames] (London, 1598) pp. 157–63.

25. Larry S. Champion, *Tragic Patterns in Jacobean and Caroline Drama* (Knoxville: University of Tennessee Press, 1977) p. 139, notes that the Duchess's conduct in the opening scene hardly justifies Antonio's idealistic praise.

26. For a very different interpretation of this scene, see Lever, *The Tragedy of State*, p. 91, and Murray, *A Study of John Webster*, pp. 124–7. Both critics see the wooing-and-wedding as a beautiful and entirely harmonious ritual.

27. On the tragic implications of the concept of original sin, see Geoffrey Brereton, *Principles of Tragedy: A Rational Examination of the Tragic Concept in Life and Literature* (London: Routledge, 1968) pp. 41, 53–5.

28. I am not the first to question this view. See Clifford Leech, *John Webster: A Critical Study* (London: The Hogarth Press, 1951) p. 77; Joyce E. Peterson, *Curs'd Example: 'The Duchess of Malfi' and Commonweal Tragedy* (Columbia, Mo., and London: University of Missouri Press, 1978) pp. 3, 9. See also Bradbrook, *Webster: Citizen and Dramatist* who remarks: 'Had she said, "I am Giovanna Bologna still", she would have more truthfully disclosed the way in which her marriage had severed her public role from her private person' (p. 154).

29. Brown's edn of *The Duchess of Malfi*, p. 4.

30. Cf. Lucas, in *The Complete Works of John Webster*, II 22.

31. Lipsius, *Two Bookes of Constancie*, pp. 15–16. On the title page of Stradling's translation, Lipsius's work is described as 'A Comfortable Conference, in common calamities . . . a singular consolation to all that are priuately distressed, or afflicted, either in mind or body.' This is indicative of the way in which Christian Stoicism had been assimilated to the religious tradition of providing spiritual 'comfort' for the dying and the distressed (cf. Thomas More's *A Dialogue of Comfort against Tribulation*, 1534).

32. Browne's edn of *The Duchess of Malfi*, p. 125 (note on IV.ii.173). See also Lucas, in *The Complete Works of John Webster*, II 185–6.

33. Cf. Ornstein, *The Moral Vision of Jacobean Tragedy*, p. 129: 'her death is a touchstone as well as a turning point in the lives of the other characters'.

34. In his challenging and valuable essay, 'The Tragedies of Webster, Tourneur and Middleton: Symbols, Imagery and Conventions', *Sphere History of Literature in the English Language: English Drama to 1710*, ed. Christopher Ricks (London: Sphere, 1971) pp. 306–51, Christopher Ricks argues that Webster's imagery-and-symbolism is obtrusive and imperfectly integrated. I hope that what I have to say here on the relationship in the two tragedies between character, theme, myth, and both non-verbal and verbal imagery goes some way towards refuting this claim. Broadly speaking, Professor Ricks appears to me to pick out imagery which is not

fully integrated but also – and this is because Webster is so very *unobtrusive* in his finest effects – to ignore much that is.

35. Berry, *The Art of John Webster*, p. 111; cf. Moody Prior, *The Language of Tragedy* (New York: Columbia University Press, 1950) p. 124.

36. Ovid, *Metamorphoses*, trs. Innes, p. 38.

37. Cf. Ferdinand: 'I'll crawl after like a sheep-biter' (v.ii.50), and Bosola: 'They are out of thy howling' (v.v.13).

38. *Seneca his Tenne Tragedies*, I 90; cf. p. 88 ('faythfull bonde of peace and love'). This translation is also available in *Five Elizabethan Tragedies*, ed. A. K. McIlwraith (London: Oxford University Press, 1938).

39. See Inga-Stina Ekeblad, 'The "Impure Art" of John Webster', *RES*, new ser., IX (1958), repr. in *John Webster, A Critical Anthology*, pp. 202–21.

40. Discussing the possibility that Ferdinand is driven by incestuous feelings, Clifford Leech (*Webster: 'The Duchess of Malfi'*, pp. 58–60) notes that 'confusion about motive . . . is an essential element in the play'.

41. See *OED*, s.v. 'counsel', senses 5b, 6, and 8.

CHAPTER SIX. THOMAS MIDDLETON

1. Cf. Una Ellis-Fermor, who in *The Jacobean Drama*, p. 152, remarks that Middleton's tragedies 'reveal the operation of natural laws about the destruction of those who unawares have broken them'.

2. A number of critics have drawn attention to 'moral equivocation', 'self-delusion', or 'moral confusion' as a salient feature of Middleton's characters. See, for example, Ornstein, *The Moral Vision of Jacobean Tragedy*, p. 196; Ribner, *Jacobean Tragedy*, pp. 129, 138; R. B. Parker, 'Middleton's Experiments with Comedy and Judgement', in *Jacobean Theatre*, SUAS I, p. 193; Dorothea Krook, *Elements of Tragedy*, pp. 176, 180; Dorothy M. Farr, *Thomas Middleton and the Drama of Realism* (Edinburgh: Oliver and Boyd, 1973) pp. 51, 75; J. R. Mulryne, in his edn of *Women Beware Women*, pp. liii–lix *passim*.

3. Ellis-Fermor, *The Jacobean Drama*, p. 151.

4. Several critics have claimed that Middleton's tragedies lack metaphysical implication; see, for example, N. W. Bawcutt, in his edn of *The Changeling*, p. xlvii; Ornstein, *The Moral Vision of Jacobean Tragedy*, p. 171. This view, however, is more often implied than stated. It has been vigorously rejected by Irving Ribner, who sees the tragedies as vehicles of a rigid Calvinist determinism, with protagonists who are evil and damned from the start. Ribner's interpretation, however, seems to me to offer an unbalanced view of two tragedies which leave intact the mysteries of free will, divine judgement, and grace, much as Marlowe does in *Faustus*: Anglican, Roman Catholic, and Puritan could all have interpreted these plays in the light of their own theological convictions.

5. One contemporary who comes close to Middleton in the way he relates sexuality to the Fall is Donne:

> How witty's ruin, how importunate
> Upon mankind! it labour'd to frustrate
> Even God's purpose, and made woman, sent
> For man's relief, cause of his languishment:

> They were to good ends, and they are so still,
> But accessory, and principal to ill;
> For the first marriage was our funeral;
> One woman at one blow then kill'd us all,
> And singly one by one they kill us now,
> And we delightfully ourselves allow
> To that consumption; and, profusely blind,
> We kill ourselves to propagate our kind.
>
> ('The First Anniversary')

6. *The Works of Thomas Middleton*, ed. A. H. Bullen (London, 1885–7) VII 224–5. The identification of James with an ideal, peaceful order is figured also in the unity of 'the Four Kingdoms (viz. England, Scotland, France, Ireland)' and – and within the King himself – of 'the Four Cardinal Virtues' (pp. 222–3).

7. *Works of Thomas Middleton*, VII 195–7.

8. *The Changeling*, v.i.1, 11, 67, iii.12; *Women Beware Women*, v.ii.198–200.

9. Bawcutt, in his edn of *The Changeling*, p. xxxix. On the relationship between plot and subplot, see William Empson, *Some Versions of Pastoral* (London: Chatto and Windus, 1935) pp. 48–52; Bradbrook, *Themes and Conventions of Elizabethan Tragedy*, pp. 213, 221–4; Karl Holzknecht, 'The Dramatic Structure of *The Changeling*', in *Renaissance Papers*, ed. A. H. Gilbert (Columbia, South Carolina: University of South Carolina Press, 1954) pp. 77–87; Richard Levin, *The Multiple Plot in English Renaissance Drama*, pp. 34–48.

10. Helen Gardner, 'Milton's Satan and the Theme of Damnation in Elizabethan Tragedy', in *Elizabethan Drama: Modern Essays in Criticism*, pp. 328–31.

11. Ornstein, *The Moral Vision of Jacobean Tragedy*, pp. 171–81.

12. For these minor echoes, see III.iii.48–50, 77–8, IV.iii.1–4. On the myth of the labyrinth in *A Midsummer Night's Dream* see D. Ormerod, '*A Midsummer Night's Dream*: The Monster in the Labyrinth', *ShakS*, XI (1978) 39–52; M. E. Lamb, '*A Midsummer Night's Dream*: The Myth of Theseus and the Minotaur', *TSLL*, XXI (1979) 478–91.

13. The symbolic function of the castle (as an image of 'strength and order') has been remarked by T. B. Tomlinson in *A Study of Elizabethan and Jacobean Tragedy* (Cambridge: Cambridge University Press, 1964) pp. 186, 192. (Tomlinson mistakenly assumes that the asylum is within the castle.)

14. Bradbrook, *Themes and Conventions of Elizabethan Tragedy*, p. 214.

15. *OED*. The quotation illustrating the penultimate sense is from Fuller (1642).

16. Tomlinson, *Elizabethan and Jacobean Tragedy*, pp. 194, 203, comments on the labyrinth symbol, but does not identify De Flores as the monster. He notes a comparable use of the symbol in Racine's *Phèdre*. Seneca's *Hippolytus* (or *Phaedra*) would be a more appropriate comparison. It was from this tragedy that Renaissance dramatists – and Racine – learned to connect disordered sexual relationships (especially incest) with the symbol of the labyrinth, as well as with riddling, equivocal language. (The second connection is evident also in Seneca's *Oedipus*.) Seneca intimates in the *Hippolytus* that when Theseus returns from his travels he finds in his own palace, where his wife is secretly in love with his son by a previous marriage, a labyrinth more confusing and monstrous than the one he conquered in Crete (there is nothing of this in Euripides's *Hippolytus*, on which Seneca's tragedy

is based). There are echoes of Seneca's *Hippolytus* in *A Midsummer Night's Dream*, *Richard III*, *Hamlet*, *The Revenger's Tragedy*, and *The Duchess of Malfi* – as well as in *The Changeling* and *Women Beware Women*.

17. See Harriet Hawkins, *Likenesses of Truth in Elizabethan and Jacobean Drama*, pp. 27–38.

18. Gardner, in *Elizabethan Drama: Modern Essays in Criticism*, pp. 329–30.

19. S. Gorley Putt, 'The Tormented World of Middleton', *TLS*, 1974, pp. 833–34. Ornstein and Ribner were among the first critics to place emphasis on the affinity between Beatrice and De Flores.

20. See, for example, Baldassare Castiglione, *The Book of the Courtier*, trs. Sir Thomas Hoby, Everyman Library (London: Dent, 1966) pp. 95, 134, 142, 168, 188, 190; George Puttenham, *The Arte of English Poesie*, facsimile repr. (Menston, Yorks: Scolar Press, 1968) pp. 231–49.

21. See above, p. 239, n. 19.

22. For the 'distress' pun, see p. 133.

23. Sir Philip Sidney, *An Apology for Poetry*, ed. Shepherd, p. 117. The echo of Sidney has been observed by Bawcutt in his edn of *The Changeling* (note on v.iii.7–9).

24. See III.iii.119–20, 185–9, 231–3; VI.iii.13–23.

25. Ellis-Fermor, *The Jacobean Drama*, pp. 139–40; Richard Hindry Barker, *Thomas Middleton* (New York: Columbia University Press, 1958) pp. 140–41; R. B. Parker, 'Middleton's Experiments with Comedy and Judgement', in *Jacobean Theatre*, SUAS I pp. 195–6.

26. Inga-Stina Ewbank notes that these three scenes are 'nodal points in the structure of the play' – 'Realism and Morality in *Women Beware Women*', *E&S*, new ser., XXII (1969) 69. On the constructional formula, see above p. 41.

27. On the destruction of family bonds, see also Ewbank, in *E&S*, new ser., XXII 65–6; and Mulryne, in his edn of *Women Beware Women*, pp. lv–lvi.

28. Barker, *Thomas Middleton*, p. 140.

29. See Christopher Ricks, 'Word-Play in *Women Beware Women*', *RES*, new ser., XII (1961) 237–50.

30. On the symbolic significance of the names Duessa (=two) and Una (=one), see Alistair Fowler, *Spenser and the Numbers of Time* (London: Routledge, 1964) pp. 6–8.

31. Synonyms and antonyms are: 'war', 'conflict', 'strive', 'strife', 'quarrel', 'insurrection', 'commotion', 'rebel', 'force', 'wrangle', 'discontent', 'disease (dis-ease)', 'fret', 'gnaw', 'vex', 'incense', 'rage', 'fury', 'noise', 'storm', 'thunder', 'tempest'; 'peace', 'appease', 'ease', 'quiet(-ness)', 'still', 'low', 'content', 'rest', 'shelter', 'comfort', 'harmony', 'music', 'consent'. Mulryne has commented on some of the ironic implications of the 'peace' motif in his edn of *Women Beware Women*, pp. lxix–lxx.

32. Synonyms and antonyms are: 'well', 'good', 'goodly', 'godly', 'virtuous', 'virtue', 'charity', 'benefactor', 'right', 'moral', 'honest', 'comely', 'handsome', 'meet', 'innocent', 'conscionable', 'conscience', 'perfect(-ion)', 'saint(-ish)', 'bless(-ing)'; 'ill', 'evil', 'malice', 'mischief', 'corruption', 'sin', 'blame', 'wrong', 'forbidden', 'guilt(y)', 'chide', 'curse', 'reprehension', 'defect', 'fault', 'blemish', 'mar', 'spoil', 'base(-ness)', 'unseemly', 'vile', 'villain', 'reprobate', 'black', 'devil', 'Hell', 'damnation', 'damned'.

33. Consider: 'good mother', 'good brother', 'good sister', 'good aunt', 'good

niece', 'good sir', 'good lord', 'good horsewoman', 'good name', 'good fortune', 'good cheer', 'good appetite', 'good thoughts', 'good counsel', 'good will', 'good comfort', 'good sport', 'good parts', 'good qualities', 'good works', 'good hearing', 'good last' (= 'shape'), 'good perfection' (= 'conclusion')! Apart from these largely stereotyped adjective-noun phrases, there are idiomatic expressions in which the crucial epithet is similarly fossilised: 'as good be blind', 'much good may't do her', 'that's a good way to . . . ', etc.

34. But she curses him in deadly earnest at IV.ii.49–54.

35. Synonyms and antonyms: 'bright', 'white', 'fair', 'glorious', 'glistering', 'immaculate', 'pure', 'chaste'; 'black', 'dull', 'dark', 'obscure', 'plain', 'blemished', 'deformed', 'leprous'.

36. Bianca's name is the subject of an extended dialogue ('What should be her name, sir?) at III.ii.13ff. One critic has commented on the pervasive temple imagery ('it evidently carries a key significance'), another has noted the symbolic significance of the name 'Bianca'; neither has detected the symbolism of 'Capella' or the New Testament allusions. See Farr, *Thomas Middleton and the Drama of Realism*, p. 87; John Potter, '"In Time of Sports": Masques and Masking in Middleton's *Women Beware Women*', *PLL*, XVIII (1982) 369. The Revels editor has caught the New Testament allusions but does not connect them with Bianca's names. See his notes on III.ii.17–18 and IV.iii.43. As he observes, Middleton cites the Pauline passage in full – giving chapter and verse – in his entertainment on James 'the Peacemaker'.

37. See Ricks, in *RES*, new ser., XII 239–40.

38. See Edward Engleberg, 'Tragic Blindness in *The Changeling* and *Women Beware Women*', *MLQ*, XXIII (1962) 23–8.

39. Blindness is not referred to in *The Changeling* except by ironic implication: all direct reference is to the eye and seeing. In *Women Beware Women*, continual interplay between the antithetical terms reinforces the sense of endemic confusion and the specific paradox mentioned above. In general the development of the blindness theme is more varied and more complex in *Women Beware Women* than in *The Changeling*. (Engleberg's otherwise admirable essay makes no distinction between the two plays in regard to this theme; nor does it note the theme's antithetical structure.)

40. Synonyms and antonyms are: 'free(dom)', 'liberty', 'consent', 'agree', 'release', 'openness', 'largeness', 'liberal', 'flowing', 'wander', 'prodigal', 'licentious', 'break into'; 'restrain(t)', 'content', 'confined', 'in compass', 'law', 'decree', 'command', 'ordained', 'forbid', 'force', 'compel', 'curb', 'check', 'cased up', 'mewed up', 'subjection', 'bound', 'chained up', 'oppressed', 'thraldom', 'captivity', 'prisoner'. The imagery of locks, keys and treasure chests belongs to this antithesis; it is punningly and ironically encapsulated in the word 'wedlock' when Leantio discovers to his dismay that his stolen bride cannot be hidden away with the same security as a jewel – III.ii.5, 190.

41. In my quotations on the Fortune theme, I have thought it appropriate to capitalise the Revels editor's 'fortune'.

42. There are some apt comments on 'forgetfulness' in Dorothea Krook's analysis of the play – *Elements of Tragedy*, p. 182.

43. See IV.i.1–18. For the (impatient and hasty) Duke as 'sun', see II.ii.319, III.ii.195, IV.ii.2, 21; for the irony of this comparison, see IV.i.128–33, 229–330, 270–8.

44. On this aspect of Middleton's art, see Barker, *Thomas Middleton*, p. 142; Ribner, *Jacobean Tragedy*, pp. 139, 152.

45. Cf. Inga-Stina Ewbank, who in *E&S*, new ser., XXII 68, stresses the importance of 'double action and double talk' in this scene.

46. Cf. the symbolic use of four characters in Kyd's playlet, in *Tamburlaine*, *A Midsummer Night's Dream*, and *Julius Caesar* (see pp. 75, 96–7, 251). Note also the personification of the four elements, virtues, and kingdoms in the Dekker-Middleton *Entertainment* for James 'the Peacemaker' (p. 194 and n. 6). In Jonson's marriage masque *Hymenaei* the four humours and affections are represented as antimasque figures emerging from a microcosm or globe representing man (they are later curbed by reason). It seems almost certain that when four characters appear together on the Renaissance stage, either divided or united, an analogy with the whole system of nature is implied.

47. For defence, see Ribner, *Jacobean Tragedy*; Ewbank, in *E&S*, new ser., XXII; Margot Heinemann, *Puritanism and Theatre: Thomas Middleton and Opposition Drama under the Early Stuarts* (Cambridge: Cambridge University Press, 1980) pp. 196–7; Mulryne, in his edn of *Women Beware Women*, pp. lvi–lvii; Potter, in *PLL*, XVIII. At the time of writing this chapter, I have been unable to consult Sarah P. Sutherland's *Masques in Jacobean Tragedy*, due for publication in 1983 by the AMS Press, but not yet available in this country.

48. Cf. Samuel Schoenbaum, *Middleton's Tragedies* (New York: Columbia University Press, 1955) p. 102.

Index

Whitman, Robert F., 238, 240
Wilson, F. P., 82, 251, 253
Wind, Edgar F., 237, 243, 252
Wordplay (and equivocation), 49,
 50, 52; the 'deed' pun, 38, 133,
 154, 167, 203, 254; the 'maze' pun,
 see Labyrinth, symbol of; the

'violence' pun, 4, 49, 138, 139, 163,
 201
World picture, world view, *see*
 Cosmology
Wright, Thomas, 240

Yeats, W. B., 238, 241